Knowledge Management in the Development of Data-Intensive Systems

Edited by
Ivan Mistrik, Matthias Galster, Bruce R. Maxim, and
Bedir Tekinerdogan

CRC Press
Taylor & Francis Group

AN AUERBACH BOOK

First edition published 2021
by CRC Press
6000 Broken Sound Parkway NW, Suite 300, Boca Raton, FL 33487-2742

and by CRC Press
2 Park Square, Milton Park, Abingdon, Oxon, OX14 4RN

ISBN: 978-0-367-43078-8 (hbk)
ISBN: 978-1-032-01597-2 (pbk)
ISBN: 978-1-003-00118-8 (ebk)

Typeset in Garamond
by codeMantra

Contents

PART III CLOUD SERVICES FOR DATA-INTENSIVE SYSTEMS

PART IV CASE STUDIES

Foreword

Introduction

Big data systems are becoming ubiquitous. The world produces a huge amount of data and software systems to make effective use of this data required more than ever. However deciding what a data-intensive system should do, architecting and designing it, building and deploying it, and evolving it over time are all still very challenging activities [11].

Part of the cause of this challenge is the diverse knowledge needed to achieve an effective data-intensive system, the diverse team usually needed to develop and deploy the solution, and the ever-changing system and data landscape.

In this foreword, I briefly characterize these challenges for data-intensive systems that the chapters of this book address in various ways.

Big Data

The concept of "big data" has become commonplace not only in software development but also in the society [1]. We produce ever-growing amounts of data that range from transport systems, health systems, energy infrastructure, social media, gaming, education, government services, leisure and tourism, scientific research, industry 4.0, and smart buildings and homes we live and work in [1,2,17]. Increasingly individuals, teams, organizations, and governments want and indeed need to leverage this data to improve performance, security, outcomes, lifestyle, and well-being.

Several "V"s of big data – volume, variety, velocity, veracity, validity, volatility, value – are critical to support any data-intensive system [6,14]. Volume typically refers to the size and complexity of data, which has grown almost exponentially in recent years. This includes social media data (e.g., video, text, images), health data (e.g., more precise genomics, MRI, etc., capture), transport and energy data (e.g., smart grids and smart transport systems), sensor data (e.g., a wide range of Internet of Things (IoT)-based systems increasingly collected from factories, buildings, hospitals, and houses), and government data of many sorts. Velocity refers to speed with which data is produced by such systems. For example, modern vehicles have hundreds of sensors, smart buildings thousands. Even individuals generate increasing data from wearables, smart homes, social media, and work practices. Data comes in increasingly diverse varieties, in part due to the increasingly diverse systems generating the data. Combining and using this wide variety of data representations is an increasingly important yet challenging problem. Veracity concerns data quality, accuracy, reliability, and the robustness of systems capturing, processing, and storing data. Lack of trust in news media, sensor data, fake news, social media content, industrial control system data, security and privacy issues, and ethical use of data are all major challenges. Validity is critical to data chosen to solve the problem at hand. There is almost too much data in the world and care is needed to determine which combinations of data sets will actually address the data-intensive software system's user needs. Data is volatile in that while some data is stable, e.g., geographic locale, topology, population characteristics, physical structures, etc., some is highly dynamic and changeable, e.g., traffic and people movement, power consumption, individual health measurements, new social media data, etc. Finally, data analysis needs to add value – how can data be combined, new information and knowledge mined, new insights be derived – to enable the data-intensive system to aid its users.

Data-Intensive Software Systems

Data-intensive software systems are characterized by their high dependence on diverse data that is critical to the system's functionality but also many nonfunctional issues [6,11,18]. Data has to be sourced from a wide range of sensors, devices, and other systems. This might include a range of IoT sensors; health systems; energy, transport, utility, grid, etc., systems; building management systems; variety of government systems; Geographic Information Systems; industrial control systems; personal sensors; and social media systems [9]. Some data is simple and low volume, but much is complex and high volume and high frequency. This means the data-intensive system may need to do a lot of processing of the data to turn it into a form that is useful.

Data from diverse sources needs to be integrated and "harmonized" to link up similar/same data items and produce a unified new set of data for further processing and usage [3]. This activity can include data wrangling, format changes, merging, splitting, joining data, and – often complex and imprecise – harmonizing similar concepts, terms, formats, and ontologies distributed across diverse source data sets.

Integrated data may need to be stored, but some large, complex, or restricted access data might need to be retrieved as needed from source systems [4]. Network constraints may impact data-intensive system performance. A variety of data processing are typically needed – machine learning, pattern recognition, information retrieval, and other techniques used to find information and extract knowledge from integrated data sets [21].

Decision support is a critical aspect of most data-intensive systems. Decisions may vary from large-scale traffic analysis and control, smart building management systems, smart hospitals, industry 4.0 control rooms, and government policymaking to individual and team decision-making, including AI-supported project management, smart homes, travel planning, and health and well-being decision-making [7]. Many of these need to be supported by complex data visualization systems, presented analyzed data sets in forms end users can interpret and make use of.

Software Engineering for Data-Intensive Systems

A range of challenging software engineering issues present in building and maintaining such data-intensive systems [6,12]. What process should be used is an interesting question – many projects have adopted Agile techniques, and at first glance, this would seem a good fit where the range of data sources, data processing, and use of data may vary over time. But many data-intensive systems are safety- and security-critical, and having many iterations, refactorings, and sprint-based delivery might not be the best fit approach.

Identifying requirements for data-intensive systems is a challenge as both end users and data sources are likely to be volatile over the life of the project development and evolution. This means requirements may be quiet emergent – new data source formats, greater volume, frequency, and variable quality (improve or even reduce) may all significantly impact the system under development. Nonfunctional requirements can be very challenging. Disparate data size, frequency, variety, and quality of data put high demands on systems. This includes performance and response time constraints; reliability and robustness where connected systems may be unpredictable in availability and their own performance; rapidly changing data volume and quality; updated connectors to source data; updated platforms hosting data-intensive systems and processing algorithms; new users with new visualization and data processing requirements; and evolving security and privacy requirements.

A data-intensive system often has extensive architecting and design challenges [18,19]. In order to interface to diverse data sources, it needs to realize a range of technology connectors. In order to retrieve, filter/wrangle, transform, integrate, harmonize, and store all/part of source system data, a range of data processing and management technologies may be required. In order to analyze collected data, a range of machine learning, information retrieval, indexing, natural language processing, image processing, and other advanced techniques, algorithms, platforms, and solutions need to be used. Visualization solutions may require extensive UI design and implementation effort and, depending on the technology desired by users, may also require significant platform resources, e.g., for VR-based support [4].

Knowledge Management

Data-intensive systems are usually built not by software engineers alone but by teams of domain experts, data scientists, organizational managers, and cloud/compute platform engineers [18]. Such a multidisciplinary team puts a lot of demands not only on software engineering process and project management, but also on knowledge management.

Current approaches to capturing, evaluating, and using requirements for data-intensive systems are not well suited to such multidisciplinary teams. Approaches used are often focused on one or two stakeholder groups and do not suit or fit the needs of others. There are no agreed standards to describe data, data processing, and data visualization [18]. The architecture and implementation of data-intensive systems are necessarily often very complex, and multistakeholder input is even needed to engineer the system (e.g., AI experts, software engineers, cloud and grid computing experts, IoT experts, and database experts). Best practices for creating and sharing such diverse knowledge across such a team are still being developed for data-intensive software system engineering [23].

As noted above, due to the several V's in big data domain, data-intensive systems inherently live in a changing environment. New data is made available. Data quality, volatility, and veracity change. Validity and value of data used may change as stakeholder needs change. Most data-intensive systems exhibit various degrees of emergent requirements, where these new/changed data sources and new/changed stakeholder needs severely impact on the system in many ways. Handling these emergent requirements is still extremely challenging [9].

Other Concerns

Many other issues present when engineering next-generation, data-intensive systems. Security and privacy are increasing challenges. Users expect data to be collected and used for specific purposes, but the interconnectedness of systems, and ability to transfer sensitive data from one system to another and lose data provenance, exposes many privacy concerns [10,23]. Many data-intensive systems are security-critical and safety-critical, in that they deal with utility, transport, health, manufacturing, and other high-value, high-criticality system domains. Due to the rapid evolution of data-intensive systems brought on by the changing nature of the underlying big data domain, many technical debt challenges present [12]. Choosing particular approaches to data sourcing, wrangling, storage, processing, and visualization may seem appropriate at one time, but then incur a variety of serious technical debt implications down the track. Ethics and wider human value issues relating to data-intensive systems represent important new areas of research and practice. Sociotechnical issues present an interesting challenge in this domain. As well as the multidisciplinary team, data-intensive systems are often used by a wide variety of stakeholders, e.g., citizens, patients. They have a wide range of diverse human factors impacting on their likely ability to use and take up the system that needs approaches to adequately incorporate into development and evolution [16]. Finally, due again to the nature of the big data domain and its volatility, data-intensive systems are almost never "finished," with new data sources, changes to data availability, quality, and volume being inherent in the domain. This makes evolving data-intensive systems even more challenging than conventional software systems [8,14].

This book provides diverse chapters addressing many of the outstanding issues in the domain of knowledge management for data-intensive software system engineering. I do hope that you find them helpful in your understanding and development of next-generation software-intensive systems!

John Grundy
Monash University
Melbourne, Australia
john.grundy@monash.edu

References

1. Al Nuaimi, E., Al Neyadi, H., Mohamed, N., & Al-Jaroodi, J. (2015). Applications of big data to smart cities. *Journal of Internet Services and Applications*, 6(1), 25.
2. Al-Ali, A. R., Zualkernan, I. A., Rashid, M., Gupta, R., & AliKarar, M. (2017). A smart home energy management system using IoT and big data analytics approach. *IEEE Transactions on Consumer Electronics*, 63(4), 426–434.
3. Avazpour, I., Grundy, J., & Zhu, L. (2019). Engineering complex data integration, harmonization and visualization systems. *Journal of Industrial Information Integration*, 16, 100103.
4. Benzaken, V., Fekete, J. D., Hémery, P. L., Khemiri, W., & Manolescu, I. (2011). EdiFlow: data-intensive interactive workflows for visual analytics. In *2011 IEEE 27th International Conference on Data Engineering* (pp. 780–791). IEEE.
5. Cai, H., Xu, B., Jiang, L., & Vasilakos, A. V. (2016). IoT-based big data storage systems in cloud computing: perspectives and challenges. *IEEE Internet of Things Journal*, 4(1), 75–87.
6. Chen, C. P., & Zhang, C. Y. (2014). Data-intensive applications, challenges, techniques and technologies: A survey on Big Data. *Information sciences*, 275, 314–347.
7. Chen, M., Mao, S., & Liu, Y. (2014). Big data: A survey. *Mobile networks and applications*, 19(2), 171–209.
8. Cleve, A., Mens, T., & Hainaut, J. L. (2010). Data-intensive system evolution. Computer, (8), 110–112. IEEE.

9. Demirkan, H., & Delen, D. (2013). Leveraging the capabilities of service-oriented decision support systems: Putting analytics and big data in cloud. *Decision Support Systems*, *55*(1), 412–421.

10. Dong, X. L., & Srivastava, D. (2013). Big data integration. In *2013 IEEE 29th International Conference on Data Engineering (ICDE)* (pp. 1245–1248). IEEE.

11. Fernandez, E. B. (2011). Security in data intensive computing systems. In *Handbook of Data Intensive Computing* (pp. 447–466). Springer, New York, NY.

12. Foidl, H., Felderer, M., & Biffl, S. (2019). Technical Debt in Data-Intensive Software Systems. In *2019 45th Euromicro Conference on Software Engineering and Advanced Applications (SEAA)* (pp. 338–341). IEEE.

13. Furht, B., & Escalante, A. (Eds.). (2011). *Handbook of Data Intensive Computing*. Springer Science & Business Media, Berlin.

14. Goeminne, M., Decan, A., & Mens, T. (2014). Co-evolving code-related and database-related changes in a data-intensive software system. In *2014 Software Evolution Week-IEEE Conference on Software Maintenance, Reengineering, and Reverse Engineering (CSMR-WCRE)* (pp. 353–357). IEEE.

15. Gorton, I., Greenfield, P., Szalay, A., & Williams, R. (2008). Data-intensive computing in the 21st century. *Computer*, *41*(4), 30–32.

16. Kaisler, S., Armour, F., Espinosa, J. A., & Money, W. (2013). Big data: Issues and challenges moving forward. In *2013 46th Hawaii International Conference on System Sciences* (pp. 995–1004). IEEE.

17. Kato, J., Igarashi, T., & Goto, M. (2016). Programming with examples to develop data-intensive user interfaces. *Computer*, *49*(7), 34–42.

18. Khalajzadeh, H., Abdelrazek, M., Grundy, J., Hosking, J. G., & He, Q. (2019). Survey and analysis of current end-user data analytics tool support. *IEEE Transactions on Big Data*.

19. Khalajzadeh, H., Simmons, A., Abdelrazek, M., Grundy, J., Hosking, J., & He, Q. (2020). An end-to-end model-based approach to support big data analytics development. *Journal of Computer Languages*, 100964.

20. Kim, G. H., Trimi, S., & Chung, J. H. (2014). Big-data applications in the government sector. *Communications of the ACM*, *57*(3), 78–85.

21. Kleppmann, M. (2017). *Designing Data-Intensive Applications: The Big Ideas Behind Reliable, Scalable, and Maintainable Systems*. O'Reilly Media, Inc., Newton, MA.

22. Mattmann, C. A., Crichton, D. J., Medvidovic, N., & Hughes, S. (2006). A software architecture-based framework for highly distributed and data intensive scientific applications. In *Proceedings of the 28th International Conference on Software Engineering* (pp. 721–730).

23. Mattmann, C. A., Crichton, D. J., Hart, A. F., Goodale, C., Hughes, J. S., Kelly, S., and Medvidovic, N. (2011). Architecting data-intensive software systems. In *Handbook of Data Intensive Computing* (pp. 25–57). Springer, New York, NY.

24. Smith, M., Szongott, C., Henne, B., & Von Voigt, G. (2012) Big data privacy issues in public social media. In *2012 6th IEEE International Conference on Digital Ecosystems and Technologies (DEST)* (pp. 1–6). IEEE.

25. Zaharia, M., Xin, R. S., Wendell, P., Das, T., Armbrust, M., Dave, A.,… & Ghodsi, A. (2016). Apache spark: a unified engine for big data processing. *Communications of the ACM*, *59*(11), 56–65.

Preface

Data-intensive systems are software applications that process and potentially generate big data. In general, data-intensive systems are characterized by the seven V's: volume (large amounts of data), velocity (continuously processed data in real time), variety (unstructured, semistructured, or structured data in different formats and from multiple and diverse sources), veracity (uncertainty and trustworthiness of data), validity (relevance of data to the problem to solve), volatility (constant change of input data), and value (how data and its analysis add value).

Data-intensive systems receive and process data from various diverse (usually distributed) sources, such as sensors, devices, whole networks, social networks, mobile devices, or devices in an Internet of Things. Data-intensive systems support the use of large amounts of data strategically and efficiently to provide additional intelligence. For example, examining industrial sensor data or business process data can enhance production, guide proactive improvements of development processes, or optimize supply chain systems. Furthermore, data-intensive systems support targeted marketing, identify new markets, or improve customer service through the analysis of customer data, social media, or search engine data. Other examples are the use of big data in science to identify disease patterns (using machine learning and artificial intelligence) or online multimedia to provide video streaming services to millions of users. Also, our society can benefit from data-intensive analytics through intelligent healthcare monitoring, cyber-security efforts, and data manipulation in smart cities. Data-intensive software systems are typically not static constructs, but flexible and adaptive systems where a single system or a platform needs to support a variety of usage scenarios. Supporting different usage scenarios means that software must be able to accommodate different (and maybe even unforeseen) features and qualities (e.g., faster response for premium customers).

Software engineering is the application of a systematic approach to designing, operating, and maintaining software systems and the study of all the activities involved in achieving the same. The software engineering discipline and research into software systems flourished with the advent of computers and the technological revolution ushered by the World Wide Web and the Internet. Software systems have grown dramatically to the point of becoming ubiquitous. They have a significant impact on the global economy and on how we interact and communicate with each other and with computers using software in our daily lives. However, there have been major changes in the type of software systems developed over the years. In the past decade owing to breakthrough advancements in cloud and mobile computing technologies, unprecedented volumes of hitherto inaccessible data, referred to as big data, have become available to technology companies and business organizations farsighted and discerning enough to use it to create new products, and services generating astounding profits. In data-intensive systems, dealing with data and the V's is at the center of many challenges in today's system design. Data-related issues such as functionality, modifiability, availability, dependability, durability, interoperability, portability, security, predictability, scalability, consistency, reliability, efficiency, and maintainability of software systems need to be addressed. In particular, one challenge when designing data-intensive software systems is to determine what forms domain objects and knowledge delivery should take for this particular domain.

Designing data-intensive software systems is difficult because distribution of knowledge across stakeholders creates a symmetry of ignorance, because shared vision of the future requires development of new knowledge that extends and synthesizes existing knowledge. Knowledge plays a key role in software development. Knowledge has been called "the raw material of software design teams," while the "thin spread of application domain knowledge" is often cited as the reason for software project failures.

The idea of constructing knowledge is based on a constructionist framework that focuses on the role of artifacts in learning, communicating, and designing. Knowledge construction in software design is concerned with two forms of knowledge: (a) knowledge that is shared by stakeholders and (b) knowledge that is made explicit in the design products. The goal is for the shared understanding of stakeholders to be reflected in design products.

Products that are created to support knowledge construction in software design are called representations for mutual understanding. These representations become mutually meaningful as they are discussed and refined by stakeholders. The shared understanding and the design products coevolve as the design progresses. Thus, representations for mutual understanding are the vehicle for knowledge construction in software design and the product of software design.

Three processes have been identified as crucial in the development of data-intensive software systems: activation of existing knowledge, communication between stakeholders, and envisioning of how a new system will change work practices.

- Activation brings existing knowledge to the forefront by making it explicit;
- Communication builds shared understanding among stakeholders; and
- Envisioning builds shared visions of how the tradition of a work practice should be changed in the future.

Goals of the Book

The book addresses new challenges arising from knowledge management in the development of data-intensive software systems. These challenges concern requirements, architectural design, detailed design, implementation, and maintenance. Furthermore, the environment in which the software will operate is an important aspect to consider when developing high-quality software. That environment has to be taken into account explicitly. A software product may be appropriate (e.g., secure) in one environment, but inadequate (e.g., not sufficiently secure) in a different environment. While these considerations are important for every software development task, there are many challenges specific to variability-intensive systems. In this book, our goal is to collect chapters on knowledge management in the development of data-intensive software systems and more specifically, how to construct, deploy, and maintain high-quality software products.

The book covers the current state and future directions of knowledge management in the development of data-intensive software systems. The book features both academic and industrial contributions, which discuss the role software engineering can play for addressing challenges that confront developing, maintaining, and evolving systems; cloud and mobile services data-intensive software systems; and the scalability requirements they imply. The book intends to feature software engineering approaches that can efficiently deal with data-intensive systems and to learn more about applications and use cases benefiting from data-intensive systems.

This book focuses on several research challenges of knowledge management when developing data-intensive software systems, in particular by:

■ surveying the existing software engineering literature on applying software engineering principles into developing and supporting data-intensive systems;
■ identifying the fields of application for data-intensive software systems;
■ investigating the software engineering knowledge areas that have seen research related to data-intensive systems;
■ revealing the gaps in the knowledge areas that require more focus for data-intensive systems development; and
■ determining the open research challenges in each software engineering knowledge area that need to be met.

The analysis and results obtained from research in this field reveal that recent advances made in distributed computing, nonrelational databases, and machine learning applications have lured the software engineering research and business communities primarily into focusing on system design and architecture of data-intensive systems. Despite the instrumental role played by data-intensive systems in the success of several businesses organizations and technology companies by transforming them into market leaders, developing and maintaining stable, robust, and scalable data-intensive systems is still a distant milestone. This can be attributed to the paucity of much deserved research attention into more fundamental and equally important software engineering activities such as requirements engineering, testing, and creating good quality assurance practices for data-intensive systems.

Reasons for a New Book and How This Book Differs from Other Books in this Area

Online media is filled with stories describing the promise and problems associated with the Internet of Things and autonomous vehicles. Context-aware computing practices have long been important to the creation of personalized mobile device user experience designs. The recent interest in augmented reality and virtual reality, cybersecurity, ultra-large-scale and data-intensive system, and "intelligent" systems (using AI, big data, etc.) has raised the bar on how hard it is to engineer software that is truly adaptable to large number of users and diverse environments. Software engineers are being told to update their knowledge of both artificial intelligence and big data analytic techniques. Software products are being designed to control mission critical systems (such as vehicles and personal robot assistants) without any consideration of the complexities involved in adapting them to constantly changing real-world situations. Most practitioners are woefully uninformed about best practices. All of these things are involved in software engineering and knowledge management for data-intensive systems. Comprehensive knowledge is needed to understand software engineering challenges involved in developing and maintaining these systems. Many books on data-intensive systems focus on the technical details of AI and machine learning. This makes it difficult to gain a comprehensive understanding of the various dimensions and aspects involved in building data-intensive systems. Here we address this gap by providing a comprehensive reference on the notion of data-intensive systems from a technical and nontechnical perspective. It focuses uniquely on the software engineering and knowledge management in the design and maintenance of data-intensive systems. The book covers constructing (i.e., planning, designing, implementing, evaluating), deploying, and maintaining high-quality software products and software engineering in and for dynamic and flexible environments. This book provides a holistic guide for those who need to understand the impact of variability on all aspects of the software life cycle, i.e., the problem space, design space, and solution space of data-intensive systems. It leverages practical experience and evidence to look ahead at the challenges faced by organizations in a fast-moving world with increasingly fast-changing customer requirements and expectations and explores the basis of future work in this area. Contributions from leading researchers and practitioners ensure scientific rigor and practical relevance of the content presented in the book.

Unique Features and Benefits for the Reader

- Familiarizes readers with essentials about knowledge management in the development of data-intensive systems
- Presents a consolidated view of the state-of-the-art (techniques, methodologies, tools, best practices, guidelines) and state-of-practice from different domains and business contexts
- Covers knowledge management at all levels and stages of development in data-intensive software systems, including software design, implementation, and verification of data-intensive software systems
- Provides useful leads for future research in established and emerging domains
- Includes case studies, experiments, empirical validation, and systematic comparisons of approaches in research and practice

Each chapter considers the practical application of the topic.

Contents

An introductory chapter by the editors explores the application of established software engineering process models and standard practices, enhanced with knowledge management techniques, to develop data-intensive systems.

Part I reviews key concepts and models for knowledge management in the development of data-intensive software systems. This includes software artifact traceability in data-intensive systems, architecting software model management and analytics framework, and variability in data-intensive systems from an architecture perspective.

Part II focuses on knowledge discovery and management in the development of data-intensive software systems. This includes the knowledge management via human-centric domain-specific visual languages, augmented analytics for data-mining and managing big data refactoring for design improvement, and knowledge discovery in systems-of-systems.

Part III presents cloud services in the development of data-intensive software systems. This includes the challenging landscape for cloud monitoring, machine learning as a service for software application categorization, and workflow-as-a-service cloud platform and deployment of bioinformatics workflow.

Part IV presents two case studies in the development of data-intensive software systems. This includes application-centric real-time decisions in practice and industrial evaluation of an architectural assumption documentation tool.

Chapter 1: Data-Intensive Systems, Knowledge Management, and Software Engineering by Bruce R. Maxim, Matthias Galster, Ivan Mistrik, and Bedir Tekinerdogan

Data-intensive computing is a class of parallel computing applications that use data-parallel approaches to process large volumes of data (terabytes or petabytes in size). The advent of big data and data-intensive software systems present tremendous opportunities (e.g., in science, medicine, healthcare, finance) to businesses and society. Researchers, practitioners, and entrepreneurs are trying to make the most of the data available to them. However, building data-intensive systems is challenging. Software engineering techniques for building data-intensive systems are emerging. Focusing on knowledge management during software development is one way of enhancing traditional software engineering work practices. Software developers need to be aware that creation of organizational knowledge requires both social construction and sharing of knowledge by individual stakeholders. This chapter explores the application of established software engineering process models and standard practices, enhanced with knowledge management techniques, to develop data-intensive systems

Part I: Concepts and Models

Chapter 2: Software Artifact Traceability in Big Data Systems by Erik M. Fredericks and Kate M. Bowers

This chapter discusses software traceability in the presence of big data. First, software traceability is discussed in terms of developing and maintaining links between software artifacts, specifically requirements and test cases, using a requirements traceability matrix. Second, the effects of big data on software traceability are presented concerning uncertainty and five common big data dimensions. Third, an exemplar application and the process for defining traceability links for that application are presented. Fourth, the state of the art in traceability and big data are reviewed. Finally, an extension of existing research in self-adaptation is presented to enable traceability links to be defined and/or recovered at runtime while a system is executing.

Chapter 3: Architecting Software Model Management and Analytics Framework by Bedir Tekinerdogan, Cagatay Catal, and Önder Babur

Model management and analytics (MMA) aims to use models and related artifacts to derive relevant information to support the decision-making process of organizations. Various different models, as well as analytics approaches, could be identified. In addition, MMA systems have different requirements and, as such, apply different architecture design configurations. Hence, a proper architecture for the MMA system is important to achieve the provided requirements. So far, no specific reference architecture has been defined that is dedicated to MMA in particular. This chapter borrows from and elaborates on existing data analytics architectures to devise and discuss a reference architecture framework that is customized for MMA. It discusses the current key data analytics reference architectures in the literature and the key requirements for MMA. Subsequently, the chapter provides the approach for deriving an application architecture of the MMA. The framework is illustrated using a real-world example.

Chapter 4: Variability in Data-Intensive Systems from an Architecture Perspective by Matthias Galster, Bruce R. Maxim, Ivan, Mistrik, and Bedir Tekinerdogan

This chapter discusses variability in data-intensive systems. It first provides an overview of why variability matters for data-intensive systems. Then, it explores variability in data-intensive systems from a software architecture perspective and discusses potential high-level solutions to addressing variability in data-intensive systems. Here, it first investigates reference architectures as a more traditional way of managing variability in data-intensive systems. It then discusses more technology-oriented approaches, including cloud computing and related concepts. Finally, the chapter discusses serverless architectures as a more recent trend in software engineering and how it relates to data variability in intensive systems. The chapter concludes with a brief reflection on ethical considerations related to variability in data-intensive systems.

Part II: Knowledge Discovery and Management

Chapter 5: Knowledge Management via Human-Centric, Domain-Specific Visual Languages for Data-intensive Software Systems by John Grundy, Hourieh Khalajzadeh, Andrew Simmons, Humphrey O. Obie, Mohamed Abdelrazek, John Hosking, and Qiang He

This chapter describes the use of a suite of human-centric, domain-specific visual languages to manage knowledge for data-intensive systems. The authors use two exemplar system case studies – a smart home to support aging people and a set of smart city technologies – to motivate the need for such an approach. The chapter describes aspects of these two example systems from abstract requirements to specific data analysis, implementation, and deployment choices using the proposed BiDaML representation. The chapter discusses the strengths and limitations of the approach and key directions for further work in this area.

Chapter 6: Augmented Analytics for Datamining: A Formal Framework and Methodology by Charu Chandra, Vijayaraja Thiruvengadam, and Amber MacKenzie

Since the emergence of business intelligence in decision-making, efforts to automate decision-making capabilities relating to data preparation, data analysis, and data visualization have continued with varying degrees of success. Many of these activities have been independently performed, lacking an architecture for integrated development and implementation. Such decision-making environment, besides remaining largely manual, is also prone to individual biases. As the need to process data volumes is increasing exponentially and sourced cross-functionally, decision-making is increasing in complexity. Further, as the dimensionality of data is increasing owing to number of variables driving an outcome or best action, it is becoming either impossible or impractical to gain valuable insights in decision-making using existing analytics approaches. This has led to biased, inferior, and untimely decision-making. The primary objective of this open research challenge is to explore the promising area of Augmented Analytics in big data that has the promise to harness features and capabilities of both machine learning and natural language processing to offer an integrated toolbox that enables executing search-based analytics and conversational analytics in unison. In this chapter, a framework and methodology for Augmented Analytics is described that has its roots in machine learning and natural language processing fields of research. It unifies capabilities of machine language algorithms and natural language processing to offer a new and innovative paradigm of augmented analytics in decision-making.

Chapter 7: Mining and Managing Big Data Refactoring for Design Improvement. Are We There Yet? by Eman Alomar, Mohamed Wiem Mkaouer, and Ali Ouni

Refactoring is the art of improving the internal structure of a program, without altering its external behavior. With the rise of continuous integration and the awareness of the necessity of managing technical debt, refactoring has become more popular in recent software builds. If we consider refactorings performed across multiple projects, this refactoring knowledge represents a rich source of information that can be useful for practitioners to understand how refactoring is being applied in practice. However, mining, processing, and extracting useful information, from this refactoring armada, seem to be challenging. This chapter takes a dive into how refactoring can be mined and preprocessed and discusses design concepts that can be used to understand the impact of these refactorings. It investigates many practical challenges for such extraction. The volume, velocity, and variety of extracted data require careful organization. The chapter outlines the techniques from many available technologies for such system implementation.

Chapter 8: Knowledge Discovery in Systems-of-Systems: Observations and Trends by Bruno Sena, Frank José Affonso, Thiago Bianchi, Pedro Henrique Dias Valle, Daniel Feitosa, and Elisa Yumi Nakagawa

Systems-of-Systems (SoS) are playing an important role in many critical sectors of our society as an answer to the ever-growing complexity of software-intensive systems. Resulting from the interoperability among independent constituent systems, SoS can perform more complex and larger missions, not achievable by any of the constituents operating individually. Moreover, the amount of data produced by the constituents can be put together to discover essential knowledge to more adequately achieve the SoS missions. This chapter analyzes the evolution of previous and recent approaches for knowledge discovery in SoS and compares them with existing ones for monolithic systems. The chapter distills some conclusions and new insights and presents an agenda for future research in this ever-growing topic.

Part III: Cloud Services for Data-Intensive Systems

Chapter 9: The Challenging Landscape of Cloud-Monitoring by William Pourmajidi, Lei Zhang, Andriy Miranskyy, Tony Erwin, David Godwin, and John Steinbacher

Model management and analytics (MMA) aims to use models and related artifacts to derive relevant information to support the decision-making process of organizations. Different models, as well as analytics approaches, could be identified. In addition, MMA systems have different requirements and, as such, apply different architecture design configurations. Hence, a proper architecture for the MMA system is important to achieve the provided requirements. So far, no specific reference architecture has been defined that is dedicated to MMA in particular. This chapter borrows from and elaborates on existing data analytics architectures to devise and discuss a reference architecture framework that is customized for MMA. It discusses the current key data analytics reference architectures in the literature and the key requirements for MMA. Subsequently, the chapter provides the approach for deriving an application architecture of the MMA. The framework is illustrated using a real-world example.

Chapter 10: Machine Learning as a Service for Software Application Categorization by Cagatay Catal, Besme Elnaccar, Ozge Colakoglu, and Bedir Tekinerdogan

In this chapter, the authors write that Catal et al. present a data-intensive software system that automatically classifies software projects into corresponding categories in a software repository. Since manual categorization of applications is time-consuming, error-prone, and costly for companies that manage the software repositories, the use of automated software systems is an effective and efficient solution. As such, the authors apply several machine learning algorithms on public data sets, which are created based on software projects hosted on the SourceForge repository. The best algorithm in terms of accuracy parameter is identified, the prediction model that uses the best algorithm is transformed into a web service and deployed on the cloud platform. From the knowledge management perspective, the prediction model of this data-intensive system is the critical knowledge that must be managed in the cloud platform, and thanks to the infrastructure support of current cloud computing platforms, monitoring and troubleshooting of these services are easily performed. The authors conclude that cloud-based application categorization is promising, and practitioners can build their own prediction services to manage their own software repositories.

Chapter 11: Workflow-as-a-Service Cloud Platform and Deployment of Bioinformatics Workflow Applications by Muhammad Hafizhuddin Hilman, Maria Alejandra Rodriguez, and Rajkumar Buyya

Workflow management systems (WMSs) support the composition and deployment of workflow-oriented applications in distributed computing environments. They hide the complexity of managing large-scale applications, which includes controlling data pipelining between tasks, ensuring the application's execution, and orchestrating the distributed computational resources to get a reasonable processing time. With the increasing trends of scientific workflow adoption, the demand to deploy them using a third-party service begins to increase. Workflow-as-a-service (WaaS) is a term representing the platform that serves the users who require to deploy their workflow applications on third-party cloud-managed services. This concept drives the existing WMS technology to evolve toward the development of the WaaS cloud platform. Based on this requirement, the chapter extends CloudBus WMS functionality to handle the workload of multiple workflows and develop the WaaS cloud platform prototype. This chapter discusses an implementation of the Elastic Budget-constrained resource Provisioning and Scheduling algorithm for Multiple workflows (EBPSM) that is capable of scheduling multiple workflows and evaluating the platform using two bioinformatics workflows. Experimental results show that the platform is capable of efficiently handling multiple workflows execution and gaining its purpose to minimize the makespan while meeting the budget.

PART IV: Case Studies

Chapter 12: Instrumentation and Control for Real-Time Decisions in Software Applications: Findings and Knowledge Management Considerations by Patrick Tendick, Audris Mockus, and Wen-Hua Ju

Analytical methods such as machine learning and predictive models can improve the way interactive applications behave in real time. However, integrating analytical methods into apps is difficult. There are many people involved, including software developers and data scientists. These apps are almost always event-driven, which can make it difficult to apply analytical models. The authors have implemented a framework that instruments an app with decision points that capture data and control the application. The data can be used to train models that can then be linked back to the decision points to control the app to improve behavior. The chapter shows that the framework is feasible and provides an easy way to gain an understanding of the application and to generate training data. The framework provides crucial knowledge, including the decisions made in the application and the data available in real time.

Chapter 13: Industrial Evaluation of an Architectural Assumption Documentation Tool: A Case Study by Chen Yang, Peng Liang, Paris Avgeriou, Tianqing Liu, and Zhuang Xiong

Documenting architectural assumptions effectively and systematically is of paramount importance in software development. However, the lack of tool support is a critical problem when practitioners manage these assumptions in their daily work. To fill this gap, this chapter proposes the Architectural Assumptions Manager (ArAM) – a tool dedicated to Architectural Assumption Documentation, which aims at alleviating this problem. ArAM was developed as a plugin for Enterprise Architect and provides integration with UML modeling. ArAM was evaluated in terms of its perceived usefulness and ease of use, through a case study with 16 architects from ten companies in China. The results indicate that ArAM is generally useful and easy to use, both in Architectural Assumption Documentation and in software development in general. Moreover, there are several points for improvement, including support for automated analysis (e.g., finding missing relationships between assumptions) and verification (e.g., verifying the correctness of existing assumptions).

Readership of this Book

The book is primarily targeted at researchers, practitioners, and graduate students of software engineering who would like to learn more about the current and emerging trends in knowledge management in the development of data-intensive software systems and in the nature of these systems themselves. The book is especially useful for practitioners who are interested in gaining deeper understanding, knowledge, and skills of sound software engineering practices in developing data-intensive systems and using data-intensive systems to develop other software-intensive systems. The book is also interesting for people working in the field of software quality assurance and adaptable software architectures.

The book also targets upper-/middle-level IT management, to learn more about trends and challenges in knowledge management in the development of data-intensive systems and how such systems may impact their business and operations.

MATLAB® is a registered trademark of The MathWorks, Inc. For product information, please contact:

The MathWorks, Inc.
3 Apple Hill Drive
Natick, MA 01760-2098 USA
Tel: 508-647-7000
Fax: 508-647-7001
E-mail: info@mathworks.com
Web: www.mathworks.com

Acknowledgments

The editors would like to sincerely thank the many authors who contributed their works to this collection. The international team of anonymous reviewers gave detailed feedback on early versions of chapters and helped us to improve both the presentation and accessibility of the work. Finally, we would like to thank the CRC Press management and editorial teams for the opportunity to produce this unique collection of articles covering the very wide range of areas related to knowledge management in the development of data-intensive software systems.

Editors

Ivan Mistrik is a researcher in software-intensive systems engineering. He is a computer scientist who is interested in system and software engineering and in system and software architecture, in particular: life cycle system/software engineering, requirements engineering, relating software requirements and architectures, knowledge management in software development, rationale-based software development, aligning enterprise/system/software architectures, value-based software engineering, agile software architectures, and collaborative system/software engineering. He has more than 40 years of experience in the field of computer systems engineering as an information systems developer, R&D leader, SE/SA research analyst, educator in computer sciences, and ICT management consultant. During the past 40 years, he has been primarily working at various R&D institutions in USA and Germany and has done consulting on a variety of large international projects sponsored by ESA, EU, NASA, NATO, and UNESCO. He has also taught university-level computer sciences courses in software engineering, software architecture, distributed information systems, and human–computer interaction. He is the author or coauthor of more than 90 articles and papers in international journals, conferences, books, and workshops. He has written a number of editorials, over 120 technical reports, and presented over 70 scientific/technical talks. He has served in many program committees and panels of reputable international conferences and organized a number of scientific workshops. He has published the following scientific books: *Rationale Management in Software Engineering, Rationale-Based Software Engineering, Collaborative Software Engineering, Relating Software Requirements and Architectures, Aligning Enterprise, System, and Software Architectures, Agile Software Architecture, Economics-driven Software Architecture, Relating System Quality and Software Architecture, Software Quality Assurance in Large-Scale and Complex Software-Intensive Systems, Managing Trade-offs in Adaptable Software Architecture, Software Architecture for Big Data and the Cloud,* and *Software Engineering for Variability Intensive Systems.*

Matthias Galster is an associate professor in the Department of Computer Science and Software Engineering at the University of Canterbury in Christchurch, New Zealand. Previously he received a PhD in Software Engineering. His current work aims at improving the way we develop high-quality software, with a focus on software requirements engineering, software architecture, development processes and practices, and empirical software engineering. He has published in leading journals and conferences and worked with a range of software companies on applied research projects. He is a frequent reviewer for top-tier international journals and conferences and serves on organizing committees of top-tier international conferences.

Bruce R. Maxim has worked as a software engineer, project manager, professor, author, and consultant for more than 40 years. His research interests include software engineering, user experience design, game development, AR/VR/XR, social media, artificial intelligence, and computer science education. Bruce R. Maxim is a full professor of computer and information science and collegiate professor of engineering at the University of Michigan – Dearborn. He established the GAME Lab in the College of Engineering and Computer Science. He has published more than 70 papers on computer algorithm animation, game development, software engineering practice, and engineering education. He has supervised several hundred industry-based software development projects as part of his work at UM – Dearborn. His professional experience includes managing research information systems at a medical school, directing instructional computing for a medical campus, working as a statistical programmer, and serving as the chief technology officer for a game development company. He has taught university courses on software engineering, game design, artificial intelligence, and user experience design. He is the recipient of several distinguished teaching awards and two distinguished service awards. He is a member of Sigma Xi, Upsilon Pi Epsilon, Pi Mu Epsilon, Association of Computing Machinery, IEEE Computer Society, American Society for Engineering Education, Society of Women Engineers, and International Game Developers Association. He has published the following books: *Software Engineering: A Practitioner's Approach*, *Software Architecture for Big Data and the Cloud*, *Software Engineering for Variability Intensive Systems*, *Software Requirements Analysis and Design*, *Software Design and Data Structures Using Turbo Pascal*, and *Turbo Pascal: Problem Solving and Program Design with Advanced Topics*.

Bedir Tekinerdogan is a full professor and chair of the Information Technology group at Wageningen University & Research in the Netherlands. He received his PhD degree in Computer Science from the University of Twente, the Netherlands. He has more than 25 years of experience in information technology and software/systems engineering. He is the author of more than 300 peer-reviewed scientific papers. He has been active in dozens of national and international research and consultancy projects with various large software companies, where he has worked as a principal researcher and leading software/system architect. Hence, he has got broad experience in software and systems engineering in different domains such as consumer electronics, enterprise systems, automotive systems, critical infrastructures, cyber-physical systems, satellite systems, defense systems, production line systems, command and control systems, physical protection systems, radar systems, smart metering systems, energy systems, and precision farming. He has taken a holistic, systemic, and multidisciplinary approach to solve real industrial problems. With this, he has ample experience in software and systems architecting, software and systems product line engineering, cyber-physical systems, model-driven software engineering, aspect-oriented software engineering, global software development, systems engineering, system-of-systems engineering, data science, and artificial intelligence. All of these topics, he is also actively teaching. He has developed and taught around 20 different academic courses and has provided software/systems engineering courses to more than 50 companies in the Netherlands, Germany, and Turkey. He has graduated more than 60 MSc students and supervised more than 20 PhD students. He has reviewed more than 100 national and international projects and is a regular reviewer for more than 20 international journals. He has also been very active in scientific conferences and organized more than 50 conferences/workshops on software engineering topics.

Contributors

Mohamed Abdelrazek
Faculty of Science, Engineering, and Built
  Environment
Deakin University
Melbourne, Victoria, Australia

Frank José Affonso
Department of Statistics, Applied
  Mathematics and Computation
State University of São Paulo
Rio Claro, Brazil

Eman Abdullah AlOmar
Rochester Institute of Technology
Rochester, New York

Paris Avgeriou
Department of Mathematics and Computing
  Science
University of Groningen
Groningen, the Netherlands

Önder Babur
Eindhoven University of Technology
Eindhoven, the Netherlands

Thiago Bianchi
IBM Brazil
São Paulo, Brazil

Kate Bowers
Oakland University
Rochester, Michigan

Rajkumar Buyya
University of Melbourne
Melbourne, Victoria, Australia

Cagatay Catal
Department of Computer Science
Qatar University
Doha, Qatar

Charu Chandra
College of Business
University of Michigan
Dearborn, Michigan

Ozge Colakoglu
DHL Supply Chain
Istanbul, Turkey

Pedro Henrique Dias Valle
Department of Computer Systems
University of São Paulo
São Carlos, Brazil

Besme Elnaccar
De Facto Software Development Group
Istanbul, Turkey

Tony Erwin
IBM Watson and Cloud Platform
Austin, Texas

Daniel Feitosa
Department of Mathematics and Computer
  Science
University of Groningen
Leeuwarden, the Netherlands

Erik Fredericks
Grand Valley State University
Allendale, Michigan

David Godwin
IBM Canada Lab
Toronto, Ontario, Canada

John Grundy
Faculty of Information Technology
Monash University
Melbourne, Victoria, Australia

Qiang He
School of Software and Electrical Engineering
Swinburne University of Technology
Melbourne, Victoria

Muhammad Hilman
Faculty of Computer Science
Universitas Indonesia
Depok, Indonesia

John Hosking
Faculty of Science
University of Auckland
Auckland, New Zealand

Wen-Hua Ju
Avaya Inc.
Morristown, New Jersey

Hourieh Khalajzadeh
Faculty of Information Technology
Monash University
Melbourne, Victoria, Australia

Peng Liang
School of Computer Science
Wuhan University
Wuhan, China

Tianqing Liu
School of Computer Science
Wuhan University
Wuhan, China

Amber MacKenzie
Information and Technology Services -
    Analytics and Decision Support
University of Michigan
Ann Arbor, Michigan

Andriy Miranskyy
Department of Computer Science
Ryerson University
Toronto, Ontario, Canada

Mohamed Wiem Mkaouer
Rochester Institute of Technology
Rochester, New York

Audris Mockus
University of Tennessee
Knoxville, Tennessee

Elisa Yumi Nakagawa
Department of Computer Systems
University of São Paulo
São Carlos, Brazil

Humphrey O. Obie
Faculty of Information Technology
Monash University
Melbourne, Victoria, Australia

Ali Ouni
Ecole de Technologie Supérieure
University of Quebec
Montreal, Quebec, Canada

William Pourmajidi
Department of Computer Science
Ryerson University
Toronto, Ontario, Australia

Maria Rodriguez
The University of Melbourne
Melbourne, Victoria, Australia

Bruno Sena
Department of Computer Systems
University of São Paulo
São Carlos, Brazil

Andrew J. Simmons
Faculty of Science, Engineering, and Built
  Environment
Deakin University
Melbourne, Victoria, Australia

John Steinbacher
IBM Canada Lab
Toronto, Ontario, Canada

Patrick Tendick
Ingredion, Inc.
Bridgewater, New Jersey

Vijayaraja Thiruvengadam
Information and Technology Services -
  Analytics and Decision Support
University of Michigan
Ann Arbor, Michigan

Zhuang Xiong
School of Computer Science
Wuhan University
Wuhan, China

Chen Yang
School of Computer Science
Wuhan University
Wuhan, China
and
Department of Mathematics and Computing
  Science
University of Groningen
Groningen, the Netherlands
and
IBO Technology (Shenzhen) Co., Ltd
Shenzhen, China

Lei Zhang
Department of Computer Science
Ryerson University
Toronto, Ontario, Canada

Chapter 1

Data-Intensive Systems, Knowledge Management, and Software Engineering

Bruce R. Maxim
University of Michigan

Matthias Galster
University of Canterbury

Ivan Mistrik
Independent Researcher

Bedir Tekinerdogan
Wageningen University & Research

Contents

1.1 Introduction

Data-intensive computing is a class of parallel computing applications which use a data-parallel approach to process large volumes of data (terabytes or petabytes in size). The advent of big data and data-intensive software systems (DISSs) presents tremendous opportunities (e.g., in science, medicine, health care, finance) for businesses and society. Researchers, practitioners, and entrepreneurs are trying to make the most of the data available to them. However, building data-intensive systems is challenging. Software engineering techniques for building data-intensive systems are emerging. Focusing on knowledge management during software development is one way of enhancing traditional software engineering work practices. Software developers need to be aware that creation of organizational knowledge requires the social construction and sharing of knowledge by individual stakeholders. In this chapter, we explore the application of established software engineering process models and standard practices, enhanced with knowledge management techniques, to develop data-intensive systems.

1.1.1 Big Data – What It Is and What It Is Not?

Big data is concerned with extracting information from several data spanning areas such as science, medicine, health care, engineering, and finance. These data often come from a various sources (Variety) such as social media, sensors, medical records, surveillance, video archives, image libraries, and scientific experiments. Often these data are unstructured and quite large in size (Volume) and require speedy data input/output (Velocity). Big data is often considered to be of high importance (Value), and there is a need to establish trust for its use in decision-making (Veracity). This implies the need for high data quality (Mistrik et al., 2017).

Big data work involves more than simply managing a data set. Indeed, the data sets are often so complex that traditional data processing applications may be inadequate. Reports generated from traditional data warehouses can provide insight to answering questions about what happened in the past. Big data tries to make use of advanced data analytics and a variety of data sources to understand what can happen in the future. An organization may use big data to enrich its understanding of its customers, competitors, and industrial trends. Data alone cannot predict the future. A combination of well-understood data and well-designed analytical models can allow reasonable predictions with carefully defined assumptions. There are many software products, deployment patterns, and alternative solutions that should be considered to ensure a successful outcome for organizations attempting to implement big data solutions (Lopes et al., 2017).

1.1.2 Data Science

Data science might be thought of as an umbrella term for any data-driven approaches for finding heuristic solutions to difficult problems. Data science incorporates tools from several disciplines to transform data into information, information into knowledge, and knowledge into wisdom. Figure 1.1 shows that data science might be considered as the intersection of three major areas: software engineering, statistics, and knowledge management (Conway, 2010). A data scientist

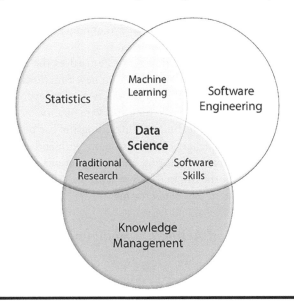

Figure 1.1   Data science Venn diagram.

must be interested in more than just the data. Using knowledge of statistics along with domain-specific knowledge helps the data scientist determine whether the particular data and proposed experiments are properly designed for a particular problem. Good software engineering skills are needed to apply these capabilities to other application scenarios (Grosky and Ruas, 2020).

Many data science projects involve statistical regression techniques or machine learning approaches. A data science project focused on data analytics would consist of the following steps (Grosky and Ruas, 2020):

1. **Data collection:** identifying data needed to satisfy the goals of the project
2. **Data cleaning:** identifying and repairing problem data elements (e.g., missing or corrupt data)
3. **Data transformation:** standardizing data formats to make them suitable for downstream analytic tasks
4. **Data analysis:** examining the data to determine the best analytic approach for predictive or inferential purposes
5. **Training set fabrication:** generating a good training set that will allow the creation of prediction models capable of generalizing data beyond those used to build the model

These steps would typically be used to establish the training set in a machine learning project or a regression-type study.

1.1.3 Data Mining

Data mining is a form of search that might be defined as the process of discovering patterns in large data sets involving methods at the intersection of machine learning, statistics, and database systems (ACM SIGKDD, 2006). Many activities in software engineering can be stated as optimization problems which apply metaheuristic search techniques to software engineering problems. Search-based software engineering is devised on the premise that it is often easier to check a candidate solution that solves a problem than to construct an engineering solution from scratch (Kulkarni, 2013). Lionel Briand (2009) believes that evolutionary and other heuristic search techniques can be easily scaled to industrial-size problems.

Search-based software engineering techniques can be used as the basis for genetic improvement of an existing software product line by grafting on new functional and nonfunctional features (Harman et al., 2014). Successful software products need to evolve continually. However, this evolution must be managed to avoid weakening software quality.

Search-based software engineering techniques (including the use of genetic algorithms) have been used to generate and repair sequences of refactoring recommendations. A dynamic, interactive approach can be used to generate refactoring recommendations to improve software quality while minimizing deviations from the original design (Alizadeh, 2018). Search-based techniques have been used to design test cases in regression testing.

1.1.4 Machine Learning and Artificial Intelligence

Machine learning, like data mining, is an integral part of data science. Creating a data set, as described in Section 1.2, is necessary to drive the machine learning process. In *supervised* machine learning, the user interacts with the training process either by providing training criteria used as a target or by providing feedback on the quality of the learning exhibited. *Unsupervised* machine learning is purely data-driven and typically processes the training data until the learning model reaches an equilibrium state, if one exists (Grosky and Ruas, 2020).

Classification problems and *regression* problems are two broad classes of supervised machine learning tasks addressed by data scientists. In classification problems, the goal is to determine ways to partition the data into two or more categories (e.g., valid vs invalid refactoring operations) and assign numeric values to the likelihood that an unknown data value would be assigned the correct classification by the trained system. In regression problems, the goal is to predict the value of an output variable given the values of several input variables (e.g., trying to predict useful lifetime of a software system based on static quality attributes of its source code). Popular techniques used for supervised learning include linear regression, logistic regression, discriminant analysis, decision trees, and neural networks. Neural networks may also be used for unsupervised learning, along with clustering and dimensional reduction (Grosky and Ruas, 2020).

Neural networks embody the connectionist philosophy of artificial intelligence (AI) developers who believe that an architecture formed by connecting multiple simple processors in a massive parallel environment is one way to duplicate the type of learning that takes place in human being. This view argues that learning takes place by forming connections among related brain cells (processors). Good connections are reinforced during learning and become stronger. Bad connections will become weaker over time, but not completely forgotten.

The power of neural networks is that the same network can be used to solve many different problems. The neural network might be thought of as a way of modeling one or more output variables as a nonlinear function; it includes its input variables and may in some cases also include values from hidden layer variables (see Figure 1.2). Specifying a neural network involves using soft links to specify the connectivity among the nodes. The strength of each connection is specified as

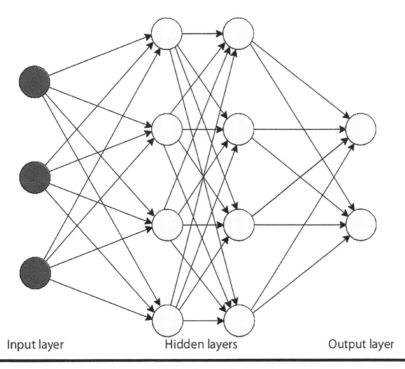

Input layer   Hidden layers   Output layer

Figure 1.2 Neural network with two hidden layers diagram.

a numeric value, which is to grow and shrink as the system processes each member of the training set one at a time. In supervised learning, feedback will be provided to help the network adjust its connection values.

The weakness of neural networks is that they cannot explain how or why the connections caused them to make their predictions for the output variables. This leads people to being skeptical of their use when making critical decisions. Nonetheless, they have been able to solve some difficult problems. Neural networks have been used to predict software reliability (Singh and Kumar, 2010) and make recommendations on code readability (Mi et al., 2018).

1.2 Data-Intensive Systems

Data is one of the many design challenges facing software engineers today. The term "data-intensive" is often used to describe systems that not only deal with huge volumes of data but also exhibit computational-intensive properties (Gokhale et al., 2008). Several difficult issues such as scalability, consistency, reliability, efficiency, and maintainability need to be figured out for these systems. One of the fundamental challenges facing the developers of data-intensive systems is the need to manage and process exponentially growing data volumes by developing new algorithms that scale to process massive amounts of data (Middleton, 2010). Data-intensive processing requirements are often linearly scalable and can be amenable to parallel processing using cloud computing techniques (Buyya et al., 2009).

1.2.1 What Makes a System Data-Intensive?

Data-intensive systems can be described as software systems that handle, generate, and process a large volume of data, which vary in their nature and may have obtained from a variety of sources over time using different technologies. The goal for using data-intensive systems is to extract value from this data for different types of businesses (Felder et al., 2019). There are several characteristics of DISSs that distinguish them from other software applications.[1]

1. Minimizing data movement – to achieve high-performance computing data-intensive systems, try to reduce data movement by ensuring the algorithms execute on the same nodes where the data reside whenever possible
2. Machine-independent programming model – applications are expressed as high-level data operations and data flows using shared libraries of programming abstractions, allowing the runtime systems to control scheduling, execution, load balancing, communications, and data movement
3. Fault-resistant – data-intensive systems are designed with a focus on reliability and availability, by making use of redundant data storage, storage of intermediate results, automatic error detection, and the ability to perform selective recomputation of results
4. Inherent scalability – data-intensive systems can be scaled in a linear manner to accommodate any volume of data or to meet time-critical performance requirements by adding more processors

---

[1] https://en.wikipedia.org/wiki/Data-intensive_computing (accessed July 12, 2020)

1.2.2 *Cloud Computing*

The ability to capture and store vast amounts of structured and unstructured data has grown at an unprecedented rate. Hence, traditional data management techniques and tools did not scale with the generated mass scale of data and the need to capture, store, analyze, and process this data within acceptable time.

To cope with the problems of rapidly increasing volume, variety and velocity of the generated data novel technical capacity and the infrastructure have been developed to aggregate and analyze big data. One of the important approaches is the integration of cloud computing with big data. Big data is now often stored on a distributed storage based on cloud computing rather than local storage. Cloud computing is defined as the dynamic provisioning of computer system resources, especially data storage (cloud storage) and computing power, without direct active management by the user.

Cloud computing is based on services that are hosted on providers over the Internet. Hereby, services are fully managed by the provider, whereas consumers can acquire the required amount of services on demand, use applications without installation, and access their personal files through any computer with Internet access. Cloud computing provides a powerful technology for data storage and data analytics to perform massive-scale and complex computing. As such, cloud computing eliminates the need to maintain expensive computing hardware, dedicated storage, and software applications.

In general, three types of cloud computing models are defined: Infrastructure as a Service (IaaS), Platform as a Service (PaaS), and Software as a Service (SaaS). The IaaS model shares hardware resources among the users. Cloud providers typically bill IaaS services according to the utilization of hardware resources by the users. The PaaS model is the basis for the computing platform based on hardware resources. It is typically an application engine similar to an operating system or a database engine, which binds the hardware resources (IaaS layer) to the software (SaaS layer). The SaaS model is the software layer, which contains the business model. In the SaaS layer, clients are not allowed to modify the lower levels such as hardware resources and application platform. Clients of SaaS systems are typically the end users that use the SaaS services on-demand basis. We can distinguish between thin clients and rich clients (or thick/fat clients). A thin client is heavily dependent on the computation power and functionality of the server. A rich client is a computer that provides itself rich functionality independent of the central server.

In principle, SaaS has a multitier architecture with multiple thin clients. In Figure 1.3, the multiplicity of the client nodes is shown through the asterisk symbol (*). In SaaS systems, the thin clients rent and access the software functionality from providers on the Internet. As such the cloud client includes only one-layer User Layer, which usually includes a web browser and/or the functionality to access the web services of the providers. This layer includes, for example, data integration and presentation. The SaaS providers usually include the layers of Distribution Layer, Presentation Layer, Business Service Layer, Application Service Layer, Data Access Layer, Data Storage Layer, and Supporting Service Layer.

The **Distribution Layer** defines the functionality for load balancing and routing. The **Presentation Layer** represents the formatted data to the users and adapts the user interactions. The **Application and Business Service Layers** represent services such as identity management, application integration services, and communication services. The **Data Access Layer** represents the functionality for accessing the database through a database management system. The **Data Storage Layer** includes the databases. Finally, the **Supporting Service Layer** includes functionality that supports the horizontal layers and may include functionality such as monitoring, billing, additional security services, and fault management. Each of these layers can be further decomposed into sublayers.

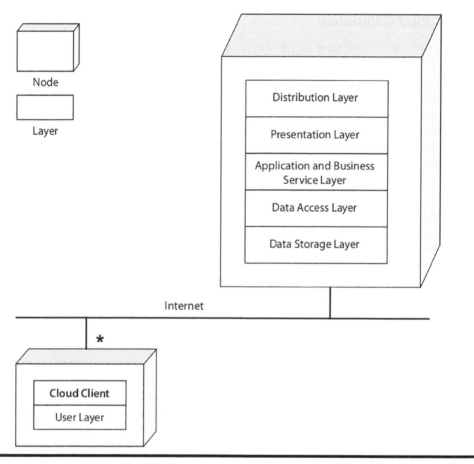

Figure 1.3 SaaS reference architecture.

1.2.3 *Big Data Architecture*

Cloud computing is often integrated with big data. Hence, an appropriate big data architecture design will play a fundamental role to meet the cloud data processing needs. Several reference architectures are now being proposed to support the design of Big Data systems, among which we will focus on the Lambda architecture defined by Marz and Warren (2015). The Lambda architecture is a big data architecture that is designed to satisfy the needs for a robust system that is fault-tolerant, both against hardware failures and human mistakes. Hereby it takes advantage of both batch- and stream-processing methods. In essence, the architecture consists of three layers: batch processing layer, speed (or real-time) processing layer, and serving layer (Figure 1.4).

The batch processing layer has two functions: (a) managing the master data set (an immutable, append-only set of raw data) and (b) precomputing the batch views. The master data set is stored using a distributed processing system that can handle very large quantities of data. The batch views are generated by processing all available data. As such, any errors can be fixed by recomputing based on the complete data set and subsequently updating existing views.

The speed layer processes data streams in real time and deals with recent data only. In essence, there are two basic functions of the speed layer: (a) storing the real-time views and (b) processing

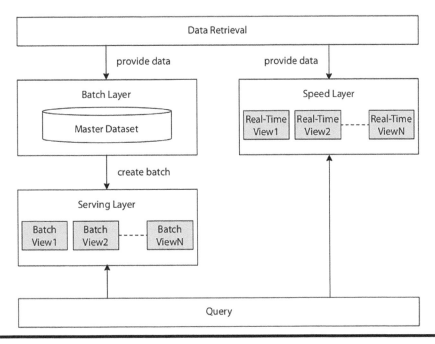

Figure 1.4 Lambda architecture for big data system.

the incoming data stream so as to update those views. It compensates for the high latency of the batch layer to enable up-to-date results for queries. The speed layer's view is not as accurate and complete as the ones eventually produced by the batch layer, but they are available almost immediately after data is received.

The serving layer indexes the batch views so that they can be queried in low-latency, ad-hoc way. The query merges result from the batch and speed layers to respond to ad-hoc queries by returning precomputed views or building views from the processed data.

1.3 Knowledge Management

Knowledge Engineering is a field within AI that develops knowledge-based systems. Such systems are computer programs that contain large amounts of knowledge, rules, and reasoning mechanisms to provide solutions to real-world problems (Ferraggine et al., 2009). Knowledge Engineering is the process of eliciting an expert's knowledge, in order to construct a knowledge-based system or an organizational memory.

Knowledge Management enables the knowledge sharing between people, where one person translates their knowledge to another one (Hansen et al., 1999). Knowledge Management in Software Engineering embraces all aspects of software construction at the intersection of Knowledge Management and Software Engineering. There are many different knowledge management frameworks in existence (Rubenstein-Montano et al., 2001). We discuss several common knowledge management activities in this section (see Figure 1.5). A full discussion of knowledge management in software engineering appears in the seminal book edited by Aurum et al. (1998).

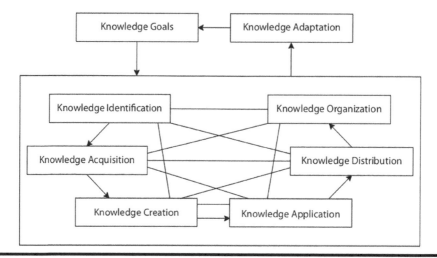

Figure 1.5 KM processes.

1.3.1 Knowledge Identification

Knowledge identification refers to the process of proactively identifying internal organization knowledge needed for the task at hand. Once relevant knowledge has been identified, knowledge can be acquired, created, and shared (Tow et al., 2015). The knowledge management process begins once an organization is able to state its business strategies and objectives. Knowledge requirements are identified to meet these goals. The difference between the knowledge needed and what the software organization needs is called the *knowledge gap* (Yip et al., 2012). Software developers many spend between 0% and 10% of their development time on knowledge identification. Developers may make use of lessons learned in previous projects to identify knowledge needed for the current project (Aurum et al., 2008).

1.3.2 Knowledge Creation

A software development organization develops knowledge through learning, problem-solving, innovation, and importing it from outside sources. Learning is an important part of knowledge management because developers need to internalize shared knowledge before they can perform specific tasks. Software developers learn by doing, learn from each other, and learn from self-study. Iterative knowledge processing is essential to organizations. An organization can only learn what has already been known by its members (Rus and Lindvall, 2002). Software engineers may spend 10%–25% of their development time on knowledge creation. This information may be captured as documents following postmortem meetings where developers describe their lessons learned (Aurum et al., 2008).

1.3.3 Knowledge Acquisition

To be useful, software engineers need to acquire or capture knowledge in explicit forms. Documented explicit assets might include manuals, client directories, competitor intelligence, patents, licenses, and project artifacts. There may also be undocumented assets such as skills, experiences, and knowledge of the organization's people that need to be made explicit (Rus and Lindvall, 2002).

Developers spend 10%–20% of their development time on knowledge acquisition activities. Often knowledge acquisition is facilitated by technical review activities. Many developers regard colleagues as their most valuable source of knowledge (Aurum et al., 2008).

1.3.4 Knowledge Organization

Software engineers organize and transform knowledge both in written form and in digital knowledge repositories. The benefits of making knowledge explicit are that it can be organized and shared with third parties without the involvement of the original knowledge creator (Rus and Lindvall, 2002). Developers may spend 5%–30% of their time on knowledge organization. Sadly, many developers insist that they keep knowledge in their heads. Even when standards and mandated documents from previous projects have been created, it is often difficult to locate and search within the documents. This may be true for online documents as well (Aurum et al., 2008).

1.3.5 Knowledge Distribution

A software development organization distributes or transfers knowledge to others though training programs, automated knowledge repositories, or social networks of experts. One of the goals of knowledge management is to transform an individual's knowledge into knowledge that can be used by the organization. Sharing experiences among developers and customers may benefit both parties (Rus and Lindvall, 2002). Software developers spend <10% of their time on knowledge distribution. The sources of knowledge shared are both implicit and explicit as each developer often has multiple sources of knowledge (Internet, magazines, colleagues, etc.) about company policies and procedures for developing software (Aurum et al., 2008).

1.3.6 Knowledge Application

The goal of knowledge management is to be able to retrieve and apply the knowledge whenever and wherever it is needed. Software development is both a people- and knowledge-intensive activity. It is important for individuals to have access to the correct information and knowledge needed to complete a task or make a decision (Rus and Lindvall, 2002). Developers may spend 10%–35% of their project time on knowledge application. Developers like to reuse their existing software development knowledge in many new scenarios. The use of third-party knowledge is important as software developers will often spend a great deal of time searching for knowledge suitable to their needs (Aurum et al., 2008).

1.3.7 Knowledge Adaption

Like all software engineering artifacts, knowledge needs to be managed and maintained, if knowledge is to evolve and remain current. One of the big problems facing knowledge management is forgetting knowledge when it becomes obsolete or proven in correct. Often one piece of knowledge generates another during the course of a project. A common task during process improvement activities is determining the root cause for a defect. Without a way of tracing the decisions that caused the defect, it is hard to make sure the bad decisions are not repeated. Many developers find the task of updating a knowledge base to be a tedious and time-consuming activity, and it is often not assigned a high priority by project managers. Software engineers spend between 5% and 20% of their development time on knowledge adaptation (Aurum et al., 2008).

1.4 Relating Data-Intensive Systems, Knowledge Management, and Software Engineering

The field of software engineering is facing new challenges at a time when it has never been easier to generate or access large bodies of online data. These challenges span a wide range of technical and social issues, often requiring careful consideration of complicated design trade-offs. These trade-offs emphasize the importance of using multidisciplinary teams, highly iterative life cycle models, and deep understanding of the technologies required when developing data-intensive systems. To move beyond data processing, software engineers need to be committed to understanding the system's application domain, as well as the needs and culture of its users (Anderson, 2015).

1.4.1 Relating Knowledge Life Cycle to Software Development Life Cycle

Software projects typically generate lots of documents, code modules, and developer communication (e.g., emails) to document the work completed. There are also informal discussions between developers that may or may not be documented. All of these are sources of information for knowledge refinement (data to information and information to knowledge). Knowledge management aims at individuals and the information that flows between them (Carreteiro et al., 2016).

The knowledge management life cycle defines the phases of organizational knowledge as (using the terminology from the last section): identification (locating internal and external knowledge sources), acquisition (documenting all knowledge), and creation (mapping knowledge to an interpretable form). After it has been documented and organized, it can be applied and used by others. The new knowledge must be distributed to others to be useful. To use the knowledge in new domains, it may need to be adapted, which will provide a new knowledge source. Much of the knowledge life cycle fits nicely into an iterative software development process model (Figure 1.6).

Requirements specification requires software engineers to interpret the clients' implicit and explicit needs, similar to the task of knowledge acquisition. Design attempts to transform the requirements into a plan, which is like the task of knowledge creation. In coding, the plan is

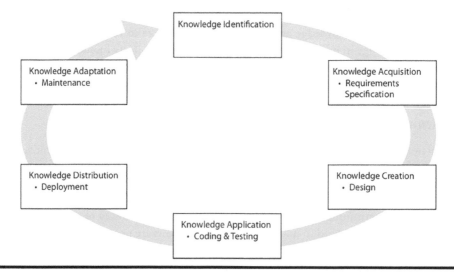

Figure 1.6   Relating the knowledge life cycle to the software development life cycle.

implemented in a manner that allows its application to be tested. When software is deployed, it is distributed to end users. During maintenance, the software is adapted to the end user's changing needs. In the case of knowledge, it is desirable to apply the knowledge to new problems and projects, if possible (Carreteiro, et al. 2016).

1.4.2 Artificial Intelligence and Software Engineering

The synergies between AI and software engineering can be thought of in two ways: the role of AI in software engineering (intelligent software engineering) and the use of software engineering in the development of AI tools and applications (intelligent software). Intelligent software engineering focuses on adding intelligence to various software engineering tasks to accomplish high effectiveness and efficiency. Intelligence software engineering focuses on the tasks required to creating AI software (Xie, 2018).

Harman (2012) claims there are three dominant uses of AI in software engineering work: probabilistic reasoning, machine learning for prediction, and search-based software engineering. Probabilistic reasoning can be used to model software reliability. Machine learning can be used to predict the presence of defects in software before failures occur. Search-based software engineering may be used to assist developers in creating test cases that may be used to automate regression testing (Pressman and Maxim, 2020). We may also use natural language interfaces to allow developers to converse with virtual assistants to improve developer productivity as they perform various software engineering tasks. As software engineering repositories become commonplace, software engineering tools may gain continuous-learning capabilities and increase their competence over time (Xie, 2018).

Software engineering for intelligence software is coming into focus as the intelligent assistants become common in consumer devices. Assuring that the dependability and reliability of intelligence software are important is critical to software safety. Formulating proper requirements for intelligence software remains a challenge for the research community. In addition, intelligence software suffers from the "no oracle" problem, which means the system may only work correctly on the training examples. This can result in a machine predicting the wrong label in a learned classification model (Xie, 2018).

1.4.3 Knowledge Repositories

There is a significant number of documents (user stories, models, developer notes, etc.) and artifacts (storyboards, code, test cases, etc.) produced during all phases of the software development life cycle. This is true even for lean agile software processes. Accessing this information and determining the contexts in which it may be useful to developers on future projects can be challenging if this knowledge is widely dispersed. It would be desirable to store this knowledge in digital repository. The knowledge is often recorded in many different data formats, making it challenging to combine into a single database table. The knowledge, even if documented, can be challenging to update without knowing the provenance of each artifact (Carreteiro et al., 2016). This is where data science may provide some assistance in organizing and searching these repositories.

1.5 Management of Software Engineering Knowledge

A software organization's main asset is its intellectual capital, especially the experience of its employees and the numerous artifacts they generate. Software development is a rapidly changing, knowledge-intensive business often involving a large number of people working on numerous activities. For a software development organization to remain competitive, it is important to establish a culture where software engineers focus on learning, capturing, and reusing these experiences in a manner that allows this knowledge to be shared with others. Knowledge management needs to support that the software engineers working in the organization need to know-how, know-who, know-what, know-when, and know-why (Rus and Lindvall, 2002). Improving the use of this software engineering knowledge is challenging for many organizations.

1.5.1 Software Engineering Challenges in a Data-Intensive World

The development of data-intensive systems has many significant social and technical challenges. As with any design problem, these challenges come as a complicated set of design trade-offs that must be considered when devising a software engineering solution. Anderson (2015) lists several challenges facing software engineers developing date-intensive systems:

- Software engineering is a tool-intensive field, yet there are very few tools to support the development of data-intensive systems.
- Data-intensive systems are often full-stack applications requiring the use of a multidisciplinary team to get the diverse skills needed (e.g., user experience design, software engineering, data analysis, information retrieval, distributed computing, natural language processing (NLP), and application domain expertise).
- The big data work requires highly iterative life cycle models with teams committed to understanding the application domain along the needs and culture of its targeted end users.
- Data-intensive system development requires a deep understanding of the available distributed system frameworks in order to select the best match for a system to be developed.
- It is hard to scale up functionality (e.g., sorting, maintaining model consistency, or data visualization) that works well for small data sets housed on mobile devices to processing data sets that may be so large that the entire file cannot ever be loaded in the device memory at the same time.
- Appropriate data modeling is important to allow developers to collect the types of data needed to answer user questions and storing this data in a way to allow questions to be answered efficiently,

Many of these challenges are related to an inherent problem with big data applications that are very CPU-intensive and have poor throughput rates. The digital information explosion has created the situation that current data processing techniques often cannot provide real-time results using existing computing hardware. Knowledge discovered using data mining techniques may be suspected if the data searched is inconsistent or incomplete. Often the data is organized after it is collected. The data engineering (cleaning, transformation, integration, reduction) required to create well-structured data sets can be very labor-intensive task. The security challenges required to maintain the data integrity and availability are also significant (Chen and Zhang, 2014).

Hummel and his collaborators identified 26 engineering challenges in the big data system development (Hummel et al., 2018). Many of these challenges would be familiar to developers of large systems of any type. Requirements can be unclear since stakeholders can imagine neither the capabilities of the system nor their future desires inspired after using the system. Scope creep may be hard to manage as new requirements emerge from the data and knowledge discovery operation. Privacy and security issues may need to dominate the design activities for some application domains. The trade-offs between quality and performance may cause conflicts among stakeholders.

Architectural issues can arise for system developers since they are often pervasively distributed, making testing and debugging difficult. Design patterns for data-intensive systems are immature. There is no unified modeling support for big data systems. Developers are often forced to use unfamiliar programming paradigms in big data work. Big data systems have high dimensionality, making it hard to design visualizations that help the user understand the data relationships. Correctness of results is often fuzzy since results may need to be expressed in probabilistic terms.

1.5.2 Communication Practices

There are many reasons software projects get in trouble. The scale of many development projects is large – leading to complexity due to scale, uncertainty causing requirement changes, and interoperability issues. To deal with these concerns effectively requires effective methods of coordinating people doing the work. This requires an effective means of managing the knowledge contained in formal and informal communications (Pressman and Maxim, 2020).

Communication is one of the key elements of successful software development. For large software engineering teams and organizations, communication is critical in gathering information, sharing knowledge, and creating functioning products. Informal and ad-hoc communication (e.g., oral, written, electronic, social media) takes significant portions of developers' working time (Reinhardt, 2009). It is important for this informal knowledge to be shared through communication. Nonaka and Takeuchi (1995) proposed a spiral knowledge sharing model (Figure 1.7) as a means by which knowledge is passed to members of an organization using the

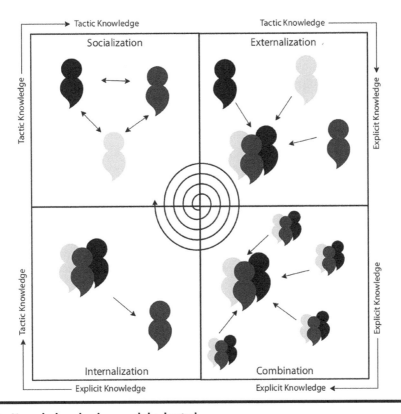

Figure 1.7   Knowledge sharing model adapted.

phases of socialization, externalization, combination, and internalization (SECI) to make implicit knowledge explicit.

The continuous knowledge cycle starts with socialization where implicit knowledge is transferred among individuals during socialization. During externalization, individuals make their implicit knowledge explicit by creating a knowledge or software engineering artifact. Explicit knowledge is combined and transformed to more mature knowledge. Lastly, this explicit knowledge is absorbed by individuals who combine it with their own knowledge and experience to create new implicit knowledge. This SECI model fosters communications and organizational learning by the continuous externalization and internalization of knowledge artifacts by individual project stakeholders (Nonaka and Takeuchi, 1995).

In software development, communication means that different people working on a common project agree to a common definition of what they are building, share information, and mesh their activities (Kraut and Streeter, 1995). Collaboration is a central activity in software engineering. Software engineering collaboration is based on three key insights: it is model-based and centered on a shared meaning within the project artifacts containing models describing the final system; software project management is a cross-cutting concern that creates organizational structures that foster collaboration; and global software engineering introduces spatial, temporal, and social–cultural distance into the pathways of collaboration (Whitehead et al., 2010). Usually regular face-to-face communication is considered the best way to spread knowledge and build trust in a team. Software quality seems to rise when two team members collaborate. New communication channels created in software engineering should try to foster the feeling of working in a common room (Reinhardt, 2009).

Experience indicates that as the number of people on a software development team increases, the overall productivity of the team suffers. Breaking team into smaller working groups helps to compartmentalize the problem but makes communication among the teams more challenging as the number of working groups grows larger. The purpose of communication in software engineering is knowledge transfer and acquisition. If the software engineering community is to deal effectively with the communication dilemma, we will need better ways of communicating among stakeholders. Search engines and knowledge repositories are becoming more sophisticated, social media and crowdsourcing are impacting software development processes. This will affect greatly the ways software developers acquire and use knowledge (Pressman and Maxim, 2020).

1.5.3 Engineering Practices

Design is critical to successful software engineering, and many developers want to begin programing as soon as they create a few use cases. While it is possible to do analysis, design, and implementation by creating prototypes incrementally, it is not wise to ignore the design trade-off considerations needed to create an appropriate and extensible architecture for the evolving software product. *Technical debt* is a software engineering term that refers to the costs (effort, time, and resources) associated with rework caused by choosing a "quick and dirty" solution to an immediate problem rather than looking for a better approach that might scale better as the product becomes larger later in the project. It is impossible to avoid creating technical debt when building a product using incremental prototypes. A good software development team understands how to pay down this debt by taking the time to refactor and redocument their code on a regular basis (Pressman and Maxim, 2020).

When agile software developers are pushed to produce new code faster and faster, they often forget to spend time managing their technical debt. Inexperienced agile teams tend to produce more defects than they might using a more controlled development process and may not be documenting their decision-making processes adequately. This can doom developers to repeat their mistakes on future projects. None of these issues are impossible to control, but developers need to capture their lessons learned and be aware of them as they make plans to manage their sprints (Elbanna and Sarker, 2016). The use of technical reviews is one way to identify defects early, but it is also important to document the root causes of these defects in a manner that makes them easily accessible to future developers.

Agile software development advocates constant interactions and information exchanges among stakeholders. Software development relies on a set of software engineering practices (unit testing, continuous integration, and refactoring) and management practices (iterative development, pair programming, daily meetings, story boards, visual management) that emphasize transparency, feedback, collaboration, and adaptation to changes. The tools used for unit testing and continuous integration can create permanent feedback on code development practices in addition to decreasing problems related to late code verification. Agile development practices can provide a context in which team members are predisposed to combining, creating, and sharing their knowledge. However, it is difficult to move this knowledge from being informally documented to formally documented without recording them in an electronic repository (e.g., wiki or database) of some kind during the sprint or spring retrospective meeting (Khalil and Khalil, 2019).

One strategy to keep technical debt under control without halting development is to make use of the design practices of diversification and convergence. *Diversification* is the process of early identification of possible design alternatives suggested by the customer's user stories. Convergence is the process of evaluating and rejecting design alternatives that do not meet the constraints imposed by the nonfunctional requirements defined for any solution the software problem being considered. The effectiveness of diversification and convergence is highly dependent on the experience and intuition of the development team members if they wish to avoid creating throwaway prototype (Pressman and Maxim, 2020). This suggests that it is important to capture the knowledge acquired by developers as the product evolves.

Most research on technical debt has focused on software architecture, code, and artifacts. There is a continuously increasing demand to use big data in science and industry, and developers of DISSs are under, at that same time, pressures as the developers of any other software product. The trade-offs between system quality and shortening development times must be considered when designing DISSs. Due to the heterogeneous nature of DISS, it is likely that technical debt can be incurred when developing its different parts (i.e., software system, data storage system, data). The components of a DISS are often tightly coupled; hence, shortcuts taken in one part may have long-term problems in another. This may require the consequences incurred by a shortcut to be paid by involving experts from other disciplines (e.g., a database shortcut may affect software engineers). If database schema or code defects could be captured in a manner that would allow all members of the multidisciplinary development team to anticipate the actions needed to avoid or resolve the defects, it might be possible to reduce the technical debt incurred while designing the system (Foidl et al., 2019).

A *design pattern* can be defined as three-part rule containing a context, a problem, and a solution (Alexander, 1979). Patterns have been defined for all types of design problems (architecture, data, component, user interface, testing). *Anti-patterns* describe commonly used solutions to design problems that have negative effects on software quality. Design patterns are usually written from the bottom up starting with the solution to a common problem and adding context elements of the situation in which it is to be applied. Anti-patterns are written from the top down, taking a recurring problem and listing its symptoms, its negative consequences, and then possible mitigation steps to reduce these consequences (Brown et al., 1998). To be useful patterns (and anti-patterns) need to be housed in a searchable repository to allow developers to find solutions applicable to the problems needed to be solved (Ampatzoglou et al., 2013). Software patterns can be described as best practice solutions to known problems, this information is valuable to people creating or maintaining similar systems. Sadly, this information is often lost due to poor documentation practices of the original developers. There has been some work on using machine learning techniques to discover new patterns present, but undocumented, in existing software products (Alhusain, 2013).

The way in which software engineering is organized has changed a lot over the last 40 years, but many of its knowledge management issues have not. According to Edwards (2003), among the principle concerns yet to be faced are:

- How to share analysis and design knowledge between projects.
- How to retain knowledge about how to make a stop/go decision following a feasibility study
- How to ensure that development and maintenance knowledge are shared between individuals and teams.
- High workloads and repaid turnover of staff make it difficult to find time for knowledge sharing and reflective activities such as knowledge sharing.
- Software engineering knowledge contains many layers of expertise from general to very specific, making it difficult to reuse.
- Organization culture must encourage a bottom-up "buy in" to knowledge management strategies employed from the top down.

Despite these problems, effective knowledge management of software engineering knowledge is possible, with the right combination of technology, people, and process. There need to be opportunities to document and personalize the knowledge management strategy used by the individuals in an organization.

1.6 Knowledge Management in Software Engineering Processes

Software engineering is a knowledge-intensive profession. Knowledge management is relevant to several software engineering aspects: strategic, organization, and technical. Knowledge management is useful to software engineering actives like these listed below (Edwards, 2003).

- Cost and time estimation
- Project management
- Stakeholder communication
- Developer use of software patterns
- Code reuse
- Staff training
- Maintenance and support

Each of these activities requires recording and being able to access historic software development data relevant to a particular software process improvement goal. The management of knowledge and experience is key to systematizing software engineering and software process improvement.

Quality continues to be an issue of concern to all software engineers. Knowledge management provides organizations with tool to deal with the challenges inherent in software development. Organizational leadership practices, available tools/technology, developer culture, and effective use of measurement have been found to be enablers for using knowledge management processes in software engineering (Ward and Aurum, 2004).

1.6.1 Requirements Engineering

A well-known problem in requirements engineering is communication among stakeholders with different backgrounds. Sometimes this communication problem is attributable to differences in the stakeholders' domain knowledge. Sometimes it is caused by a reluctance of stakeholders to share their knowledge. Requirements engineering might be described as a spiral knowledge management process where tacit knowledge is made explicit (Figure 1.3). Getting stakeholders to focus on sharing their knowledge during requirements engineering is essential to effective requirements engineering. Sometimes sharing can be facilitated, then teams make use of evolutionary prototypes for the purpose of explicit representation of the codified requirements knowledge (Pilat and Kaindl, 2011).

Requirements tracing can be a knowledge management technique that helps align the evolving system with changing stakeholder needs. Experience reuse is necessary to control quality, costs, and time, especially on teams with high developer turnover. Requirements tracing lays the groundwork for knowledge management in large software organizations. Requirements engineering has three dimensions: managing the convergence of stakeholder interests on system goals and constraints, achieving a shared understanding of the issues involved in realizing the system vision, and documenting in formats sharable among humans and machines. When seen as a knowledge product, a traceability artifact must capture all three dimensions of the requirements engineering process. Establishing and maintaining requirements traceability can be an expensive and politically sensitive task (Jarke, 1998).

A software requirements specification is usually a product that evolves during the requirements engineering process. The software requirements specification has a high impact on the ensuing software development activities, even in incremental software process models. The knowledge management activities used to construct and evolve the software requirements should be organized in a manner to discover and understand the knowledge, both implicit and explicit, possessed by all stakeholders. This information is essential to understanding the problem and designing a solution to it. Explicit knowledge is relatively easy to identify since it is often written down. Implicit knowledge often is based on personalized visions and expectations, which makes it hard for stakeholders to integrate into their understanding of the project. Serna et al. (2017) identified three approaches to knowledge management in requirements engineering:

1. Social interaction process approach in which individual knowledge acquisition is transferred to collective knowledge where it can be organized and shared within the software organization using negotiation as the primary means of integrating disparate interests.
2. An AI modeling approach for ensuring the quality of requirements elicitation by focusing on principles used to create recommendation systems (identifying people willing and able to provide complete requirements descriptions that are available for reuse in the evolving system) and fuzzy logic systems (using automatic discovery of implicit connections in the organizations knowledge repository and historic records to enhance organization memory).

3. Gamification approach in which the stakeholders are encouraged to treat barriers (such as cultural, temporal, geographical, social–economic diversity) to stakeholder communication and knowledge transfer as obstacles that must be overcome.

Requirements represent a description of decision alternatives made regarding system quality and functionality. Engineering and implementing requirements are collaborative problem-solving activities where stakeholders produce and consume lots of knowledge. We have discussed techniques for eliciting and sharing requirements knowledge earlier in this chapter. It is also important to consider the importance of representing requirements knowledge for reuse and how to reason about requirements to create new knowledge.

Representing requirements knowledge has two main challenges: providing efficient access to all stakeholders and supporting reuse when similar issues arise at later times. Many requirements tasks are repetitive, labor-intensive, and time-consuming (e.g., hazard analysis for a critical system or creating usability requirements for a mobile app). Instead of using copy and paste technology to reuse text-based requirements in similar projects, it would be wiser to capture this knowledge as models, patterns, cases, and ontologies. NLP is improving, but it is a cumbersome way to capture knowledge that is searchable and reusable (Maalej and Thurimella, 2013).

Reasoning about requirements means considering requirements and a collection and analyzing their interdependencies to derive new knowledge and discover inconsistencies. Requirements planned for the same release should be compatible. Requirements incompatibilities are triggered when not enough time is available to check for inconsistencies. Pairwise comparisons of all requirements are not feasible for large projects. Stakeholders need to settle for focusing on traceability maintenance among critical requirements. A promising technique for reasoning about requirements uses sematic wiki technologies, which allow all stakeholders to collect and semantically enrich requirements. Requirements should be associated with the stakeholders who design and maintain them. Semantic wiki-based environments used for requirements engineering have huge setup overhead and would benefit from the creation of tools to assist in their use (Maalej and Thurimella, 2013).

1.6.2 Architectural Design

Software architectural knowledge consists of architectural design, design decisions, assumptions, contextual information, and other nonfunctional requirements associated with a particular software design. Except for the architecture design and nonfunctional requirements, most architectural knowledge remains hidden in the minds of the software architects. It is likely that explicit representation of this architectural knowledge would be helpful to other developers seeking to build and evolve similar high-quality systems that would be desirable. It would also be desirable to store this architectural knowledge base (e.g., patterns, anti-patterns, ontologies, use cases, design decisions) in a searchable repository. A major problem to overcome with such repository is how to visualize architectural knowledge in a meaningful way. Meaningful ways of representing design decisions would be especially valuable. Linking the ontology of design decisions to the contents of actual design documents would allow for data mining techniques to uncover meaningful traceability relationships. This type of traceability would also allow for easier evaluation as part of change impact analysis (Kruchten et al., 2006).

Knowledge-based approaches can be used to facilitate software architecting activities such as architectural evaluation. Knowledge capture and representation using an ontology to describe architectural elements and relationships is the most popular approach used in architecting activities. Knowledge recovery activities such as documenting past architectural design activities are seldom used in software architecture work. Knowledge-based approaches are most used in architectural evaluation, but not used much in architecture impact analysis or architecture implementation (Li et al., 2013).

1.6.3 Design Implementation

Software development is a series of knowledge-intensive activities that include requirements gathering, problem analysis, design, coding, testing, and supporting software. Agile software development teams need highly valuable knowledge to carry out software design implementation activities. Agile teams are cross-functional teams that make use of frequent face-to-face interaction, effective communication, and customer collaboration as a means of sharing project knowledge. Knowledge sharing can be challenging for distributed agile team due to spatial, temporal, and cultural barriers to communication. The knowledge required for agile development is context-dependent and may be difficult to transfer among different agile teams even within the same organization. Critically analyzing knowledge before trying to reuse it is critical to successful implementation of knowledge management systems. Several knowledge management processes are useful in distributed software development. Knowledge acquisition is facilitated during project inception, customer collaboration, formal training, and self-study. Knowledge organization occurs as developers translate implicit knowledge into explicit forms such as Wiki articles, design documents, and presentation materials stored in a knowledge repository. Knowledge sharing among members of distributed teams (using electronic communication as needed) is facilitated during daily scrum meetings, site visits, pair programming, task rotation, and informal discussions. This shared and stored knowledge is integrated with each individual's knowledge to create new knowledge that may be used in software projects with similar contexts (Dorairaj et al., 2012)

Dingsøyr and Smite (2014) describe five approaches to knowledge management that might be used by software engineers working on global software development projects.

- The systems approach focuses on storing knowledge in shared repositories, because this knowledge has been codified – this approach works well to minimize spatial and temporal distances, but cultural challenges are not easily addressed.
- The cartographic approach focuses on using knowledge maps and creating knowledge directories – this approach works well when temporal distances are small and knowledge can be transferred orally and is also subject to cultural distance issues.
- The engineering approach focuses on organization processes and knowledge flows – this approach relies heavily on explicit knowledge, and it is not affected by temporal or spatial distance, but again cultural difference may cause process knowledge to be interpreted differently by different developers.
- The organizational approach focuses on the use of networks or communities of practice for sharing (pooling) knowledge; explicit knowledge change is less formal than found in repositories and is often communicated orally in physical or virtual meeting – meaning that this approach can suffer from issues caused by all three distances (spatial, temporal, and cultural).
- The spatial approach focuses on using the design of an office space (e.g., whiteboards, Kanban boards, task charts, open office layouts, etc.) to facilitate knowledge management – this approach requires colocation of team members and is only practical for small agile teams.

Dingsøyr and Smite (2014) suggest companies planning to manage global software projects consider several factors. First, they need to identify the specific barriers to knowledge management caused by spatial, temporal, or social distancing. Next, they need to define what should be shared locally and globally (these may differ among the various development sites). For local knowledge management, use approaches (spatial, organizational, cartographic) that require fewer resources first. For global knowledge management, select an approach after evaluating the challenges inherent in the development – cross-site collaboration does not happen without opportunities to learn how to use tools available. Avoid repository approaches that restrict the availability of knowledge to certain sites and avoid premature standardization of practices based on experiences from a single development site.

The use of open-source software has become a popular means of software implementation. Software engineers benefit from reduced development costs for large projects and full access to the source code for components utilized. Managing knowledge in open-source software development can be difficult. It is crucial to allow developers to capture, locate, and share knowledge on code and methods used to implement the open-source project. Open-source software may or may not have much explicit knowledge recorded other than the source code comments. There is often considerable implicit knowledge that exists only in the heads of developers and shared among members of a community of practice. This can make it challenging to integrate open-source software into the knowledge management processes used by development organizations. Knowledge sharing and collaborations among members of a community of practice can be the basis for creating knowledge networks that could be the basis for open-source knowledge management practices (Lakulu et al., 2010).

Designing the software architecture of a software-intensive system is a knowledge-intensive process. The knowledge produced and consumed is complex and needs to be shared and reused among various stakeholders across several software engineering activities. The traditional view is that software architectures are determined by their functional requirements and differentiated from one another during trade-off analysis by assessing how well they accommodate the most important nonfunctional requirements. One view of software architecture is that it is the union of a set of design decisions and that documenting these decisions would be a valuable source of knowledge for future developers. The most valuable decision documentation is the rationale behind the decision, not just the decision result. The rationale behind a particular architectural decision may only reside in the heads of the decision-makers. It is important to provide mechanisms for codifying knowledge in different forms and to focus on leveraging knowledge communities and office spaces to become arenas for knowledge sharing. Learning, both individual and corporate, can be viewed as the process of converting knowledge from implicit to explicit representations (Dingsøyr and van Vliet, 2009).

1.6.4 Verification and Validation

In software engineering, *verification* refers to the set of tasks performed to ensure that a product correctly implements its function as defined by its requirement specification. *Validation* refers the set of tasks undertaken to ensure that the delivered software functions are traceable to the customer's needs and wants. Boehm (1981) described the differences by asking two questions. For verification, are developers building the software correctly? For validation, are developers building the correct product? These questions cannot be answered by testing alone. Verification and validation involve many software quality activities such as feasibility studies, reviews, audits, testing, algorithm analysis, change management, and support. Quality cannot be added at the end and must be incorporated into a software product throughout the process of software engineering (Pressman and Maxim, 2020). Verification and validation activities generate lots of data and many documents. This information needs to be captured and managed as knowledge to make it useful to developers through the software development process.

Verification and validation of engineering designs are important because they influence the performance of delivered products, definition of product functionality, and customer perception of product quality. This makes design verification and validation activities highly valued by software development organizations, though they do not always receive sufficient time or resources in lean software development processes. For mission-critical software development, especially products that require external certification, there is great interest in developing new measurement, inspection, modeling, and planning methods to support software verification and validation. The development of knowledge management capabilities for codifying and capturing verification data will be important to the industrial adoption and implementation of new design verification and validation methods (Maropoulos and Ceglarek, 2010).

Weak alignment of requirements engineering with verification and validation practices can lead to problems in delivering required products on time and with the right levels of quality. For example, failing to communicate requirements changes to testers can result in new requirements not being verified properly or incorrect verification of old requirements that are no longer valid. Efficient development of large-scale software systems requires the coordination of people, activities, and artifacts. Bjarnason and her colleagues (Bjarnason et al., 2014) make four observations on the alignment between requirements engineering and testing activities. Communication and coordination among stakeholders are vital and need to continue throughout the software development process. Getting the quality and accuracy of the requirements right is a crucial starting point for testing the evolving software in-line with the defined and agreed-upon software requirements. The size of the software development organization and its products is a key source of variability for the challenges and practices associated with the alignment of requirements engineering with verification and validation activities. Tools and practices are often not scalable and need to be selected to suit the size of the company and its tasks. Lastly, alignment practices such as good requirements documentation and traceability seem to be applied thought external enforcement for safety-critical systems development. This is in contrast to the development of less critical systems where the only internal motivation for alignment of these practices is seen, even when developers have observed delays and wasted effort caused by poor alignment practices. This suggests that many companies may benefit from making semiautomated knowledge management practices part of their corporate culture.

Fanmuy and his colleagues (Fanmuy et al., 2014) found in a study of requirements written by professional software developers that about 25% of the requirements contained one or more of the following grammatical defects: absence of the word "shall" (8%–10%), use of forbidden works (10%–15%), use of multiple design object (15%), and incorrect grammar (50%). Their observation is that classical review techniques are not performing as expected and that use of lexical and syntactic analysis processing tools could quickly identify several bad requirements earlier. They also suggest the use of ontologies and requirements templates as a way to do better requirements engineering and an easier way to reuse knowledge. Automated tools can assist by finding requirements that are missing, ambiguous, inconsistent, or contain noise.

1.6.5 Maintenance and Support

Software maintenance and support activities begin during requirements engineering and do not end until the software product is formally retired. If the goal of software engineering is to deliver high-quality software products that meet customer needs in a timely manner, software

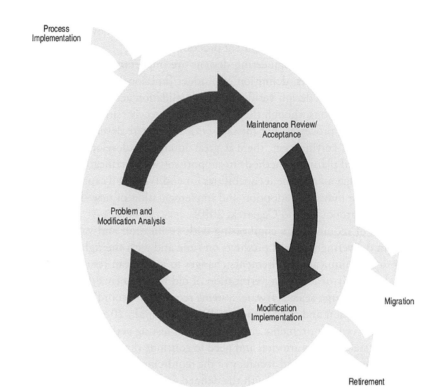

Figure 1.8 Software maintenance and support.

maintenance and support must be performed proactively. It should not be driven solely by correcting defects identified by end users in bug reports. It is important to avoid unnecessary rework, which can happen when defects are repaired in isolation. Supporting software requires software engineers to create tools and processes that allow them to identify potential issues and resolve them before they become problems. A generic process model for proactive maintenance is shown in Figure 1.8. Developers need to search for indicators suggesting that a product may have quality problems and attempt to resolve them through product refactoring or reengineering (Pressman and Maxim, 2020). This suggests that maintenance and support activities may benefit from improved use of software analytics and knowledge management.

For analytics to be useful, they must be actionable based on their proven predictive value. Mining historic information housed in software repositories can help developers determine which analytics are useful and how they might target their software support activities. Zhang et al. (2013) report several lessons learned when using software analytics for proactive maintenance tasks:

■ To get buy-in from developers, analytics must be used to identify meaningful development problems.
■ Analytics need to make use of application domain knowledge to be useful to developers.
■ Developing analytics requires iterative and timely feedback from users.
■ Make sure analytics are scalable to larger problems and customizable to incorporate new discoveries.
■ Evaluation criteria must be correlated with real software engineering practices.

One of the obstacles found in software maintenance is the lack of knowledge contained in the software itself. Research has shown that as much as 60% of the maintenance effort is devoted to understanding the software to be modified (Budiardjo et al., 2016). Proponents of requirements traceability claim that it allows for easier program comprehension and support for software maintenance. Requirements-to-code traceability can reflect the knowledge of how the requirements have been implemented in the code. Capturing and maintaining this knowledge is important to better code comprehension and support for software maintenance. At least one study found that providing software developers use case to code traceability information allowed them to perform maintenance tasks 21% faster and create 60% more correct solutions than developers without traceability information (Mäder and Egyed, 2012).

Knowledge of software operation in the field is acquired by many software organizations in order to improve their software maintenance processes. One of the most challenging tasks is trying to set priorities for software maintenance tasks. To move past personal opinion, it is helpful to have information on the frequency and severity of the reported failures as well as the developer's goals and available resources when trying to set maintenance priorities. Having access to data and knowledge of software operation in the field can make it easier for developers to reach consensus when setting maintenance priorities (van der Schuur et al., 2011).

1.6.6 Software Evolution

In complex software development, projects planning and communication among stakeholders are crucial to effective collaboration throughout the entire software life cycle. Software evolution might be defined as a broader term that encompasses both software development and software maintenance. Adopting knowledge practices would improve both software development and software maintenance activities. A lot of knowledge needed may be documented but a lot of knowledge remains in the minds of the developers. Often knowledge management approaches to software engineering focus on the early activities such as requirements engineering and ignore the knowledge needed for maintenance and reengineering (de Vasconcelos et al., 2017). Figure 1.9 shows a set of activities that take place in cyclic software evolution model.

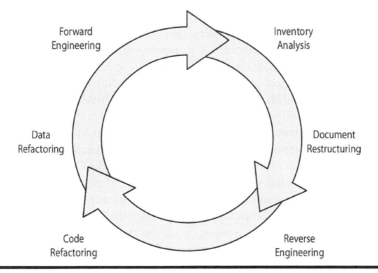

Figure 1.9   Software evolution process model.

The software evolution includes six knowledge-intensive activities (Pressman and Maxim, 2020):

- Inventory analysis – every software organization should have an inventory of all software applications and libraries; storing this information in a searchable repository makes software easier to track and reuse
- Document restructuring – weak documentation is common in legacy systems that have been changed many times. It may be too expensive to create documentation when none exists; the better practice is to determine the level of documentation needed to develop and maintain the software and ensure that the software evolves with each incremental prototype
- Reverse engineering – it is the process of design recovery where developers extract data, architecture, and procedural details from an existing software representation
- Code refactoring – source code is analyzed for violations of good design practices and rewritten to improve software quality without changing its functionality
- Data refactoring – current data architecture is dissected and new data models are created; once new data objects and attributes are defined, the existing data structures are reviewed for quality
- Forward engineering – it recovers design information from existing software and tries to reconstitute the system to improve both its quality and capability

1.7 Development of Data-Intensive Systems

Knowledge plays a key role in software development. Knowledge has been called "the raw material of software design teams" (Walz et al., 1993), while the "thin spread of application domain knowledge" (Curtis et al., 1988) is often cited as the reason for software project failures. In the context of software development, the idea of constructing knowledge is based on a constructionist framework that focuses on the role of artifacts that support learning about, communicating, and designing software-intensive systems (Méndez et al., 2019). More specifically, constructing knowledge in data-intensive systems is about creating direct or indirect business value for the users of the data-intensive system. Here, knowledge construction is concerned with two forms of knowledge: (a) knowledge that is shared by stakeholders (e.g., developers, end users, etc.) and (b) knowledge that is in the design products (i.e., in data-intensive software systems and related artifacts, such as code or documentation). The goal is for the shared understanding of stakeholders to be reflected in design products (Reeves and Shipman 1992; Shipman 1993). The development of data-intensive systems needs to consider both forms of knowledge.

Most, if not all, major software development companies (such as Microsoft, Google, Facebook, and Netflix) develop data-intensive systems and services. For example, at Microsoft, product teams have used machine learning in applications such as Bing Search, the Cortana virtual assistant, the Microsoft Translator for real-time translation, and the Azure AI platform to enable customers to build their own "smart" applications (Amershi et al., 2019; Salvaris et al., 2018). However, developing such applications is highly complex and often involves challenges (and solutions) not known from other types of software-intensive systems. To address these challenges, development teams at Microsoft build software applications with customer-focused AI features by integrating existing agile software engineering processes with AI-specific workflows. These are often informed by prior experiences with early AI and data science applications (Amershi et al., 2019).

In general, designing, implementing, and maintaining data-intensive systems affect not only characteristics of the software product (i.e., what we build – a business intelligence system for a global insurance company) but also the development process (i.e., how we build it –how we ensure systematic quality assurance and validation despite highly complex data and data processing). This raises software engineering issues related to requirements, design, implementation, evaluation, deployment, and maintenance. Sculley et al. discuss challenges for building machine learning systems as one type of data-intensive systems and point out that poor engineering choices can be very expensive (Sculley et al., 2015). In this section, we outline some of the challenges involved in developing data-intensive systems.

1.7.1 Software Engineering Challenges

In general, data-intensive systems are systems where data, and in particular big data, and related challenges contribute essential influences to the analysis, design, implementation, deployment, and evolution of the software-intensive system. Just as software engineering is primarily about the creation and maintenance of code, data-intensive systems are all about the data and the code that utilizes the data to enable features, business goals, and business models. Software engineering in general is about building systems that are elegant, abstract, modular, and simple. By contrast, the data in data-intensive systems are voluminous, context-specific, heterogeneous, and often complex. This results in problems when designing software features to collect, analyze, and present data (e.g., machine learning models) and when integrating these features into software systems at scale (Amershi et al., 2019).

- Requirements engineering: Typical functional requirements of data-intensive systems include storing, managing, accessing, and processing data. This typically includes features related to searching, analyzing, mining, and visualizing data as information. Examples of such systems include health and medical information systems, energy and transportation systems, Geographic Information Systems, industrial control systems in factories and manufacturing plants, and social media platforms (Dong and Srivastava 2013). In particular, determining what forms domain objects and knowledge delivery should take is challenging. The distribution of relevant knowledge across stakeholders creates a symmetry of ignorance, because shared vision of the future requires development of new knowledge that extends and synthesizes existing knowledge (Reeves and Shipman, 1992; Shipman, 1993).
- Architecture and design: It can be more difficult to maintain strict module boundaries between the parts of the system that handle the data than for software engineering modules. For example, if a data-intensive software system uses machine learning models, these can be connected in complex ways that cause them to affect one another during training and tuning of the data required for a feature, even if developers intended them to remain isolated from one another (Amershi et al., 2019).
- Debugging, testing, and evolution: When debugging data-intensive systems, we need to look for not only programming bugs, but also inherent issues that arise from model errors and uncertainty (Amershi et al., 2019; Kulesza et al., 2015). These issues become more important as data-intensive systems, the data they handle, and their analysis become more complex. Furthermore, just like any other software-intensive system, data-intensive systems go through frequent revisions, often initiated by changes in the data, data models, models, or parameters (e.g., used in machine learning or AI-based techniques). These revisions may impact system performance. In particular, fast-paced model development and iterations require frequent deployment.

■ Data management: As developers at Microsoft found, the amount of effort and rigor it takes to discover, source, manage, and version data is inherently more complex and different than doing the same with software code (Amershi et al., 2019). Also, many data analysis techniques used in data-intensive systems, such as machine learning techniques, rely on large data sets for learning. Therefore, the success of data-intensive systems relies on data availability, quality, and management (Polyzotis et al., 2017).

Further challenges are related to the required experience and training of those who develop data-intensive systems. Building customizable and extensible models of data requires teams to not only have software engineering skills but almost always require deep enough knowledge of advanced data analysis and processing techniques (Amershi et al., 2019). For example, "data-intensive" features based on AI and machine learning are more visible in customer-facing products (e.g., machine learning components in email clients and word processing) and embedded systems (e.g., edge computing) (Amershi et al., 2019). As a consequence, developers may need to learn new techniques and tools or learn how to work with specialists in these areas.

1.7.2 Building and Maintaining Data-Intensive Systems

When building and maintaining data-intensive systems, software engineers need a proper understanding, suitable methods, and tools for representing, managing, and reasoning about the data, its characteristics, and its purpose. Therefore, software engineers typically need to collaborate with data scientists. Furthermore, data-related challenges need to be considered by many different stakeholders (clients, acquirers, business analysts, requirements engineers, system and software architects, designers, technology experts, domain experts, service providers, subcontractors, end users, coders, testers). Therefore, software development practices for data-intensive systems impact all types of software development activities and all phases of a software product life cycle. We discuss some implications on building and maintaining data-intensive systems in the following subsections.

1.7.2.1 Requirements Engineering

Requirements engineering activities need to be able to explore the problem space and to identify foreseeable and potentially unforeseeable data, data needs, and data analysis; capture these in an appropriate format and specification; and maintain these specifications throughout the lifetime of a system. Developers would decide which data is needed and is useful for a product. This means, during requirements engineering, we need to identify different types of requirements, including requirements about data quality and quantity, provenance, monitoring, and protected classes and attributes (Vogelsang and Borg, 2019). Requirements engineers need to identify a suitable measure of accuracy to mediate between end users and those who are experts in handling the data (i.e., data scientists). Also, during the requirements stage, engineers need to think about viable data sources, the value of the data, as well as use cases for the data and analysis results.

Requirements engineering for data-intensive systems also requires establishing data governance policies. Data governance is a cross-cutting type of activity related to establishing and maintaining the goals of data, the data analysis, and aligning them with enterprise goals and strategies of an organization, or the purpose of a data-intensive product and service. For example, an organization may decide to analyze consumer behavior to design experiments for product evaluation. Data governance would ensure that this goal is maintained throughout the development of a data-intensive software product or service.

1.7.2.2 *Architecture and Design*

Developers need to decide what types of data models are the most appropriate ones for modeling the required data as well as analyzing them, given the constraints of AI and machine learning techniques typically used in data-intensive systems. The required data and data models need to be supported by proper data collection techniques (e.g., at the requirements stage, developers may look at existing data sets or discuss ways to collect their own and new data during the lifetime of a system). Here, developers may use available data sets and analysis techniques. For example, when designing software for autonomous cars, they might decide to use generic data sets for training a partial model (e.g., ImageNet for object detection (Amershi et al., 2019)) and then apply transfer learning together with more specialized data to train a more specific model (e.g., to detect pedestrians in a software-intensive system for autonomous cars).

Design also involves exploring processes, techniques, and tools for data cleaning to remove inaccurate or noise data from the data stored and processed. This includes exploring technologies, frameworks, etc., to handle large amounts of diverse and frequently arriving data (databases, analytical models, etc.). Below we outline generic activities for the data-centric part of the design of a data-intensive software system:

- Collect and track data: Data need to be collected, typically from multiple data sources. This means that the architecture and design need to support adding, replacing, or removing data sources. Data sources could be hardware sensors or software monitors. Furthermore, due to the rapid iteration involved in data-intensive systems, the data schema (and the data) changes frequently, even many times per day. These changes need to be tracked.
- Clean and curate data: Cleaning (or cleansing data) is about detecting, correcting, or removing corrupt data from a data set (e.g., incomplete, incorrect, inaccurate, or irrelevant parts of the data). Data-intensive systems need to include features to support interactive data wrangling, batch processing, and scripting (Wu, 2013). Curating data is about organizing and integrating the data that has been collected from different sources. It includes "all the processes needed for principled and controlled data creation, maintenance, and management, together with the capacity to add value to data" (Miller, 2014). For data-intensive systems, curation is prominent when processing high-volume and complex data (Furht and Escalante, 2011). Data curation attempts to determine what information is worth saving and for how long (Borgman, 2015).
- Filter data: Filtering data is about selecting a smaller part of the data set (or data sets) and using that set (or sets) for further analysis. Filtering can be temporary. This means that the complete data set is kept (typically, all raw data is kept), but only the subset is used for a certain operation, depending on the user needs and goals. For example, we can filter to investigate data for a particular period of time, or groups of interest, or to exclude erroneous observations, or to train and validate statistical models for data analysis.
- Store data: Data rarely have explicit schema definitions to describe the columns and characterize their statistical distributions. Engineers need to choose tools and infrastructure, such as Microsoft Azure or Amazon AWS. Storing data also impacts data and knowledge sharing within a data-intensive system. In particular, when a data-intensive system uses machine learning–based data analysis procedures, sharing preprocessed data is crucial. For example, since labeling for supervised machine learning techniques is expensive and time-consuming, it is important to make data available within the company and to reuse it as much as possible (Polyzotis et al., 2017).

■ Version data: Developers need to be aware of the rapid evolution of data sources and continuous changes in data due to operations initiated by the developers themselves or incoming new data (e.g., from sensors or user interactions). This requires rigorous data versioning and sharing techniques. For example, models and data sets can be tagged with information about which data is used for training and the origin. However, while there are very well-designed technologies to version code, the same is not true for data. A given data set may contain data from several different schema regimes. When a single engineer gathers and processes this data, they can keep track of these unwritten details, but when project sizes scale, maintaining this tribal knowledge can become a burden. To codify this information into a machine-readable form, Gebru et al. propose to use data sheets inspired by electronics to transparently and reliably track the metadata characteristics of these data sets (Amershi et al., 2019; Gebru et al., 2018).

1.7.2.3 Debugging, Evolution, and Deployment

To support debugging, developers need more interpretable models or visualization techniques that make "black-box" models more interpretable (Gunning, 2017, Weld and Bansal, 2018). Modularized, layered, and tiered software architecture to simplify error analysis and debuggability can help for large multi-model systems. Testing needs to be supported by infrastructure for A/B testing (which is a good foundation and frequently used for testing ML systems in production), as practiced at Google and Facebook (Tang et al., 2010; Bakshy et al., 2014).

To support evolution and deployment, developers can employ rigorous and agile techniques to evaluate systems. Also, automating tests is as important in data-intensive systems as in any software-intensive system. Still it is important that the human remains in the loop (Amershi et al., 2019). To ensure that deployment goes smoothly, we need to not only automate the deployment pipeline, but also integrate building the models needed for analysis into the pipeline and the rest of the software (e.g., by using common versioning repositories for both data-intensive and non-data-intensive codebases).

1.7.2.4 Organizational Aspects and Training

Data scientists need to work with software engineers (Kim et al., 2017) and in multidisciplinary teams, since data-intensive systems typically require not only knowledge of software engineering, data science, computer science, math, and statistics but also domain or discipline knowledge (e.g., biology, geography, linguistics, or health sciences). At the organizational level, software developing organizations could support this by hosting internal conferences on data science, machine learning, and AI to introduce the basic technologies, algorithms, tools, and best practices in these areas. Also, open forums in organizations on more advanced topics such as deep learning can bring developers together and learn more about new ways of building software. Internal communication channels such as mailing lists, online forums, wikis, and Slack channels can further enable developers ask questions and share new ideas (Amershi et al., 2019).

1.7.3 Ensuring Software Quality in Data-Intensive Systems

Software quality is a critically important yet very challenging aspect of building data-intensive software systems. It is widely acknowledged as a fundamental issue for enterprise, web, and mobile software systems. However, assuring appropriate levels of software quality when building data-intensive software systems is even more of a challenge. According to Webster's Dictionary, "quality" is "a degree of excellence; a distinguishing attribute." That is, quality is the degree to which a software product lives up to the modifiability, availability, durability, interoperability, portability, security, predictability, and other attributes that a customer expects. These quality attributes are the key to ensuring the quality of data-intensive software systems.

Ever since we started to develop "programs" for the very first computer systems, quality has been not only a laudable goal but also very challenging one to actually obtain. Quality may come at significant cost to build-in and maintain. However, substandard quality may come with far greater costs: correcting defects, fixing up business data or processes gone wrong, and sometimes very severe, even life-threatening consequences of lack of appropriate quality.

Defining quality is challenging. Typically, a system or system architecture is thought to have a range of quality attributes. These are often termed nonfunctional requirements. A great range has been developed over many decades in systems engineering. When considering the design and implementation of systems, we often think in terms of reusability, modifiability, efficiency, testability, composability, and upgradability, among many others. Users of software systems are often concerned with usability, along with associated quality issues of performance, robustness, and reliability. Developmental processes wish to ensure repeatability, efficiency, and quality of the process itself. As data-intensive software systems get larger, more complex, and more diverse, many if not all of these quality attributes become harder to ensure.

Many software quality attributes are discussed in the seminal work on Software Architecture in Practice by Bass, Clements, and Kazman (2010). The authors use the key concept of architecture-influencing cycles. Each cycle shows how architecture influences, and is influenced by, a particular context in which architecture plays a critical role. Contexts include technical environments, the life cycle of a project, an organization's business profile, and the architect's professional practices. Quality attributes remain central to their architecture philosophy. Rosanski and Woods in their book *Software Systems Architecture* show why the role of the architect is central to any successful information systems development project and, by presenting a set of architectural viewpoints and perspectives, provide specific direction for improving organization's approach to software systems architecture (Rosanski and Woods, 2011). In particular, they use perspectives to ensure that an architecture exhibits important qualities such as performance, scalability, and security. *The Handbook of Software Quality Assurance* by Schulmeyer and McManus serves as a basic resource for current software quality assurance knowledge (Schulmeyer and McManus, 2007). It emphasizes the importance of CMMI and key ISO requirements and provides the latest details on current best practices and explains how SQA can be implemented in organizations large and small. Galin provides an overview of the main types of Software Quality Assurance models (Galin, 2004). This includes reviewing the place of quality assurance in several software process models and practices. An emphasis is on metrics as these are crucial to permitting an objective assessment of a project's system quality as well as progress. The edited book on *Software Quality Assurance in Large Scale and Complex Software Intensive Systems* by Mistrik, Soley, Ali, Grundy, and Tekinerdogan makes a valuable contribution to this existing body of knowledge in terms of state-of-the-art techniques, methodologies, tools, best practices, and guidelines for Software Quality Assurance and points out directions for future software engineering research and practice (Mistrik et al., 2016). It covers all aspects of Software Quality Assurance, including novel and high-quality research-related approaches that relate the quality of software architecture to system requirements, system architecture, and enterprise architecture, or software testing.

With the large interest and focus on complex software architectures over the past two decades, describing and ensuring software quality attributes in architecture models has become of great interest. This includes developing quality attribute metrics to enable these attributes to be measured and assessed, along with trade-off analysis where ensuring a certain level of quality on one dimension may unintentionally impact others. From a related viewpoint, how design decisions influence the quality of a system and its software architecture are important. It has been well recognized that requirements and architecture/design decisions interplay, especially in domains where the actual deployed system architecture, components, and ultimately quality attributes are unknown or at least imprecise.

There is a strong need to better align enterprise, system, and software architecture from the point of view of ensuring total quality of data-intensive systems. One key concern in data-intensive systems is the quality of data. Here, we can differentiate various data quality attributes that a data-intensive system must maintain (Amershi et al., 2019). These include accessibility; accuracy; authoritativeness; explainability; fairness; latency; learning time, cost, scalability; structuredness; and robustness.

Breck et al. explore different aspects of quality assurance in projects that utilize machine learning, beyond just model and data quality. They also provide some examples and a checklist of quality assurance steps, based on practical experience at Google (Breck et al., 2017). In addition to typical software quality attributes, some organizations also established principles around data-intensive systems and in particular AI-enabled systems in an open world (Amershi et al., 2019). For example, Microsoft's principles include fairness, accountability, transparency, and ethics (Amershi et al., 2019). Details about Microsoft's commitment are described elsewhere.[2]

Many diverse methods and processes have been developed for evaluating quality in software processes, architectures, and implementations. To make them practical, almost all require some degree of tool support to assist in defining quality expectations, taking appropriate measures, and making complex analysis of this data. Software testing methods and tools are a critical component applied at varying levels of software artifacts and at various times. Robust empirical validation of quality has become an important research and practice activity. For example, Zhou et al. studied operational issues of large MapReduce clusters (Zhou et al., 2015). MapReduce is a programming model and associated implementation used in data-intensive systems for processing and generating big data sets with parallel, distributed algorithms on a cluster (Lämmel, 2008). They concluded that most hardware failures are not captured by redundancy mechanisms (Zhou et al., 2015).

Furthermore, there has been strong demand for effective quality assurance techniques to apply to legacy systems and third-party components and applications. As these very often come with "pre-defined" quality measures, understanding these and their impact on other components – and wider system quality – is often critical in engineering effective data-intensive systems. However, many quality constraints and sometimes compromises may need to be made. Understanding and balancing are critical.

Finally, the emergence of data-intensive systems such as enterprise, cloud-enabled, and mobile applications has resulted in much more volatile enterprise system platforms where new services and apps are dynamically deployed and interacted with. There is growing interest in engineering context-aware systems that incorporate diverse knowledge about role, task, social, technological, network, and platform information into ensuring quality systems. "Internet of Thing" brings with it increasing need to ensure the quality of a great many interconnected and interactive software systems.

---

[2] https://www.microsoft.com/en-us/ai/our-approach-to-ai

1.7.4 Software Design Principles for Data-Intensive Systems

As Menzies writes, "Much of the current SE knowledge will be relevant and useful, since a significant amount of the engineers' time will be spent outside of the core AI tools" (Menzies, 2020). This also applies to data-intensive systems in general, which heavily rely on AI for data analysis. Hulten discusses a broad range of software engineering aspects involved in building machine learning systems, including requirements, architecture, quality assurance, and related processes (Hulten, 2018). For example, Hulten suggests implementing an "Intelligence Runtime" responsible for interfacing with the rest of an "intelligent system," gathering the information needed to execute the system's intelligence, loading and interpreting the intelligence, and connecting the intelligence's predictions back to the rest of the system. Also, Hulten suggests including "Intelligence Telemetry" to collect observations about how users are interacting with the data-intensive system and sending some or all of these observations back to the system.

Similarly, Kleppmann provides recommendations of how to balance scalability, consistency, reliability, efficiency, and maintainability, as well as choosing between an overwhelming variety of tools, including relational databases, NoSQL data stores, stream or batch processors, and message brokers (Kleppmann, 2017). Kleppmann explores batch processing, stream processing, partitioning, and replication as design decisions for data-intensive systems. Also, Kleppmann compares different query languages that developers can use in data-intensive systems, storage engines, and data encoding.

To design data-intensive systems, software engineers can collaborate with data scientists. For example, software engineers typically build a product; are concerned about cost, performance, stability, etc.; and identify quality through customer satisfaction. They are aware not only that solutions must scale, but also that software products must be maintainable and evolve over longer periods. They value security, safety, fairness, etc. Data scientists on the other hand can focus on data, the collection of data, data sets, training of models, and the evaluation of models. They are experts in modeling techniques and feature engineering.

Regarding the knowledge in the development of data-intensive systems, three processes have been identified as crucial in development of data-intensive software systems: activation of existing knowledge, communication between stakeholders, and envisioning of how a new system will change work practices. Activation brings existing knowledge to the forefront by making it explicit; communication builds shared understanding among stakeholders; and envisioning builds shared visions of how the tradition of a work practice should be changed in the future. Constraints on the possibilities for transcending the existing tradition of a work practice come from the work organization, the limits of technology, project budgets, and so forth. Visions at some point have to be tested against reality to avoid envisioning what is not possible. Another challenge to envisioning is the fact that future is a moving target. Users are not passive receivers of technology, but instead are themselves designers, who use and adapt technology to their own needs (Simon, 1981; Greenbaum and Kyng, 1991; Mackay, 1992). Therefore, it is important that visions of the future are not regarded as static goals to be attained, but rather as the starting point for continual change and adaptation.

In summary, software development is seen as a cooperative effort between users, who know the practices and implicitly know what a new system should do, and developers, who know the technological possibilities for new systems but not know what technologies are appropriate for the worker's practices. The problem for system development of data-intensive systems could be framed as a movement from a tacit and distributed understanding of existing practices toward a shared vision of what new practices should be (Shipman, 1993).

1.7.5 Data-Intensive System Development Environments

Developers need to integrate data analysis and machine learning development support into traditional software development infrastructures (Amershi et al., 2019). Developers typically want to ensure seamless development across different stages of software development. However, machine learning components, for example, have different characteristics compared to more traditional software components. For example, variation in the uncertainty of data-driven learning algorithms and complex component relationships caused by hidden feedback loops can lead to substantial changes, which were previously well understood in software engineering (Sculley et al., 2015; Nushi et al., 2017). Unifying and automating the day-to-day workflow of software engineers can reduce overhead.

Therefore, building and maintaining data-intensive systems requires the support from suitable tools and development and deployment infrastructures. For example, at Microsoft, developers leverage internal infrastructure or build pipelines specialized to their needs (Amershi et al., 2019). Such pipelines need to be able to continuously load and massage data, enabling engineers to experiment with many variations of AI algorithms. The goal of infrastructures and environments is to help developers discover, gather, ingest, understand, and transform data and then train deploy and maintain models. These pipelines are automated and support training, deployment, and integration of models with the product they are a part of. Examples of openly available IDEs to enable Microsoft's customers to build and deploy their models are Azure Machine Learning for Visual Studio Code and Azure Machine Learning Studio. Tools, platforms, and environments need to be customizable to make them easier to use for developers with varying levels of experience. Furthermore, developers may blend data management tools with machine learning or AI frameworks to avoid the fragmentation of data and modeling activities (Amershi et al., 2019).

1.8 Outlook and Future Directions

Ian Gorton and his colleagues (Gorton et al., 2016) describe several design challenges facing software engineers who seek to create scalable data-intensive systems.

- ■ Pervasive distribution – need to make use of geographically distributed systems to achieve high scalability and availability
- ■ Write heavy workloads – need to use data partitioning and distribution across disks to allow replication to provide high availability
- ■ Variable request loads – need to provide elastic cloud services to avoid the costs of overengineering the system to handle spike requests
- ■ Computationally intensive analytics – need a strategy mixing rapid response requests with long-running requests that involve significant amounts of data
- ■ High availability – need to use distributed software and data replication to make the system resilient

The massive scale brings on other software engineering challenges. It becomes difficult to optimize testing times because of the resources required. New business requirements may impact hundreds of system components, making planning and coordination challenging. Engineering must be able to work independently without interference from centralized management. These challenges will need careful trade-offs requiring new software architectures, design strategies, engineering techniques, and approaches to deployment.

The explosion of interest in AI caused software engineers to look at the synergies possible between AI and software engineering. AI techniques are being added as software engineering processes, in particular natural processing and machine learning (Xie, 2018). NLP is being used to help software engineers mine change requests and customer complaints to guide refactoring efforts. In the future, NLP and machine learning might be able to assist in knowledge recovery activities by mining software engineering artifacts. Software engineering techniques can be used to improve the dependability, reliability, and security of AI software tools used in critical systems.

Harman suggests that several challenges lie ahead for the use of AI in software engineering (Harman, 2012). Many applications of AI to SE have focused on the solution of specific problem instances rather than devising strategies for finding solutions and knowledge discovery. Parallelism is needed for efficient processing in data-intensive systems, to make this technology accessible to large numbers of practitioners, new AI techniques are needed to automatically partition data and schedule parallel process execution. In self-adaptive systems, it would be useful if optimization process could be dynamically added to the deployed software. Some AI techniques have already proved themselves superior to humans in several software engineering activities. The use of AI in program comprehension and design recovery are active areas of research. If AI can be used to identify defects and apply fixes automatically, then software engineering processes will need to be modified to take this into account so to ensure that corporate knowledge repository is updated when the fix goes into the released software.

Data-intensive software systems are often developed under extreme schedules and strict delivery schedules. Developers often need to make technical compromises to meet business constraints. In the future, AI techniques may help developers manage their repository of architectural decisions. Use of AI will not eliminate the need to take technical debt into account when data-intensive systems are evolved. AI techniques may help practitioners identify database schema smells in data-centric software systems (Foidl et al., 2919).

Software development is a knowledge-intensive process. A lot of this knowledge is documented, but a lot of knowledge exists only in the developers' heads. Being able to document this knowledge for use and reuse is challenging for all organizations. Integrating knowledge management practices with software engineering activities may help resolve this problem, if AI-based tools are created (de Vasconcelos et al., 2016)

References

ACM SIGKDD (2006), Data Mining Curriculum 2006-04-30, https://www.kdd.org/curriculum/index. html, Retrieved 2020-04-11.

Alexander, C. (1979) *The Timeless Way of Building*, Oxford University Press, Oxford, UK, 1979.

Alhusain, S. (2013) "Towards machine learning based design pattern recognition", *Proceedings of 13th UK Workshop on Computational Intelligence*, September 2013, pp. 244–251.

Alizadeh, V., M. Kessentini, W. Mkaouer, M. Ocinneide, A. Ouni, and Y. Cai (2018) "An interactive and dynamic search-based approach to software refactoring recommendations," *IEEE Transactions on Software Engineering*, 2018, available at: https://ieeexplore.ieee.org/document/8477161

Amershi, S., Begel, A., Bird, C., DeLine, R., Gall, H., Kamar, E., Nagappan, N., Nushi, B., and Zimmermann, T. (2019) "Software engineering for machine learning: A case study", *2019 IEEE/ACM 41st International Conference on Software Engineering: Software Engineering in Practice (ICSE-SEIP)*, pp. 291–300.

Ampatzoglou, A., et al. (2013) "Building and mining a repository of design pattern instances: Practical and research benefits", *Entertainment Computing*, vol. 4, pp. 131–142.

Anderson, K. (2015) "Embrace the challenges: Software engineering in a big data world", *2015 IEEE/ACM 1st International Workshop on Big Data Software Engineering, Florence*, pp. 19–25.

Aurum, A., Jeffery, R., Wohlin, C., and Handzic, M. (Eds.), (1998) *Managing Software Engineering Knowledge*, Springer, Berlin, Heidelberg, New York.

Aurum, A., Daneshgar, F., and Ward, J. (2008) "Investigating knowledge management practices in software organizations – An Australian experience", *Information and Software Technology*, vol. 50, pp. 511–528.

Bakshy, E., Eckles, D., and Bernstein, M. (2014) "Designing and deploying online field experiments", *Proceedings of the 23rd International Conference on World Wide Web*, pp. 283–292.

Bass, L., Clements, P., and Kazman, R. (2010) *Software Architecture in Practice* (3rd edition) Addison-Wesley Professional, Boston, MA.

Bjarnason, E., Runeson, P., Borg, M. et al. (2014) "Challenges and practices in aligning requirements with verification and validation: A case study of six companies", *Empirical Software Engineering*, vol. 19, pp.1809–1855. doi:10.1007/s10664-013-9263-y.

Boehm, B. (1981) *Software Engineering Economics*, Prentice Hall, Englewood Cliffs, NJ, 1981.

Borgman, C. (2015). *Big Data, Little Data, No Data: Scholarship in the Networked World*, MIT Press, Cambridge, MA.

Breck, E., Cai, S., Nielsen, E., Salib, M., and Sculley, D. (2017) "The ML test score: A rubric for ML production readiness and technical debt reduction", *IEEE International Conference on Big Data (Big Data)*.

Briand, L. (2009) "Model-driven development and search-based software engineering: an opportunity for research synergy", *2009 1st International Symposium on Search Based Software Engineering*, Windsor, pp. xix–xix.

Brown, W.J., et al., (1998) *AntiPatterns - Refactoring Software, Architectures, and Projects in Crisis*, Wiley, New York.

Budiardjo, E., Zamzami, E., Ramadhan, G., and Musa, M. (2016) "Ontology-based knowledge management system model for R3ST software maintenance environment", *Proceedings of the Fifth International Conference on Network, Communication and Computing (ICNCC '16)*. Association for Computing Machinery, New York, NY, USA, pp. 198–202. doi:10.1145/3033288.3033340.

Buyya, R., Yeo, C.S., Venugopal, S., Broberg, J., and Brandic, I. (2009) "Cloud computing and emerging IT platforms: Vision, hype, and reality for delivering computing as the 5th utility", *Future Generation Computer Systems*, vol. 25 (6), pp. 599–616.

Carreteiro, P., de Vasconcelos, J.B., Barão, A., and Rocha, Á. (2016) "A Knowledge Management Approach for Software Engineering Projects Development". In: Rocha, Á., Correia, A., Adeli, H., Reis, L., and Mendonça Teixeira, M. (eds.) *New Advances in Information Systems and Technologies. Advances in Intelligent Systems and Computing*, vol. 444. Springer, Cham. doi: 10.1007/978-3-319-31232-3_6.

Chen, C., and Zhang, C. (2014) "Data-intensive applications, challenges, techniques and technologies: Asurvey on big data", *Information Sciences*, vol. 275, pp. 314–347. Elsevier.

Conway, D. (2010) The Data Science Venn Diagram, available at: http://drewconway.com/zia/2013/3/26/the-data-science-venn-diagram.

Curtis, B., Krasner, H., and Iscoe, N. (1988) "A field study of the software design processes for large systems", *Communications of the ACM*, vol. 31(11), pp. 1268–1287.

de Vasconcelos, J., Kimble, C., Carreteiro, P., and Rocha, A. (2017) "The application of knowledge management to software evolution", *International Journal of Information Management*, vol. 37(1), Part A, pp. 1499–1506. doi:10.1016/j.ijinfomgt.2016.05.005.

Dingsøyr, T., and van Vliet, H. (2009) "Introduction to software architecture and knowledge management". In: Babar, M.A., Dingsøyr, T., Lago, P., van Vliet, H. (eds.), *Software Architecture Knowledge Management*. Springer, Berlin, pp. 1–17.

Dingsøyr, T., and Smite, D. (2014) "Managing knowledge in global software development projects", *IT Professional*, vol. 16(1), pp. 22–29, Jan.-Feb. 2014, doi:10.1109/MITP.2013.19.

Dong, X., and Srivastava, D. (2013) "Big data integration", *2013 IEEE 29th International Conference on Data Engineering (ICDE)*. IEEE, pp. 1245–1248.

Dorairaj, S., Noble, J., and Malik, P. (2012) "Knowledge management in distributed agile software development", *2012 Agile Conference, Dallas, TX*, 2012, pp. 64–73, doi:10.1109/Agile.2012.17.

Edwards, J. (2003) "Managing software engineers and their knowledge". In: Aurum, A., Jeffery R., Wohlin C., and Handzic M. (eds.), *Managing Software Engineering Knowledge*, Springer, Berlin, Heidelberg, New York.

Elbanna, A., and Sarker, S. (2016) "The risks of agile development: Learning from adopters", *IEEE Software*, vol. 33(5), September-October 2016, pp. 72–79.

Fanmuy G., Fraga A., and Llorens J. (2014) "Requirements verification in the industry". In: Hammami O., Krob, D., and Voirin, J.L. (eds.) *Complex Systems Design & Management*. Springer, Berlin, Heidelberg.

Felderer, M., Russo, B., and Auer, F. (2019) "On testing data-intensive software systems". In: Biffl, S., et al. (ed.) *Security and Quality in Cyber-Physical Systems Engineering*. Springer International Publishing, pp. 129–148.

Ferraggine, V. E., Doorn, J. H., and Rivero, L. C. (2009). *Handbook of Research on Innovations in Database Technologies and Applications: Current and Future Trends* (2 Volumes) (pp. 1–1124). IGI Global, Hershey, PA. doi:10.4018/978-1-60566-242-8.

Foidl, H., Felderer, M., and Biffl, S., (2019) "Technical debt in data-intensive software systems", *2019 45th Euromicro Conference on Software Engineering and Advanced Applications (SEAA)*, Kallithea-Chalkidiki, Greece, pp. 338–341.

Furht, B., and Escalante, A. (2011). *Handbook of Data Intensive Computing*, Springer Science & Business Media, Berlin. p. 32. ISBN 9781461414155.

Galin, D. (2004) *Software Quality Architecture: From Theory to Implementation*, Pearson Education, London.

Gebru, T., Morgenstern, J., Vecchione, B., Vaughan, J., Wallach, H., Daumé III, H., and Crawford, K. (2018) "Datasheets for datasets", CoRR, vol. abs/1803.09010, 2018.

Gokhale, M., Cohen, J., Yoo, A., and Miller, W. (2008) "Hardware technologies for high-performance data-intensive computing", *IEEE Computer*, vol. 41 (4), pp. 60–68.

Gorton, I., Bener, A.B., and Mockus, A. (2016) "Software engineering for big data systems", *IEEE Software*, vol. 33(2), pp. 32–35. doi:10.1109/MS.2016.47.

Greenbaum, J., and Kyng, M. (1991) *Design at Work: Cooperative Design of Computer Systems*, Lawrence Erlbaum Associates, Hillsdale, NJ.

Grosky, W., and Ruas, T. (2020) "Data science for software engineers". In: Pressman, R., and Maxim, B. (eds.) *Software Engineering: A Practitioner's Approach* (9th Edition), McGraw-Hill, New York, NY.

Gunning, D. (2017) "Explainable artificial intelligence (XAI)", Defense Advanced Research Projects Agency (DARPA).

Hansen M.T., Nohria N., and Tierney T. (1999) "What's your strategy for managing knowledge?", *Harvard Business Review*, vol. 77, pp. 106–116.

Harman, M. (2012) "The role of artificial intelligence in software engineering", *Proceedings of the First International Workshop on Realizing AI Synergies in Software Engineering (RAISE '12)*. IEEE Press, Piscataway, NJ, USA, pp. 1–6.

Harman, M., et al. (2014) "Search based software engineering for product line engineering: A survey and directions for future work", *Proceedings of the 18th International Software Product Line Conference*, SPL14, Florence, Italy, vol. 1, September 2014, pp. 5–18.

Hulten, G. (2018) *Building Intelligent Systems: A Guide to Machine Learning Engineering*, Apress, New York.

Hummel, O. et al. (2018) "A Collection of Software Engineering Challenges for Big Data System Development," *2018 44th Euromicro Conference on Software Engineering and Advanced Applications (SEAA)*, Prague, 2018, pp. 362–369, doi: 10.1109/SEAA.2018.00066.

Jarke, M. (1998) "Requirements tracing", *Communications of the Association of Computing Machinery*, vol. 41 (12), pp. 32–36.

Khalil, C., and Khalil, S. (2019) "Exploring knowledge management in agile software development organizations", *International Entrepreneurship and Management Journal*. doi:10.1007/s11365-019-00582-9.

Kim, M., Zimmermann, T., DeLine, R., and Begel, A. (2017) "Data scientists in software teams: State of the art and challenges". *IEEE Transactions on Software Engineering*, vol. 44(11), pp. 1024–1038.

Kleppmann, M. (2017) *Designing Data-Intensive Applications: The Big Ideas Behind Reliable, Scalable, and Maintainable Systems*, O'Reilly, Newton, MA.

Kruchten, P., et al. (2006) "Building up and reasoning about architectural knowledge", *International Conference on Quality of Software Architectures*. Springer, pp. 43–58.

Kulesza, T., Burnett, M., Wong, W., and Stumpf, S. (2015) "Principles of explanatory debugging to personalize interactive machine learning", *Proceedings of the 20th International Conference on Intelligent User Interfaces*, pp. 126–137.

Kulkarni, V. (2013) "Model driven software development". In: Van Gorp, P., et al. (ed.) *Modelling Foundations and Applications. ECMFA 2013*. Lecture Notes in Computer Science, vol. 7949, Springer, Heidelberg.

Kraut, R., and Streeter, L. (1995) "Coordination in Software Development", *Communications of the Association of Computing Machinery*, vol. 38(1), pp. 69–81.

Lakulu, M., et al. (2010) "A framework of collaborative knowledge management system in open source software development environment", *Journal of computer and Information Science*, vol. 3(1), pp. 81–90.

Lämmel, R. (2008). "Google's map reduce programming model — Revisited", *Science of Computer Programming*, vol. 70, pp. 1–30. doi:10.1016/j.scico.2007.07.001.

Li, Z., et al. (2013) "Application of knowledge-based approaches in software architecture: A systematic mapping study", *Information and Software Technology*, vol. 55, pp. 777–794.

Lopes, D., Palmer, K., and O'Sullivan, F. (2017) "Big Data: A Practitioners Perspective". In: Mistrik, I., Bahsoon, R., Ali, N., Heisel, M., and Maxim, B. (eds.) Software Architecture for Big Data and the Cloud (pp. 167–179). Morgan Kaufman Publishers, Cambridge, MA. doi: 10.1016/b978-0-12-805467-3.00010-7.

Maalej, W., and Thurimella, A.K. (2013) "An Introduction to Requirements Knowledge". In: Maalej, W., and Thurimella, A. (eds.) *Managing Requirements Knowledge*. Springer, Berlin, Heidelberg.

Mackay, W.E. (1992) "Co-adaptive Systems: Users as Innovators", *CHI'92 Basic Research Symposium*.

Mäder, P., and Egyed, A. (2012) "Assessing the effect of requirements traceability for software maintenance", *2012 28th IEEE International Conference on Software Maintenance (ICSM)*, Trento, 2012, pp. 171–180. doi: 10.1109/ICSM.2012.6405269.

Maropoulos, P., and Ceglarek, D. (2010) "Design verification and validation in product lifecycle", *CIRP Annals – Manufacturing Technolgy*, vol. 59(2), pp. 740–759. doi:10.1016/j.cirp.2010.05.005.

Marz, N., and Warren, J. (2015) *Big Data: Principles and Best Practices of Scalable Realtime Data Systems*, Manning Publications Co., Shelter Island, NY.

Méndez F., Böhm, W., and Vogelsang, A., et al. (2019) "Artifacts in software engineering: A fundamental positioning", *Software System Model*, vol. 18, pp. 2777–2786. doi:10.1007/s10270-019-00714-3.

Menzies, T. (2020) "The five laws of SE for AI", *IEEE Software*, vol. 37, pp. 81–85. doi:10.1109/MS.2019.2954841.

Mi, Q., Keung, J., Xiao, Y., Mansah, S., and Gao, Y. (2018) "Improving code readability classification using convolutional neural networks", *Information and Science Technology* vol. 104, pp. 60–71.

Middleton, A.M. (2010) "Data-intensive technologies for cloud computing". In *Handbook of Cloud Computing*, Springer, New York, pp. 83–136.

Miller, R. (2014) "Big data curation", *20th International Conference on Management of Data (COMAD) 2014*, Hyderabad, India, December 17–19, 2014.

Mistrik, I., Bahsoon, R. Ali, N., Heisel, M., and Maxim, B. (2017) *Software Architecture for Big Data and the Cloud*, Morgan Kaufman Publishers, Cambridge, MA.

Mistrik, I., Soley, R., Ali, N., Grundy, J., and Tekinerdogan, B. (Eds.) (2016) *Software Quality Assurance*, Morgan Kaufmann (an imprint of Elsevier), Waltham, MA.

Nonaka, I., and Takeuchi, H. (1995) *The Knowledge Creating Company: How Japanese Companies Create the Dynamics of Innovation*, Oxford University Press, Oxford, UK.

Nushi, B., Kamar, E., Horvitz, E., and Kossmann, D. (2017) "On human intellect and machine failures: Troubleshooting integrative machine learning systems", *in AAAI, 2017*, pp. 1017–1025.

Pilat, L. and Kaindl, H. (2011) "A knowledge management perspective of requirements engineering", *2011 Fifth International Conference on Research Challenges in Information Science*, Gosier, 2011, pp. 1–12, doi:10.1109/RCIS.2011.6006849.

Polyzotis, N., Roy, S., Whang, S., and Zinkevich, M. (2017) "Data management challenges in production machine learning", *Proceedings of the 2017 ACM SIGMOD*, 2017, pp. 1723–1726.

Pressman, R., and Maxim, B. (2020), *Software Engineering: A Practitioner's Approach* (9th Edition), McGraw-Hill, New York.

Reeves, B.N., and Shipman, F. (1992) "Supporting communication between designers with artifact-centered evolving information spaces", *Proceedings of the Conference on Computer-Supported Cooperative Work (CSCW'92)*, ACM, 1992, pp. 394–401.

Reinhardt, W., (2009). "Communication is the key – Support durable knowledge sharing in software engineering by microblogging". In: Münch, J. & Liggesmeyer, P. (Hrsg.), *Software Engineering 2009-Workshopband*. Gesellschaft für Informatik e.V, Bonn, pp. 329–340.

Rosanski, N. and Woods, E. (2011) *Software Systems Architecture: Working with Stakeholders Using Viewpoints and Perspectives*, Addison-Wesley, Boston, MA.

Rubenstein-Montano, B., et al. (2001) "A systems thinking framework for knowledge management", *Decision Support Systems*, vol. 31, pp. 5–16.

Rus, I. and Lindvall, M. (2002) "Knowledge management in software engineering", *IEEE Software*, vol. 19(3), pp. 26–38.

Salvaris, M., Dean, D., and Tok, W. (2018) "Microsoft AI platform". In: *Deep Learning with Azure*. Apress, Berkeley, CA, pp. 79–98.

Schulmeyer, G. and McManus, J. (2007) *Handbook of Software Quality Assurance* (4th edition), Artech House Publishers, Norwood, M.

Sculley, D., Holt, G., Golovin, D., Davydov, E., Phillips, T., Ebner, D., Chaudhary, V., Young, M., Crespo, J., and Dennison, D. (2015) "Hidden technical debt in machine learning systems", In *NIPS, 2015*.

Serna, E., Bachiller, O., and Serna, A. (2017) "Knowledge meaning and management in requirements engineering", *International Journal of Information Management*, vol. 37 (3), pp. 155–161. doi:10.1016/j.ijinfomgt.2017.01.005.

Shipman, F. (1993) Supporting Knowledge-Base Evolution with Incremental Formalization, PhD-Thesis, University of Colorado, Department of Computer Science.

Simon, H.A. (1981) *The Science of the Artificial*, The MIT Press, Cambridge, MA.

Singh, Y., and Kumar, P. (2010) "Application of fee-forward neural networks for software reliability prediction", *ACM SIGSOFT Software Engineering Notes*, vol. 35(5), pp. 1–6.

Tang, D., Agarwal, A., O'Brien, D., and Meyer, M. (2010) "Overlapping experiment infrastructure: More, better, faster experimentation", *Proceedings of the 16th ACM SIGKDD International Conference on Knowledge Discovery and Data Mining*, pp. 17–26.

Tow, W., Venable, J., and Dell, P. (2015) "Developing a theory of knowledge identification effectiveness in knowledge management", *PACIS 2015 Proceedings*. http://aisel.aisnet.org/pacis2015/85.

van der Schuur, H., Jansen, S., and Brinkkemper, S. (2011) "Sending out a software operation summary: leveraging software operation knowledge for prioritization of maintenance tasks", *2011 Joint Conference of the 21st International Workshop on Software Measurement and the 6th International Conference on Software Process and Product Measurement*, Nara, 2011, pp. 160–169. doi:10.1109/IWSM-MENSURA.2011.14.

Vogelsang, A., and Borg, M. (2019) "Requirements engineering for machine learning: Perspectives from data scientists", *Proceedings of the 6th International Workshop on Artificial Intelligence for Requirements Engineering (AIRE)*, 2019.

Walz, D.B., Elam, J.J., and Curtis, B. (1993) "Inside a software design team: Knowledge acquisition, sharing, and integration", *Communications of the ACM*, vol. 36(10), pp. 63–76.

Ward, J., and Aurum, A. (2004) "Knowledge management in software engineering - describing the process", *2004 Australian Software Engineering Conference, Proceedings*, Melbourne, Victoria, Australia, 2004, pp. 137–146, doi: 10.1109/ASWEC.2004.1290466.

Weld, D. and Bansal, G. (2018) "Intelligible artificial intelligence," arXiv preprint arXiv:1803.04263.

Whitehead J., Mistrík I., Grundy J., and van der Hoek A. (2010) "Collaborative software engineering: Concepts and techniques". In: Mistrík, I., Grundy, J., Hoek, A., Whitehead, J. (eds.) *Collaborative Software Engineering*. Springer, Berlin, Heidelberg.

Wu, S. (2013), "A review on coarse warranty data and analysis", *Reliability Engineering and System*, vol. 114, pp.1–11.

Xie, T. (2018) "Intelligent software engineering: Synergy between AI and software engineering", *Proceedings of the 11th Innovations in Software Engineering Conference (ISEC'18)*. ACM, New York, NY, USA, Article 1.

Yip, M., Ng, A., and Din, S. (2012) "Knowledge management activities in small and medium enterprises/industries: A conceptual framework", *Proceedings of 2012 Conference on Innovation and Information Management (ICIIM 2012)*, IPCT vol. 36, Singapore, pp. 16–19.

Zhang, D., et al. (2013) "Software analytics in practice", *IEEE Software*, vol. 30(5), pp. 30–37.

Zhou, H., Lou, J., Zhang, H., Lin, H., Lin, H., and Qin. T. (2015) "An empirical study on quality issues of production big data platform", *IEEE/ACM 37th IEEE International Conference on Software Engineering*.

CONCEPTS AND
MODELS

Chapter 2

Software Artifact Traceability in Big Data Systems

Erik M. Fredericks
Grand Valley State University

Kate M. Bowers
Oakland University

Contents

Chapter Points

■ Software traceability is an important engineering process for applications comprising varying levels of data.
■ Traceability links can enhance assurance that software is being validated.
■ Traditional strategies for managing traceability links must be extended for big data systems, as demonstrated in this chapter.

2.1 Introduction

The rate at which big data scales is growing exponentially in accordance with the amount of data collected on a daily basis (Marr 2018). While the definition of what constitutes "big" data changes as the amount of data generated increases (i.e., from gigabytes to zettabytes), the concerns inherent must be handled by software. If we consider big data to comprise five "V's,"[1] then the applications designed to manage that data set must consider its *velocity, veracity, volume, value,* and *variety.* If we extrapolate further and consider the design and implementation of such an application from a software engineering perspective, then we are also concerned with designing requirements, test cases, and other artifacts generally necessary for the creation of a reliable system, albeit in the context of big data. Given that these artifacts must scale in complexity to reflect big data concerns, so too must the *traceability links* between such artifacts scale in complexity.

Consider a sample application specified in Figure 2.1. This application is tasked with consuming multiple types of input from web services streaming data, Internet of Things (IoT) sensors continuously broadcasting information, and sporadic user input. The information gathered by the application is stored in a document database (e.g., MongoDB, CouchDB, etc.[2]) for later analytics.

This application must contend with inputs that provide data at varying rates, types, encodings, etc. For instance, a web service may send a packet of data as JSON that is encoded in ISO-8859-1 text formatting, whereas user input is encoded via a user interface such as UTF-8. Moreover, the data streamed from the web service may be scraped at routine intervals; however, user input appears on an event-driven basis. Such concerns can be typical for big data applications. Each of

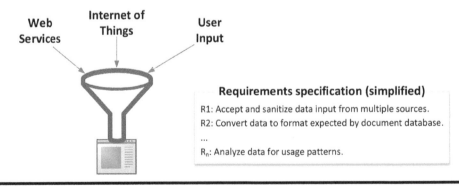

Figure 2.1 Example big data application with sample requirements.

---

[1] The number of V's that define big data tends to fluctuate based on the application.
[2] See https://www.mongodb.com/ and https://couchdb.apache.org/.

these use cases will generally be covered by a software requirement that specifies what is to be performed and how. While the requirements in Figure 2.1 are generalized for presentation purposes, a requirement such as R1 would specify where data would be generated and its expected format. To ensure R1 is properly implemented, *traceability links* from the requirement to various software artifacts would be created. For example, a link would be generated between a set of test cases that provide adequate coverage of R1 and R1 itself. Moreover, links would be generated from R1 to the design decisions that necessitated its creation. Effectively, traceability provides a path from high-level software design to low-level implementation details such that each software artifact is properly managed (Cleland-Huang 2006; Gotel and Finkelstein 1994).

Big data is being leveraged to make decisions based on analytics, trends, and predictions via numerous advanced methods, including artificial intelligence (Chen, Mao and Liu 2014) and machine learning (Najafabadi 2015). Software traceability is often considered to be an approach for following a requirement from its inception to its implementation and beyond (Gotel and Finkelstein 1994). However, few articles exist as of now that discuss the additional concerns that big data can impart upon a rigorous traceability activity. Specifically, traceability analysis is traditionally a manually intensive task, whereas introducing big data concepts and concerns to an application can both exponentially increase the amount of time required for an engineer to undergo the traceability process and significantly increase the risk of introducing errors into the developed traceability links.

This chapter focuses on the design and implementation of software traceability in the context of a big data application. Given that the data contained within a big data set may fluctuate among its various dimensions (i.e., velocity, veracity, etc.), we argue that the application using the data set must be flexible in response to managing the sheer scale of the uncertainties inherent within each dimension. To this end, we will discuss how to enable flexibility in traceability via adaptation, where links may come and go as the application requires. Moreover, this activity requires elevating traceability to be a first-class citizen in the overall software engineering process. To enable traceability adaptation, we introduce an adaptive traceability matrix (ATM), an extension to existing techniques for visualizing traceability (Hariri and Fredericks 2018).

The remainder of this chapter is organized as follows. Section 2.2 discusses relevant background information in software requirements, traceability, and big data. Section 2.3 introduces uncertainty in the context of big data, and Section 2.4 discusses how software artifacts may be translated to big data applications. Section 2.5 examines the state of the art with respect to traceability. Section 2.6 then introduces how adaptive properties can be introduced into traceability for big data applications. Finally, Section 2.7 summarizes this chapter and presents future directions for research.

2.2 Background

This section introduces our representation of software requirements, including how to derive their performance metrics, how traceability factors in, discusses big data from a software engineering perspective, and then overviews the impact of uncertainty in big data applications.

2.2.1 Software Requirements Representation

Requirements engineering (RE) is an aspect of the software development process, generally performed during the early stages of a software development life cycle (Pohl 1993) that is concerned with defining, specifying, verifying, and validating requirements according to an accepted process (where this process varies by organization). This area is very broad in and of itself, and in this chapter, we are assuming that a formal RE process has already been conducted to accurately define and constrain a system to an expected operating procedure.

We now provide our definition of a software requirement to be used in this chapter as a basis for enabling traceability procedures. Requirement 1 (R1), as is next specified, will provide a *functional* requirement (i.e., can be empirically measured) that specifies how a smart home IoT sensor application is tasked with sending monitored data to a server for collection.

```
R1: Device shall sample temperature and humidity readings and transmit
the sampled readings to the server every 30 seconds.
```

R1 above would typically be supported by several similar requirements ensuring the health of the device and calibration of sensors, how to package sensor readings, and the ability to transmit on the network. For illustrative purposes, we will focus on this single measurable requirement. Generally, R1 would be followed as a guideline for implementation and validation, with rigorous quality assurance activities ensuring correct behavior. However, in the context of systems that can be considered *safety-critical* (i.e., must continuously function accurately and correctly), run-time methods for measuring its performance are necessary. One method for introspecting upon a software requirement is via utility functions, as is next described.

Utility Functions: Utility functions are mathematical formulae that can be used to quantify how well requirements are being satisfied during system execution (Walsh et al. 2004; DeGrandis 2009). A utility function is specific to each requirement (or other software artifact, such as an iStar goal) and typically normalized on [0.0, 1.0]. A value of 1.0 indicates complete satisfaction, or that the requirement is behaving as expected. A value of 0.0 indicates a violation, and any value in between is the level of satisfaction. For example, consider R1 from Section 2.2.1. To quantify this requirement, we can define a Boolean formula as shown in Equation 2.1 related to R1:

$$\text{util}_{R1} = \begin{cases} 1.0 \text{ iff sensor readings successfully transmitted every 30 s} \\ 0.0 \text{ else} \end{cases} \tag{2.1}$$

Equation 2.1 displays a sample utility value based on an application's behavior. For instance, R1 states that the application must sample and transmit every 30 seconds. If this action successfully occurs, then the utility value is 1.0 and R1 is considered *satisfied*. If the timing constraint is not met, R1 is considered *violated* and results in a utility value of 0.0 (Figure 2.2).

Quantifying requirements at run time enables software to introspect upon itself, changing its behavior as necessary (see Section 2.6). A violated requirement that is detected at run time can be

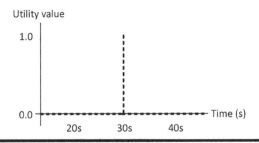

Figure 2.2 Sample Boolean utility function values.

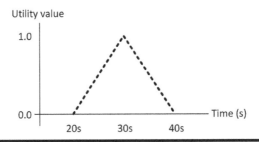

Figure 2.3   Utility values with RELAX operator applied to `R1`**.**

mitigated by changes to the application's configuration or expressed behaviors, assuming that the violation is transient and does not cause critical failure. Such a change ideally would result in the requirement being satisfied again.

Utility functions can also be leveraged to adapt traceability links. For instance, a violated requirement may trigger an adaptation in the system, resulting in a broken traceability link. If the system has the capability to self-reconfigure, then either an existing or a newly derived traceability link can be set to ensure that no links are missing. Moreover, additional flexibility can be introduced into utility functions to provide plasticity in performance monitoring. For instance, `util`$_{R1}$ can be modified to use a fuzzy logic function (i.e., via the RELAX specification language (Whittle et al. 2009; Ramirez et al. 2012)) that provides a continuous value (see Equation 2.2), rather than a discrete value (see Equation 2.1). Such flexibility could be used to modify behaviors or configurations at run time to yield a more optimal performance.

$$\mathrm{util}_{R1} = \mathrm{AS\,CLOSE\,AS\,POSSIBLE\,TO}\left(30\ \mathrm{seconds}\right) \qquad (2.2)$$

Figure 2.3 shows the change in utility value when the RELAX operator has been applied to `R1`. The resulting utility value is no longer Boolean, but rather a range of values between [0.0, 1.0] that depicts the degree of satisfaction that `R1` may take. This range can be used to proactively update a program at run time, rather than wait for a violation to occur (e.g., adapt behavior when a utility value is below a threshold or degrades at a specific rate).

2.2.2 Traceability

Software traceability is an oft-overlooked engineering practice that is required in the field, given its importance for various auditing practices (Cleland-Huang 2006). Traceability, in essence, ensures that each software artifact is linked to a related software artifact at a different level of abstraction (Spanoudakis and Zisman. 2005). For instance, a design decision must be linked to at least one software requirement that must in turn be linked to at least one test case, where each test case must be linked to a test report. Figure 2.4 demonstrates a sample traceability path between a requirement (`R1`) and three test cases (`TC1–3`).

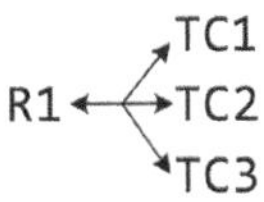

$$R1 \longleftarrow \begin{array}{l} \nearrow TC1 \\ \rightarrow TC2 \\ \searrow TC3 \end{array}$$

Figure 2.4   Sample traceability links between a requirement and associated test cases.

Table 2.1 Sample Requirements Traceability Matrix

Requirement ID	Requirement Description	Test Case IDs / Status	
R1	*Device shall sample temperature and humidity readings and transmit the sampled readings to the server every 30 seconds.*	TC1	PASS
		TC2	PASS
		TC3	FAIL
		...	...
		TCn	PASS
...	...	...	
Rm	...	...	

Traceability is an activity that ensures that no requirement is left untested, that no test case is irrelevant, and that no architectural element is redundant. While it is impossible for software to remain free from bugs or logic errors, traceability will ensure that the proper *process* for specifying and testing a system is followed. The distinction is important, as verification and validation activities are intended to reduce the number of bugs in a system, whereas traceability ensures that the process for specifying and employing verification and validation activities are correctly followed (Cleland-Huang 2006; Winkler Pilgrim. 2010; Borg, Runeson and Ardö 2014). Moreover, traceability is extremely important for safety-critical systems where certifications (e.g., ISO, CMMI, etc.) are required to demonstrate that no untraceable code exists (Cleland-Huang 2006).

Multiple traceability approaches exist, with common software packages such as IBM DOORS[3] and PTC Integrity Lifecycle Manager[4] providing an interface for generating traceability links between software artifacts at different levels of abstraction. A general visualization of traceability is to create a *requirements trace matrix* (RTM). An example of an RTM is below in Table 2.1.

Table 2.1 demonstrates how a requirement (R1) is linked to a set of test cases (TC1,2,3,n) that test various aspects of the requirement to ensure correct implementation. For this example, TC3 is marked as failed, meaning that the implementation, requirement, and test case itself must be reviewed. For brevity, Table 2.1 has only listed out three columns; however, a full implementation would also link fields such as responsible parties, known defects, boundary ranges, etc.

2.2.3 Big Data

Every day, massive volumes of data are created, modified, and retrieved around the world. In 2018, 2.5 quintillion bytes of data were generated globally (Marr 2018). Google supports 40,000 searches per second, or 3.5 billion searches every 24 hours (Marr 2018). Every 60 seconds, Facebook users update 293,000 statuses, post 510,000 comments, and upload 136,000 images (Noyes 2020). Such massive data sets introduce challenges in the collection, storage, analysis, and extraction of useful information, as traditional techniques are unable to support the main characteristics of big data.

---

[3] See https://www.ibm.com/support/knowledgecenter/en/SSYQBZ_9.6.1/com.ibm.doors.requirements.doc/topics/c_welcome.html

[4] See https://www.ptc.com/en/products/plm

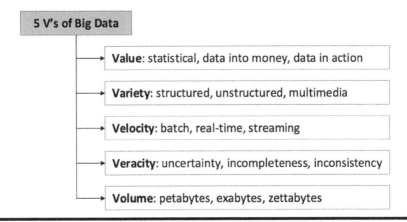

Figure 2.5   Big data dimensions (Hariri, Fredericks and Bowers 2019).

Initially, big data was defined with three characteristics: (a) volume, (b) velocity, and (c) variety (Laney 2001). However, this definition has been extended to include (d) value and (e) veracity (Gantz and Reinsel 2011; Jain 2016; IBM 2020). Although other characteristics of big data have been introduced (Borne 2014), big data is still generally defined using the 5 V's, shown in Figure 2.5.

The *value* characteristic encompasses the usefulness of the data or how it can effectively be used in decision-making. For example, Amazon may analyze millions of purchase records to recommend new products and further increase sales. Similarly, Netflix can evaluate trends in what their users watch and suggest shows or movies to encourage customers to use their services more frequently. Unlike the other four V characteristics, the value of big data offers an advantage over small data sets, rather than represent the challenges that big data imposes.

The *variety* characteristic refers to the challenge of big data where the data sets comprise non-uniform formats. The format of big data sets is generally described as structured, semistructured, and unstructured. Structured data includes information that can be stored in a relational database where fields can be sorted. Semistructured data uses tags instead of fields to group records in a less organized way than a relational database. Unstructured data, such as multimedia content, cannot be sorted or organized. Data cleaning, integrating, and transformation techniques can preprocess unstructured data and convert it to semistructured or structured data (Han, Pei and Kamber 2011; Xiong et al. 2006).

The *velocity* characteristic indicates the speed that the data is received, categorized into batch, real-time, near-real-time, and streaming. The primary challenge associated with the velocity characteristic is to analyze the data as quickly as it is generated (Chen, Mao and Liu 2014). As the amount of data produced grows, the analytic techniques are often unable to evaluate the data quickly enough. Furthermore, in safety-conscious systems, any delays in processing emergency situations can lead to injury or death.

The *veracity* characteristic comprises the quality of the data. Massive data sets often include incomplete or missing fields and records that contribute to inefficient analytic techniques. Veracity includes poor quality at the data collection and data analytic stages.

The *volume* characteristic refers to size, the most common challenge of big data. There is no defined threshold that defines a data set to be large enough to be classified as big data (Gandomi and Haider 2015); however, data sets that meet the exabyte or zettabyte ranges are generally considered as big data (Chen, Mao and Liu 2014; Vajjhala, Strang and Sun 2015). The volume characteristic also changes over time and can depend on the size analytic techniques are expected to process at once. The growing volume of big data also presents challenges in database management techniques, as databases must increase capacity to match the data received. Next, we will discuss how uncertainty can impact big data applications.

2.3 Uncertainty in Big Data

Uncertainty is an insidious problem inherent to all applications (Ziv, Richardson and Klösch 1997; Esfahani and Malek 2013), regardless of data size and application type. For big data, however, uncertainty presents additional concerns related to not only the application but the data set as well. To contextualize how big data can impact the traceability analysis process, we highlight some of the more common types of uncertainty we may face in this domain, focusing on the big data dimensions that were previously introduced.

2.3.1 Value

The value characteristic focuses on the benefits provided by big data rather than the challenges that big data imposes. Corporations can take advantage of big data analytics by monitoring user trends and participation to provide targeted advertising, predict user preferences, provide product recommendations, and overall make more profitable business decisions (Court 2015). Examples of uncertainty in the value characteristic include incorrect analytics decisions and misinterpreted data.

2.3.2 Variety

Data is generally expected to be organized into structured formats for application consumption. However, big data applications may experience semistructured data (e.g., NoSQL databases), unstructured data (e.g., text and multimedia content), and structured data (e.g., objects, SQL databases) within the same data stream. Traditional analysis techniques typically expect data to be in a known format; however, noise or unexpected aberrations in received data can lead to challenges in analysis (Chen, Mao and Liu 2014). Data cleaning, integrating, and transforming techniques can be used to mitigate uncertainty in data (Xiong et al. 2006); however, there still exists the possibility that noise will remain or that the data will be improperly cleaned.

2.3.3 Velocity

The variable speed at which data can be received is a major challenge for big data applications, as data ideally needs to be analyzed as quickly as it is produced (Chen, Mao and Liu 2014). For example, a smart home environment tasked with monitoring a patient's biometrics must quickly and accurately make decisions on the received data. The system must be able to distinguish an emergency situation from a normal situation (e.g., a heart attack vs. heart rate from normal activity) in data that is being instantly transmitted via biometric sensors, where such data also is impacted by the other big data dimensions in parallel (veracity, volume, etc.).

2.3.4 Veracity

Uncertainty in veracity is a concern relating to the quality of data. Noise in data can manifest as a result of faulty or limited sensors, data rot, or problems with transmission from source to receiver. For example, if a microphone is monitoring a person's voice (e.g., Google Home, Amazon Alexa, etc.[5]) and there is a large amount of background noise, then analytics performed on the received audio stream must take this into account. In the same domain, a patient being monitored by a microphone may slur their speech (i.e., a stroke-related symptom); however, issues relating to the quality of the microphone may mask such a symptom. Such uncertainties denote problems with veracity at the data collection, transmission, and analysis stages.

2.3.5 Volume

There is no accepted threshold of how much data is considered to be big data (Gandomi and Haider 2015); however, data sets within the exabyte (EB) or zettabyte (ZB) size ranges are usually categorized as big data sets (Chen, Mao and Liu 2014; Vajjhala, Strang and Sun 2015). The scalability of techniques and tools is a problem that must be considered, as many that exist cannot handle the scale of data to be managed (Chen, Mao and Liu 2014; Saidulu and Sasikala 2017). Programs can run out of memory, become difficult to sort through in the case of an end user, or no longer return optimal/accurate results. There are also a number of uncertainty factors impacting the data collection stage, the data analysis, and the type of technique used. Other techniques aim to model the amount or type of uncertainty inherent in the data under analysis.

2.4 Software Artifacts in the Big Data World

There are numerous examples of applications in the wild that actively use massive data sets including social media (e.g., Twitter/Facebook graphs), Q&A websites (e.g., StackOverflow), and content delivery (e.g., YouTube) (Madhavji, Miranskyy and Kontogiannis 2015). While the underlying representation for data may be quite different (i.e., graph databases, document databases, OLAP, etc.), the software engineering concepts are similar. Each application needs to be appropriately specified in terms of requirements, test cases, design decisions, etc., where software artifacts play an important role in the various development processes (Fernández 2019). To this end, we describe how big data can impact such artifacts in terms of a motivating example in an IoT healthcare application tasked with monitoring and supporting in-home patient care (Fredericks, Bowers et al. 2018). We focus on requirements and test cases in this section; however, other types of artifacts are relevant as well (e.g., software architectures, UML diagrams, etc.).

The Cognitive Assisted Living (CAL) framework is a smart home that supports the needs of early-stage Alzheimer's patients in terms of monitoring cognitive state over time. Figure 2.6 depicts the high-level architecture of the system comprising various types of users, cloud services, local servers, and local devices.

The amount of data collected by CAL is considered to be big data, as large numbers of records are added over time. One aspect of CAL performs analytics on measured sensor data to provide an analysis of patient interactions with the system, where such data is collected in various formats and at various times. Such sensor data includes patient biometrics and responses to questions asked autonomously by the system, where responses include audio, text, and images.

---

[5] See https://store.google.com/product/google_home and https://developer.amazon.com/alexa.

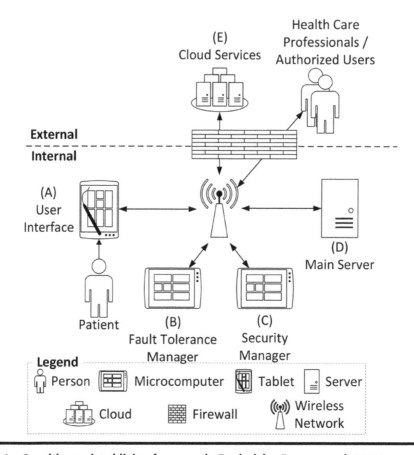

Figure 2.6 Cognitive assisted living framework (Fredericks, Bowers et al. 2018).

Development of software artifacts follows a similar pattern, even though CAL spans the cyber-physical, IoT, and big data domains. Specifically, requirements and test cases must be derived to specify and validate system behaviors, respectively. Traceability links must be generated as well to ensure that all requirements are tested satisfactorily. A requirement for CAL ($R1_{CAL}$) can be derived to state that "CAL shall randomly select three questions to be asked each morning at 8:00am," where additional requirements can specify the method of delivery (e.g., via tablet, home automation device, etc.). A test case for $R1_{CAL}$ ($TC1_{CAL}$) may be derived such that the "Random question generator returns three unique questions." Given the complexity of the system, many more requirements and test cases would need to be derived to fully specify the system, and an RTM would be created to ensure that all requirements are tested.

2.5 Automated Traceability Techniques (State of the Art)

Traceability has been a very important topic in software engineering for many years and must continue to adapt alongside the changing needs of the domain. Given its relative complexity, manual generation of an RTM is a time-consuming and error-prone process that will most likely not scale well with applications that must manage massive amounts of data. Recently, a mapping study highlighted many traceability techniques that were supplemented with empirical study (Charalampidou 2020). For the purposes of this chapter, we focus on automated techniques. To this end, we now highlight two cutting-edge techniques for managing traceability concerns in terms of automated traceability generation and link discovery using semantic techniques.

2.5.1 Automated Traceability Generation

Traceability is often considered to be an arduous process, given that a software engineer must first determine which artifacts are related and then insert manual links into an RTM or similar software tool. As such, automated techniques are attractive to reduce the burden on the software engineer, including machine learning, natural language processing, and search-based approaches. Machine learning approaches, for instance, can be used to automatically classify links (Mills 2017) or combine program analysis with classification for link discovery (Grechanik, McKinley and Perry 2007). Natural language processing and information retrieval methods have been used to improve link recovery (i.e., reconstruction of links between artifacts) and accuracy using multiple techniques (Ali, Guéhéneuc and Antoniol 2013; Borg, Runeson and Ardö 2014). Search-based techniques such as genetic algorithms (Panichella et al. 2013) and multiobjective optimization (Ghannem, Hamdi et al. 2017) have been used to model traceability link recovery as an optimization problem.

2.5.2 Semantic Link Discovery and Recovery

Another approach for automatically managing traceability leverages semantic analysis (Kchaou et al. 2019). While we will leave an in-depth discussion of language semantics to other publications (Falessi, Cantone and Canfora 2013), semantic analysis generally involves trying to find similarities between texts written in a natural language (i.e., the intent of the phrase rather than focusing on pure syntax). For an RE process, semantic analysis is attractive in that a well-formed semantic search can find overlapping requirements written by multiple engineers or discover missing requirements. In the case of (Kchaou et al. 2019), the authors use a semantic model to automatically discover the impact that requirements updates can have on UML models, including class, sequence, and use case diagrams. Such impacts directly correlate to traceability links between requirements and other aspects of the software design lifecycle. The intent behind traceability is to ensure a rigorous software engineering process that is applicable to all types of applications regardless of domain. However, we envision that big data applications may cause additional problems that must also be addressed. We next describe an approach for introducing self-adaptive properties into the traceability process.

2.6 Traceability Adaptation

One commonality between all concerns introduced so far in this chapter is uncertainty, from unexpected data types to missing blocks of data. In other domains, adaptation has been used to mitigate uncertainty at the application level in the form of self-adaptive systems (SASs) (Kephart and Chess 2003). An SAS can reconfigure itself, in terms of configurable parameters or expressed behaviors, to mitigate unexpected situations for which it was not explicitly designed. This behavior is generally enabled via a control loop that introspects upon the system and provides adaptive mechanisms. For instance, the *MAPE-K (Monitor-Analyze-Plan-Execute-Knowledge)* feedback loop

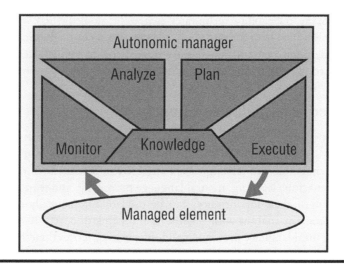

Figure 2.7   MAPE-K feedback loop (Kephart and Chess 2003).

provides a framework for a system to (a) *monitor* itself via internal and external sensors, (b) *analyze* sensor data to determine if a reconfiguration is necessary, (c) generate a safe *plan* to transition the system from one state to another, and then (d) safely *execute* the specified transition plan. Each step is linked together via common *knowledge* to ensure that all aspects of the loop are aware of the other aspects. Figure 2.7 presents the standard form of the MAPE-K loop from (Kephart and Chess 2003). Note that other forms of adaptive feedback loops have also been developed.

Given that the notion of adaptation has been shown to effectively combat uncertainty at the application level, we can extrapolate that adaptation can also be used at the traceability level. Therefore, we posit that adaptation can be introduced to support the changing nature of the data sets underlying big data applications. To do so, we will extend Table 2.1 to be adaptive in nature, allowing traceability links to be added and removed at run time, as necessary. Table 2.2 illustrates this concept of an ATM, an extension of the work performed by (Hariri and Fredericks 2018), where an ATM adds adaptive capabilities onto the standard RTM. Effectively, an ATM extends a generic RTM to comprise a three-dimensional traceability matrix that can add in the system configuration as a dimension, enabling traceability links to be enabled/disabled as well as added/removed as the system self-reconfigures. While Table 2.2 is visualized as a two-dimensional table, consider that the derivation of R1 (to R1′ and beyond) comprises a third dimension.

An ATM can be realized as follows for the self-adaptive smart home application model. From the previous smart home example, consider a situation in which the temperature of each individual room must be reported to ensure both the safety and comfort of the inhabitant (i.e., the inhabitant is elderly or requires medical supervision). If the temperature is too hot or too cold, then the inhabitant can experience discomfort that negatively impacts their living state. If a temperature sensor fails in a room, then the smart home may reconfigure itself to ensure that a proper temperature reading is still available. The system may use a secondary sensor (e.g., from a device not normally tasked with monitoring the full room temperature such as a smart vacuum) or request that an administrator add a new sensor. Regardless, there will be a requirement to monitor the temperature of each room that does not necessarily specify how that requirement is fulfilled, so long as the requirement is satisfied. This requirement will be linked to test cases that ensure proper behavior. One or more of these test cases can become violated as a result of differing sensor

Table 2.2 Sample Adaptive Traceability Matrix

Requirement ID	Requirement Description	Test Case IDs / Status	
R1	*Device shall sample temperature and humidity readings and transmit to the server every 30 seconds.*	TC1	PASS
		TC2	PASS
		TC3	FAIL
		...	...
		TCn	PASS
R1′	*Device shall sample temperature and humidity readings and transmit to the server AS CLOSE AS POSSIBLE TO (30 seconds).*	TC1	PASS
		TC2′	PASS
		TC3′	PASS
		...	...
		TCn	PASS

accuracy, placement, or even communication protocol. As such, a standard RTM would indicate a traceability link violation, as there exists a requirement with a failing test case.

While techniques exist for introducing flexibility into RE (Whittle et al. 2009; Ramirez et al. 2012) and software testing (Fredericks, DeVries and Cheng 2014), an ATM can introduce flexibility at the traceability level. Consider an ATM to act as a many-to-many multiplexor of sorts. For instance, consider requirement R1 and its associated test cases TC1, TC2, and TC3. To enable self-adaptation, variations of each of these artifacts may be derived to satisfy the various configuration states that the system may enable at run time. R1 may have three variations (R1′, R1″, and R1″), and each test case may have one variation each (for brevity, TC1′, TC2′, and TC3′). A traceability link can be derived between each artifact as input/output conditions allow (for instance, R1″ may only be linked to TC2′, etc.). As such, an ATM describing this model would be visualized as follows in Figure 2.8.

Note that this is a limited example for illustrative purposes. In reality, there would be many requirements and many test cases by themselves (i.e., in a standard RTM). An ATM may comprise an exponentially larger number of connections, each of which *may be active or inactive* based on the state of the system itself.

Now we can bring this concept full circle. Thus far we have considered how traceability applies to the SAS domain; however, we have not applied it to the big data domain. Given the difficulties and uncertainties previously discussed regarding management of a big data application, we may consider that applying self-adaptive characteristics to a big data application may hold some benefit.

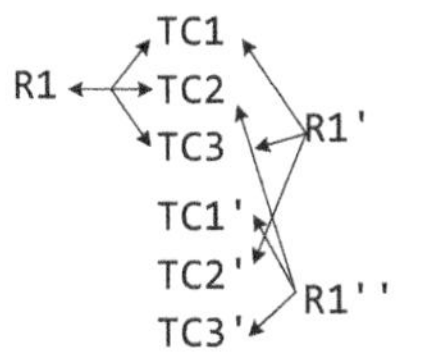

Figure 2.8 Adaptive requirements traceability example.

Table 2.3   RTM Defined for CAL

Requirement ID	Requirement Description	Test Case IDs / Status	
$R1_{CAL}$	CAL shall randomly select three questions to be asked each morning at 8:00am	$TC1_{CAL}$	PASS

Table 2.4   ATM Defined for CAL

Requirement ID	Requirement Description	Test Case IDs / Status	
$R1_{CAL}$	CAL shall randomly select three questions to be asked each morning at 8:00am	$TC1_{CAL}$	PASS
$R1_{CAL}'$	CAL shall randomly select three questions to be asked each morning after the patient is awake.		

For example, if we focus on the *velocity* property of big data, we can derive a requirement and set of test cases in a similar fashion to our adaptive smart home CAL. Consider the requirement and test case previously defined for CAL, aggregated in an RTM (Table 2.3):

However, now consider that we add a new third-party device (e.g., a biometric smart watch) that also must have its data consumed by our managing application. This particular smart watch measures a patient's heart rate, blood oxygen levels, and activity level. For this example, we are interested in the activity level, as that value can be monitored to determine whether the patient is awake or asleep.

To support this new device, a suite of requirements, test cases, and traceability links should be added to the existing specifications and matrices. As such, we can derive a new version $R1_{CAL}$ ($R1_{CAL}'$) to state that "CAL shall randomly select three questions to be asked each morning after the patient is awake." TC1CAL would not need to change, as it specifies the behavior of the random question generator. However, any test cases that focus on the time of day may need adjustment. To avoid a complete tear-up of the system and its software artifacts, we can apply self-adaptive characteristics to our application. For this case, CAL can select its run-time requirements configuration to use the biometric sensor for monitoring patient activity. In the absence of such a device (e.g., the device is powered off or disconnected), CAL could revert to its former configuration. A traceability analysis would find that $R1_{CAL}$ is satisfied in some form, given that at minimum one of its variations is active and test cases attached are passing. An ATM can be described as follows in Table 2.4:

While this may be a contrived example, ideally such an application could be significantly extended to comprise numerous configurations of requirements, test cases, and traceability links. Moreover, derivations of requirements for varying application configurations can be either manually or automatically generated, depending on the necessity and effort of the generation activity.

Threats to Validity. The research presented in this section is intended as a proof of concept to highlight the concepts of traceability adaptation in real-world systems. As such, we have identified the following threats to validity. First, an empirical study is necessary to demonstrate that adaptation is feasible in terms of software traceability (i.e., that "plasticity" is a positive property).

Second, further study is necessary to ensure that the presence of big data characteristics (i.e., velocity, variety, etc.) impacts traceability links. Third, we focus on software requirements and test cases in this chapter. As such, further study is required for the many other types of software artifacts present in the software development life cycle.

2.7 Discussion

This chapter has discussed the traceability problem in the context of big data. First, we introduced traceability and its implications for required software engineering processes. Next, we discussed our interpretation of big data and how uncertainty can impact big data applications in the more common V's. We then illustrated how software artifacts can be extended to the big data domain and presented the state of the art with respect to software traceability in big data applications. We also proposed an approach for extending software traceability to the big data domain via self-adaptive characteristics. Specifically, we posit that enabling traceability to adapt alongside a reconfigurable system can help maintain traceability in the face of uncertainty.

Future work for this line of research includes discovering new traceability links at run time via semantic search, automated refinement of software artifacts as traceability links are discovered and/or updated, and introducing formal methods to verify the correctness of a system as a result of automated or adaptive traceability.

Acknowledgments

The authors gratefully thank Natalie Fredericks for her support with state-of-the-art industrial traceability techniques and Reihaneh Hariri for her initial research on adaptive requirements traceability. This work was also supported by NSF grant CNS-1657061 and Oakland University. Any opinions, findings, and conclusions or recommendations expressed in this material are those of the authors and do not necessarily reflect the views of Grand Valley State University, Oakland University or other research sponsors.

References

Ali, Nasir, Yann-Gaël Guéhéneuc, and Giuliano Antoniol. 2013. "Trustrace: Mining software repositories to improve the accuracy of requirement traceability links." *IEEE Transactions on Software Engineering* 39: 725–741.

Borg, Markus, Per Runeson, and Anders Ardö. 2014. "Recovering from a decade: A systematic mapping of information retrieval approaches to software traceability." *Empirical Software Engineering* 19: 1565–1616.

Borne, Kirk. 2014. *Top 10 Big Data Challenges – A Serious Look at 10 Big Data V's.* https://mapr.com/blog/top-10-big-data-challenges-serious-look-10-big-data-vs/.

Charalampidou, Sofia and Apostolos Ampatzoglou, and Evangelos Karountzos, and Paris Avgeriou. 2020. "Empirical studies on software traceability: A mapping study." *Journal of Software: Evolution and Process*, 32: e2294.

Chen, Min, Shiwen Mao, and Yunhao Liu. 2014. "Big data: A survey." *Mobile Networks and Applications* (Springer) 19: 171–209.

Cleland-Huang, Jane. 2006. "Just enough requirements traceability." *30th Annual International Computer Software and Applications Conference (COMPSAC'06)*, pp. 41–42.

Court, David. 2015. "Getting big impact from big data." *McKinsey Quarterly* 1(1): 52–60.

DeGrandis, Paul and Valetto, Giuseppe. 2009. "Elicitation and utilization of application-level utility functions." *Proceedings of the 6th International Conference on Autonomic Computing.* Barcelona, Spain: ACM, pp. 107–116.

Esfahani, Naeem, and Sam Malek. 2013. "Uncertainty in self-adaptive software systems." In: de Lemos, R., Giese H., Müller H.A., Shaw M. (eds.) *Software Engineering for Self-Adaptive Systems II*, pp. 214–238. Springer, Heidelberg.

Falessi, Davide, Giovanni Cantone, and Gerardo Canfora. 2013. "Empirical principles and an industrial case study in retrieving equivalent requirements via natural language processing techniques." *IEEE Transactions on Software Engineering* 39: 18–44.

Fernández, Daniel Méndez, Wolfgang Böhm, Andreas Vogelsang, Jakob Mund, Manfred Broy, Marco Kuhrmann, and Thorsten Weyer. 2019. "Artefacts in software engineering: A fundamental positioning." *Software & Systems Modeling* 18 (5): 2777–2786.

Fredericks, Erik M., Byron DeVries, and Betty H. C. Cheng. 2014. "Towards run-time adaptation of test cases for self-adaptive systems in the face of uncertainty." *Proceedings of the 9th International Symposium on Software Engineering for Adaptive and Self-Managing Systems*, Hyderabad, India.

Fredericks, Erik M., Kate M. Bowers, Katey A. Price, and Reihaneh H. Hariri. 2018. "CAL: A smart home environment for monitoring cognitive decline." *2018 IEEE 38th International Conference on Distributed Computing Systems*, pp. 1500–1506.

Gandomi, Amir, and Murtaza Haider. 2015. "Beyond the hype: Big data concepts, methods, and analytics." *International Journal of Information Management* (Elsevier) 35: 137–144.

Gantz, John, and David Reinsel. 2011. "Extracting value from chaos." *IDC iView* 1142: 1–12.

Ghannem, Adnane, Mohamed Salah Hamdi, Marouane Kessentini, and Hany H. Ammar. 2017. "Search-based requirements traceability recovery: A multi-objective approach." *2017 IEEE Congress on Evolutionary Computation (CEC)*, pp. 1183–1190.

Gotel, Orlena C. Z., and Anthony C. W. Finkelstein. 1994. "An analysis of the requirements traceability problem." *Proceedings of the First International Conference on Requirements Engineering*, pp. 94–101.

Grechanik, Mark, Kathryn S. McKinley, and Dewayne E. Perry. 2007. "Recovering and using use-case-diagram-to-source-code traceability links." *Proceedings of the 6th Joint Meeting of the European Software Engineering Conference and the ACM SIGSOFT Symposium on the Foundations of Software Engineering*, pp. 95–104.

Han, Jiawei, Jian Pei, and Micheline Kamber. 2011. *Data Mining: Concepts and Techniques.* Elsevier, Waltham, MA.

Hariri, Reihaneh H., and Erik M. Fredericks. 2018. "Towards traceability link recovery for self-adaptive systems." *Workshops at the Thirty-Second AAAI Conference on Artificial Intelligence.*

Hariri, Reihaneh H., Erik M. Fredericks, and Kate M. Bowers. 2019. "Uncertainty in big data analytics: survey, opportunities, and challenges." *Journal of Big Data* (Springer) 6: 44.

IBM. 2020. *Extracting business value from the 4 V's of big data.* https://www.ibmbigdatahub.com/infographic/extracting-business-value-4-vs-big-data.

Jain, Anil. 2016. *The 5 V's of big data.* https://www.ibm.com/blogs/watson-health/the-5-vs-of-big-data/.

Kchaou, Dhikra, Nadia Bouassida, Mariam Mefteh, and Hanêne Ben-Abdallah. 2019. "Recovering semantic traceability between requirements and design for change impact analysis." *Innovations in Systems and Software Engineering* (Springer) 15: 101–115.

Kephart, Jeffrey O., and David M. Chess. 2003. "The vision of autonomic computing." *Computer* 36: 41–50.

Laney, Doug. 2001. "3D data management: Controlling data volume, velocity and variety." *META Group Research Note* 6: 1.

Madhavji, Nazim H., Andriy Miranskyy, and Kostas Kontogiannis. 2015. "Big picture of big data software engineering: With example research challenges." *2015 IEEE/ACM 1st International Workshop on Big Data Software Engineering*, pp. 11–14.

Marr, Bernard. 2018. *How much data do we create every day?* https://www.forbes.com/sites/bernardmarr/2018/05/21/how-much-data-do-we-create-every-day-the-mind-blowing-stats-everyone-should-read.

Mills, Chris. 2017. "Automating traceability link recovery through classification." *Proceedings of the 2017 11th Joint Meeting on Foundations of Software Engineering*, pp. 1068–1070.

Najafabadi, Maryam M. and Villanustre, Flavio and Khoshgoftaar, Taghi M. and Seliya, Naeem and Wald, Randall and Muharemagic, Edin. 2015. "Deep learning applications and challenges in big data analytics." *Journal of Big Data* (Springer) 2 (1): 1.

Noyes, Dan. 2020. *Top 20 facebook statistics*. https://zephoria.com/top-15-valuable-facebook-statistics/.

Panichella, Annibale, Bogdan Dit, Rocco Oliveto, Massimiliano Di Penta, Denys Poshyvanyk, and Andrea De Lucia. 2013. "How to effectively use topic models for software engineering tasks? An approach based on genetic algorithms." *Proceedings of the 2013 International Conference on Software Engineering*, pp. 522–531.

Pohl, Klaus. 2010. *Requirements Engineering: Fundamentals, Principles, and Techniques*. Springer Publishing Company, Incorporated, New York.

Pohl, Klaus. 1993. "The three dimensions of requirements engineering." *International Conference on Advanced Information Systems Engineering*, pp. 275–292.

Ramirez, Andres J., Erik M. Fredericks, Adam C. Jensen, and Betty H. C. Cheng. 2012. "Automatically RELAXing a goal model to cope with uncertainty." In Gordon Fraser and Jerffeson Teixeira de Souza (eds.) *Search Based Software Engineering*, Vol. 7515, pp. 198–212. Springer, Heidelberg.

Saidulu, D. and Sasikala, R. 2017. "Machine learning and statistical approaches for Big Data: issues, challenges and research directions." *International Journal of Applied Engineering Research* 12 (21): 11691–11699.

Spanoudakis, George, and Andrea Zisman. 2005. "Software traceability: A roadmap." *Handbook of Software Engineering and Knowledge Engineering* 3: 395–428.

Vajjhala, Narasimha Rao, Kenneth David Strang, and Zhaohao Sun. 2015. "Statistical modeling and visualizing open big data using a terrorism case study." *2015 3rd International Conference on Future Internet of Things and Cloud*, pp. 489–496.

Walsh, W.E., G. Tesauro, J.O. Kephart, and R. Das. 2004. "Utility functions in autonomic systems". In: Proceedings of the First IEEE International Conference on Autonomic Computing. pp. 70–77. IEEE Computer Society.

Whittle, Jon, Pete Sawyer, Nelle Bencomo, Betty H. C. Cheng, and Jean-Michel Bruel. 2009. "RELAX: Incorporating uncertainty into the specification of self-adaptive systems." *17th IEEE International Requirements Engineering Conference (RE'09)*, pp. 79–88.

Winkler, Stefan, and Jens Pilgrim. 2010. "A survey of traceability in requirements engineering and model-driven development." *Software \& Systems Modeling* (Springer) 9: 529–565.

Xiong, Hui, Gaurav Pandey, Michael Steinbach, and Vipin Kumar. 2006. "Enhancing data analysis with noise removal." *IEEE Transactions on Knowledge and Data Engineering* (IEEE) 18: 304–319.

Ziv, Hadar, Debra Richardson, and René Klösch. 1997. "The uncertainty principle in software engineering." *submitted to Proceedings of the 19th International Conference on Software Engineering (ICSE'97)*.

Chapter 3

Architecting Software Model Management and Analytics Framework

Bedir Tekinerdogan
Wageningen University & Research

Cagatay Catal
Qatar University

Önder Babur
Eindhoven University of Technology

Contents

3.1 Introduction

Currently, many businesses have searched for extracting information from data to yield new insights and make smarter decisions and thus, create business value. With the advancement in computing, the current ability to capture and store vast amounts of data has grown at an unprecedented rate, which soon did not scale with traditional data management techniques. Yet, to cope with the rapidly increasing volume, variety, and velocity of the generated data, we can now adopt the available novel technical capacity and the infrastructure to aggregate and analyze big data. This situation has led to new and unforeseen opportunities for many organizations. Big Data has now indeed become a very important driver for innovation and growth for various industries such as health, administration, agriculture, and education [14,16,17].

Big data is usually characterized using six V's, that is, volume, variety, velocity, veracity, value, and variability. Volume is the key characteristic of Big Data indicating the large amount of data that usually does not fit on one computer [14,18,19]. Variety relates to the different data types including structured data, semistructured data, and unstructured data. Velocity refers to the speed at which the data is generated as well as it is being processed. Veracity refers to the trustworthiness of the data. Value refers to the valorization of data and how big data gets better results from stored data. Finally, variability describes the variety of data that is being stored and still needs to be processed and analyzed.

With big data, different types of data have been addressed including text, audio, and video. A different type of data that did not get much attention in data analytics yet is the whole set of models that are used in various engineering and science disciplines. A model hereby is an abstract representation of some elements of the considered domain. In science, models can relate to, for example, physical and chemical models. In engineering, models can relate to the intermediate artifacts for realizing the eventual system. In software engineering, models are, for example, the UML design artifacts such as use case models, package diagrams, class diagrams, sequence diagrams, and state diagrams.

In this context, model management and analytics (MMA) aims to use models and related artifacts to derive relevant information to support the decision-making process of organizations [2–6,20]. Various different models, as well as analytics approaches, could be identified. In addition, MMA systems will have different requirements, different platforms [21] and, as such, apply different architecture design configurations. Hence, a proper architecture for the MMA system is important to achieve the provided requirements. So far, no specific reference architecture has been defined that is dedicated to MMA in particular. Designing such an architecture is important since models have additional, different properties than conventional data. This might also imply the need for novel analytics approaches.

In this chapter, we elaborate on existing data analytics architectures to devise and discuss a reference architecture framework that is customized for MMA. We discuss the current key data analytics reference architectures in the literature and the key requirements for MMA. Subsequently, we provide the approach for deriving an application architecture of the MMA. We illustrate the framework using a real-world example.

The remainder of the chapter is organized as follows. In Section 3.2, we discuss the background. Section 3.3 describes the approach for deriving reference architecture for model analytics. Section 3.4 describes the features of a big data architecture using a feature diagram. Section 3.5 presents the selected big data reference architectures. Section 3.6 explains the approach to derive the MMA application architecture by utilizing the feature model for big data. Section 3.7 provides the related work and finally, Section 3.8 concludes the chapter.

3.2 Preliminaries

In this section, we provide the necessary background for the architecture design of MMA. For this, we shortly discuss big data analytics in Section 3.2.1 and then proceed with the background on software architecture design in Section 3.2.2.

3.2.1 Big Data Analytics

Data analytics is the discovery, interpretation, and communication of meaningful patterns in data [14]. With data analytics, data is examined in order to derive insight, from which one can make decisions and take actions that lead to effective outcomes. Hence, the goal of analytics is usually to improve the business by gaining knowledge, which can be used to make improvements or changes. Traditionally, data analytics predominantly refers to a various set of applications, such as basic business intelligence (BI), online analytical processing (OLAP), and various forms of advanced analytics. Data analytics is related to the term business analytics, with the difference that the latter is focused on business uses, while data analytics has a broader focus.

Data analytics is important to support decision-making and likewise help organizations better achieve their business goals. Different types of analytics can be distinguished including descriptive analytics, diagnostic analytics, predictive analytics, and prescriptive analytics. Each of these types of analytics can be understood quite simply as using data to answer different types of questions. Descriptive analytics uses historical data to provide insight into what has happened. Diagnostics analytics again uses historical data to answer why something has happened. Predictive analytics elaborates on the insight of the analyzed data and answers what can happen. Finally, prescriptive analytics that usually builds on, and uses the other types of analytics, answers the question of what to do.

In the case of data analytics, the source is the traditional data (e.g. text, audio, video, etc.). With model analytics, we assume that the analytics takes as input a set of models to support the decision-making process. Model analytics can thus be considered as a subcategory of data analytics orienting particularly on model artifacts (Figure 3.1).

3.2.2 Architecture Design

Software architecture defines the gross-level structure of a software system. Architecture modeling is important to enhance the understanding of the software system, support the communication among stakeholders, and guide the development process [22,24]. A common practice of modeling architecture is using different architectural views that address the concerns of a

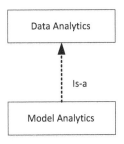

Figure 3.1   Model analytics vs. data analytics.

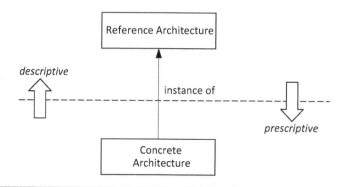

Figure 3.2   The relation between reference architecture and concrete architectures.

specific group of stakeholders. Architectural views document the architectural design decisions from a specific viewpoint. That means, the designs documented in an architectural view follow the conventions, including models and notations, defined in the corresponding architectural viewpoint. From a given architectural viewpoint, one or more architectural views can be designed.

When dealing with a family or domain of systems, we can define a reference architecture. Several definitions of reference architecture exist in the literature. Often it is applied as a product line architecture in the product line engineering process [25,26,27]. A reference architecture is often defined as a generic architecture for a class of information systems that are being used as a foundation for the design of concrete architectures from this class [1]. A reference architecture presents the architectural best practices by various means such as standards, design patterns, and can be employed by software architects as a base from the beginning of the project to the end of it. A concrete architecture is an instantiation of the reference architecture that defines the boundaries and constraints for the implementation and is used to analyze risks, balance trade-offs, plan the implementation project, and allocate tasks. A reference architecture can be derived upfront from scratch or be derived from the knowledge and experiences accumulated in designing concrete architectures in the past. The concrete architectures differ from one case to the next depending on the requirements of the stakeholders involved. In essence, reference architectures can be either descriptive to capture the essence of existing architectures or prescriptive to guide the development of new ones. Figure 3.2 depicts the relations between reference architecture and concrete architectures.

3.3 Approach for Deriving Reference Architecture

Our key objective in this study is to support the MMA by adopting a reference architecture and support the development of application architecture. For this, we have followed a systematic domain analysis approach, which is shown in Figure 3.3. The domain analysis process consists of a domain scoping and domain modeling process. In the domain scoping process, the domain of investigation and the concrete knowledge sources are identified. In the domain modeling phase, the data is extracted from the identified knowledge sources. In our case, the domain of interest is the big data reference architecture. As it is also shown in the figure, after we have defined the

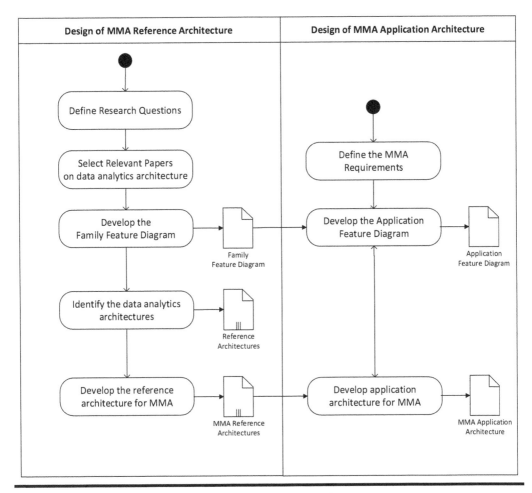

Figure 3.3 Adopted approach for deriving reference architecture.

research question for developing a reference architecture, we have searched for the relevant primary studies that relate to data analytics architectures. The list of papers that we have used in the domain analysis process is shown in Table 3.1.

We did not adopt a heavy systematic literature review process for this study since this was not our concrete goal. Rather than identifying and deriving a particular reference architecture in our study, we aimed to explore the use of existing big data reference architectures and investigate their usage for MMA.

Based on the selected papers, domain modeling is started, which results in a domain model. The domain model is typically derived using a commonality and variability analysis on the concepts of the selected papers. Among the domain modeling approaches, feature modeling is extensively used. A feature is a system property that is relevant to some stakeholders and is used to capture commonalities or discriminate between features [12]. A feature model is a model that defines features and their dependencies. Feature models are usually represented in feature diagrams (or tables). A feature diagram is a tree with the root representing a concept (e.g., a software system),

Table 3.1   List of Papers to Derive the Reference Architecture of Data Analytics (in alphabetical order)

C. Ballard, C. Compert, T. Jesionowski, I. Milman, B. Plants, B. Rosen, & H. Smith. Information Governance Principles and Practices for a Big Data Landscape, IBM Redbooks, 2014 [8].
W.L. Chang, D. Boyd, O. Levin. NIST Big Data Interoperability Framework: Volume 6, Reference Architecture, Special Publication (NIST SP) - 1500-6r2, 2019 [9].
B. Geerdink. A reference architecture for big data solutions introducing a model to perform predictive analytics using big data technology. In Internet Technology and Secured Transactions (ICITST), pp. 71–76), 2013 [11].
M. Maier. A. Serebrenik, and I. T. P. Vanderfeesten. Towards a Big Data Reference Architecture, 2013 [13].
N. Marz, and J. Warren. Big Data: Principles and best practices of scalable realtime data systems, Manning Publications Co., 2015 [14].
Oracle, Information Management and Big Data A Reference Architecture, An Oracle White Paper, February, 2013 [15].
P. Pääkkönen, and D. Pakkala. Reference Architecture and Classification of Technologies, Products and Services for Big Data Systems. Big Data Research, 2015 [16].
S. Soares, Big Data Governance: An Emerging Imperative, MC Press, 2012 [19].

and its descendent nodes are features. In addition, the feature model identifies the constraints on the allowed combinations of features, and as such, a feature model defines the feasible models in the domain.

From the identified primary studies, we have also derived the data analytics architectures and subsequently, design the reference architecture. In the application engineering process, the family feature model and the reference architecture are used to derive the application architecture for a given MMA project. The family feature model covers the features of the overall big MMA system domain. To describe the features of a particular big data project, we derive the *application feature model* from the family feature model. The application architecture is derived using the application feature model and the reference architecture. For this, the domain design rules are executed based on the selected features. Hence, a selection of different application feature models trigger different domain design rules, which lead to a different application architecture. We define the family feature model as well as the application engineering process in more detail in the following sections.

3.4 Big Data Analytics Feature Model

Based on the identified papers and the big data literature, we have derived the family feature model for big data systems, as shown in Figure 3.4. This has been adopted from our earlier work on a feature-based analysis in product line engineering [23,24] and of big data systems [17]. Since the variability model represents the domain of big data systems, we term this as a family feature diagram that can be used to derive concrete feature diagrams representing the required features for a concrete big data system.

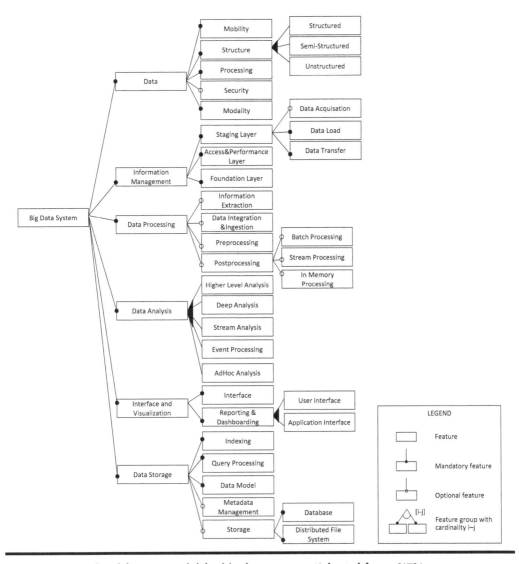

Figure 3.4   Top-level feature model for big data system. (Adapted from: [17].)

3.5 Big Data Analytics Reference Architectures

From the literature, we could indeed identify multiple different big data reference architectures [9,14,17]. In the following, we discuss the ones that we have selected in this study. In principle, other reference architectures could be selected.

3.5.1 Lambda Architecture

The Lambda architecture is a big data architecture that is designed to satisfy the needs of a robust system that is fault-tolerant, against both hardware failures and human mistakes [14]. A conceptual model is shown in Figure 3.5.

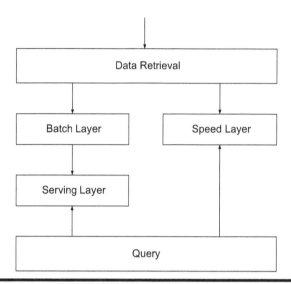

Figure 3.5 Conceptual architecture of big data system.

In essence, the architecture consists of three layers including batch processing layer, speed (or real-time) processing layer, and serving layer. The batch processing layer has two functions: (a) managing the master data set (i.e., an immutable, append-only set of raw data) and (b) to precompute the batch views. The master data set is stored using a distributed processing system that can handle very large quantities of data. The batch views are generated by processing all available data. As such, any errors can be fixed by recomputing based on the complete data set and subsequently updating existing views. The speed layer processes data streams in real time and deals with recent data only. In essence, there are two basic functions of the speed layer: (a) storing the real-time views and (b) processing the incoming data stream to update those views. It compensates for the high latency of the batch layer to enable up-to-date results for queries. The speed layer's view is not as accurate and complete as the ones eventually produced by the batch layer, but they are available almost immediately after data is received. The serving layer indexes the batch views so that they can be queried in low-latency and in an ad-hoc way. The query merges result from the batch and speed layers to respond to ad-hoc queries by returning precomputed views or building views from the processed data.

3.5.2 Functional Architecture

Another big data reference architecture that we adopt is functional architecture, as shown in Figure 3.6. The reference architecture distinguishes six key modules including *Data Extraction, Data Loading and Preprocessing, Data Processing, Data Analysis, Data Loading and Transformation,* and *Interfacing and Visualization.* The reference architecture can be used to describe many different big data systems.

3.6 Application Model Analytics Features

After developing the feature model and the selection/development of a reference architecture in essence, we can start with the application architecture design for MMA. To this aim, we have performed a case study on the model analytics framework, SAMOS (Statistical Analysis of

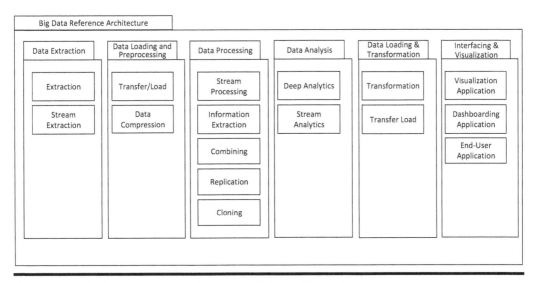

Figure 3.6   Big data reference architecture. (Adapted from: [16].)

Models) [4–6], with the objectives of validating the reference architecture, as well as describing SAMOS and identifying potential features for future development. SAMOS is a tool developed for analyzing large sets of artifacts in Model-Driven Engineering, such as models and metamodels (representing languages). It has been used for a variety of artifact types, such as Ecore metamodels[1], UML and feature models, and domain-specific industrial models. Several application areas falling under the broad term *Model Analytics* that SAMOS was exploited include model repository management and exploration, clone detection, and architectural analysis.

While SAMOS has been used in a wide range of settings, its development as an emerging *big-data-ready* model analytics framework is still in an early stage. We outline the configuration of the model analytics reference architecture (i.e., the feature model) in Figure 3.7 and discuss the existing and planned features of SAMOS.

We summarize the features of SAMOS in terms of the top-level features of Data, Data Processing, Data Analysis, Interface and Visualization, and finally, Data Storage. The features of Information Management, notably with respect to the data access and performance, are left as a long-term goal for extending the framework.

- **Data:** Most sources of data we deal with in SAMOS contain structured data (e.g., models adhering to schematic metamodels). However, models can contain unstructured data in the form of model element names (i.e., short chunks of text) and annotations (i.e., potentially long, free-form text). In all cases, the data to be analyzed is a batch (i.e., not streaming) and textual (i.e., not audio or visual).
- **Data Processing:** SAMOS extensively addresses this feature and offers options for extracting various types of information from MDE artifacts: text, metrics, and structural chunks such as trees. Various components deal with the preprocessing of data; notably natural language processing aspects such as tokenization, synonym detection, and tree/graph filtering, and topological sorting. Furthermore, we plan to integrate model transformations for

---

[1] https://www.eclipse.org/modeling/emf/

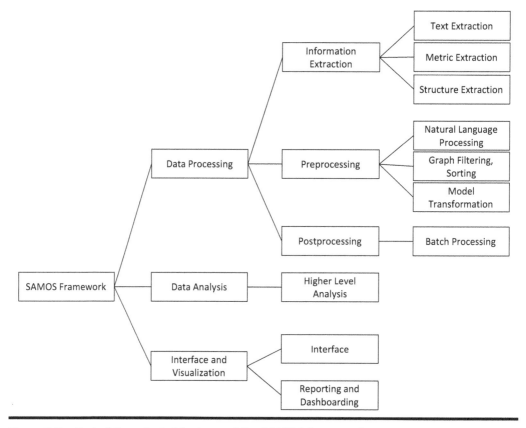

Figure 3.7 Part of the selected features of the SAMOS framework.

preprocessing other (possibly heterogeneous) types/sets of MDE artifacts into SAMOS for analysis. Finally, SAMOS offers exclusively batch mode postprocessing.

- **Data Analysis:** The second large component of SAMOS deals with various types of analyses on the extracted data. This ranges from simple descriptive statistical analyses for empirical studies on those artifacts to more advanced text/data mining and machine learning techniques (e.g., clone detection and architectural reconstruction on the MDE artifacts).
- **Interface and Visualization:** Reporting and dashboarding are essential for inspecting and visualizing the analysis results. An example would be the hierarchical clustering of MDE repositories to explore their content. Furthermore, in a new version of SAMOS (currently under development), it is integrated into the KNIME[2] data mining environment; hence, enabling a large set of graphical user and application interfaces to operate SAMOS [4].
- **Data Storage:** SAMOS does not deal with indexing and querying of MDE data, unlike some dedicated tools such as Hawk. While in the usual operation of SAMOS, the data is stored in local file systems, a recent experimental extension to SAMOS explores the distributed data storage and processing for model analytics [6].

---

[2] https://www.knime.com/

Based on the above feature selections, we could now derive the application architecture. Our discussion so far mostly focused on applying and validating the feature model. Another angle involves guiding future development and evolution of SAMOS as a mature model analytics framework. Following Figure 3.4, we can identify potential improvements for SAMOS. We observe security, for instance, to become an issue as SAMOS is used in industrial settings where models are considered confidential. As for the Information Management feature group, SAMOS currently tackles all the different activities in an ad-hoc way; it would be beneficial to adopt a clear layered approach and streamline the activities, e.g., data staging and access. Furthermore, we are planning to integrate state-of-the-art types of analyses from data mining and machine learning domains, notably deep analyses, into SAMOS. Last but not the least, with the help of the feature model, we are recently investigating how to incorporate data storage and querying for models in SAMOS. The current file-based approach (even when distributed) had quite a few limitations, which could be potentially mitigated using, e.g., a graph or document database.

3.7 Related Work and Discussion

In the literature, we can identify different approaches for defining reference architectures. Galster and Avgeriou [10] propose a methodology to define empirically grounded reference architectures. The approach consists of the following steps: decision on type of reference architecture, selection of design strategy, empirical acquisition of data, construction of reference architecture, enabling the reference architecture variability, and finally, evaluation of the reference architecture.

Architectural tactics [7] aim at identifying architectural decisions related to a quality attribute requirement and composing these into architecture design. Defining explicit viewpoints for quality concerns can help to model and reason about the application of architectural tactics.

Architectural Perspectives [8] are a collection of activities, tactics, and guidelines to modify a set of existing views to document and analyze quality properties. Architectural perspectives as such are basic guidelines that work on multiple views together. It might be interesting to look at integrating the guidelines provided by the Architectural Perspectives and the design of big data architectures.

Several software architecture analysis approaches have been introduced for addressing quality properties. The goal of these approaches is to assess whether or not a given architecture design satisfies desired concerns including quality requirements. The main aim of the viewpoint definitions in our approach, on the other hand, is to communicate and support the architectural design with respect to quality concerns. As such, our work can directly support the architectural analysis to select feasible design alternatives.

In our earlier work, we have also focused on the domain-driven design of big data architectures [17,18]. This study builds on these earlier results but is different in the sense that we explicitly focus on MMA. We could state that despite the concrete focus, the large part of the big data architectures can be reused.

Data analytics is a broad domain in which some functions might not be easily isolated as it is defined in the current reference architectures. Some of the concerns might be cross-cutting and not easily modularized [2]. For this case, we might need to use aspect-oriented development approaches. We consider this as part of our future work.

The adoption of a reference architecture and feature modeling is a reuse-based approach that is often applied in the product line engineering context [25,26] to reduce the cost of development, reduce the time to market, and increase the quality of the products. In our future work, we will focus on the product line engineering approach for MMA.

3.8 Conclusion

MMA can be considered as a special case of data analytics in which the purpose is to analyze the data and extract information to support the decision-making process. Models are now extensively used in different science and engineering disciplines. Beyond archiving these models, there is also a need for analyzing these models to extract the necessary information for providing important insight into the science and engineering processes. Based on the existing data analytics reference architectures, we have described the common and variable features regarding MMA and discussed the need for developing or using the corresponding reference architecture. Hence, we have proposed a reuse-based approach for developing MMA architectures based on existing big data architectures. Adopting a reference architecture appeared to be quite useful together with the feature diagrams for big data systems. The reference architecture can be used in two different ways. On the one hand, it can be used to describe existing MMA projects and likewise also indicate the gaps or complementary issues. On the other hand, it can be used to guide the engineer in developing an MMA framework. We have illustrated the usage of the reference architecture for a case study on analyzing UML models. In general, we can state that existing big data reference architectures together with the accompanying feature modeling approaches can also be used for MMA. Our future work will further advance the reference architecture and apply it to multiple different case studies. In particular, we aim to apply MMA for agriculture business risk management, marketing and consumer behavior, and stock market domains.

References

1. S. Angelov, P. Grefen, and D. Greefhorst. A classification of software reference architectures: Analyzing their success and effectiveness. In *Proc. of European Conference on Software Architecture (WICSA/ECSA)*, pp. 141–150, 2009.
2. J. Bakker, B. Tekinerdogan, and M. Aksit. Characterization of early aspects approaches. In *Proceedings of the Early Aspects Workshop at AOSD*, The Netherlands, 2005.
3. Ö. Babur, L. Cleophas, and M. van den Brand. Hierarchical clustering of metamodels for comparative analysis and visualization. In *Proc. of the 12th European Conf. on Modelling Foundations and Applications*, pp. 2–18, 2016.
4. C. Babur. Model analytics and management. PhD thesis, Technische Universiteit Eindhoven, 2019. Proefschrift.
5. Ö. Babur, L. Cleophas, and M. van den Brand. Metamodel clone detection with SAMOS. *Journal of Computer Languages*, vol. 51, pp. 57–74, 2019. doi:10.1016/j.cola.2018.12.002.
6. Ö. Babur, L. Cleophas, and M. van den Brand. Towards distributed model analytics with Apache Spark. In *Proc. of the 6th Int. Conf. on Model-Driven Engineering and Software Development*, 2018, pp. 767–772, 2018.
7. F. Bachmann, L. Bass, and M. Klein. Architectural Tactics: A Step toward Methodical Architectural Design. Technical Report CMU/SEI-2003-TR-004, Pittsburgh, PA, 2003.
8. C. Ballard, C. Compert, T. Jesionowski, I. Milman, B. Plants, B. Rosen, and H. Smith. *Information Governance Principles and Practices for a Big Data Landscape*, IBM Redbooks, 2014.
9. W.L. Chang, D. Boyd, and O. Levin. NIST Big Data Interoperability Framework: Volume 6, Reference Architecture, Special Publication (NIST SP) -1500-6r2, 2019. D. Chapelle. Big Data & Analytics Reference Architecture, An Oracle White Paper, 2013.
10. M. Galster, and P. Avgeriou. Empirically-grounded reference architectures: A proposal. In *Proceedings of the Joint ACM SIGSOFT Quality of Software Architectures (QoSA)*, pp. 153–158). 2011. doi:10.1145/2000259.2000285.

11. B. Geerdink. A reference architecture for big data solutions introducing a model to perform predictive analytics using big data technology. In *Internet Technology and Secured Transactions (ICITST)*, pp. 71–76. 2013.

12. K. Kang, S. Cohen, J. Hess, W. Nowak, and S. Peterson. Feature-Oriented Domain Analysis (FODA) Feasibility Study. Technical Report, CMU/SEI-90-TR-21, Software Engineering Institute, Carnegie Mellon University, Pittsburgh, Pennsylvania, November 1990.

13. M. Maier, A. Serebrenik, and I.T.P. Vanderfeesten, Towards a Big Data Reference Architecture, 2013.

14. N. Marz, and J. Warren. *Big Data: Principles and Best Practices of Scalable Realtime Data Systems*, Manning Publications Co, Shelter Island, New York, 2015.

15. Oracle, Information Management and Big Data: A Reference Architecture, An Oracle White Paper 2013.

16. P. Pääkkönen, and D. Pakkala. Reference architecture and classification of technologies, products and services for big data systems, *Big Data Research*, vol. 2, Issue 4, 2015, pp. 166–186. ISSN 2214-5796. doi:10.1016/j.bdr.2015.01.001.

17. C. Salma, B. Tekinerdogan, and I. Athanassiadis. Domain-driven design of big data systems based on a reference architecture. In: I. Mistrik, R. Bahsoon, N. Ali, M. Heisel, and B. Maxim (Eds.), *Software Architecture for Big Data and the Cloud*, Morgan Kaufmann, Burlington, MA, pp. 49–68, 2017. doi:10.1016/B978-0-12-805467-3.00004-1.

18. C. Salma, B. Tekinerdogan, and I. Athanassiadis. Feature driven survey of big data systems. *Proceedings of the International Conference on Internet of Things and Big Data (IoTBD 2016)*, Rome, SciTePress - ISBN 9789897581830, pp. 348–355, 2016.

19. S. Soares. *Big Data Governance: An Emerging Imperative*, MC Press, 2012.

20. B. Tekinerdogan, Ö. Babur, L. Cleophas, M. van den Brand, and M. Aksit. *Model Management and Analytics for Large Scale Systems*, Elsevier, Academic Press, 2019. ISBN: 9780128166499.

21. B. Tekinerdogan, S. Bilir, and C. Abatlevi. Integrating platform selection rules in the model driven architecture approach. In: U. Aßmann, M. Aksit, and A. Rensink (Eds.) *Model Driven Architecture*, LNCS, vol. 3599. Springer, Berlin, Heidelberg, 2005.

22. B. Tekinerdogan. Software Architecture. In: T. Gonzalez, and J.L. Díaz-Herrera (Eds.) *Computer Science Handbook*, Second Edition, Volume I: Computer Science and Software Engineering, Taylor and Francis, Milton Park, 2014.

23. B. Tekinerdogan, Ö. Özköse Erdoğan, and O. Aktuğ. Supporting incremental product development using multiple product line architecture, *International Journal of Knowledge and Systems Science (IJKSS)* 5(4), 2014. doi:10.4018/ijkss.2014100101.

24. B. Tekinerdogan, and M. Aksit. Classifying and evaluating architecture design methods. In: M. Aksit (Eds.) *Software Architectures and Component Technology*, Springer, Boston, MA, pp. 3–27, 2002.

25. B. Tekinerdogan, and K. Öztürk. Feature-driven design of SaaS architectures. In: Mahmood, Z., and Saeed, S. (Eds.), *Software Engineering Frameworks for the Cloud Computing Paradigm*. Computer Communications and Networks. Springer, London, 2013. doi:10.1007/978-1-4471-5031-2_9.

26. E. Tüzün, B. Tekinerdogan, M.E. Kalender, and S. Bilgen. Empirical evaluation of a decision support model for adopting software product line engineering, *Information and Software Technology*, Elsevier, vol. 60, pp. 77–101, April 2015.

27. E. Tüzün, and B. Tekinerdogan, Analyzing impact of experience curve on ROI in the software product line adoption process, *Information and Software Technology*, vol. 59, pp. 136–148, 2015. ISSN 0950-5849. doi:10.1016/j.infsof.2014.09.008.

Chapter 4

Variability in Data-Intensive Systems: An Architecture Perspective

Matthias Galster
University of Canterbury

Bruce R. Maxim
University of Michigan-Dearborn

Ivan Mistrik
Independent Researcher

Bedir Tekinerdogan
Wageningen University and Research

Contents

4.1 Introduction

Today's users of modern software-intensive systems (i.e., systems "where software contributes essential influences to the design, construction, deployment, and evolution of the system as a whole to encompass individual applications" [1]) expect flexible and adaptive products and services. Also, many software-intensive systems are "data-intensive" to enable new business models to provide enhanced user experience and customer value. As Kim writes, "We are at a tipping point where software companies are generating large-scale telemetry, machines, quality, and user data [2]." Furthermore, data-intensive systems are "a technological building block supporting Big Data and Data Science application [3]." For example, Microsoft's Bing Search, the Cortana virtual assistant, the Microsoft Translator for real-time translation, and the Azure AI platform to enable customers to build and customize their own "smart" applications all utilize data-intensive machine learning technologies [4]. Similarly, Google's search engine indexes millions of web pages and provides search results in milliseconds. Another example is Facebook. In 2012, the social media page was already generating more than 500 terabytes of data every day[1] (including around 2.7 billion "likes" and 300 million photos). Our final example is Netflix [5]. Much of the success of Netflix is due to its high customer retention rates. This is only possible by collecting data from their millions of subscribers and implementing data analytics to discover customer behavior and patterns (e.g., to generate personalized recommendations for movies or TV shows). Netflix models each customer and their interactions to create a detailed user profile that goes beyond personas created through conventional user modeling. For example, Netflix records diverse and large amounts of data, including the time and date a subscriber watched a show, the device used to watch a show, if the show was paused, if viewers resume after pausing, if viewers finish an entire TV show, how long it takes for viewers to finish a show, etc.

Therefore, to succeed in today's competitive and innovation-driven markets, modern data-intensive systems must enable and support variability to accommodate different deployment and usage scenarios. Supporting variability and different usage scenarios in data-intensive systems means that software must accommodate changing and often unforeseen functional requirements and in particular changing quality requirements related to volume, variety, veracity, and velocity of data. As a consequence, variability in data-intensive systems differs from variability in conventional software engineering or software product lines. Challenges that arise in the context of variability in data-intensive systems concern the overall software engineering life cycle, including requirements, architecture, detailed design, implementation, and maintenance of those systems. In this chapter, we explore why and how variability matters in data-intensive systems and take an architecture perspective to discuss potential high-level solutions to addressing variability in data-intensive systems.

4.2 Variability in Data-Intensive Systems

Variability in software-intensive systems is typically understood as the ability of a software system or software artifact (e.g., components, modules, libraries) to be adapted to changing needs so that they fit a specific context [6]. It is an issue in all types of modern software systems [7] and current systems can be adapted in various aspects: hardware, software, data, or processes. Therefore,

---

[1] https://techcrunch.com/2012/08/22/how-big-is-facebooks-data-2-5-billion-pieces-of-content-and-500-terabytes-ingested-every-day/.

variability is about adapting software functionality, behavior, qualities as well as the underlying structure of the software. These adaptations are enabled through a combination of variation points in software development artifacts and variants as options that can be chosen to resolve variability at variation points. Systematically identifying and appropriately managing variability and commonalities among different software products and services distinguishes variability from other approaches that support reuse and product versions [8]. Designing for, implementing, and maintaining variability in software systems not only affect what we build (i.e., software products and services), e.g., systems with "continuous configuration management" from compile time and deployment time to runtime. It also affects how we build products and services (i.e., the development process), e.g., systematic quality assurance and validation of highly complex designs and solution spaces [7].

4.2.1 How Variability Occurs in Data-Intensive Systems

In general, today's data-intensive systems can be adapted in various system elements:

- **Hardware**: Data-intensive systems typically require powerful hardware and reliable data storage technologies. Many software-intensive systems control hardware or interact with hardware (for example, embedded systems or systems that comprise mechanical parts, such as Internet-of-Things/IoT systems). In contrast to software variability, variability in hardware is more about a system's manufacturing or deployment than system functionality. Different CPU or memory configurations affect performance and memory consumption, variation in network capacity, etc.
- **Infrastructure software**: Infrastructure software in data-intensive systems include middleware, database management systems, cloud computing infrastructures, etc. These are typically chosen as out-of-the-box solutions and then configured for a particular context.
- **Application software**: Application software is the "customized" software (often written from scratch) that supports the business processes and models of an organization. Such software often implements AI or machine learning pipelines. Variability in application software also depends on variability in business processes, i.e., in the collection of related and structured activities or tasks that produce a specific output (e.g., when dynamically adapting and updating workflows of a business process by selecting and replacing variants).

In data-intensive systems, variability not only raises issues related to the application, the hardware required for its deployment and necessary infrastructure and application software as discussed above, but also the data that the applications handle. Therefore, regarding the data in data-intensive systems, variability concerns the following aspects that are typically associated with "big data" systems (Laney originally proposed three "V's" – volume, variety, and velocity [9], but this list has been expanded over time [10]; below we do not consider other "V's," such as value, viscosity, etc.):

- **Volume (amount of data processed)**: Volume can change over time and across variants of a system. There is no agreed definition of what defines data to be large to be considered "big" [11]. In general, data in the exabyte or zettabyte ranges are generally considered "big" [12].
- **Variety (types of data handled by a system)**: Data can be structured (e.g., data objects), unstructured (e.g., text, multimedia content), or semistructured. Sometimes, different types of data may appear in the same data stream and their format may be unknown, making the

analysis of such data difficult [12]. This requires sophisticated data cleaning, transformation, and integration techniques.

- **Velocity (speed at which data are generated)**: Variability occurs since data can be generated in different ways, often categorized into batch, real-time, near-real-time, and streaming [12]. Systems may support one or more of these categories of data. The speed at which data arrives can vary over time and also across variants of a system.
- **Veracity (degree to which data can be trusted)**: Data in data-intensive systems is often incomplete. This may require data collection and analysis techniques to handle such data efficiently. Variability occurs since different types and categories of data might be of different quality.

Despite variability in the above points, data-intensive systems still need to support quality attributes discernible at run time (e.g., performance, security, availability) and quality attributes not discernible at run time (e.g., modifiability, portability, reusability) [13]. Examples of situations in which large data-intensive systems did not meet these quality attributes include the Netflix outage on Christmas Eve in 2012,[2] Amazon's August 19, 2013 downtime of 45 minutes that resulted in millions of dollars loss in revenue,[3] and Google's homepage that went offline for 5 minutes on August 16, 2013.[4]

Given the increasing size and heterogeneity of data-intensive systems (e.g., software ecosystems, cyber-physical systems, systems of systems, ultra-large-scale systems), new and emerging application domains (e.g., unmanned aerial vehicles, smart health and e-health applications, large-scale surveillance systems, social networking apps), dynamic operating conditions (e.g., availability of resources in edge computing and IoT), fast-moving and highly competitive markets (e.g., gaming, mobile apps, business intelligence, and data analytics), and increasingly powerful computing infrastructures (e.g., cloud computing, serverless computing, distributed XaaS platforms), the complexity caused by variability becomes more difficult to handle [14]. Also, since variability is pervasive, software engineers need a proper understanding, suitable methods and tools for representing, managing, and reasoning about variability [15]. Furthermore, variability needs to be considered by many different types of stakeholders (clients, acquirers, business analysts, requirements engineers, system and software architects, designers, technology experts, domain experts, data scientists, statisticians, service providers, infrastructure providers, sub-contractors, service users, end users, coders, testers).

4.2.2 Types of Variability in Data-Intensive Systems

Regarding types of variability, based on our previous work [16], we differentiate (a) level of anticipation, (b) intentional versus unintentional variability, (c) involved artifacts, and (d) triggers. Variability in data-intensive systems can be anticipated, i.e., the data-intensive system is designed in a way to facilitate variability in volume, variety, veracity, and velocity. On the other hand, variability may also be unanticipated, i.e., not anticipated during the initial design, development, and deployment of a data-intensive system. Similarly, variability might be intentional or unintentional. Intentional variability in data-intensive systems means that variability is planned and based on conscious design decisions. On the other hand, unintentional variability means that variability

---

[2] https://netflixtechblog.com/a-closer-look-at-the-christmas-eve-outage-d7b409a529ee.

[3] https://www.latimes.com/business/la-xpm-2013-aug-19-la-fi-tn-amazon-website-down-20130819-story.html.

[4] https://www.cnet.com/news/google-goes-down-for-5-minutes-internet-traffic-drops-40/.

is caused by forces and influences that are not controlled by project stakeholders. Moreover, variability in data-intensive systems can arise from the following artifacts or impact these artifacts: (a) There can be variability in the business process(es) supported by the data-intensive system, and (b) the architecture of a data-intensive system can be subject to variability, or even help achieve variability in data-intensive systems. Finally, the trigger for variability could be stakeholders who demand certain data or data analyses. Another trigger could be the environment, e.g., changes in the deployment context.

4.2.3 Variability Management in Data-Intensive Systems

Variability management includes tasks related to managing dependencies between variabilities, maintenance, and continuous population of variant features with new variants, removing features, the distribution of new variants to customers [17]. More specifically, this includes variability conceptualization, implementation, and evaluation. Variability conceptualization to identify solutions that address variability-related stakeholder concerns and to achieve relevant requirements [7]. Variability implementation is about implementing (i.e., codifying and documenting) variability in a system, based on concepts defined during variability conceptualization activities. Finally, during variability evaluation, we need to determine the extent to which systems meet their objectives and address variability.

4.2.4 A Business Perspective

Data-intensive systems support transformations of businesses across various layers (see Figure 4.1). Businesses transform from being providers of data-intensive digital products (e.g., electronic newspapers, music and movies; see Layer 1 in Figure 4.1) to providers of data-intensive digital processes and services (e.g., online payment, travel booking; see Layer 2 in Figure 4.1) to providers and enablers of digital business models (e.g., Twitter, Spotify, Netflix, Indiegogo; see Layer 3 in Figure 4.1). Digital business models typically handle data-intensive digital products (e.g., movies, music) and processes (e.g., online payment for movies and music). In particular, digital ecosystems (such as smart farming, smart mobility, smart health; see Layer 4 in Figure 4.1) are facilitated by data-driven business models, digital business processes, and new and innovative services and products. Finally, such data-intensive ecosystems (i.e., businesses that work as a unit to exchange information and resources and interact with a shared market and based on a common technological

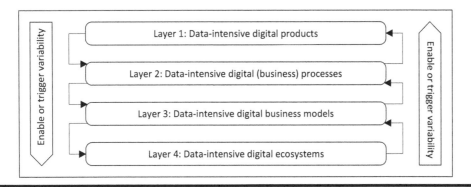

Figure 4.1   Variability in different layers of data-intensive systems.

platform [18]) aggregate different business models, processes, products, and services. Systems that occur in and support these layers are not only data-intensive, but also variability-prone in any of the layers shown in Figure 4.1.

In Figure 4.1, the arrows indicate that variability can occur in any layer and then trigger or enable variability in another one. For example, to support variability in digital products, we may also need to adapt digital business processes. On the other hand, variability in data-intensive digital business models may be enabled by variability in data-intensive digital business processes.

4.3 The Role of Architecture in Data-Intensive Systems

The software architecture of a data-intensive system plays a crucial role for achieving adaptable data-intensive systems [19]. In fact, it has been noted that one of the top three requirements for data-intensive solutions is a flexible architecture.[5] Also, as Gorton and colleagues argue, data-intensive systems must be able to sustain write-heavy workloads [20], and the architectural design impacts how well a system can support such workloads. In general, the software architecture represents the high-level system design. When making architectural design decisions, engineers are forced to reason about a system, its software elements, the relations between them and properties of both, and the system's attributes, including any trade-offs [21]. To address the challenges involved in architecting data-intensive systems, the Software Engineering Institute at Carnegie Mellon initiated QuABase, a knowledge base for architectural knowledge for data-intensive systems.[6]

Consider a scenario in which the high-level business goal is to increase market share. In this scenario, a data-intensive system needs to be scalable and reliable to accommodate variability and growth in data volume, capacity, and variety without exploding system costs. Also, the architecture design solutions for variability-intensive architectures of such a data-intensive system need to consider workload patterns [22], availability, and performance. If not designed well, the data-intensive system may suffer from data communication bottlenecks under certain loads and difficulties when integrating and testing new data analysis features. In this scenario, choosing frameworks, open-source code, databases and data storage technologies, cloud infrastructures, and technology stacks are examples of architectural decisions that impact quality attributes and variability. Typically, data-intensive systems need to support different types of data storage (e.g., relational data for structured data; NoSQL solutions for semistructured data; data warehouses[7]). For example, many data-intensive systems use NoSQL databases (e.g., Cassandra, Riak, and MongoDB). However, these databases are not all equal in terms of scalability because they support different data models or query models. Furthermore, data-intensive systems, such as IoT systems, are distributed systems, so the networks to connect IoT devices need to consider throughput expectations.

Over the years, software architecture design solution concepts have been emerging. For example, architectural patterns, tactics, and styles provide reusable solutions for design; component-based approaches follow a "container" strategy with interfaces; company-specific product line architectures allow us to manage the variation and at the same time capitalize on commonality between software products and services; frameworks and platforms form the basis of software ecosystems. In the context of data-intensive systems, Mattmann et al. point out architectural challenges, such as data volume, data dissemination, data curation, use of open source, searching,

---

[5] https://visual.ly/community/Infographics/technology/cios-big-data.

[6] https://quabase.sei.cmu.edu/mediawiki/index.php/Main_Page.

[7] Systems built as layer on top of databases to make analytics fast and efficient for online analytical processing.

processing and analyzing data, and information modeling [23]. Architecture design concepts for data-intensive systems need to consider these challenges in addition to enabling variability. Mattmann et al. also provide examples of data-intensive systems and architectures to illustrate architectural concepts in data-intensive systems [23]. Architecture-related design concepts need to help reduce, or if at all possible, avoid technical debt. Therefore, Foidl et al. discuss technical debt in the context of data-intensive systems and propose a conceptual model for technical debt in data-intensive systems [24]. This conceptual model is based on decomposing data-intensive systems into three parts consisting of "Software Systems" (e.g., traditional software and machine learning applications), "Data Storage Systems" (databases, distributed file systems, data models, and storage), and "Data" [24]. Technical debt can emerge and impact each of these parts [24]. In the following sections of this chapter, we discuss some architecture-related design concepts.

4.4 Reference Architectures to Support Data-Intensive Systems

One way to systematically handle variability in data-intensive system is to utilize reference architectures. In general, reference architectures capture the essence of the architecture of systems that belong to a certain technology domain (e.g., service-based systems), application domain (e.g., automotive systems), or problem domain (e.g., image processing) [25]. Reference architectures offer one way to systematically reuse existing architecture knowledge when developing new software systems or new versions of similar products [26]. The purpose of a reference architecture is to facilitate the development of concrete architectures for new systems, to help with the evolution of a set of systems that stem from the same reference architecture, and to ensure standardization and interoperability of different systems. Examples of generic reference architectures for service-oriented architecture and service-based systems include IBM's foundation architecture [27] and Nexof [28]. On the other hand, examples of more specific reference architectures include reference architectures for e-contracting [29], security [30,31], and web browsers [32].

In the context of data-intensive systems, Oracle's reference architecture for Big Data systems [33] promotes a unified vision for information management and analytics. The reference architecture defines a set of architecture principles that are commonly accepted as best practices in industry. It is described in terms of components that achieve capabilities typically required by organizations. The reference architecture supports hot-pluggable "Knowledge Modules" to provide out-of-the-box modularity, flexibility, and extensibility. More specifically, Weyrich and Ebert discuss reference architectures for IoT systems (one type of data-intensive systems), where advanced data analytics are the "front end" for users [34]. One key issue in these reference architectures is flexibility so that products can autonomously adapt to usage scenarios such as assisted living, intelligent buildings, smart transportation, energy, healthcare, transportation, or entire supply chains [34].

Related to reference architectures is the concept of product line architectures [35]. A product line architecture describes concepts and structures to achieve variation in features of different products that belong to the same market domain, while sharing as many parts as possible in the implementation [36]. Thus, the product line architecture captures the central design of all products of the product line [37] and addresses variability explicitly through "features," "variation points," "variants," etc. [38]. While traditional product lines instantiate products at design times, dynamic product lines provide adaptability of systems during run time [39,40].

Reference architectures are sometimes considered the same as product line architectures [26] or as one type of reference architecture (besides platform-specific architectures, industry-specific architectures, and industry-cross-cutting architectures) [41]. Others have argued that product line architectures are less abstract than reference architectures [42,43], but more abstract than concrete architectures [44]. To generalize the relationship between reference architecture and product line architecture, one may assume that each product line architecture is a reference architecture, but not all reference architectures are product line architectures. We provide a more detailed comparison of product line architectures and reference architectures in previous work [7]. In the context of data-intensive systems, product line architectures and reference architectures may consider the distributed nature of systems. As Gorton et al. argue, due to scalability and availability needs of data-intensive systems, distribution occurs in all tiers, from webserver farms and caches to back-end storage [20].

4.5 Service-Oriented Architecture and Cloud Computing

Service-oriented architecture and cloud computing can be combined to provide solutions for variability in data-intensive systems. Service-oriented architecture (SOA) [45] is a standard-based and technology-independent distributed computing paradigm for discovering, binding, and assembling loosely-coupled software services. SOA typically supports variability through dynamic service retrieval and binding [46]. Here, the right level of service granularity can support variability. Coarse-grained services are distinguished from fine-grained services that offer less functionality [47]. Fine-grained services offer more possibilities to handle variability [47,48].

Similarly, cloud computing provides on-demand availability of data storage and computing power, without direct active management by the user [49]. Large clouds often have functions distributed on computers over multiple locations. An advantage of cloud computing is the sharing of resources to achieve economies of scale, scalable deployment, redundancy and reliability, and minimized up-front IT costs. Cloud applications are often offered as Software-as-a-Service and allow the use of computational capability through web services. Some popular examples of cloud computing are Amazon's Elastic Compute Cloud, Google's App Engine, and Microsoft's Azure, which allow users to rent "virtual computers" on which they run their own applications. When building cloud-based data-intensive systems, we need to consider the roles and needs of both cloud consumers and cloud providers. Cloud consumers need to architect the systems to account for a lack of full control over important quality attributes. Cloud providers on the other hand have to design and architecture infrastructures and systems that provide the most efficient way to manage resources and to keep promises made in service-level agreements. For example, cloud providers need to optimize reliability and provide consistent computational power to cloud users. At the same time, they have to consider energy efficiency (they are paying for electricity and cooling of massive server farms).

A more recent trend related to cloud computing is edge computing. In edge computing, we push the computation, the data, and the analysis to the very edge of the network, to the people who are using computing (and often mobile) devices as end users. Examples for such systems include systems for early responders, which have a mobile device and need to do some analysis and require computational power, data staging, and a way to get data from the cloud. In such scenarios, we can apply surrogates (e.g., nearby laptops) that allow us to augment the capabilities of the mobile device so we can offload some of the computation or data staging, so the data coming from the cloud can in transit be hosted on this surrogate and then move to the mobile device.

Looking at IoT systems as an example of data-intensive systems, cloud and edge computing could enhance these systems. IoT describes software-intensive systems of connected computing devices, mechanical and digital machines, animals or people and with the ability to transfer data over a network without human involvement [50]. IoT typically integrates multiple technologies, real-time analytics, machine learning, commodity sensors, wireless sensor networks, control systems, and embedded systems. A popular example of IoT technology are smart homes, which integrate devices and appliances (such as lighting fixtures, thermostats, home security systems and cameras, and other home appliances) that can be controlled via devices, such as smartphones and smart speakers. To handle variability in data-intensive systems, cloud computing and IoT could be combined [51]. We can utilize synergies between IoT and cloud computing to overcome limitations of IoT while extending the scope of cloud computing platforms to include physical devices. One limitation of IoT is that devices in an IoT have limited resources (e.g., processing power, storage, energy). Therefore, complex computing tasks or permanent storage of data generated and processed by IoT devices cannot be performed on the devices themselves. Hence, when combining cloud computing and IoT, cloud computing platforms may act as back-end solutions (e.g., to share huge amounts of data in IoT to different distributed consumers).

4.6 Serverless Architectures for Data-Intensive Systems

Serverless architectures represent a more recent trend to support variability in data-intensive systems. Generally speaking, serverless architectures do not require the provision or management of any servers [52]. Serverless computing platforms provide Function(s)-as-a-Service (FaaS) to end users while promising reduced hosting costs, high availability, fault tolerance, and dynamic hosting of individual functions known as microservices. Serverless computing environments, unlike Infrastructure-as-a-Service (IaaS) cloud platforms, abstract infrastructure management including the creation of virtual machines, operating system containers, and load balancing from users. For a service or platform to be considered serverless, it should provide the following capabilities[8]:

- **No server management**: There is no need to provide or maintain any servers. There is no software or run time environment to install, maintain, or administer [53].
- **Flexible scaling**: Applications can scale automatically or by adjusting capacity through toggling the units of consumption (e.g., throughput, memory) rather than units of individual servers [53].
- **High availability**: Serverless applications have built-in availability and fault tolerance. Developers are not required to architect for these capabilities because services provide them by default [53].
- **No idle capacity**: Users no dot need to pay for idle capacity. There is no need to preprovision or overprovision capacity (e.g., for storage or computing power). Users are not charged when their code is not running [53].

A concrete example of a serverless architecture for data-intensive systems and out-of-the-box cloud storage solutions is Amazon's S3 (Simple Storage Service)[9] together with Amazon's serverless computing platform Lambda.[10] Such solutions can be part of a pipeline where data are uploaded into a "bucket" (i.e., a namespace or a database table or a disk drive), transformed, and then moved to another "bucket." Furthermore, solutions such as Amazon's S3 also support the processing of large amounts of data, storing potentially huge objects and binary unstructured data, and only

---

[8] https://d1.awsstatic.com/whitepapers/serverless-architectures-with-aws-lambda.pdf.
[9] https://aws.amazon.com/s3/.
[10] https://aws.amazon.com/lambda/.

processing individual objects at a time [54]. For storing small bits of structured data, with minimal latency, and potential need to process groups of objects in atomic transactions, developers may choose a document database or a NoSQL database designed for storing structured textual data, such as Amazon's DynamoDB[11] database [54]. Moreover, developers may utilize design principles to ensure secure data in cloud-based environments. For example, "protect data in transit and at rest" means that data are classified into sensitivity levels and mechanisms, such as encryption, tokenization, and access control are used where appropriate [22]. Similarly, "keep people away from data" means that mechanisms and tools need to be created to reduce or eliminate the need for direct access or manual processing of data. This reduces the risk of loss or modification and human error when handling sensitive data [22]. More architectural issues for cloud-based data-intensive systems using concrete use cases can be found online.[12,13]

4.7 Ethical Considerations

In data-intensive systems and when using related technologies and techniques, such as machine learning and AI, ethical considerations and wider human and societal values become first-class citizens [55]. Examples of data-intensive systems that violated such considerations and values include Amazon's recruitment software that became biased against women [56]. In general, data-intensive systems handle tremendous amounts of data. Therefore, questions related to data governance are important [57], and developers need to consider many "non-technical" architectural decisions related to a larger data (retention) life cycle management process and how and where the data will be collected, processed, preserved, archived, versioned, or deleted. More specifically, while data-intensive systems allow firms to rapidly capture, analyze, and exploit information, it can also enable access to data that compromises an individual's privacy [58]. Ville et al. summarize key principles in ethics and group them into principles related to the development organization (accountability, responsibility) and principles related to the system itself (transparency, predictability, fairness, and trustworthiness) [57]. For example, transparency is about understanding the data and how algorithms change the data, and predictability is about the confidence that the system does what it is supposed to. Fairness concerns fairness in data or bias as well as who benefits from the analyzed data. From a variability point of view and software development, ethics could be considered a "non-functional" requirement [57]. Many examples of data-intensive systems that are subject to variability need to consider ethical constraints, e.g., self-driving cars.

4.8 Conclusions

Today's data-intensive software systems are subject to variability terms of purpose, application domain, complexity, size, novelty, adaptability, required qualities, and life span. This chapter provided an overview of variability in data-intensive systems. In this chapter, we had a closer look at variability in data-intensive systems from the perspective of the architecture of those systems. In particular, we explored why variability in data-intensive systems matters and investigated various high-level solutions toward handling variability in data-intensive systems.

---

[11] https://aws.amazon.com/dynamodb/.
[12] https://aws.amazon.com/architecture/well-architected/.
[13] https://aws.amazon.com/architecture/icons/.

References

1. ISO/IEC/IEEE, "Systems and Software Engineering - Architecture Description." vol. ISO/IEC/IEEE 42010 Geneva, Switzerland, 2011.
2. M. Kim, "Software engineering for data analytics," *IEEE Software*, vol. 37, pp. 36–42, 2020.
3. T. Wiktorski, *Data-intensive Systems: Principles and Fundamentals using Hadoop and Spark*. Berlin: Springer, 2019.
4. S. Amershi, A. Begel, C. Bird, R. DeLine, H. Gall, E. Kamar, N. Nagappan, B. Nushi, and T. Zimmermann, "Software engineering for machine learning: A case study," In *International Conference on Software Engineering: Software Engineering in Practice (ICSE-SEIP)*, Montreal, Canada: ACM, 2019, pp. 291–300.
5. N. Diamantopoulos, J. Wong, D. I. Mattos, I. Gerostathopoulos, M. Wardrop, T. Mao, and C. McFarland, "Engineering for a science-centric experimentation platform," In *International Conference on Software Engineering (ICSE-SEIP)*, Seoul, Korea: IEEE, 2020, pp. 1–10.
6. J. van Gurp, J. Bosch, and M. Svahnberg, "On the notion of variability in software product lines," In *Working IEEE/IFIP Conference on Software Architecture*, Amsterdam, The Netherlands: IEEE Computer Society, 2001, pp. 45–54.
7. M. Galster, I. Mistrik, and B. Maxim, "Variability-intensive software systems: Concepts and techniques," In *Software Engineering for Variability Intensive Systems*, I. Mistrik, M. Galster, and B. Maxim, Eds. New York: CRC Press, 2019, pp. 1–38.
8. J. Bosch, G. Florijn, D. Greefhorst, J. Kuusela, J. H. Obbink, and K. Pohl, "Variability issues in software product lines," In *4th International Workshop on Software Product Family Engineering*, Bilbao, Spain: Springer Verlag, 2002, pp. 303–338.
9. D. Laney, *3D Data Management: Controlling Data Volume, Velocity, and Variety*, Stamford, CT: META Group Inc., 2001.
10. R. Hariri, E. M. Fredericks, and K. M. Bowers, "Uncertainty in big data analytics: Survey, opportunities, and challenges," *Journal of Big Data*, vol. 44, pp. 1–16, 2019.
11. A. Gandomi, and M. Haider, "Beyond the hype: Big data concepts, methods, and analytics," *International Journal of Information Management*, vol. 35, pp. 137–144, 2015.
12. M. Chen, S. Mao, and Y. Liu, "Big data: A survey," *Mobile Networks and Applications*, vol. 19, pp. 171–109, 2014.
13. P. Bourque, and R. E. Fairley, *Guide to the Software Engineering Body of Knowledge, Version 3.0*, Washington, D.C.: IEEE Computer Society, 2014.
14. M. Galster, D. Weyns, M. Goedicke, U. Zdun, R. Rabiser, G. Perrouin, and B. Zhang, "Variability and complexity in software design - towards a research agenda," *ACM Software Engineering Notes*, vol. 41, pp. 27–30, 2016.
15. M. Galster, and P. Avgeriou, "Handling variability in software architecture: Problems and implications," In *9th IEEE/IFIP Working Conference on Software Architecture*, Boulder, CO: IEEE Computer Society, 2011, pp. 171–180.
16. M. Galster, D. Weyns, D. Tofan, B. Michalik, and P. Avgeriou, "Variability in software systems - a systematic literature review," *IEEE Transactions on Software Engineering*, vol. 40, pp. 282–306, 2014.
17. M. Svahnberg, J. van Gurp, and J. Bosch, "A taxonomy of variability realization techniques," *Software - Practice and Experience*, vol. 35, pp. 705–754, April 2005.
18. D. Messerschmitt, and C. Szyperski, *Software Ecosystem: Understanding an Indispensable Technology and Industry*. Cambridge, MA: MIT Press, 2003.
19. B. Tekinerdogan, and H. Sozer, "Variability viewpoint for introducing variability in software architecture viewpoints," In *Joint Working IEEE/IFIP Conference on Software Architecture (WICSA) and the Sixth European Conference on Software Architecture (ECSA) - Companion Volume*, Helsinki: ACM, 2012, pp. 163–166.
20. I. Gorton, A. B. Bener, and A. Mockus, "Software engineering for big data systems," *IEEE Software*, vol. 33, pp. 32–35, 2016.
21. L. Bass, P. Clements, and R. Kazman, *Software Architecture in Practice*. Boston, MA: Addison-Wesley, 2012.

22. Amazon, "AWS Well-Architected Framework," 2019.

23. C. Mattmann, D. Crichton, A. Hart, C. Goodale, S. Hughes, S. Kelly, L. Cinquini, T. Painter, J. Lazio, D. Waliser, N. Medvidovic, J. Kim, and P. Lean, "Architecting data-intensive software systems," In *Handbook of Data Intensive Computing*, B. Furht and A. Escalante, Eds. Berlin: Springer, 2011, pp. 25–57.

24. H. Foidl, M. Felderer, and S. Biffl, "Technical debt in data-intensive software systems," In *45th Euromicro Conference on Software Engineering and Advanced Applications (SEAA)*, Kallithea-Chalkidiki, Greece: IEEE, 2019, pp. 338–341.

25. R. Cloutier, G. Muller, D. Verma, R. Nilchiani, E. Hole, and M. Bone, "The concept of reference architectures," *Systems Engineering*, vol. 13, pp. 14–27, March 2010.

26. K. Pohl, G. Boeckle, and F. van der Linden, *Software Product Line Engineering - Foundations, Principles, and Techniques*. Berlin / Heidelberg: Springer Verlag, 2005.

27. R. High, S. Kinder, and S. Graham, "IBM's SOA Foundation - An Architectural Introduction and Overview," IBM, White Paper November 2005.

28. V. Stricker, K. Lauenroth, P. Corte, F. Gittler, S. D. Panfilis, and K. Pohl, "Creating a reference architecture for service-based systems - a pattern-based approach," In *Towards the Future Internet*, G. Tselentis, A. Galis, A. Gavras, S. Krco, V. Lotz, E. Simperl, B. Stiller, and T. Zahariadis, Eds. Amsterdam: IOS Press, 2010, pp. 149–160.

29. S. Angelov, and P. Grefen, "An E-contracting reference architecture," *Journal of Systems and Software*, vol. 81, pp. 1816–1844, November 2008.

30. T. E. Faegri, and S. Hallsteinsen, "A software product line reference architecture for security," In *Software Product Lines*, T. Kakola and J. C. Duenas, Eds. Berlin / Heidelberg: Springer Verlag, 2006, pp. 275–326.

31. M. Hafner, M. Memon, and R. Breu, "SeAAS - A reference architecture for security services in SOA," *Journal of Universal Computer Science*, vol. 15, pp. 2916–1936, 2009.

32. A. Grosskurth, and M. Godfrey, "A reference architecture for web browsers," In *International Conference on Software Maintenance Budapest*, Hungary: IEEE Computer Society, 2005, pp. 661–664.

33. Oracle, "Big Data & Analytics Reference Architecture," 2013.

34. M. Weyrich, and C. Ebert, "Reference architectures for the internet of things," *IEEE Software*, vol. 33, pp. 112–116, 2016.

35. F. Ahmed, and L. F. Capretz, "The software product line architecture: An empirical investigation of key process activities," *Information and Software Technology*, vol. 50, pp. 1098–113, October 2008.

36. M. Jazayeri, F. van der Linden, and A. Ran, *Software Architecture for Product Families: Principles and Practice*. Reading, MA: Addison-Wesley, 2000.

37. M. Verlage and T. Kiesgen, "Five years of product line engineering in a small company," In *27th International Conference on Software Engineering*, St. Louis, MO: ACM, 2005, pp. 534–543.

38. J. Bayer, O. Flege, P. Knauber, R. Laqua, D. Muthig, K. Schmid, T. Widen, and J.-M. DeBaud, "PuLSE: A methodology to develop software product lines," In *Symposium on Software Reusability*, Los Angeles, CA: ACM, 1999, pp. 122–131.

39. H. Shokry, and M. Ali Babar, "Dynamic software product line architectures using service-based computing for automotive systems," In *2nd International Workshop on Dynamic Software Product Lines*, Limerick, Ireland: Lero International Science Centre, 2008, pp. 53–58.

40. S. Hallsteinsen, S. Jiang, and R. Sanders, "Dynamic software product lines in service-oriented computing," In *3rd International Workshop on Dynamic Software Product Lines*, San Francisco, CA, 2009, pp. 28–34.

41. O. Vogel, I. Arnold, A. Chughtai, E. Ihler, T. Kehrer, U. Mehlig, and U. Zdun, *Software-Architektur - Grundlagen - Konzepte - Praxis*. Berlin/Heidelberg: Spektrum Akademischer Verlag, 2009.

42. S. Angelov, P. Grefen, and D. Greefhorst, "A classification of software reference architectures: Analyzing their success and effectiveness," In *Joint Working IEEE/IFIP Conference on Software Architecture & European Conference on Software Architecture (WICSA/ECSA)*, Cambridge, UK: IEEE Computer Society, 2009, pp. 141–150.

43. E. Y. Nakagawa, P. O. Antonino, and M. Becker, "Reference architecture and product line architecture: A subtle but critical difference," In *5th European Conference on Software Architecture*, Essen, Germany: Springer Verlag, 2011, pp. 207–211.

44. S. Angelov, J. Trienekens, and P. Grefen, "Towards a Method for the Evaluation of Reference Architectures: Experiences from a Case," In *Second European Conference on Software Architecture*, Paphos, Cyprus: Springer, 2008, pp. 225–240.

45. M. H. Dodani, "SOA 2006: State of the art," *Journal of Object Technology*, vol. 5, pp. 41–48, November–December 2006.

46. R. Kazhamiakin, S. Benbernou, L. Baresi, P. Plebani, M. Uhlig, and O. Barais, "Adaptation of service-based systems," In *Service Research Challenges and Solutions for the Future Internet*, M. P. Papazoglou, K. Pohl, M. Parkin, and A. Metzger, Eds. Berlin / Heidelberg: Springer Verlag, 2010, pp. 117–156.

47. M. Galster, and E. Bucherer, "A business-goal-service-capability graph for the alignment of requirements and services," In *IEEE Congress on Services*, Honolulu, HI: IEEE Computer Society, 2008, pp. 399–406.

48. R. Haesen, M. Snoeck, W. Lemahieu, and S. Poelmans, "On the definition of service granularity and its architectural impact," In *20th International Conference on Advanced Information Systems Engineering (CAiSE'08)*, Montpellier, France: Springer, 2008, pp. 375–389.

49. R. Buyya, J. Broberg, and A. M. Goscinski, *Cloud Computing: Principles and Paradigms*. Hoboken, NJ: Wiley, 2011.

50. L. Atzori, A. Iera, and G. Morabito, "The internet of things: A survey," *Computer Networks*, vol. 54, pp. 2787–2805, 2010.

51. A. Botta, W. de Donato, V. Persico, and A. Pescapé, "Integration of cloud computing and internet of things: A survey," *Future Generation of Computer Systems*, vol. 56, pp. 684–700, 2016.

52. T. Lynn, P. Rosati, A. Lejeune, and V. Emeakaroha, "A preliminary review of enterprise serverless cloud computing (Function-as-a-Service) platforms," In *International Conference on Cloud Computing Technology and Science (CloudCom)*, Hong Kong: IEEE, 2017, pp. 162–169.

53. Amazon, "Serverless Architectures with AWS Lambda: Overview and Best Practices," 2017.

54. G. Adzic, *Running Serverless: Introduction to AWS Lambda and the Serverless Application Model*. London, UK: Neuri Consulting LLP, 2019.

55. J. Whittle, M. A. Ferrario, W. Simm, and W. Hussain, "A case for human values in software engineering," *IEEE Software*, vol. 38, pp. 106–113, 2020.

56. J. Dastin, "Amazon Scraps Secret AI Recruiting Tool that Showed Bias Against Women," In *Reuters Technology News*, 2018.

57. V. Vakkuri, K.-K. Kemell, J. Kultanen, and P. Abrahamsson, "The current state of industrial practice in artificial intelligence ethics," *IEEE Software*, vol. 37, pp. 50–57, 2020.

58. R. Herschel, and V. M. Miori, "Ethics & big data," *Technology in Society*, vol. 49, pp. 31–36, 2017.

KNOWLEDGE DISCOVERY AND MANAGEMENT

Chapter 5

Knowledge Management via Human-Centric, Domain-Specific Visual Languages for Data-Intensive Software Systems

John Grundy and Hourieh Khalajzadeh
Monash University

Andrew J. Simmons
Deakin University

Humphrey O. Obie
Monash University

Mohamed Abdelrazek
Deakin University

John Hosking
The University of Auckland

Qiang He
Swinburne University of Technology

Contents

5.1 Introduction

Smart living applications are increasingly in demand. These range from smart homes – for general-purpose use or specific tasks, e.g. supporting aged care, disability or rehabilitation; smart transport systems; smart grid and other utility-oriented systems; autonomous vehicles; 'smart living' robotics; industry 4.0-supporting applications; smart hospitals and schools; and smart buildings in general [1–3].

For example, Figure 5.1 shows two exemplar smart living solutions, a smart home to support ageing people living in their homes and a smart urban environment. Both are composed of a number of sensors and interactors. Both have a range of diverse end users with diverse end-user requirements. The sensors generate significant amounts of heterogeneous data that needs to be stored, processed and presented. Some of the data processing is done 'on the edge' [4]. Other is uploaded and done 'on the cloud' [5]. These lead to a need for careful algorithm selection for the data processing, choice of deployment of algorithms and management of security, privacy, reliability, performance and robustness constraints.

Such systems come with a number of serious challenges in the engineering of the system. By their very nature, they need to incorporate a wide range of users and use cases, leading to challenging requirements engineering tasks. This includes determining the high-level requirements of the system, key processes it needs to support, key data sources, data storage and data processing and required system and user interactions [6]. Architecting such systems is challenging [7], given the wide range of hardware and application software platforms needed. Many design decisions relate to the data-intensive nature of the system: how to obtain, wrangle, transform, integrate, harmonise and store diverse data; choice of machine learning techniques to process and extract key information from the data; and appropriate large-scale data visualisation techniques needed to support diverse decision-making.

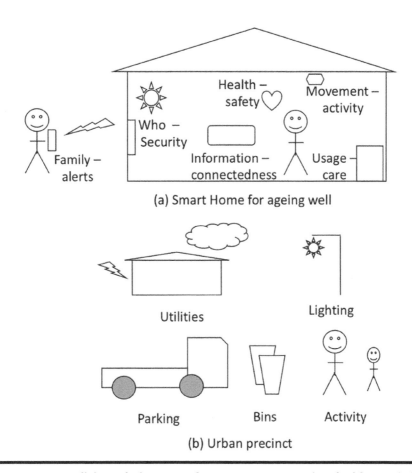

Figure 5.1   Two smart living solution examples (© IEEE 2021, reprinted with permission).

We have developed a suite of domain-specific visual languages to assist in supporting the development of such data-intensive systems, BiDaML [8]. BiDaML provides a set of visual languages to capture high level to detailed requirements, data-oriented design decisions, deployment scenarios and detailed data representation and processing formats and algorithms. In this chapter, we illustrate the use of our BiDaML approach to support the development of two exemplar smart living systems.

5.2 Motivation

Consider the example from Figure 5.1 of a 'smart home' to assist ageing people. Such a smart living solution aims to provide ageing people with support for physical and mental challenges as they age, but want to stay in their own home longer and be safe and secure [9]. Key features of this system – with a focus on the data-intensive system aspects – include, but are not limited to:

■ Sensors that detect the ageing person's movements throughout the smart home – data generated needs to be stored, processed to determine regular behaviour patterns; deviation from these can alert carers that the elderly person is unwell, has a fall, etc.

- Sensors that detect device usage and activity, e.g. stove, lights, tap, fridge, etc. – as above, this data is integrated, possibly with movement data, to help build the occupant's behaviour profile. It may also be used to support health-related reminders, e.g. 'Have you had a glass of water recently?'
- Health-related data captured via, e.g., Bluetooth-enabled scales, blood pressure monitor, wearable, augmented medicine container, etc. – these can check that the elderly person is, e.g., taking medication, there are no serious outlier health indicators and data can be shared with remote clinician.
- Communication devices to connect to family, carer and community, such as tablets, smart TVs, etc. – these also may provide important behaviour monitoring, but also support connectedness and combat loneliness and anxiety especially of living alone. Smart home features such as heating, lighting, windows, doors, etc. – these support environment management especially for physically challenged individuals.

Other smart living devices may be added or removed or reconfigured. Other data analysis may be carried out with multiple data input sources. Data privacy, physical and electronic security and reliability are all critical requirements in this domain.

Smart cities have become a greatly increasing area of research but also of practice [10–12]. Consider the example from Figure 5.1 of a smart city solution which includes diverse data feeds to assist urban precinct operation and strategic planning. A local government instruments a wide variety of its artefacts to assist in providing services and in overall planning and management of services. These might include but are not limited to:

- Smart parking – parking spaces and parking buildings indicate free/occupied spaces. These may be used to provide real-time parking space availability to users, overstaying vehicles to traffic wardens and over time large-scale parking usage statistics for urban planners.
- Smart lighting – which adapts to both ambient light and weather conditions to save power, but also usage information to reduce lighting when unused or increase on demand as pedestrian movement is detected.
- Smart rubbish bins – these proactively monitor rubbish bin space usage, smells, liquids and ask for collection when needed. They also can give long-term indications of space usage for planning purposes.
- Space usage sensors – these detect pedestrian and vehicular traffic and can be used to inform different usage patterns according to date, time, correlation to events, etc.
- Traffic flow monitoring and control – these provide very detailed information about road usage and may provide highly localised and adaptive control of vehicle traffic lights and pedestrian crossings.
- Pedestrian activity including movement, density, use of communal tables, chairs, benches, etc. – these allow low-level monitoring and even proactive intervention, e.g. to help enforce social distancing for COVID-19, along with larger-scale data analysis for the usage of footpaths, crossings, communal facilities, blockages, etc.
- Building usage and control – these provide the ability to optimise building utility usage to reduce costs and environment impact and larger-scale data on usage, access needs, etc.
- Park management including smart watering systems
- Smart utility management

Local government is continually looking for ways to better manage complex resources and balance demands of retailers, pedestrians, vehicle users, manufacturers, householders, etc. Smart living solutions such as the above provide both low-level, on-the-spot ways to monitor and control government facilities, but also larger-scale over time and distance analysis of usage patterns and demand [13]. Unlike the smart home scenario, the users are very large in number and very diverse. The technologies are also more diverse, needing a wider range and scale of platforms and networks to achieve. Privacy and security issues still present but are both individual and group challenges. Scaling to thousands of devices with very large data capture, storage and processing become major challenges.

In both of these systems, a range of stakeholders and developers are needed to develop, deploy and maintain the solution. These range from customers and end users, managers, data scientists, software engineers and edge- and cloud-platform engineers. Sometimes a very wide range of these stakeholders are needed producing a wide variety of heterogeneous devices, servers, networks, dashboards, interfaces, etc. A critical need is for a knowledge management approach that can support this diverse team.

5.3 Approach

To design data-intensive systems such as those above, we developed the BiDaML suite of visual languages to model key knowledge required [8]. BiDaML provides a set of domain-specific visual languages using five diagram types at different levels of abstraction to support key aspects of big data analytics. These five diagram types cover the whole data analytics software development life cycle from higher-level requirement analysis and problem definition through the low-level deployment of the final product. These five diagrammatic types are:

- *Brainstorming diagram* provides an overview of a data analytics project and all the tasks and sub-tasks that are involved in designing the solution at a very high level. Users can include comments and extra information for the other stakeholders;
- *Process diagrams* specify the key analytics processes/steps including key details related to the participants (individuals and organisations), operations and conditions in a data analytics project capturing details from a high level to a lower level;
- *Technique diagrams* show the step-by-step procedures and processes for each sub-task in the brainstorming and process diagrams at a low level of abstraction. They show what techniques have been used or are planned to be used and whether they were successful or there were any issues;
- *Data diagrams* document the data and artefacts that are produced in each of the above diagrams at a low level, i.e. the technical AI-based layer. They also define in detail the outputs associated with different tasks, e.g. output information, reports, results, visualisations and outcomes;
- *Deployment diagrams* depict the run-time configuration, i.e. the system hardware, the software installed on it and the middleware connecting different machines to each other for development-related tasks.

Figure 5.2 shows an overview of our BiDaML framework in the left side and its notations on the right side. Users including domain experts, business owner, data scientists and software engineers brainstorm, design and analyse the problem and requirements by defining tasks through

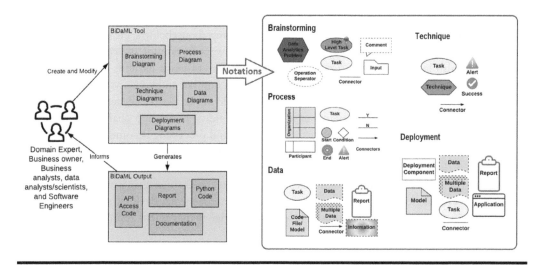

Figure 5.2   BiDaML overview and notations.

visual-based drag-and-drop of the notations through a brainstorming diagram. Business owners and business analysts with the help of the other users would then create a process diagram by specifying the details related to the organisations and participants involved in the project. Users can generate reports and iterate through the different aspects of the projects in order to come up with a plan for the project. Data analysts and data scientists will then focus on data, feature and model engineering parts of the project by further breaking down the tasks to more detailed tasks and connecting them to the data items and techniques. Data analysts and data scientists can generate Python code or connect to the ML tools' APIs in this step. They can embed their Python code to reuse in future projects in this step. Once models are created and finalised, data analysts and data scientists can work with the software engineers to walk them through the models, how they work, the input and outputs of the models and the requirements to access the models.

In the following sections, we use the two representative data-intensive system examples above to show how BiDaML is used to capture and represent key knowledge needed to successfully build each of the systems.

5.4 High-Level Requirements Capture

5.4.1 Brainstorming

A brainstorming diagram is used to capture the key goals of a data-intensive system expressed at a high level. There are no rules as to how abstractly or explicitly a context is expanded. The diagram overviews a system in terms of the specific problem it is associated with and the tasks and sub-tasks to solve the specific problem. It supports interactive brainstorming and collaboration between interdisciplinary team members to identify key aspects of a system such as its requirements implications, analytical methodologies and specific tasks. Figure 5.3 shows the brainstorming diagram for the smart city system.

In Figure 5.3, the root node, illustrated as a red hexagon, represents the data analytics problem the project aims to address, i.e. the smart city project. High-level tasks are illustrated as orange ellipses with fixed pins to highlight their importance. These include nodes labelled *define objectives*,

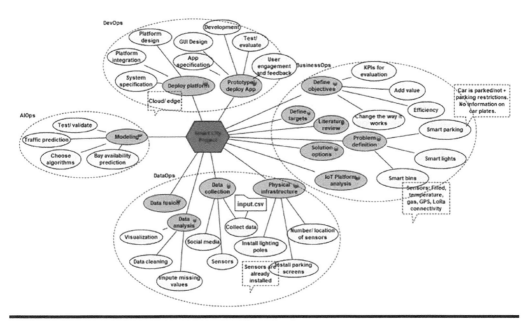

Figure 5.3   Smart city brainstorming diagram.

data collection, *data fusion*, etc. All other tasks, which are children of high-level tasks, are called *low-level* tasks. These are drawn using yellow ellipses, such as *KPIs for evaluation* and *collect data*. A task (both high- and low-level) may be labelled with useful information such as *input* files or *comments* for carrying out the requisite tasks. For instance, the low-level task *Collect data* is labelled by the input file *input.csv*. Comments are illustrated as dialogue boxes with a broken border.

Figure 5.4 shows the brainstorming diagram for the smart home system. A red hexagon icon represents the Smart Home system, and the orange ellipses show the five key to-do tasks with which the problem is associated. High-level tasks connected directly to the problem are automatically

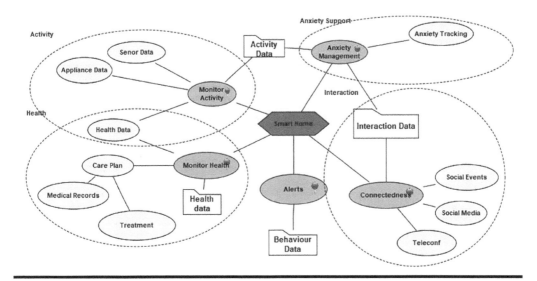

Figure 5.4   Smart home brainstorming diagram.

changed to bright orange notes with fixed pins to highlight their importance. In this example, *Monitor Activity* is one of the key high-level tasks which is further broken down to *Sensor Data*, *Appliance Data* and *Health Data* capture and processing tasks as lower-level to-do tasks to achieve this. An input icon representing the *Activity Data* is shown to be produced by this *Monitor Activity* feature. Other key tasks that make up this example smart home include *Health Monitoring*, support for *Anxiety Monitoring*, supporting *Connectedness* to family, friends and carers and providing *Alerts*, e.g. if collected and processed behaviour data indicates that the elderly person is unwell.

These brainstorming diagrams provide a high-level conceptual model of the overall system requirements. We drill down from the tasks, sub-tasks and data sets to define more details of the solution.

5.4.2 Process Definition

A high-level process diagram for our smart city use case is shown in Figure 5.5. In this diagram type, we use an adapted Business Process Model and Notation (BPMN) process diagram representation that captures (a) key organisations as 'pools' (blue boxes); (b) key stakeholders involved as 'swimlanes' (white boxes); (c) key process tasks as yellow ovals; (d) process start (green circle) and stop (red circle) points; (e) decision points (diamonds); (f) and process task flows links. The idea is to capture a range of high-level, key data processing steps in the system.

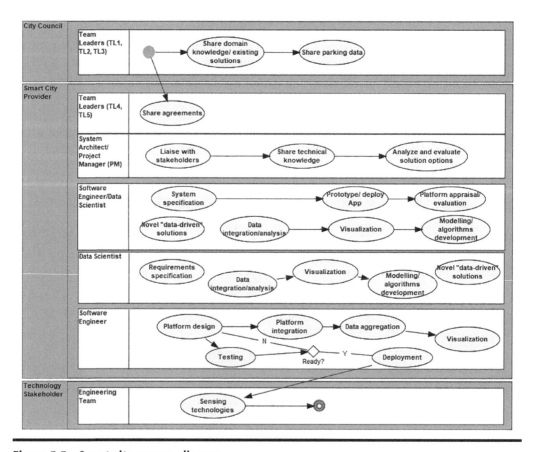

Figure 5.5   Smart city process diagram.

For this example, the smart city project starts when the team leaders from the city council share domain knowledge and the existing solutions as well as the parking data with the other stakeholders (top pool/swimlane). The project ends when the engineering team (bottom pool/swimlane), as the technology stakeholders, implements the required sensing technologies. These diagrams clarify the different responsibilities of stakeholders. In this example, the team working with the council and technology stakeholders is made up of several individuals with different responsibilities on the project. This includes *platform design, platform integration,* etc. tasks. A decision point is modelled shown by diamonds with Y/N connectors specifying different conditions that can change the order and priority of the tasks performed. In this example, whether the platform is ready based on the results of the *Testing* task.

For a different usage of these process diagrams, Figure 5.6 shows a process diagram for part of the smart home scenario. Here, the clinician identifies a need for a smart home configuration for the elderly person. A 'care plan' is set up for them which defines the monitoring to be undertaken, the devices to be used and key tasks used to realise the monitoring. The smart home provider engineers do appropriate installations, configurations and device log monitoring. The elderly user – possibly with assistance – may set some preferences around the devices used, data captured and give consent. Devices capture appropriate data and store it. Family and friends communicate with the elderly person via appropriate device(s). Some alerts are modelled – the clinician is alerted to health data parameters indicating a possible health issue. Engineers are informed of device malfunction. Friends are alerted when an elderly person misses a requested or scheduled connection. Some of the tasks are ongoing, such as *Monitor Health* and *Monitor Logs* and therefore, only have an 'N' arrow or are actually intermediate start/end events such as *Initiate Talk Request* and *Accept Talk Request*

Multiple process diagrams can be defined and can capture different perspectives on data-intensive system requirements. Some process diagrams may be very high-level, while others focus on more detailed processes and tasks within the system.

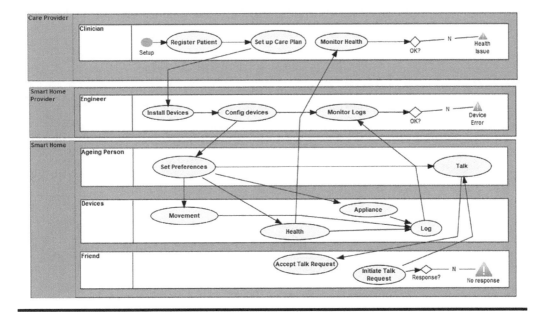

Figure 5.6   Smart home process diagram.

5.5 Design

5.5.1 Data Management

Data is a critical component of all data-intensive systems. Data is sourced, typically from a wide range of other systems, devices, users and existing datasets. New data is synthesised when wrangling, integrating and harmonising diverse data sets. New data is also synthesised when applying data processing algorithms within the system. A BiDaML data diagram extends a task notation from the process or brainstorming diagrams with additional attributes or labels about data. This can include sources of data, algorithms used to manage data and the key producers and consumers of specific data within the data-intensive system.

A sample data diagram for our smart city project is shown in Figure 5.7. The task icon is reused from the brainstorming and process diagrams to show key producers/consumers of data. Data is represented as green dashed icons, models/code as blue icons and reports as 'clipboard' icons. In this data diagram, we focus on the algorithms associated with the smart parking sub-system. Here the task node titled 'Modelling/algorithms development' represents a project task relating to several models that need to be produced to support smart parking facilities. This task generates different models such as *parking occupancy model*, *short-term availability model*, *long-term availability model* and *turnover rate model*. These models are then fed to the *prototype/deploy app* task, which uses them to generate the corresponding data and reports to show on a smart parking app.

A data diagram used to model the movement monitoring aspect of the smart home is shown in Figure 5.8. Here we use the data captured from the movement and appliance sensors installed in the smart home to formulate a 'behaviour model' over time of the elderly person. This behaviour model is then used by the alerting sub-system to determine anomalous situations that may require informing the elderly people themselves, e.g. missed a meal or medication; their friends and family, e.g. less movement than expected, missed meal or delayed activity indicating perhaps anxious or unwell; and carer or emergency services, e.g. had a fall, no movement at all, in darkness but not gone to bed, etc.

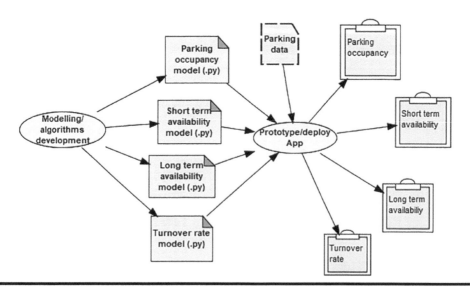

Figure 5.7   Smart city data diagram.

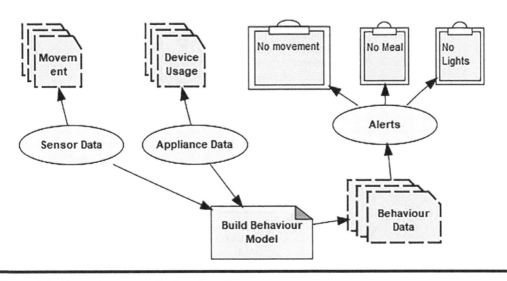

Figure 5.8 Smart home monitoring data diagram.

With brainstorming and process diagrams, we can define data diagrams at varying levels of detail, define multiple data diagrams for different aspects of the system and drill down further into processes in terms of the way the data is obtained, wrangled, processed, stored, etc.

5.5.2 Data Processing

We define a number of technique diagrams to specify the details of how data is processed using BiDaML. Technique diagrams capture the choice of data transformation, wrangling, harmonisation, integration and processing approaches used in a data-intensive system. This includes the choice of feature selection, outlier identification, data preparation for input into a third-party library or package, post-processing extraction of data items and choice of data analysis algorithms. Yellow ovals again represent tasks from brainstorming, process and/or data diagrams. Green hexagons represent technique choices and how these are chained together to implement the data processing required. Occasionally, techniques used produce errors, which are flagged by suitable alerts.

Figure 5.9 shows a technique diagram for the smart city system again focusing on the smart parking aspects. In this diagram, *average parking duration*, *bay occupancy* and *turnover rate* are some example analyses used to realise the *data analysis*. The alert and tick icons attached to the techniques show whether these methods were useful or there were any issues in adopting them. We can create such diagrams for every task and sub-task in the brainstorming and process diagrams as needed. The techniques can be further broken down into sub-techniques used.

Figure 5.10 shows a technique diagram describing how the behaviour model will be built up from sensor and appliance usage information. In this technique implementation, we build up a movement event history model and correlate this with appliance usage and key locale information from within the smart home, e.g. kitchen area, bathroom(s), bedroom(s), living room, etc. We then use a Markov model to predict behavioural event sequences, durations and locations. This model is used to check if observed behaviour, e.g. movement (or lack of), appliance usage (or lack of), etc., does not correspond to the prediction of the model.

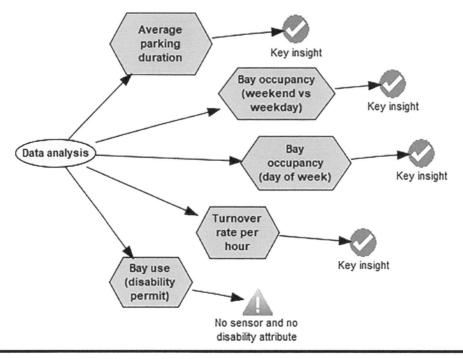

Figure 5.9 **Smart city technique diagram.**

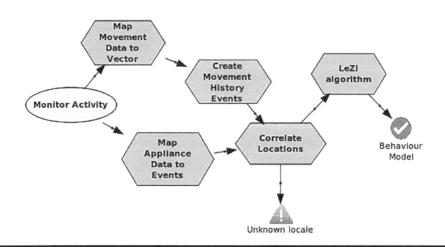

Figure 5.10 **Smart home behaviour model technique diagram.**

5.6 Deployment

We adapt the UML deployment diagram concept to describe how our data-intensive system components will be deployed in the field. We use BiDaML data, report and task icons to illustrate key locations in the deployment scenario. Devices, servers, networks, etc. can be modelled. Multiple deployment diagrams can be used to define complex systems from different perspectives.

Figure 5.11 shows a part of the deployment diagram for the smart city project. Vertical stacking denotes layering of *infrastructure nodes* that describe the technology stack, e.g. a general computing infrastructure is used to run scheduler and workflow monitor that supports the Jupyter notebook server. Horizontal linkages, such as the Restful API/ODBC edge between the service and browser or *mobile*, allow interactions between different technology stacks. Task nodes and attributes from other diagrams are mapped to infrastructure nodes that host them. For instance, the task node 'Train models' and the attribute 'Parking data' have incoming edges from the service node.

Figure 5.12 shows an example deployment diagram for part of the smart home system. A smart home 'edge server' – represented as a blue box – is used to communicate with the variety of sensors and interactors in the home. This also hosts several applications – represented as rounded rectangles, e.g. *Behaviour Modelling*, *Person Reminders*. Data and models are stored on the edge server, e.g. the synthesised behaviour model and raw activity, health and interaction data. A personal care plan for the elderly person is kept, developed by their clinician via their *Care Plan Client* application. A provider server hosts various servers and also holds obfuscated data about activities and health, used for population analysis purposes. Data from electronic medical records is obtained from, e.g. an EPIC system.

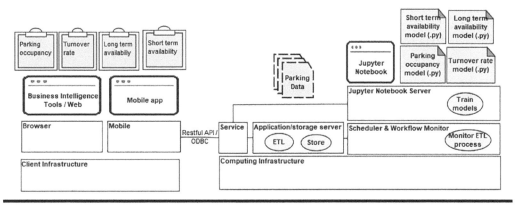

Figure 5.11   Smart city deployment diagram.

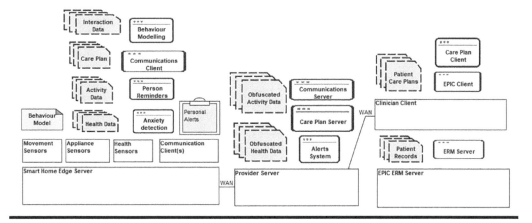

Figure 5.12   Smart home deployment diagram.

5.7 Tool Support

BiDaML is equipped with an integrated design environment for creating its five diagrams. BiDaML tool support aims to provide a platform for efficiently producing BiDaML visual models and to facilitate their creation, display, editing, storage, code generation and integration with other tools. Once all the diagrams are created and connected, users can obtain outputs and share them with other stakeholders. There are currently two sets of outputs generated from the diagrams. First, a hierarchy of the graphs can be exported to Word and HTML from any of the diagrams. However, since all the subgraphs are connected together in the overview diagram, the most comprehensive report can be generated and exported to Word/HTML through the overview diagram. The second set of outputs are Python code/BigML API and reports that are embedded in the tool and can be traced back.

An example of the tool used for creating the brainstorming diagram for the smart city project as well as a template code generated for this example is shown in Figure 5.13. In this figure, users can (a) drag and drop notations, (b) double-click on the notations to rename or modify them and finally (c) generate template Python code. Another example of the tool used for generating a report from the high-level diagram including all the diagrams created and how they are connected for the smart city project is shown in Figure 5.14. A report generated for this example is also shown in the right side. In this figure, users can (a) click on the 'Generate' option, (b) choose 'Export Graph Hierarchy to Word/HTML' to get a comprehensive report of all the diagrams and their explanations in Word/HTML format.

5.8 Discussion

5.8.1 Experience to Date

BiDaML has been applied to some other real-world, large-scale applications as well, such as a property price prediction website for home buyers, a traffic analysis project and in different health-related projects. Our aim was to evaluate and gain experience with applying our knowledge

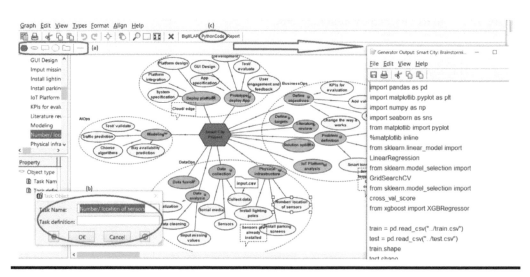

Figure 5.13 BiDaML tool support – Template code generation.

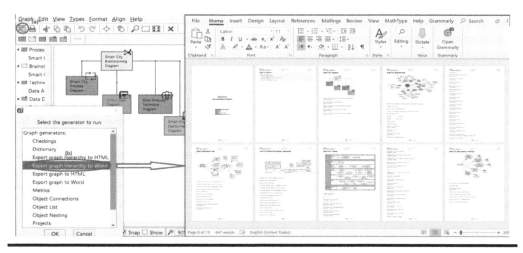

Figure 5.14   BiDaML tool support – Report generation.

management method to conduct requirements analysis and modelling part of complex data analytics applications. We found that BiDaML successfully supports complex data-intensive software systems in industrial settings and it has been practical to a variety of real-world large-scale applications. It helped communication and collaboration between team members from different backgrounds by providing a common platform with mutual language. Moreover, it helped identify and make agreements on details in the early stages and therefore, could potentially help reduce the cost and improve the speed of business understanding and requirement analysis stages. BiDaML provides automatic documentation that can be re-used for retraining and updating of the models. Based on one of our users' experience: 'As the frequency of multidisciplinary, collaborative projects is increasing, there is a clear benefit with the use of (The tool) as a tool for designing data analytics processes. Furthermore, the automatic code generation capabilities of (The tool) would greatly aid those who do not have experience in large-scale data analysis. We do see use of (The tool) in this specific project and would be interested in seeing its results'.

Based on our two smart home and smart city examples, users have the freedom to design BiDaML diagrams in different ways. For example, the smart city process diagram describes the design of the whole solution, whereas the smart home process diagram describes just the participant onboarding/monitoring process (e.g. there is no Software Engineer or Data Scientist involved). Process diagrams were initially designed in a way to cover all the steps and processes within all the organisations and participants; however, our experiences with these use cases showed that process diagram can be used in either manner (i.e. for development of the whole system or just for documenting a process). Moreover, in developing the smart home brainstorming diagram, we had the issue of tasks that are ongoing (Monitor Health, Monitor Logs) so only have an 'N' arrow or are actually intermediate start/end events (Initiate Talk Request, Accept Talk Request). Therefore, in order to reduce the number of symbols needed in BiDaML, informal usage of the intermediate events allows different users to use and specify diagrams based on the preferences (i.e. unlike BPMN, we just have start/end/alert rather than a full notation for formally specifying all the different kinds of intermediate events).

There are some notable challenges we faced while working with industrial partners on these data analytics requirement engineering problems. (a) Our tool can be accessed by all the stakeholders in different geographical locations. However, our intervention has been required so far, as the current tool depends on MetaEdit+ modelling development tool [14] and a licence required to be purchased by users; (b) Users make benefits of the early requirement engineering part; however, they continue using existing tools or programming language to develop the ML and application development parts once they have completed the requirement analysis, modelling and planning part of the project. To overcome the first challenge, we are currently working on re-implementing the tool as a stand-alone web-based tool that users can work on individually without any help from us. To overcome the second challenge, we aim to develop integration to popular existing tools to encourage users to continue using our approach through the entire development of the final product. We see considerable scope for providing back-end integration with data analytics tools such as Azure ML Studio[1], RapidMiner[2], KNIME[3], etc. Our tool can be used at an abstract level during requirements analysis and design and then connect to different tools at a low level. Therefore, BiDaML DSVLs can be used to design, implement and control a data analytics solution [15].

5.8.2 Evaluation

We have evaluated our BiDaML approach and toolset from three perspectives:

- As above, we have applied the approach and toolset to model several real-world industrial projects.
- A symbol-by-symbol evaluation of the cognitive effectiveness of the visual notation against established theoretical principles. This was performed using the Physics of Notations framework [16].
- Two user research studies with data analysts/scientists and software engineers under controlled conditions.

Physics of Notations: The BiDaML notations re-use and adapt concepts and notations from Statistics Design Language [17], BPMN [18], and UML [19]. However, we adapted these existing notations to ensure a consistent set of notations for BiDaML that were suited to the needs of multi-disciplinary teams of end users across multiple abstraction levels of modelling. In particular, to facilitate cognitive integration of the different diagrams, we re-use some of the same notational elements across the different types of BiDaML diagrams when they share a common concept.

Using the Physics of Notations framework [16], we analysed each symbol in BiDaML to ensure it was visually distinct from other symbols (e.g. different shape and colour), semantically transparent (not likely to be misinterpreted) and represented a distinct concept. After our first evaluation [15], we performed a major revision of the notations and some of the concepts used [8]. Major updates included a better definition of concept meta-models, new improved notational elements for clarity and consistency, simplification of some diagram models and notations and a variety of tool improvements.

User Research Studies: Our first evaluation [15] performed a cognitive walkthrough with three data scientists and two software engineers to perform three pre-defined modelling tasks. Our second evaluation [8], performed using the revised version of BiDaML presented in this chapter, asked 12 target end users to model a problem from their own domain. In this second evaluation, we asked users to create both a BiDaML diagram and a diagram using the notation (whether

---

[1] https://studio.azureml.net/.
[2] https://rapidminer.com/.
[3] https://www.knime.com/.

formal, textual or ad-hoc) of their choice. This allowed us to contrast the strengths and limitations of BiDaML against other techniques.

5.8.3 Strengths and Limitations

Key strengths of our BiDaML approach as evidenced by our evaluations – trials on industry problems, controlled experiments and Physics of Notations–based analysis – include: suitability for a wide range of diverse data-intensive system stakeholders and developers; facilitating communications and collaborations between multi-disciplinary team members; usefulness as a high-level brainstorming and data-intensive system requirements capture approach; assisting re-use of data analytics solutions on new projects and problems; and detailed knowledge capture from multiple perspectives of complex data-intensive system domains.

Key limitations include: for some users, concepts and notational representations take some time to understand and use and terminology is different from their domain of expertise; limitations with code recommendation and code generation in the current toolset; limitations with supporting distributed collaborative teamwork in the current toolset; bridging the gap and supporting traceability between abstraction model specifications and detailed code solutions; keeping implementations consistent with BiDaML models; and recommending the most suitable data analytics techniques or similar solution implementations from BiDaML specification models.

5.9 Summary

We have described two contemporary case studies requiring data-intensive systems – a smart home to support ageing people and a smart city solution. Both have many challenges relating to data-intensive system knowledge management. We have described the use of our BiDaML suite of domain-specific visual languages to provide development teams a variety of modelling techniques to address these issues. We have discussed experience to date with BiDaML, its strengths and limitations and identified a range of key future work directions to address these limitations.

Acknowledgment

Grundy and Khalajzadeh are supported by an Australian Laureate Fellowship FL190100035, and parts of this work have been supported by ARC Discovery Project DP170101932 and ARC ITRH IH170100013.

References

1. J. Al-Jaroodi and N. Mohamed, "Service-oriented architecture for big data analytics in smart cities," in *2018 18th IEEE/ACM International Symposium on Cluster, Cloud and Grid Computing (CCGRID)*. IEEE, 2018, pp. 633–640.
2. A. De Iasio, A. Futno, L. Goglia, and E. Zimeo, "A microservices platform for monitoring and analysis of IoT traffic data in smart cities," in *2019 IEEE International Conference on Big Data (Big Data)*. IEEE, 2019, pp. 5223–5232.
3. J. Grundy, K. Mouzakis, R. Vasa, A. Cain, M. Curumsing, M. Abdelrazek, and N. Fernando, "Supporting diverse challenges of ageing with digital enhanced living solutions," in *Global Telehealth Conference 2017*. IOS Press, 2018, pp. 75–90.

4. T. Taleb, S. Dutta, A. Ksentini, M. Iqbal, and H. Flinck, "Mobile edge computing potential in making cities smarter," *IEEE Communications Magazine*, vol. 55, no. 3, pp. 38–43, 2017.

5. Y. Liu, C. Yang, L. Jiang, S. Xie, and Y. Zhang, "Intelligent edge computing for iot-based energy management in smart cities," *IEEE Network*, vol. 33, no. 2, pp. 111–117, 2019.

6. A. Cleve, T. Mens, and J.-L. Hainaut, "Data-intensive system evolution," *Computer*, vol. 43, no. 8, pp. 110–112, 2010.

7. C. A. Mattmann, D. J. Crichton, S. Hughes, S. C. Kelly, and M. Paul, "Software architecture for large-scale, distributed, data-intensive systems," in *Proceedings. Fourth Working IEEE/IFIP Conference on Software Architecture (WICSA 2004)*. IEEE, 2004, pp. 255–264.

8. H. Khalajzadeh, A. Simmons, M. Abdelrazek, J. Grundy, J. Hosking, and Q. He, "An end-to-end model-based approach to support big data analytics development," *Journal of Computer Languages*, vol. 58, p. 100964, 2020.

9. M. K. Curumsing, N. Fernando, M. Abdelrazek, R. Vasa, K. Mouzakis, and J. Grundy, "Understanding the impact of emotions on software: A case study in requirements gathering and evaluation," *Journal of Systems and Software*, vol. 147, pp. 215–229, 2019.

10. A. Fensel, D. K. Tomic, and A. Koller, "Contributing to appliances? Energy efficiency with internet of things, smart data and user engagement," *Future Generation Computer Systems*, vol. 76, pp. 329–338, 2017.

11. L. Mora, R. Bolici, and M. Deakin, "The first two decades of smartcity research: A bibliometric analysis," *Journal of Urban Technology*, vol. 24, no. 1, pp. 3–27, 2017.

12. Z. Rashid, J. Melià-Seguí, R. Pous, and E. Peig, "Using augmented reality and internet of things to improve accessibility of people with motor disabilities in the context of smart cities," *Future Generation Computer Systems*, vol. 76, pp. 248–261, 2017.

13. H. Chourabi, T. Nam, S. Walker, J. R. Gil-Garcia, S. Mellouli, K. Nahon, T. A. Pardo, and H. J. Scholl, "Understanding smart cities: An integrative framework," in *2012 45th Hawaii International Conference on System Sciences*. IEEE, 2012, pp. 2289–2297.

14. J.-P. Tolvanen, R. Pohjonen, and S. Kelly, "Advanced tooling for domain-specific modeling: Metaedit+," in Sprinkle, J., Gray, J., Rossi, M., Tolvanen, J.P. (eds.) *The 7th OOPSLA Workshop on Domain-Specific Modeling, Finland*, 2007.

15. H. Khalajzadeh, M. Abdelrazek, J. Grundy, J. Hosking, and Q. He, "Bidaml: A suite of visual languages for supporting end-user data analytics," in *2019 IEEE International Congress on Big Data (BigDataCongress)*. IEEE, 2019, pp. 93–97.

16. D. Moody, "The "physics" of notations: Toward a scientific basis for constructing visual notations in software engineering," *IEEE Transactions on Software Engineering*, vol. 35, no. 6, pp. 756–779, 2009.

17. C. H. Kim, J. Grundy, and J. Hosking, "A suite of visual languages for model-driven development of statistical surveys and services," *Journal of Visual Languages & Computing*, vol. 26, pp. 99–125, 2015.

18. M. Chinosi, and A. Trombetta, "BPMN: An introduction to the standard," *Computer Standards & Interfaces*, vol. 34, no. 1, pp. 124–134, 2012.

19. M. Fowler, and U. Distilled, "A brief guide to the standard object modeling language," 2003.

Chapter 6

Augmented Analytics for Data Mining: A Formal Framework and Methodology

Charu Chandra, Vijayaraja Thiruvengadam, and Amber MacKenzie

University of Michigan

Contents

6.1 Introduction

Augmented Analytics invokes multidisciplinary research in broad areas of machine learning and natural language processing. Implementation of a framework and methodology based on this paradigm has the promise of enormous improvements in the quality, relevance, and timeliness of complex business decision-making in image, sound, and video data formats. Augmented Analytics is grounded in two broad areas of data science, namely data science methodology and tools, and the innovative application of data science methods in any research area.

Since the emergence of business intelligence in decision-making, efforts to automate decision-making capabilities relating to preparation, analysis, and visualization of data have continued with varying degrees of success. Much of these activities have been independently performed, lacking an architecture for integrated development and implementation. Such decision-making environment, besides remaining largely manual, is also prone to individual biases. As the need to process data volumes is increasing exponentially and sourced cross-functionally, decision-making is increasing in complexity. Further, as the dimensionality of data is increasing owing to the number of variables driving an outcome or best action, it is becoming either impossible or impractical to gain valuable insights in decision-making using existing analytics approaches. This has led to biased, inferior, and untimely decision-making.

In this chapter, it is proposed to harness the features and capabilities of both Machine Learning and Natural Language Processing to offer an integrated framework and methodology that enable executing search-based analytics and conversation-based analytics in unison. This approach to augmented analytics may be utilized for data mining applications in diverse fields, such as education, business, engineering, legal, and medical fields. It also lends to investigating further the role of Deep Learning in Machine Learning Algorithms, especially Neural Networks and Artificial Intelligence in Augmented Analytics.

The rest of the chapter is organized as follows. Next, specific aims of research in augmented analytics are discussed. Following this, the related work in augmented analytics is described, where detailed discussion on various algorithms and methods to implement it is provided. Next, an augmented analytics framework is proposed. Examples of various applications and description of a conversational analytics tool to implement the proposed framework and methodology is offered along with future directions of research on augmented analytics.

6.2 Specific Aims of Research in Augmented Analytics

Queries are an integral part of any decision-making process. Invariably, data is key to answer any business query. For instance, a frozen dessert pie distributor needs to forecast weekly sales of frozen dessert pies in order to make a major and frequently made procurement decision. To query this information, it will require access to databases related to pie sales, pricing for pies, and advertising expenses incurred on promoting pie sales. A similar case could be made for other functions, such as logistics, inventory management, production scheduling, etc. Designing queries for such ad-hoc business decisions would be logical. Data would be the key input for these queries. Since the emergence of business intelligence in decision-making, efforts to automate decision-making capabilities relating to data preparation, data analysis, and data visualization have continued with varying degrees of success. Much of these activities have been independently performed, lacking an architecture for integrated development and implementation. Such decision-making environment, besides remaining largely manual, is also prone to individual biases. As the need to process data volumes is increasing exponentially and sourced cross-functionally, decision-making is increasing in complexity. Further, as the dimensionality of data is increasing owing to the number of variables driving an outcome or best action, it is becoming either impossible or impractical to gain valuable insights in decision-making using existing analytics approaches. This has led to biased, inferior, and untimely decision-making. The combined framework and methodology proposed in this chapter is an attempt to fill this important gap.

Any research effort to define application of augmented analytics framework, methodology, and tools for data mining in enhancing decision-making capabilities in various applications must thoroughly analyze theoretical frameworks and models in search-based analytics and conversation-based analytics, the two pillars of augmented analytics. This must be done with a view to gaining insights on (a) emerging decision-making architectures and (b) recommending a formal methodology for reference and guidance in the implementation of applications in various domains. The discussion of the proposed framework and methodology described in this chapter is to fulfill this aim of bringing into complete harmony the design, modeling, and implementation components of an Augmented Analytics architecture.

Clougherty Jones and White (2019) and Sallam et al. (2017) have very aptly documented the emergence of Augmented Analytics as a significant field in offering a suite of tools available to support complex decision-making. As it finds increasing acceptance and usage among decision-makers, among the key challenges with augmented analytics decision-making modeling are:

- Speech-to-text and vice versa conversion for use in decision modeling.
- Models for specific decision-making needs are developed independently, and their integration with each other is desired to be done on an ad-hoc basis.
- Different data analytics models have different modeling requirements, which must be carefully customized for the integrated decision model.
- Model development is a complex activity and may be performed according to application domains.
- Most applications are context-dependent and require application-specific data structures.

The aim of the proposed research is to address these challenges by offering an integrated framework and methodology for augmented analytics by fusing several modeling techniques, namely query modeling, machine learning and natural language processing, and data analytics. Query modeling models query or queries required to solve the decision-making problem. The combined machine learning and natural language processing model defines the search mechanisms required to answer the query. The data analytics model is employed for very domain-specific purposes, such as for predictive analysis, optimization, etc.

Anticipated contributions from the proposed research framework and methodology are – formulation of an integrated augmented analytics model, techniques for development and configuring of such query model to support the decision-making environment, and data analytics model to support ad-hoc decision-making.

6.3 Related Work in Augmented Analytics

Augmented analytics is an emerging and a powerful paradigm that has the potential to propel decision-making capabilities to *n*th degree of business intelligence and analytics. Augmented analytics amalgamates use of machine learning and natural language processing to enhance business intelligence and data analytics. Augmented analytics has the potential of leveraging capabilities of natural language processing embedded in data analytics tools to process large data sets emanating from multiple sources, including raw data via human conversation, to process and prepare data for analysis utilizing capabilities of machine learning algorithms. The use of machine learning algorithms and natural language processing gives augmented analytics tools the ability to process and analyze data organically and gain deeper insights into the decision-making process, thereby improving timeliness and quality of decisions.

The research described in this chapter evaluates and proposes a framework and methodologies in data acquisition, data integration, data organization and management, data visualization and analysis, delivery of insights, and impact measurement for decision-making. This effort is significant and innovative due to its promise of delivering a unified approach to decision-making by harnessing the capabilities of machine learning algorithms and natural language processing in unique ways.

Conventional methods of retrieving information analyze data utilizing graphical representation, such as tables and charts. With the increased embedding of textual and speech tools in hardware devices, such as iPhone, iPad etc., retrieving information by users has taken on added meaning, whereby other visual and voice features are now being integrated. This is the genesis of a distinct branch of analytics, commonly known as Augmented Analytics, combining human and machine conversation, which integrates features of Machine Learning, Natural Language Processing, and Deep Learning, delivered through implementation as an application, such as a chatbot.

6.3.1 Axiomatic System Design

In order to design applications to implement with augmented analytics philosophy, it is important to understand the methodology of designing a system that caters to the customer's needs. Suh and Do (2000) explore and present the approach required to design systems that involve software components in industries where it is increasingly required to integrate software into reliable and error-free solutions. This design methodology extends further the methodology proposed by Kim et al. (1991) describing core aspects of axiomatic design involving, (a) the Axiom of Independence and the Axiom of Information and (b) concepts of various domains, such as the customer, functional, physical, and process domains and the need to map processes between these domains, and allow for decomposition. Figure 6.1 depicts these four domains and their relationships.

Kulak et al. (2010) review research describing applications where axiomatic design method has been utilized to reinforce the practice of using the Independence Axiom for designing most systems.

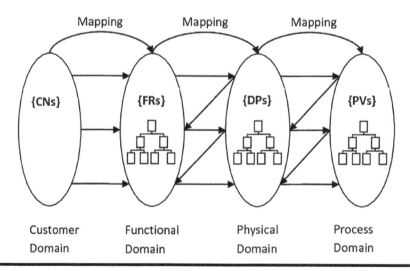

Figure 6.1 System development domains in axiomatic system design.

Brodie (1982) offers valuable insight into how axiomatic design is used in order to define a data model to aid in the proper design and utility of database design, analysis, and implementation.

6.3.2 Data Preparation and Data Modeling

Complex data requirements emanating from presentation of data in various formats for conversational software applications that are at the heart of implementing Augmented Analytics pose significant challenges in their design.

Boselli et al. (2013) analyze the process of data cleaning itself, presenting a model approach based on consistency and formal methods to cleaning data in order to make it suitable for use in analysis. In a similar vein, Prasad et al. (2011) explore techniques for data cleansing in enterprise-scale data sets with changing customer needs and requirements that do not often work with the traditional iterative nature of data improvement. These papers offer valuable insight into how data cleanup should be approached in a dynamic environment.

LaPlante (2019) discusses the growing trends in available structured and unstructured data, limitations of traditional analytics to understand such data; hence the importance and future of augmented analytics using machine learning and natural language processing. Jacob et al. (2008) look at a more direct application of augmented data, in how data obscured in large data sets can be extracted and produced to obtain new insights on data hitherto unseen. Their research helps in understanding the significance of Augmented Analytics and its ability to present data.

Hammer et al. (2013) illustrate challenges posed by huge and complex electronic data for visual analysis. They offer guidance on the use of intelligent data visualization methods covering diverse domains of complex data visualization. Andrienko and Andrienko (2013) propose a method to build time-series models for large and diverse spatial data sets. They offer various models to evaluate time-series data.

The contribution by Vellido et al. (2013) discusses nonlinear dimensionality reduction techniques to limit errors and ways to visualize, using cartograms that are suitable for topographic mapping.

Xu et al. (2013) discuss use and challenges involving dynamic graph layouts for Internet-based systems. They describe a meaningful visualization that correctly links the layout to the previous image according to each node grouping.

A study by Quispel and Maes (2014) demonstrates ways different people view and visualize graphical data based on the graphic design rate and attractiveness along with visual clarity. Results from this survey paper show the difference in design preferences between professionals and common users.

Liu et al. (2018) discuss the rapid growth of digital representation of data and various tools that can be used for data visualization of complex scholarly data sets. Authors describe the method of scholarly data collection and provide an overview of various visualization tools, such as Tableau, ICHARTS, Infogram, and Visualize Free. The paper also discusses major challenges involved with the integration of large volumes of raw data into the visualization tools to generate clean and informative results.

Goodman et al. (2018) evaluate exploratory visualization and discuss ways to promote flexible data visualization techniques capable of facilitating discovery and communication, simultaneously.

With increasing complexity and volume of the flowing data, there is a need to make visual analysis more efficient and effective. Qin et al. (2019) discuss survey techniques to make visualization more effective. They suggest defining visualization specifications according to user requirements and processing the data, which is scalable to create interactive visuals. Ko and Chang (2017) offer a real-life example of use of data visualization tools to analyze complex graphical healthcare data using Tableau. The Business Intelligence tool offered in Tableau Desktop explores visualization of information gathered from colon cancer patients. The paper aptly describes steps to use Tableau and ways to increase levels of analysis utilizing different charts.

6.3.3 Machine Learning for Data Preparation and Data Discovery

Machine learning is a method of data analysis that automates analytical model building. It is a branch of artificial intelligence based on the idea that systems can learn from data, identify patterns, and make decisions with minimal human intervention. It means developing new capabilities and helping the machine learn information and problem-solving skills. An input data is taken to teach the machine, how to answer questions, solve problems, and derive conclusion, without any human interventions. In a chatbot, machine learning is used to learn the data from user inputs. It uses Natural Language Processing for learning human language between systems. This method helps in understanding the intent from the input data and make appropriate response. This method is intended to analyze machine learning algorithms to study data for detecting patterns or applying known (or predefined rules) to (a) categorize or catalog animate or inanimate entities, (b) predict likely outcomes or actions based on identified patterns and relationships, and (c) detect unexpected behaviors.

Some of the advanced machine learning algorithms, such as deep learning algorithms, enable analysis of image, sound, and video data formats. Deep learning is a subset of machine learning. It is a model within artificial intelligence that aims to imitate the human intelligence. It solves or finds patterns from the data and uses those patterns to design new data. It allows the chatbot to learn the description of data and process new data. For a chatbot to respond, it needs to understand the intentions of the input data/message and determine what kind of response message should be sent. Deep learning helps the chatbot to gather information from data, such as gender, emotion. Sometimes, it even helps the chatbot to understand the mood of the sender by analyzing the verbal and sentence structuring.

A few advanced types of Machine Learning algorithms for data preparation and data discovery are described in Grayson et al., (2015), Kotsiantis (2007), Sebastiani (2002), and Shmueli et al. (2017). These are as follows:

- *Supervised and Semi-Supervised Learning*, where the algorithm learns via example by identifying correlations and patterns through desired inputs and outputs. Some of the common techniques in predictive analytics, such as Bayesian statistics, Decision Trees, Forecasting, Neural Networks, Random Forests, Regression Analysis, and Support Vector Machines, fall in this algorithm category.
- *Unsupervised Learning*, where learning is modeled by drawing inferences and grouping "like" entities based on unconstrained observation and intuition. Some of the common techniques in predictive analytics, such as Affinity Analysis, Clustering, K-Means Clustering, Nearest-Neighbor Mapping, Self-Organizing Maps, and Singular Value Decomposition, fall in this algorithm category.
- *Reinforcement Learning* and *Deep Learning*, where the algorithm is provided a set of allowed actions, rules, and potential end states, thereby determining what series of actions and in what circumstances will lead to an optimal result. Some of the common techniques in predictive analytics, such as Artificial Neural Network, Learning Automata, Markov Decision Process, and Q-Learning, fall in this algorithm category.

6.3.4 Natural Language Processing for Data Preparation and Data Discovery

Natural Language Processing enables machine learning algorithms to understand written language, voice commands, or both. This includes evaluating, categorizing, and recommending for each user query a natural language processing tool or tools that besides mapping the spoken words in a command to a dictionary, also helps to infer meaning or intent in order to inform the machine learning algorithm of an appropriate action or response (Gabrilovich and Markovitch, 2009; Manning and Schutze, 1998; Nadkarni et al., 2011; and Nasukawa and Yi, 2003).

Natural language processing is part of data science and artificial intelligence, which involves human language (natural language) and computer interactions. To be specific, it comes down to how computers understand and process huge volumes of natural language data. Without Natural Language Processing, there is nothing to deliver by chatbots. Natural Language Processing is what helps and allows chatbots to recognize the message and answer appropriately. When a user greets the chatbot, it is the natural language processing that helps the chatbot to know that the input given is a greeting, which in sequence lets the chatbot come up with a suitable response. The chatbot responds with a return greeting. Without Natural Language Processing, no chatbot can understand the difference between various syllables. This is because without Natural language processing, the chatbot understands it as a text input. Thus, Natural Language Processing provides context and meaning to text input and hence helps chatbot to come up with the best response.

6.3.5 Business Analytics and Data Analytics

Business Analytics and Data Analytics refer to practices, methods, and techniques developed and catalogued for investigating performance of a business to gain insights from data and improve decision-making. Common analytical methods utilized are drawn from statistical modeling and analysis, optimization, computer science, and visualization fields. Business analytics and data analytics utilize analytical modeling and numerical analysis, including explanatory and predictive modeling in decision-making.

Specifically, areas within data analytics include descriptive analytics, diagnostics analytics, predictive analytics, and prescriptive analytics. Some of the machine learning techniques utilized for each type are as follows:

■ Descriptive analytics – data mining
■ Diagnostic analytics – classification, regression, association analysis of data
■ Predictive analytics – sentimental analysis, forecasting
■ Prescriptive analytics – deep learning, neural networks

Some of the techniques utilized for business analytics are data aggregation, data mining, association and sequence identification, text mining, forecasting, predictive analytics, optimization, and data visualization.

6.4 Proposed Framework and Methodology for Research on Augmented Analytics

The primary objective of this research is to harness features and capabilities of both Machine Learning and Natural Language Processing to offer an integrated decision modeling environment that enables executing search-based analytics and conversational analytics in unison.

To this end, this section describes a framework that has its roots in machine learning and natural language processing fields of research. This framework provides the basis of formalizing a methodology that unifies capabilities of machine language algorithms and natural language processing to offer a new and innovative paradigm of augmented analytics in decision-making (Clougherty Jones and White, 2019 and Sallam et al., 2017). Algorithms and techniques from broad areas of data science, artificial intelligence, and business analytics are employed for problem-solving.

Figure 6.2 depicts the conceptual framework of the proposed Integrated Augmented Analytics Model. The Integrated Augmented Analytics Model is designed as a collection of independent modules, representing models that perform specific tasks to solve the decision-making problem based on the proposed augmented analytics approach. The **Query Model** is configured to a specific application whose domain defines the decision-making problem. The decision-making problem corresponds to the decision-making model, which invokes a combination of (a) a **Generic Model** that serves as a core model integrating the interface of machine learning and natural language processing algorithms, (b) **Data Analytics** model that invokes problem-solving algorithms from data science and business analytics areas of research and is customized to contextualize specific needs of the application domain for which the queries are designed, and (c) **Application Model,** which is specific to and is used for the decision-making problem.

A discussion on various models that make up the Integrated Augmented Analytics Model is offered below.

The decision-making problem is formally defined using **Query Model**, which captures the needs of information encapsulated in the query and being answered utilizing augmented analytics tools, specific to the Integrated Augmented Analytics Model. The Axiomatic System Design principles are utilized to design the query. As depicted in Figure 6.1, the software system design consists of four domains, namely the customer, functional, physical, and the process domain. The customer domain represents "what we want," the design domain represents "How will we satisfy what we want." The customer domain focuses on customer needs to be reflected in a product or system. The functional domain maps the customer needs (CAs) to functional requirements (FRs). These FRs are then mapped into physical domain, and the design parameters (DPs) are mapped to satisfy functional requirements. To attain the system specified with DPs, a process is developed,

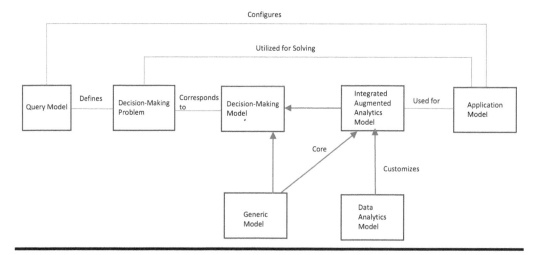

Figure 6.2 Conceptual framework of integrated augmented analytics model.

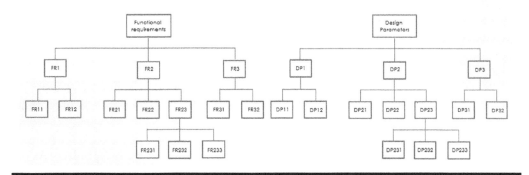

Figure 6.3   Structures of functional requirements and design parameters.

which is characterized by process variables (PVs) in the process domain. The entire software design fits into the above-mentioned domains. Therefore, this is a generalized design solution that can be applied in all design applications with four domains.

The implementation of the Axiomatic Design approach is built upon several sequential steps of system analysis and design that transform a system from its virtual to physical form, corresponding to transforming a concept (or idea) about a decision-making software application to its implementation as a decision-making tool. Figure 6.3 depicts the hierarchy tree structure of FRs and DPs.

The next step in the axiomatic design involves *mapping between domains*. The FRs designed in the FRs domain are mapped on to the physical domain, namely devising a design embodiment and recognizing the DPs. This overall mapping between FRs and DPs is depicted in Figure 6.3 and further detailed in explanations given below.

FR1 = Speech or text recognition

FR2 = Process query

FR3 = Display the output

DP1 = The speech or text can be recognized through Dialogflow

DP2 = The Dialogflow system will analyze the query content

DP3 = Collect right information from database and output the result

FR11 = Speech content can be translated into text

FR12 = Understand the meaning of the text

DP11 = Finish translation through speech recognition system in Dialogflow

DP12 = Analyze sentence structure through Natural Language Processing in Dialogflow

FR21 = Give a prompt, if query cannot be understood

FR22 = Capture the keywords

FR23 = Get exact information from database

DP21 = Training phrases will be built in the intent of Dialogflow

DP22 = Ensure the query completeness through creating entities in Dialogflow

DP23 = Get exact data through JavaScript codes written in fulfillment part in Dialogflow

FR31 = Display the result as text or voice

FR32 = Prompt the user to continue or end the conversation

DP31 = The Dialogflow gives the output

DP32 = The Dialogflow gives the prompt about the next step

The final leaves for the Axiomatic Design depicted in Figure 6.3 are represented by following set of queries:

FR231 = Locate and verify data
FR232 = Execute the query
FR233 = Remember the context for next possible query
DP231 = Find the location of the data from database through fulfillment in Dialogflow
DP232 = Some necessary calculation happens through JavaScript codes written in fulfillment
DP233 = Create a context through intent part in Dialogflow

The hierarchies of FRs and DPs in all design representations must satisfy the Independence Axiom and Information Axiom. In terms of design matrix, they are either uncoupled design or decoupled design. In addition, the entire system designed is decoupled design, as depicted in Figure 6.3.

Uncoupled or decoupled design affords the flexibility and scalability to assemble systems, whether an information system or an automobile system in a modular fashion. In this manner, while each module is designed and implemented independently, however, modules may be assembled by defining common relationships among them in a whole-part relationship.

For an **Application Model** for forecasting frozen dessert pie sales for a distributor, queries for the decision-making problem are designed with mapping respective FRs and DPs to actualize their execution utilizing appropriate machine learning and natural language processing techniques. For instance, for the above example, correspondence between FRs and DPs and queries is as follows:

FR231 = Locate and verify data -> Query 1.1: Locate Sales History database for frozen dessert pies. Identify decision variable as Pie Sales per week and independent variables as Price per pie in dollars by week and Advertising Expenses in thousands of dollars per week
FR232 = Execute the query -> Query 1.2: Retrieve Sales History database for the frozen dessert pies; apply multiple regression model to forecast weekly frozen dessert pie sales; compute sales for a given price and advertising expense value
FR233 = Remember the context for next possible query -> Query 2.1: Ascertain whether Query 1 is fully executed.
  − If option 1 or "yes" is invoked, fetch the next query.
  − If option 2 or "no" is invoked, prepare for further action required for decision-making in Query 1.
DP231 = Find the location of the data from database through fulfillment in Dialogflow -> Query 2.2: If Query 2.1, option 1 is invoked, retrieve appropriate sales history data for the next frozen dessert pie

The **Generic Model** component of Integrated Augmented Analytics Model is utilized to implement core aspects of the decision-making problem, i.e., the set of queries designed by the Query Model. It amalgamates use of machine learning and natural language processing to implement execution of queries defined within the context of a specific application domain by the Query Model.

Figure 6.4 depicts data workflow for execution of conversational queries defined in the Query Model.

Such a representation depicts obtaining the appropriate data to answer the query from data sources, preparing the data in a format that is ready for further data analysis, which may lead to valuable deep insights about the decision-making problem. Next, data is presented to the

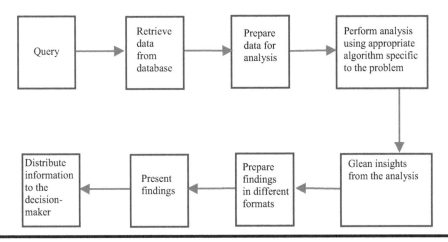

Figure 6.4   A generic data workflow of a conversational query.

decision-maker, utilizing appropriate visualization techniques. Finally, the desired information is distributed to decision-makers to facilitate problem-solving.

Conversational analytics leverages the power of machine learning, natural language processing, and deep learning techniques. Machine learning "trains" the chatbot (application available for executing a conversational query) on various interactions, it will go through and help streamline the responses it offers by way of outputs. Natural language processing enables computers to derive the meaning from user text inputs. Deep learning allows chatbots to conduct contextual dialogue.

As stated earlier, conversation analytics techniques offer technology that transcribes speech and converts it into data. It prepares indexing that makes data searchable. It offers a query and search user interface to define requirements and carry out searches and provide insights on data analyzed to the user.

The workflow of generic processing of a Conversational Query is depicted in Figure 6.5.

The Implementation of the Query Model is realized as follows. User input is recognized by either speech or text. User is prompted to get more clarity about the query input, if some relevant

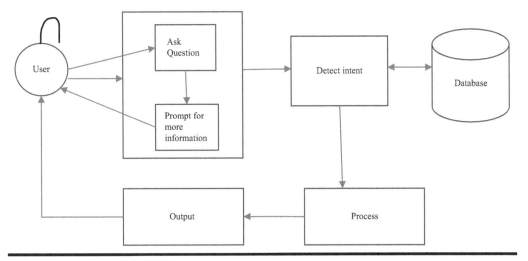

Figure 6.5   Workflow of a conversational query model.

information is missing from the initial user input. The model recognizes the intent that is needed to perform based on the user input. The database is queried through a query request and response is received. Then, values needed for the service are fetched and the output to the query is processed. Output is either displayed or conveyed through speech. Finally, the query stores in its memory the context in the last phase of query and repeats the process, if needed.

The **Data Analytics** model that invokes problem-solving algorithms from data science and business analytics areas of research is customized to contextualize specific problem-solving needs of the application domain for which queries are designed. Depending on the nature of the decision-making problem modeled in the decision-making model and contextualized for the specific application defined in the Application Model, appropriate methods and techniques are applied to solve the decision-making problem. Thus, if the original query identified by the Query Model was to analyze sales forecasts for a specific frozen dessert pie product, given price and advertising data, a multiple-regression algorithm would be chosen from the set of predictive analytics algorithms available in the Data Analytics algorithm repository.

The **Application Model,** which is specific to and is used for the decision-making problem, is a case-specific model and is used to model the decision-making needs of the application under study. Thus, tasks, such as problem formulation, defining objective function, and functional constraints for decision-making problem, would be performed by this model. Thus, for the original sales forecasting query, variables of total sales, price, advertising would be identified in this model. Also, their relationship in terms of dependent and independent variables would be established in this model. The input from Application Model would be the basis to configure the Query Model.

6.5 Applications of Augmented Analytics and Conversational Query Tool

The *physical domain*, as depicted in Figure 6.1, of the query application software design utilizing the Axiomatic Design theory, is developing an application software that enables implementation of conversational analytics by way of either a textual or a voice command input.

The implementation of the Query Model is by way of a Query Tool. One of the prominent tools available for this purpose is chatbot, which is an application that, while facilitating conversations between the human and the software system by way of a query, also synthesizes data from various sources and provides the output for such query. An example of developing a Query Model for forecasting frozen dessert pie sales for a distributor, utilizing the chatbot tool, is offered later in this section.

Chatbot can be developed in two different ways, via voice (which is using voice commands, Google Assistant, Alexa, and Siri) or text (using instant messaging applications, such as Facebook Messenger, Telegram). The chatbot model can be designed with the help of Google Dialogflow. The implementation of chatbot consists of integration of JavaScript within the Google Dialogflow.

Use of chatbot is prevalent in business as it can reduce customer service costs and handling multiple users at a time reliably (Mekni et al., 2020). A task-based chatbot is one that is developed with two aspects – predefined conversational interactions required to accomplish any task and modeling interactions required to complete the task. The challenge faced is connecting the natural language of a customer to the interactions created. The solution could be including keywords while modeling the interactions (Hoon et al., 2020).

Chatbots that are used for educational purposes are growing rapidly but are in their early stages of development. As educational chatbots are just being developed, the analysis can help in creating better chatbot teachers (Smutny and Schreiberova, 2020). The core component in implementing the dialogue system for this application was the Natural Language Understanding.

Word embedding and deep neural network architecture were some of the deep learning techniques that had been enhanced by Natural Language Understanding (Bashir et al., 2018). A deep learning model was applied in radiology to study neural networks and recurrent neural networks. The deep learning axioms from the radiology study were based on data that will be used for research and patient care. The findings were to extract required information from the text (Sorin et al., 2020).

Przegalinska et al. (2019) focus on bringing a Natural Language Processing function in a chatbot that can support deep learning as well as become more interactive. A methodology for tracking down the interactions between a chatbot and human is recorded, and the potential negative effects are identified through this tracking, and the method to overcome them is identified.

Juhn and Liu (2019) used Natural Language Processing in an electronic health record-based clinic research. They demonstrated how Natural Language Processing in Artificial Intelligence helped to extract information and narrate clinical health records. Based on this logic, it helped in learning how to extract and understand the data.

Pantano and Pizzi (2020) used Machine Learning algorithms to obtain the essential knowledge of patent files. This research developed a smart patent summarizing tool with the help of Machine Learning to summarize huge amount of data in an efficient manner. This is done involving natural language text processing inside Machine Learning algorithms.

6.5.1 Conversational Query Tool Architecture

Components and features in the development of conversational queries are as follows:

Google Cloud Platform – Google provides Google Cloud Platform services to build, manage, and deploy applications on a cloud network, which supports companies to meet their business requirements using their preferred tools and frameworks.

Google Dialogflow – Google has an inbuilt tool that supports natural language understanding, which is the Google Dialogflow. It is the tool that performs the role of a dialog manager and detects the keyword and intents from the end user's input. It plays a major role in building the chatbot using machine learning and deep learning algorithms.

Natural Language Understanding – To understand the end user's input, a parser is needed, which helps understand the input. To understand the input from the end user, it should be in the form of string added with a context for better understanding. Responses are constructed with respect to the context of the end user's request. This helps in reducing the complexity of understanding end-user queries.

Chatbot design involves the integration of following components and concepts:

Agent is the virtual agent of the chatbot that manages conversations with end users. The agent understands human language with the help of natural language. Generally, the end user's input (text or audio) is translated into structured data and sent to the application with the help of Dialogflow. It connects the back end with business logic.

Intent – All agents in the chatbot are made up of intents. Intents can be called as end user's actions because they are simply actions that every end user performs on an agent. This means that the intent maps the end user's request to what actions should be taken. They help in restructuring the sentences as end users can request in several ways; hence, these work as the access points to a

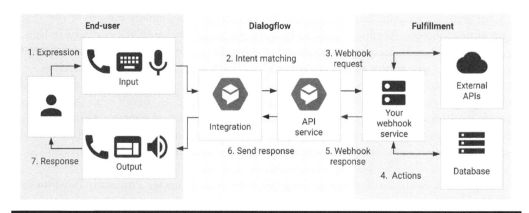

Figure 6.6 Chatbot query function flow diagram. (https://cloud.google.com/diaogflow/docs/fulfillment-overview.)

conversation. It decides what Application Programming Interface to call upon when there is an end-user request.

Entity – Entities help the agent by giving the information from where it should extract values from end user's input. All the information from a sentence is very valuable for a business logic. Thus, logics such as date, currency, distance, time, etc., are important for which Google Dialogflow provides a predefined entity, namely numbers and dates inside the system.

Context makes the chatbot genuinely conversational. The context understands what end users are referring to. To match the end user's expression, the Dialogflow must be provided with proper context in order to map the intent. The conversation flow can be controlled using the context by configuring contexts for intents. Usually, the Dialogflow matches the intents, which are configured with context.

Webhook plays a key role in performing queries. Dialogflow sends a request to webhook service with information about the matched intent. The system can perform any required actions and respond to Dialogflow with information for how to proceed.

Figure 6.6 depicts the flow diagram of chatbot query function.

To illustrate the execution of various steps to actualize the end-user query utilizing chatbot, the following example is utilized:

A distributor of frozen dessert pies wants to evaluate factors thought to influence weekly demand of frozen pies. A multiple regression model is modeled to forecast future weekly frozen dessert pie sales, with following inputs:

■ Dependent variable: pie sales, in units per week,
■ Independent variables: price, in dollars ($), and advertising expenses in thousands of dollars ($100's),

Data from sales history database for frozen dessert pie sales for 15 weeks is as show in Table 6.1.

The multiple regression equation to predict future frozen dessert pie sales is of the form:

$$\text{Predicted Sales} = b_0 + b_1(\text{Price}) + b_2(\text{Advertising}) \qquad (6.1)$$

Table 6.1 Weekly Sales History for Frozen Dessert Pie Sales

Week	Pie Sales	Price ($)	Advertising ($100s)
1	350	5.50	3.3
2	460	7.50	3.3
3	350	8.00	3.0
4	430	8.00	4.5
5	350	6.80	3.0
6	380	7.50	4.0
7	430	4.50	3.0
8	470	6.40	3.7
9	450	7.00	3.5
10	490	5.00	4.0
11	340	7.20	3.5
12	300	7.90	3.2
13	440	5.90	4.0
14	450	5.00	3.5
15	300	7.00	2.7

where,

b_0 is the intercept or constant term,

b_1 is the slope for price, and

b_2 is the slope for advertising expenses.

After the multiple regression model is solved, the regression equation is written as follows

$$\text{Predicted Sales} = 306.256 - 24.975(\text{Price}) + 74.131(\text{Advertising}) \tag{6.2}$$

where,

$b_1 = -24.975$, that is, sales will decrease, on average, by 24.975 pies per week for each $1 increase in selling price, net of the effects of changes due to advertising.

$b_2 = 74.131$, that is, sales will increase, on average, by 74.131 pies per week for each $100 increase in advertising, net of the effects of changes due to price.

Predicting sales for a week in which the selling price is $5.50 and advertising is $350 is as follows:

$$\text{Predicted Sales} = 306.256 - 24.975 * 5.50 + 74.131 * 3.50 = 428.62 \tag{6.3}$$

For this frozen dessert pie sales forecast example, steps in the query function utilizing Dialogflow are executed as follows:

Step 1: The end-user requests for service using either text or speech.

Query: Calculate sales forecast (or predicted sales) where weekly selling price is $5.50 and advertising expenditure is $350.

Action: The user request is created as an intent in the chatbot. Also, all other different ways this end-user query could be asked are used as keywords. For instance, "What is the sales forecast for weekly selling price of $5.50 and advertising dollars 350." The idea is to train chatbot to recognize different ways the end-user query with similar intent could be posed.

Step 2: Dialogflow processes the end-user request matching it for corresponding Intent.

Action: Dialogflow matches the query with existing intents in its repository. Since the specific query matches the intent or a similar phrase, it is processed further.

Step 3: Dialogflow requests webhook service with the matched intent, the action, the parameters, and the response defined for the intent.

Action: Dialogflow creates entities, namely predicted sales, price, advertising, which are set to desired parameter values, $5.50 for price and $350 for advertising for the query.

Step 4: Service performs actions as requested, such as database queries.

Action: Webhook requests are initiated as part of the fulfillment activity, whereby a database query to access weekly frozen dessert pie sales database, identified in Table 6.1, is executed. Also, an application programming interface (API) to initiate an algorithm to run a regression model on entities with their specified parameters values identified in Step 3 is invoked. With data accessed from the database, the API performs the algorithm to calculate the predicted sales in line with the multiple regression model specified in Equation 6.1 above. The final multiple regression Equation 6.2 is then used to compute the predicted sales as shown in Equation 6.3.

Step 5: Service sends webhook response to Dialogflow.

Action: Webhook service initiates a message to Dialogflow with the predicted sales calculated in Step 4.

Step 6: Dialogflow sends the output message, which is then displayed to the end user by either voice or text.

Action: Dialogflow formats the response for the query and sends the predicted sales value of $428.62 to the end user by the mode (text or voice) it was originally received in Step 1.

Augmented analytics is an approach that holds the promise of offering disruptive technology in data and analytics by harnessing the unique capabilities of (a) machine learning algorithms to understand written language, voice commands, or both with the assistance of (b) natural language processing that has the ability to translate language into a form that a machine learning algorithm can understand. It offers the promise of automating insights needed for complex decision-making in our day-to-day transactions in our personal and business needs (LeCun et al., 2015).

Augmented analytics promises to (a) improve the quality of business decision-making by offering deeper insights and unbiased recommendations, (b) drastically reduce the decision-making cycle time by offering a unified umbrella to disparate activities in data processing, (c) offer capabilities of various software tools for descriptive, diagnostic, predictive, prescriptive, and visual analytics under a unified software portal, and (d) spawn innovative data and analytics research and development. Advances in Deep Learning hold a major promise for Augmented Analytics. Neural Networks and Artificial Intelligence offer potential to advance this emerging field in decision-making analytics. As more and more data formats, such as images, sounds, and videos, are incorporated in decision-making processes, Deep Learning will play a pivotal role in achieving success in that effort and more inquiry is needed into the Deep Learning research space.

Acknowledgement

For the first author, this work is supported by the University of Michigan-Dearborn Office of Research and Sponsored Program with Project Grant No. U069087, December 2019.

References

Andrienko, N., & Andrienko, G. (2013). A visual analytics framework for spatio-temporal analysis and modelling. *Data Mining and Knowledge Discovery*, *27*(1), 55–83.

Bashir, A. M., Hassan, A., Rosman, B., Duma, D., & Ahmed, M. (2018). Implementation of a neural natural language understanding component for Arabic dialogue systems. *Procedia Computer Science*, *142*, 222–229.

Boselli, R., Cesarini, M., Mercorio, F., & Mezzanzanica, M. (2013). Improving data cleansing techniques on administrative databases. *European Conference on e-Government*, 85.

Brodie, M. L. (1982). Axiomatic definitions for data model semantics. *Information Systems*, *7*(2), 183–197.

Clougherty Jones, L., & White, A., "Hype Cycle for Enterprise Information Management, 2019," Gartner, 25 July 2019.

Gabrilovich, E., & Markovitch, S. (2009). Wikipedia-based Semantic Interpretation for Natural Language Processing. *Journal of Artificial Intelligence Research*, *34*, 443–498.

Goodman, A. A., Borkin, M. A., & Robitaille, T. P. (2018). New Thinking on, and with, Data Visualization. arXiv e-prints, arXiv:1805.11300.

Google Chatbot Query function flow diagram (https://cloud.google.com/diaogflow/docs/fulfillment-overview).

Grayson, J., Gardner, S., & Stephens, M. L., "*Building Better Models with JMP Pro*," SAS Institute, Cary, NC, 2015.

Hammer, B., Keim, D., Lawrence, N., & Lebanon, G. (2013). Preface: Intelligent interactive data visualization. *Data Mining and Knowledge Discovery*, *27*(1), 1–3.

Hoon, G. K., Yong, L. J., & Yang, G. K. (2020). Interfacing Chatbot with Data Retrieval and Analytics Queries for Decision Making. In *RITA 2018* (pp. 385–394). Springer, Singapore.

Jacob, M., Kuscher, A., Plauth, M., & Thiele, C. (2008). Automated data augmentation services using text mining, data cleansing and web crawling techniques. Paper presented at the 136–143.

Juhn, Y., & Liu, H. (2019). Artificial intelligence approaches using natural language processing to advance EHR-based clinical research. *The Journal of Allergy and Clinical Immunology*, *145*(2), 463–469.

Kim, S.-J., Suh, N. P., & Kim, S.-G. (1991). Design of software system based on axiomatic design. *CIRP Annals - Manufacturing Technology*, *40*(1), 165–170.

Ko, I., & Chang, H. (2017). Interactive visualization of healthcare data using tableau. *Healthcare Informatics Research*, 23(4), 349–354.

Kotsiantis, S. B. (2007) Supervised learning: A review of classification techniques. *Informatica*, 31, 249–268.

Kulak, O., Cebi, S., & Kahraman, C. (2010). Applications of axiomatic design principles: A literature review. *Expert Systems with Applications*, *37*(9), 6705–6717.

LaPlante, A. (2019). *What is Augmented Analytics?* (1st ed.) O'Reilly Media, Inc., Newton, MA.

LeCun, Y., Bengio, Y., & Hinton, G. (2015). Deep Learning. *Nature*, *521*, 436–444.

Liu, J., Tang, T., Wang, W., Xu, B., Kong, X., & Xia, F. (2018). A survey of scholarly data visualization. *IEEE Access*, *6*, 19205–19221.

Manning, C. D., & Schutze, H., "*Foundations of Statistical Natural Language Processing,*" MIT Press, Cambridge, MA, 1998, p. 680.

Mekni, M., Baani, Z., & Sulieman, D. (2020). A smart virtual assistant for students. In *Proceedings of the 3rd International Conference on Applications of Intelligent Systems* (pp. 1–6).

Nadkarni, P.M., Ohno-Machado, L., & Chapman, W. W. (2011). Natural language processing: An introduction. *Journal of the American Medical Informatics Association, 18* (5), 544–551.

Nasukawa, T., & Yi, J., "Sentiment analysis: Capturing favorability using natural language processing," *Proceedings of the 2nd International Conference on Knowledge Capture (K-CAP03)*, pp. 70–77, 2003, Sanibel Island, Florida, USA.

Pantano, E., & Pizzi, G. (2020). Forecasting artificial intelligence on online customer assistance: Evidence from chatbot patents analysis. *Journal of Retailing and Consumer Services, 55*, 102096.

Prasad, K. H., Faruquie, T. A., Joshi, S., Chaturvedi, S., Subramaniam, L. V., & Mohania, M. (2011). Data cleansing techniques for large enterprise datasets. Paper presented at the 135–144.

Przegalinska, A., Ciechanowski, L., Stroz, A., Gloor, P., & Mazurek, G. (2019). In bot we trust: A new methodology of chatbot performance measures. *Business Horizons, 62*(6), 785–797.

Qin, X., Luo, Y., Tang, N., & Li, G. (2019). Making data visualization more efficient and effective: A survey. *The VLDB Journal, 29*, 117–93.

Quispel, A., & Maes, A. (2014). Would you prefer pie or cupcakes? preferences for data visualization designs of professionals and laypeople in graphic design. *Journal of Visual Languages and Computing, 25*(2), 107–116.

Sallam, R., Howson, C., & Idoine, C., "Augmented Analytics Is the Future of Data and Analytics," Gartner, 27 July 2017.

Sebastiani, F. (2002). Machine Learning in Automated Text Categorization. *ACM Computing Surveys, 34* (1), 1–47.

Shmueli, G., Bruce, P. C., Stephens, M. L., & Patel, N. R., "*Data Mining for Business Analytics: Concepts, Techniques, and Applications with JMP Pro,*" Wiley, Hoboken, NJ, 2017.

Smutny, P., & Schreiberova, P. (2020). Chatbots for learning: A review of educational chatbots for the Facebook Messenger. *Computers & Education, 151*, 103862.

Sorin, V., Barash, Y., Konen, E., & Klang, E. (2020). Deep learning for natural language processing in radiology—fundamentals and a systematic review. *Journal of the American College of Radiology, 17*, 639–648.

Suh, N. P., & Do, S. (2000). Axiomatic design of software systems. *CIRP Annals - Manufacturing Technology, 49*(1), 95–100.

Vellido, A., García, D. L., & Nebot, À. (2013). Cartogram visualization for nonlinear manifold learning models. *Data Mining and Knowledge Discovery, 27*(1), 22–54.

Xu, K. S., Kliger, M., & Hero III, A. O. (2013). A regularized graph layout framework for dynamic network visualization. *Data Mining and Knowledge Discovery, 27*(1), 84–116.

Chapter 7

Mining and Managing Big Data Refactoring for Design Improvement: Are We There Yet?

Eman Abdullah AlOmar and Mohamed Wiem Mkaouer
Rochester Institute of Technology

Ali Ouni
University of Quebec

Contents

7.1 Introduction

Successful software systems undergo evolution through continuous code changes, as means to update features, fix bugs, and produce a more reliable and efficient product. Prior studies have pointed out how software complexity can be a serious obstacle preventing the ease of software evolution, as large and sophisticated modules are, in general, harder to understand and error-prone. Such patterns, located in the system design, negatively impact the overall quality of software as they are responsible for making its design inadequate for evolution.

In this context, it has been shown that software engineers spend up to 60% of their programming time in reading source code and trying to understand its functionality, in order to properly perform the needed changes without "breaking" the code. Consequently, software maintenance activities that are related to improving the overall software quality take up to 67% of the cost allocated for the project. The *de-facto* way of handling such debt is through software refactoring. By definition, refactoring is the art of improving design structure while preserving the overall external behavior. With the rise of technical debt, and developers' acknowledgment of shortage in their deliverables, refactoring stands as a critical task to maintain the existence of software and to prevent it from decay.

Projects that are known to be successful in maintaining their quality through several waves of updates and migrations across various programming paradigms and frameworks are known to be witnessing efficient refactoring strategies. Such hidden knowledge has triggered the intention of research to mine and understand how developers refactor their code in practice. In this context, several refactoring detection tools have been lately proposed to mine the development history of a given software project and extract all the information related to all refactoring operations that were performed on its code elements.

As recent refactoring tools (e.g., RefactoringMiner [24] and RefDiff [21]) have reached a high level of maturity, their usage across various large projects has triggered an explosion in the information that can be obtained regarding previously performed refactorings and their corresponding impact on the source code. Furthermore, refactoring, being by nature a code change, when batched, becomes harder to analyze. Moreover, code changes visualization is gaining more attention in software engineering research, yet visualizing refactoring is still underresearched.

For the abovementioned challenges that the plethora of refactorings have emerged, this chapter initiates the discussion about how the world of big data can provide a rich source of solutions. We detail the multiple challenges linked to refactoring indexing, analysis, and visualization, while exploring potential big data solutions. As depicted in Figure 7.1, we identify five refactoring challenges, triggering the explosion of refactoring data, which we can call *Big Data Refactoring Challenges*. These challenges are (a) detection of refactoring operations in software systems, (b) developer's documentation of refactoring activities, (c) recommendation of refactoring opportunities on existing software systems, (d) automation of refactoring execution, and (e) visualization of refactoring impact on the source code. We organize this chapter to explore each of these challenges, by detailing its existing tools and methodologies, along with discussing their limitations and how they are explicitly or implicitly linked to big data dimensions.

This chapter is organized as follows: the first section is associated with tools and techniques related to the identification of executed refactorings, the next section is dedicated to documentation. Section 7.4 summarizes the existing tools to automate the generation of refactorings. Recommendation of refactorings is also covered in Section 7.5. The need for refactoring visualization is covered in Section 7.6 before concluding in Section 7.7.

Figure 7.1 **Big data refactoring.**

7.2 Mining and Detection

The popularity of the GitHub hosting service is increasing rapidly and has been used frequently as the base of data collection in literature. Research in mining software repositories mainly relies on two GitHub services: the version and bug tracking systems. GitHub stores all versions of the source code, and any specific changes are represented by a commit that involves a textual description of the change (i.e., commit message). The bug tracking system, on the other hand, provides an interface for reporting errors. GitHub makes it possible to mine a large amount of information and different properties of open-source projects.

The challenge in this area lies in analyzing a comprehensive and large number of GitHub commits containing refactoring. Several studies have mining tools to identify refactoring operations between two versions of a software system. Dig et al. [9] developed a tool called Refactoring Crawler, which uses syntax and graph analysis to detect refactorings. Prete et al. [20] proposed Ref-Finder, which identifies complex refactorings using a template-based approach. Hayashi et al. [12] considered the detection of refactorings as a search problem. The authors proposed a graph search algorithm to model changes between software versions. Xing and Stroulia [27] proposed JDevAn, which is a UMLDiff-based, design-level analyzer for detecting refactorings in the history of Object-Oriented systems. Tsantalis et al. presented RefactoringMiner, which is a lightweight, UMLDiff-based algorithm that mines refactorings within Git commits. Silva and Valente [21] extended RefactoringMiner by combining the heuristics-based static analysis with code similarity (TF-IDF weighting scheme) to identify 13 refactoring types. Tsantalis et al. [24] extended their tool to enhance the accuracy of the 28 refactoring types that can be detected through structural constraints. A recent survey by Tan [22] compares several refactoring detection tools and shows

Table 7.1 Studied Data Set Statistics

Item	Count
Studies projects	3,795
Commits with refactorings	322,479
Refactoring operations	1,208,970
Commits with refactorings and keywords	2,312
Remove false-positive commits	1,067
Final data set	1,245

that RefactoringMiner is currently the most accurate refactoring detection tool. The choice of the mining tool is driven by accuracy; therefore, RefactoringMiner is suitable for mining and detecting refactorings and extracting big data refactoring. It is suitable for studies that require a large variety of repositories and commit volumes.

With the existence of millions of software projects, whose sizes vary from small to large, mining their refactorings could lead to an amount of data that cannot be handled by traditional means. This links mining refactoring to Big 'Data's Volume. For instance, in our recent study [2], we mined refactoring in 3,795 open-source projects. The process extracted over 1,200,000 refactoring operations, distributed in 322,479 commits. More details about this data set are in Table 7.1. We faced challenges in hosting and querying this data. To extend our study, we need to extract refactorings in over 300 000 open-source projects, and we are currently unable to perform this study, unless we seek the right framework to collect, store, and index such data.

Another interesting challenge related to such data is its heterogeneity. Refactoring operations are different from each other in their structure, target code elements, and impact on source code. For instance, the rename identifier refactoring is the act of changing the name of a given attribute. Such operation requires saving the old name of the attribute, its new name, and the path of the file containing the attribute. As for extract method, which is the splitting of a given method into two submethods, this operation requires saving the old method signature and body (and path) along with saving the signature and bodies of the newly created methods (and paths). So, each refactoring type requires a unique structure to store its information. Furthermore, various studies are interested in the reachability of the refactoring operation, to better analyze their impact on the code design. Storing refactored code elements and their corresponding dependencies may require specific data structures such as graphs. For large and complex systems, analyzing such information is challenging.

7.3 Refactoring Documentation

A number of studies have focused recently on the identification and detection of refactoring activities during the software life cycle. One of the common approaches to identify refactoring activities is to analyze the commit messages in version-controlled repositories. Prior work [2] has explored how developers document their refactoring activities in commit messages; this activity is called Self-Admitted Refactoring or Self-Affirmed Refactoring (SAR). In particular, SAR refers to the situation that shows developers' explicit documentation of refactoring operations intentionally introduced during a code change. For example, by manual inspection of the Cassandra-unit1 open-source project, AlOmar et al. [2] used this example to demonstrate SAR: "refactoring of Abstract*DataSet to delete duplicate code," which indicates that developers intentionally refactor one class to remove the redundancy antipattern that violates design principles. The authors manually analyzed commit messages by reading through 58,131 commits. Then they extracted, from these commit messages, a set of repetitive keywords and phrases that are specific to refactoring. They provided a set of 87 patterns, identified across 3,795 open-source projects. Since this approach heavily depends on the manual inspection of commit messages, in follow-up work, AlOmar et al. [3] presented a two-step approach that firstly distinguishes whether a commit message potentially contains an explicit description of a refactoring effort; then, secondly classifies it into one of the three common categories identified in a previous study [2], which is the first attempt to automate the detection and classification of self-affirmed refactorings. The existence of such patterns unlocks more studies that question the 'developers' perception of quality attributes (e.g., coupling, complexity); these results may be used to recommend future refactoring activity. For instance, AlOmar et al. [4] identified the quality models that are more in line with the 'developer's vision of quality optimization when they explicitly mention in the commit messages that they refactor to improve these quality attributes. This study shows that, although there is a variety of structural metrics that can represent internal quality attributes, not all of them can measure what developers consider to be an improvement in their source code. Based on their empirical investigation, for metrics associated with quality attributes, there are different degrees of improvement and degradation of software quality for different SAR patterns.

As stated above, developers use a variety of patterns to express their refactoring activities. Previous studies illustrate such a pattern. However, one big challenge is that it is not practical for large real-world projects to manually collect all potential keywords/phrases reported in a large number of commit messages, as developers may use various expressions to annotate how they refactor. To cope with this challenge, future research could plan to use the findings of previous studies to build a text-mining tool that will automatically support software engineers in the task of identifying, detecting, and highlighting self-affirmed refactoring in the commit messages. This detector could allow users to train their own model and integrate self-affirmed refactoring detectors into their development tools.

If we want to extend the study of AlOmar et al. [4] and analyze refactoring documentation across the data set previously described in Table 7.1, we are challenged by the volume of text that needs to be analyzed. Furthermore, this text originated from many developers, from different projects, and so, it contains various semantics, which increases the ambiguity of deciphering it. From a variability perspective, there is a need to find better formatting and indexing for this text in order to adequately extract the needed information. For instance, the rise of word2Vec [11], when combined with the appropriate vector indexing, may provide a potential solution to avoid naive string matching, which is known to generate false positives. Other topic modeling techniques can be also explored to extract textual patterns that are relevant to refactoring documentation; however, their manual validation is challenging due to the large number of potential patterns that can be generated. For instance, Table 7.2 showcases the existence of various refactoring candidate textual patterns, extracted from our data set in Table 7.1, which require manual validation.

Table 7.2 Potential Candidate Refactoring Text Patterns

BugFix	Code Smell	External QA	Functional	Internal QA
Minor Fixes	Avoid code duplication	Reusable structure	Add* feature	Decoupling
Bug* fix*	Avoid duplicate code	Improv* code reuse	Add new feature	Enhance loose coupling
Fix* bug*	Avoid redundant method	Add* flexibility	Added a bunch of features	Reduced coupling
Bug hunting	Code duplication removed	Increased flexibility	New module	Reduce coupling and scope of responsibility
Correction of bug	Delet* duplicate code	More flexibility	Fix some GUI	Prevent the tight coupling
Improv* error handling	Remove unnecessary else blocks	Provide flexibility	Added interesting feature	Reduced the code size
Fix further thread safety issues	Eliminate duplicate code	A bit more readable	Added more features	Complexity has been reduced
Fixed major bug	Fix for duplicate method	Better readability	Adding features to support	Reduce complexity
Fix numerous hug bug	Filter duplicate	Better readability and testability	Adding new feature	Reduced greatly the complexity
Fix several bug	Joining duplicate code	Code readability optimization	Addition of a new feature	Removed unneeded complexity
Fixed a minor bug	Reduce a ton of code duplication	Easier readability	Feature added	Removes much of the complexity
Fixed a tricky hug	Reduce code duplication	Improve readability	Implement one of the batch features	Add inheritance
Fix* small bug	Reduced code repetition	Increase readability	Implementation of feature	Added support to the inheritance
Fixed nasty bug	Refactored duplicate code	Make it better readable	Implemented the experimental feature	Avoid using inheritance and using composition instead
Fix some bug*	Clear up a small design flaw	Make it more readable	Introduced possibility to erase feature	Better support for specification inheritance
Fixed some minor bugs	TemporalField has been refactored	Readability enhancement	New feature	Change* inheritance
Bugfix*		Readability and support-ability improvement	Remove the default feature	Extend the generated classes using inheritance
Fix* typo*		Readability improvements	Removed incomplete Features	Improved support for inheritance
Fix* broken		Reformatted for readability	Renamed many features	Perform deep inheritance
Fix* incorrect		Simplify readability	Renamed some of the features for consistency	Remove inheritance
Fix* issue*		Improve* testability	Small feature addition	
Fix* several issue*		Update the performance	Support of optional feature	
Fix* concurrency issue* with		Add* performance	Supporting for derived features	
Fixes several issues		Scalability improvement		
Solved some minor bugs		Better performance		
		Huge performance improvement		

(Continued)

Table 7.2 (Continued)   Potential Candidate Refactoring Text Patterns

BugFix	Code Smell	External QA	Functional	Internal QA
Working on a bug	Remove commented out code	Improv* performance	Added functionality	Inheritance management
Get rid of	Removed a lot of code duplication	More manageable	Added functionality for merge	Loosened the module dependency
A bit of a simple solution to the issue	Remise* code duplication	More efficient*	Adding new functionality	Prevents circular inheritance
A fix to the issue	Remove some code duplication	Make it reusable for other	Adds two new pieces of functionality to	Avoid using inheritance
Fix a couple of issue	Removed the big code duplication	Increase efficiency	Consolidate common functionality	Add composition
Issue management	Removed some dead and duplicate code	Verify correctness	Development of this functionality	Composition better than inheritance
Fix* minor issue	Remove* duplicate rode	Massive performance improvement	Export functionality	Us* composition
Correct issue	Resolved duplicate code	Increase performance	Extend functionality of	Separates concerns
Additional fixes	Sort out horrendous code duplication	Largely resolved performance issues	Extract common functionality	Better handling of polymorphism
Resolv* problem	Remove duplicated field	Lots of performance improvement	Functionality added	Makes polymorphism easier
Correct* test failure*	Remov* dead rode	Measuring the performance	House common functionality	Beater encapsulation
Fix* all failed test	Remove some dead-code	Improv* stability	Improved functionality	Better encapsulation and less dependencies
Fix* compile failure	Removed all dead code	Usability improvements	Move functionality	Pushed dream dependencies
A fix for the errors	Removed apparently dead code	Noticeable performance improvement	Moved shared functionality	Remov* dependency
Better error handling	This is a bit of dead code	Optimizing the speed	Feature/code improvements	Split out each module into
Better error message handling		Performance boost	Pulling-up common functionality	
Cleanup error message		Performance enhancement	Push more functionality	
Error fix*		Performance improvement	Re-implemented missing functions	
Fixed wrong		Performance much improved	Refactored functionality	
Fix* error*		Performance optimization		
Fix* some error*		Performance speed-up		
Fix small error		Refactor performance test		
Fix some errors		Renamed performance test		
Fix compile error				
Fix test error				
Fixed more compilation errors				

(Continued)

Table 7.2 (Continued)   Potential Candidate Refactoring Text Patterns

BugFix	Code Smell	External QA	Functional	Internal QA
Fixed some compile errors	Removed more dead code	Speed up performance	Refactoring existing functionality	
Fixes all build errors	Fix* code smell	Backward compatible with	Add functionality to	
Fixed Failing tests	Fix* some code smell	Fix backward compatibility	Remov* function*	
Handle	Remove* some 'code smells'	Fixing migration compatibility	Merging its functionality with	
Handling error*	Update data classes	Fully compatible with	Remove* unnecessary function*	
Error* fix	Remove useless class	Keep backwards compatible	Reworked functionality	
Tweaking error handling	Removed obviously unused/- faulty code	Maintain compatibility	Removing obsolete functionality Replicating existing functionality with	
Various fix	Lots of modifications to code style	Make it compatible with	Split out the GUI function	
Fix* problem*	Antipattern bad for performances	More compatible	Add cosmetic changes	
Got rid of deprecated code	Killed really old comments	Should be backward-compatible	Add* support	
Delet* deprecated code	Less long methods	Retains backward compatibility	Implement* new architecture	
Remov* deprecated code	Removed some unnecessary fields	Stay compatible with	Update	
		Added some robustness	Additional changes for UI layout has changed	
		Improve robustness	GUI: Small changes	
		Improve usability	New UI layout	
			UI changes	
			UI enhancements	

7.4 Refactoring Automation

Maintaining large-scale code and ensuring large-scale semantically safe refactoring can be a challenging task. Many contemporary integrated development environments (IDEs) provide a limited set of automatic refactoring operations applied to a single file or package. Handling large refactoring poses a big challenge in many object-oriented development projects. Further, performing a high volume of refactoring typically takes longer and changes multiple parts of the system. If refactoring influences large chunks of the system, as a result, there is a need to break changes down into smaller parts. A few questions could be investigated when performing volume and variety of refactoring:

- How can large refactoring operations be planned?
- How can undo-functionality be implemented for large refactorings during the actual refactoring?
- How can we add more functionality during the execution of large refactorings while ensuring behavior preservation for the existing application?
- How can we integrate the plans of implementing large refactorings into the development process?
- How can we document the status of a large refactoring?

7.4.1 Refactoring Tools

Various aspects of refactoring need to be considered when automating the application of refactoring. These include, but are not limited to, automation, reliability, coverage, and scalability of refactoring tools. With regard to automation, fully automated and semiautomated refactoring tools are beneficial for developers. For example, adding support for an "undo" feature can facilitate the process of returning the software to its original state in case the effect of refactoring is not desirable. Reliability indicates whether the software guarantees behavior preservation of the refactoring transformation. A full guarantee of behavioral preservation is challenging; thus, an automated refactoring tool should define a set of pre- and post-conditions to ensure program correctness after the application of refactoring. Concerning coverage, refactoring tools should cover a wide range of refactoring activities that developers could perform, i.e., the tool should be as complete as possible. It would be worthwhile to have refactoring tools that support a complete set of refactoring operations of different levels of granularity (e.g., class, method, package) to improve the system design from different perspectives (e.g., code smell removal, adherence to object-oriented design practices such as SOLID and GRASP, etc.). Scalability is another aspect that should be taken into consideration when constructing refactoring tools.

7.4.2 Lack of Use

Despite the positive aspects of semiautomated refactoring, many developers continue to prefer to do refactoring manually, even when the opportunity to use a refactoring tool presents itself. In the realm of Extract Method refactoring, Kim et al. [13] found that 58.3% of developers chose to perform their refactorings manually. Another study by Negara et al. [18] shows that even though the majority of developers are aware of refactoring tools and their benefits, they still chose to refactor manually. Murphy-Hill et al. [16] found that only two out of 16 students in an object-oriented programming class had previously used refactoring tools. Another survey by Murphy-Hill [15] found that 63% of surveyed individuals at an Agile methodology conference used environments with refactoring tools and that they use the tools 68% of the time when one is available. This is significant, since Agile methodologies are generally predisposed to be in favor of refactoring, indicating that the general usage must be even lower. Murphy-Hill tempers this statement by noting the likelihood of bias in the 'participants' responses, as well as the survey size of 112 being nonrepresentative as it is comparatively small compared with all programmers.

Murphy-Hill also compared studies by Murphy-Hill et al. and Mäntylä et al. They show that students claim that they are more likely to perform Extract Method refactoring immediately compared with Rename refactoring, yet developers are eight times as likely to use a Rename refactoring tool than an Extract Method refactoring tool [14]. Research by Vakilian et al. and Kim et al. also indicates that the majority of developers would prefer to apply refactorings other than Rename refactoring manually [13,25]. There is no clear conclusion for this discrepancy, but it indicates either an underuse of Extract Method refactoring tools or overuse of Rename refactoring tools. Ultimately, it seems unrealistic to come to a concrete conclusion regarding the use of refactoring tools by all developers, but these findings show strong indirect evidence that refactoring tools are underutilized compared with their potential.

From a big data perspective, these studies suffer from a lack of analysis of value. There should be an alignment of how tools refactor code with what developers are expecting their code to be refactored. So far, existing tools focus on removing code smells and improving the structural design measurements; however, and as seen in Table 7.2, developers do refactor their code for various reasons that go beyond these two objectives.

7.4.3 Lack of Trust

There have been a number of studies and surveys done collecting information on 'developers' aversion to refactoring tools. Surveys by Campbell et al. [8], Pinto et al. [19], and Murphy-Hill [15] include the same barrier to entry in their findings: lack of trust. In general, this refers to when a developer is unwilling to give control over the modification of the code base to the refactoring tool due to perceived potential problems. This can manifest for a number of reasons. The developer may be unfamiliar with the tool and unwilling to risk experimenting with a tool that could modify the program in unexpected ways. The developer may be unfamiliar with the terms the tool uses, or the information it displays, or the tool may be difficult to learn or use. They may not understand exactly what the tool intends to change about their program. They may not know how the tool will affect the style or readability of the code, or they may be familiar with this and knowingly dislike what it will do to their code. Pinto et al. [19] found that some developers will avoid suggested refactorings if they would need to trade readability for atomicity. In any of these scenarios, a more trustworthy option for the developer would be to rely on their own intuition, abilities, and experience.

Developers also reported concerns that refactoring tools would implement poor design choices, due to bugs in the tool, inconsistencies with the detection algorithms, or special cases with the code base, such as reflection. Several popular refactoring tools have been shown to contain such bugs that modify program behavior without the developer ever knowing [1,26]. Veracity, or the extent to which refactorings can be trusted, is an emerging problem from a big data perspective.

7.4.4 Behavior Preservation

Today, a wide variety of refactoring tools automates several aspects of refactoring. However, ensuring the behavior preserving property when building tool-assisted refactoring is challenging.

Several formalisms and techniques have been proposed in the existing literature to guarantee the behavior preservation and correctness of refactorings. Actual source code transformation and a set of preconditions are the two main parts for any refactoring operation to be performed by automated refactorings.

7.5 Refactoring Recommendation

Performing refactoring in a large software system can be very challenging. While refactoring is being applied by various developers [5], it would be interesting to evaluate their refactoring practices. We would like to capture and better understand the code refactoring best practices and learn from these developers so that we can recommend them to other developers. There is a need to build a refactoring recommendation system to (a) identify refactoring opportunities and pinpoint design flaws and (b) apply refactoring solutions. To support future refactorings, structural, semantic, dynamic, and historical information between code components needs to be considered. Recently proposed recommenders do generate a large list of refactorings to apply. This represents a challenge for practitioners since they do not want to lose the identity of their design, also they cannot fully understand the impact of such a large set of code changes. Such a problem is mapped to big data volume and veracity. Furthermore, running such a set of refactorings requires handling several constraints. It is to satisfy the correctness of the applied refactorings. Previous studies distinguish between two kinds of constraints: structural constraints and semantic constraints. Structural constraints were extensively investigated in the literature. Fowler, for example, defined in [10] a set of pre- and post-conditions for a large list of refactoring operations to ensure structural consistency. However, software engineers should check manually all actors related to the refactoring operation to inspect the semantic relationship between them. In the next subsections, we further detail the challenges of establishing the relationship between refactoring and its corresponding target code element(s).

7.5.1 Structural Relationship

Structural relationships mean selecting quality metrics to measure system improvement before and after the application of refactoring that includes method calls, shared instance variables, or inheritance relationships. Several quality metrics have been reported in the literature to capture different aspects of internal quality attributes. For example, the coupling between object (CBO) metric correlates with coupling, i.e., the higher the CBO value, the higher the coupling between classes.

7.5.2 Semantic Relationship

To determine the semantic relationship between code components, textual similarity is measured. If the terms of two code components (i.e., class or method) are very similar, then it is probable that developers used the same terms to express the responsibilities implemented by the class or the method. For example, two methods are considered conceptually related if both of these methods perform conceptually similar actions. This information is useful for grouping similar code components together. There are a few quality metrics to capture semantic similarity (e.g., the conceptual cohesion of classes (C3) and the conceptual coupling between classes (CCBC)). For example, in order to recommend Move Class refactoring, software module classes having high CCBC values can be grouped together. Consequently, the changes can be localized easily by developers, and the software will be more manageable and maintainable.

7.5.3 Historical Information

The refactoring process can be automated, not only by using the state-of-the-art features (improving design metrics and quality attributes) but also with contextual features that simulate 'developers' presence by using refactoring operations previously performed by developers. These refactoring operations could be obtained by using refactoring-mining tools such as RefactoringMiner and RefDiff that identify refactoring applied between two subsequent versions of a software system.

7.6 Refactoring Visualization

Visualizing refactoring activity applied to the source code helps provide a big picture about refactoring. It helps gain insight into the source code and improves the understandability of the software. However, visualizing large refactoring activity presents both technical and cognitive challenges. Particularly, if the code change is complex and large, the task of detecting refactoring anomalies and looking for defects becomes more challenging. Developers could perform batch refactoring or sequence of refactoring operations. Murphy-Hill et al. [17] define batch refactorings as refactoring operations that are executed within 60 seconds of each other. Their findings show that developers repeat the application of refactoring, and 40% of refactorings performed using a refactoring tool occur in batches. Recently, Brito et al. [7] introduced a refactoring graph concept to assess refactoring over time. The authors analyzed ten Java projects, extracted 1,150 refactoring subgraphs, and evaluated their properties: size, commits, age, composition, and developers. To increase the trust between developers and the tool, Bogart et al. [6] recently extended JDeodorant tool by providing developers with the possibility of verifying their refactoring outcomes. The extended tools offer timely visualization of multiple selected refactorings and detect whether there is a conflict or not.

Visualizing big data refactoring is not deeply studied or discussed in the refactoring literature. Refactoring visualization is a vital process since it allows developers to look at the code and learn how it is organized and how it works. Further, it assists developers in pinpointing possible bad code smells that violate design principles, determining which code paths are susceptible to a bug, and saving development time.

Research in refactoring should expand on refactoring graphs at the method level and focus on class and package-level refactorings. Also, research could complement existing git-based (e.g., RefactoringMiner [24] and RefDiff [21]) and contemporary IDE refactoring tools (e.g., JDeodorant [23] and RefFinder [20]) with visualization features.

7.7 Conclusion

In this chapter, we have explored various challenges that the rise of refactoring research has been facing, which represent interesting research opportunities for the big data community. For each refactoring challenge, we explored its related studies to understand its growth and complexity, then we discussed how it is linked to big data dimensions. As we established stronger connections between refactoring and big data, we hope to see emerging studies leveraging big data techniques and frameworks to take refactoring research to the next level.

References

1. Rafi Almhana, Wiem Mkaouer, Marouane Kessentini, and Ali Ouni. Recommending relevant classes for bug reports using multi-objective search. In *2016 31st IEEE/ACM International Conference on Automated Software Engineering (ASE)*, pp. 286–295. Singapore. IEEE, 2016.

2. Eman Abdullah Alomar, Mohamed Wiem Mkaouer, and Ali Ouni. Can refactoring be self-affirmed? An exploratory study on how developers document their refactoring activities in commit messages. In *Proceedings of the 3rd International Workshop on Refactoring*, New York, NY, USA. ACM, 2019.

3. Eman Abdullah Alomar, Mohamed Wiem Mkaouer, and Ali Ouni. Toward the automatic classification of self-affirmed refactoring. *Journal of Systems and Software*, vol. 171, p. 110821, 2020.

4. Eman Abdullah Alomar, Mohamed Wiem Mkaouer, Ali Ouni, and Maroune Kessentini. On the impact of refactoring on the relationship between quality attributes and design metrics. In *2019 ACM/IEEE International Symposium on Empirical Software Engineering and Measurement (ESEM)*, pp. 1–11. Porto de Galinhas-PE, Brazil. IEEE, 2019.

5. Eman Abdullah Alomar, Anthony Peruma, Christian D Newman, Mohamed Wiem Mkaouer, and Ali Ouni. On the relationship between developer experience and refactoring: An exploratory study and preliminary results. In *Proceedings of the IEEE/ACM 42nd International Conference on Software Engineering Workshops*, pp. 342–349. Montreal, Canada. 2020.

6. Alex Bogart, Eman Abdullah Alomar, Mohamed Wiem Mkaouer, and Ali Ouni. Increasing the trust in refactoring through visualization. In *Proceedings of the IEEE/ACM 42nd International Conference on Software Engineering Workshops*, pp. 334–341. Montreal, Canada. 2020.

7. Aline Brito, Andre Hora, and Marco Tulio Valente. Refactoring graphs: Assessing refactoring over time. arXiv preprint arXiv:2003.04666, 2020.

8. Dustin Campbell and Mark Miller. Designing refactoring tools for developers. In *Proceedings of the 2nd Workshop on Refactoring Tools*, p. 9. New York, United States. ACM, 2008.

9. Danny Dig, Can Comertoglu, Darko Marinov, and Ralph Johnson. Automated detection of refactorings in evolving components. In: Thomas, D. (eds.) *ECOOP 2006 – Object-Oriented Programming*, pp. 404–428. Springer, Heidelberg, 2006.

10. Martin Fowler, Kent Beck, John Brant, William Opdyke, and Don Roberts. *Refactoring: Improving the Design of Existing Code*. Addison-Wesley Long-man Publishing Co., Inc., Boston, MA, USA, 1999.

11. Yoav Goldberg and Omer Levy. word2vec explained: deriving Mikolov et al.'s negative-sampling word-embedding method. arXiv preprint arXiv:1402.3722, 2014.

12. Shinpei Hayashi, Yasuyuki Tsuda, and Motoshi Saeki. Search-based refactoring detection from source code revisions. *IEICE Transactions on Information and Systems*, vol. 93(4), p. 754–762, 2010.

13. Miryung Kim, Thomas Zimmermann, and Nachiappan Nagappan. A field study of refactoring challenges and benefits. In *Proceedings of the ACM SIGSOFT 20th International Symposium on the Foundations of Software Engineering*, p. 50. North Carolina, United States. ACM, 2012.

14. Mika V Mäntylä and Casper Lassenius. Drivers for software refactoring decisions. In *Proceedings of the 2006 ACM/IEEE International Symposium on Empirical Software Engineering*, pp. 297–306. Rio de Janeiro, Brazil. ACM, 2006.

15. Emerson Murphy-Hill. Programmer friendly refactoring tools. 2009.

16. Emerson Murphy-Hill and Andrew P Black. Refactoring tools: Fitness for purpose. *IEEE Software*, vol. 25(5), pp. 38–44, 2008.

17. Emerson Murphy-Hill, Chris Parnin, and Andrew P Black. How we refactor, and how we know it. *IEEE Transactions on Software Engineering*, vol. 38(1), pp. 5–18, 2011.

18. Stas Negara, Nicholas Chen, Mohsen Vakilian, Ralph E Johnson, and Danny Dig. A comparative study of manual and automated refactorings. In *European Conference on Object-Oriented Programming*, pp. 552–576. Montpellier, France. Springer, 2013.

19. Gustavo H Pinto and Fernando Kamei. What programmers say about refactoring tools? An empirical investigation of stack overflow. In *Proceedings of the 2013 ACM Workshop on Workshop on Refactoring Tools*, pp. 33–36. Indiana, United States. ACM, 2013.

20. Kyle Prete, Napol Rachatasumrit, Nikita Sudan, and Miryung Kim. Template-based reconstruction of complex refactorings. In *2010 IEEE International Conference on Software Maintenance*, pp. 1–10, Timi Oara, Romania. IEEE, Sept 2010.

21. Danilo Silva and Marco Tulio Valente. Refdiff: Detecting refactorings in version histories. In *2017 IEEE/ACM 14th International Conference on Mining Software Repositories (MSR)*, pp. 269–279, Buenos Aires, Argentina. May 2017.

22. Liang Tan and Christoph Bockisch. A survey of refactoring detection tools. In *Software Engineering*, 2019.

23. Nikolaos Tsantalis, Theodoros Chaikalis, and Alexander Chatzigeorgiou. Jdeodorant: Identification and removal of type-checking bad smells. In *2008 12th European Conference on Software Maintenance and Reengineering*, pp. 329–331. IEEE, 2008.

24. Nikolaos Tsantalis, Matin Mansouri, Laleh M Eshkevari, Davood Mazinanian, and Danny Dig. Accurate and efficient refactoring detection in commit history. In *Proceedings of the 40th International Conference on Software Engineering*, pp. 483–494. Washington, DC, United States. ACM, 2018.

25. Mohsen Vakilian, Nicholas Chen, Stas Negara, Balaji Ambresh Rajkumar, Brian P Bailey, and Ralph E Johnson. Use, disuse, and misuse of automated refactorings. In *Proceedings of the 34th International Conference on Software Engineering*, pp. 233–243. Zurich, Switzerland. IEEE Press, 2012.

26. Mathieu Verbaere, Ran Ettinger, and Oege De Moor. Jungl: A scripting language for refactoring. In *Proceedings of the 28th International Conference on Software Engineering*, pp. 172–181. Shanghai, China. ACM, 2006.

27. Zhenchang Xing and Eleni Stroulia. Umldiff: An algorithm for object-oriented design differencing. In *Proceedings of the 20th IEEE/ACM International Conference on Automated Software Engineering, 'ASE'05*, New York, NY, USA, pp. 54–65. ACM, 2005.

Chapter 8

Knowledge Discovery in Systems of Systems: Observations and Trends

Bruno Sena
University of São Paulo

Frank J. Affonso
São Paulo State University

Thiago Bianchi
IBM Brazil

Pedro Henrique Dias Valle
University of São Paulo

Daniel Feitosa
University of Groningen

Elisa Yumi Nakagawa
University of São Paulo

Contents

8.1 Introduction

Systems of Systems (SoS) are a class of systems composed of distributed constituent systems that drive their resources and capabilities together to achieve missions not feasible by any of these constituents operating independently (Jamshidi 2011; Nielsen et al. 2015). Over the past years, the engineering of such systems has brought many challenges because of their size and dynamic characteristics. In general, five characteristics describe these systems (Dersin 2014): (a) operational independence: each constituent has its individual missions and continues to operate to achieve them even when decoupled from the SoS; (b) managerial independence: constituents are developed and managed by different organizations with their own structures and technologies; (c) evolutionary development: constituents constantly change to adapt to new missions and to different environment scenarios; (d) geographic distribution: constituents are not intrinsically integrated and need of means to communicate among them; and (e) emergent behavior: which refers to the SoS mission, which is accomplished by the synergistic collaboration among constituents.

This class of systems is present in several highly critical domains, such as health (Hata et al. 2017), petrochemical (Nazari et al. 2015), transportation (Zheng et al. 2013), smart cities (Batty 2012; Cavalcante et al. 2016), and civil and industrial applications (King et al. 2011). Due to the complexity of these domains, most constituents of an SoS usually generate and manage huge amounts of data, which contain relevant knowledge that belongs to a specific constituent, but are not analyzed and also used in favor of the SoS as a whole. If such knowledge is adequately identified and managed, this knowledge could improve decision-making processes helping stakeholders understand the macro behavior of the SoS and also support automated decision-making by the SoS at runtime.

When Agrawal et al. (2011) stated that "we are awash in a flood of data today," they resumed in a single sentence the Big Data context and the concern about making useful utilization of this enormous data collection. SoS are right on the spot in this context since they are related to the management and exchange of data on distributed environments (Maier 1998). Hence, Big Data and SoS seem to be part of the same context, where Big Data focuses on data processing (Beyer and Laney 2012) and SoS focus on using such data to acquire knowledge, fulfill missions, and support decision-making. Moreover, Machine Learning has been applied in SoS such as in the healthcare domain and emergency management systems, in which several techniques, e.g., statistical models, clustering, fuzzy logic, neuro-computing, data mining, pattern recognition, and evolutionary algorithms, have been used (Tannahill et al. 2013). As a result, all effort applied to the extraction of relevant information from data can be used to improve or even change the SoS missions (Silva et al. 2015). In the software industry, initiatives to acquire knowledge from data are paramount to implement systems that deliver on "smarter planet" scenarios (Spohrer and Maglio 2010), which are now present across all industry sectors (Chen et al. 2016; Paroutis et al. 2014).

As an example, in the healthcare domain (Lahboube et al. 2014; Wickramasinghe et al. 2007), constituents systems monitor the vital signs of patients (e.g., pressure, heart rate, and temperature), manage hospital information, and support nursery and emergency/ambulances. By analyzing together the data provided from these constituents, considerable gains can be achieved such as the prediction of events such as a heart attack and then trigger a specific SoS behavior before the event occurs. Another example is in the global emergency domain where different constituents monitor natural disasters (hurricanes, earthquakes, and floods). The early prediction of critical situations could help citizens evacuate regions before the disaster happens (Goswami et al. 2018) or identify regions where an emergency response may be needed. Hence, the discovery of knowledge from distributed databases of SoS constituents at runtime could prevent injuries, reduce financial losses, and save lives, preventing large disasters as those occurred in 2017 in the Caribbean Sea, USA (Issa et al. 2018) and in 2011 in the Sendai area, Japan (Luo 2012). Considering the relevance of a better discovery of knowledge in SoS, initiatives that address such discovery from distributed constituents are important. Moreover, the advancement of technologies related to Big Data, Artificial Intelligence, and Machine Learning has enabled the manipulation of large amounts of data and extraction of relevant knowledge that has changed how decisions are made.

Based on the aforementioned scenarios, this chapter presents the state of the art on Knowledge Discovery (KD) in SoS and reports on future research perspectives. We include discussions related to data collection in SoS, integration of data, and discovery of useful and critical knowledge.

This chapter is organized into seven sections. While Section 8.2 firstly provides an overview of the state of the art on how knowledge has been managed in SoS, Sections 8.3, 8.4, and 8.5 detail it based on three facets: data collection, data integration, and knowledge discovery. Finally, in Section 8.6, we summarize findings and new insights and draw our conclusions in Section 8.7.

8.2 Overview of the State of the Art on Knowledge Management in SoS

To identify the state of the art on knowledge management in SoS, we conducted a Systematic Mapping Study (SMS) following well-known guidelines proposed by Petersen et al. (2015) and found 17 studies, extracted from them information regarding the three facets (data collection, data integration, and knowledge discovery, which were selected because they represent the traditional steps of a knowledge discovery process), and performed various analyses. In turn, SMS is a type of literature review that uses systematic methods to collect, critically appraise research studies, and synthesize findings on a specific research topic (Petersen et al., 2015). To conduct this SMS, we used the search string *(systems of systems OR systems-of-systems) AND (knowledge discovery OR knowledge engineering OR knowledge acquisition OR knowledge extraction OR big data OR data mining)* in seven databases (ACM Digital Library, EI Compendex, IEEE Digital Library, ISI Web of Science, ScienceDirect, Scopus, and Springer Link.) and applied the following inclusion criteria (IC): IC1: "The study addresses collection or integration of data, or extraction of knowledge from the SoS constituents"; and IC2: "The study addresses decision-making from the knowledge of SoS." Besides that, the exclusion criteria (EC) were: EC1: "The study is not related to SoS"; EC2: "The study does not address collecting or integrating data, extracting knowledge, or supporting decision-making from the SoS constituents"; EC3: "The study is an extended abstract, table of contents, foreword, tutorial, editorial, or summary of conference"; EC4: "The study is a previous version of a more complete study about the same research"; and EC5: "The study does not have an abstract or the full text is not available." Moreover, three research questions (RQ) guided this SMS: RQ1: Which approaches have been proposed to collect data from SoS constituents?; RQ2: Which approaches have been proposed to integrate data from SoS constituents?; and RQ3: Which approaches have been proposed to extract knowledge from SoS constituents?

As observed in Table 8.1 (column "Year"), the number of studies published in this topic has remained stable throughout the last 13 years, and the first studies were published in 2005. Regarding the publication venues, most studies (14 of 17) were published in conference proceedings or workshops, while only three were published in journals, as depicted on the left side of Figure 8.1.

Table 8.1 Studies That Address KD in SoS.

ID	Title	Author	Year
S01	A Grid-Based Architecture for Earth Observation Data Access	Aloisio et al.	2005
S02	Knowledge Mining Application in ISHM Testbed	McDermott et al.	2006
S03	Rich Feeds for RESCUE	Demchak et al.	2008
S04	An Efficient Grid-Based Metadata Processing And Sharing Architecture For GEOSS	Hassan and Huh	2008
S05	Innovative Data Mining Techniques in Support of GEOSS	King et al.	2011
S06	System-of-Systems Information Interoperability using a Linked Dataspace	Curry	2012
S07	Predictive Analytics Can Facilitate Proactive Property Vacancy Policies for Cities	Appel et al.	2014
S08	The Automatic Identification System of Maritime Accident Risk Using Rule-Based Reasoning	Idiri and Napoli	2012
S09	The Seven Main Challenges of an Early Warning System Architecture	Moßgraber et al.	2013
S10	Big Data Analytic Paradigms – From PCA to Deep Learning	Tannahill and Jamshidi	2014
S11	A System-of-Systems Service Design for Social Media Analytics	Wong et al.	2014
S12	SoSE Architecture of Data-Intensive Computing for Healthcare Information System	Ni et al.	2015a
S13	Anatomy of Functional Components of Healthcare Information System	Ni et al.	2015b
S14	Urban Planning and Building Smart Cities Based on the Internet of Things Using Big Data Analytics	Rathore et al.	2016
S15	Integration of Brainstorming Platform in a System of Information Systems	Majd et al.	2016
S16	Integration of Big Data Analytics Embedded Smart City Architecture with RESTful Web of Things for Efficient Service Provision and Energy Management	Silva et al.	2017
S17	A System-of-Systems Approach to Improving Intelligent Predictions and Decisions in a Time-Series Environment	Curry et al.	2018

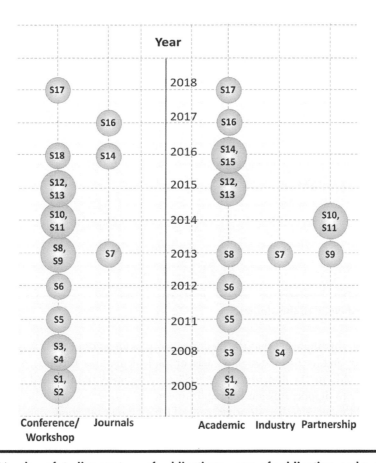

Figure 8.1   Number of studies per type of publications, years of publication, and author context/orientation.

Such results may be related to the fact that most studies are not consolidated enough to be published in a journal, which may also suggest that this is an emerging topic. Considering the venues, most of the studies were published in three general conferences or workshops: International Conference on Information Systems for Crisis Response and Management (ISCRAM), International Conference on Internet Computing for Science and Engineering (ICICSE), and IEEE Systems-of-Systems Engineering Conference (SoSE).

Considering the authorship of the studies that was obtained looking for the institution of all authors of each study, most studies were written only by academic researchers, two were written only by industry practitioners, and three studies resulted from a partnership between industry and academia. Figure 8.1 presents the study distribution in these different combinations of authors.

All studies addressed one of the following application domains: smart environments (e.g., smart cities and smart grids) (S07, S10, S14, and S16); healthcare (S02, S12, and S13); information systems (S11, S15, and S17); earth observation (S01, S04, and S05); crisis management and natural disaster contexts (S03 and S09); maritime systems (S08); and enterprise energy management (S06). The prevalence of domain-specific approaches indicates that research was tailored to particular contexts and that generalization of the findings is not still possible.

The word cloud presented in Figure 8.2, built from title, abstract, and keywords of the 17 studies, shows the frequency at which various terms appear in these studies. Terms such as data

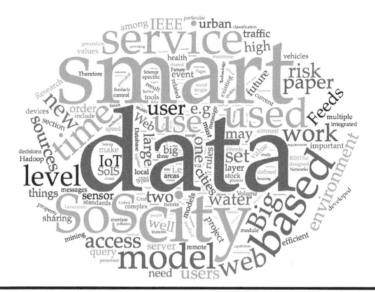

Figure 8.2 Word cloud of the studies.

and SoS stand out, highlighting that the identified works address or propose ways to handle data in SoS, whether by architectures, design models, or implementations. Other terms, such as smart, city, and service, indicate the domains where SoS were developed and the need to make such SoS smarter and ready to support mission accomplishment.

No study addressed together all aspects of KD (i.e., data collection, data integration, and knowledge discovery), but only one or two of them. Nine studies addressed data collection (S01, S02, S03, S04, S06, S11, S14, S15, and S16), six addressed data integration (S01, S02, S06, S11, S14, and S15), and 15 addressed knowledge discovery (S02, S03, S04, S05, S07, S08, S09, S10, S11, S12, S13, S14, S15, S16, and S17). Each study focused on a particular aspect and assumed the others as black boxes. Furthermore, most studies cannot be compared directly, since they present different perspectives; some studies present architectural solutions, and others present technological solutions, modeling methods, or just discussions about trends and limitations. Although there is little room for comparisons, we found that these studies can complement each other and together can support a more complete approach. The following sections detail KD in SoS from different aspects.

8.3 Data Collection in Systems of Systems

Data collection from SoS constituents has been the focus of attention, with many solutions addressing the architectural level. From a wider viewpoint, there are two distinct perspectives to collect data in SoS. The first one requires that each constituent provide its data voluntarily to a centralized platform. In this approach, data becomes available and is only collected or used by other constituents, as proposed in some studies (S04, S06, and S11). Regarding communication, the platform where the data is available can be shared among constituents if there is an agreement among them, or it may be individual. In the latter, the use of communication and control protocols among constituents is essential to know from which platforms the data can be collected and in which way the data can be used. In the second perspective, as proposed by some studies

(S01, S02, S03, S04, S14, and S15), constituents do not provide their data automatically but only when the data is requested by an external entity to fulfill a mission or other reasons. Constituents must agree in providing data to be used for a particular end and have an external interface (or service) to deal with requests systematically. The main difference between the two aforementioned perspectives lies in the key quality attribute of interest for the designed solution. In the first case, the focus is on data availability, whereas the second is focused on security since only authorized data will be shared between any two parties. In both perspectives, contracts should be well defined to not influence the business operation of the SoS.

We also found 13 quality attributes as important for data collection in SoS by systematically looking for quality attributes explicitly mentioned in each study. As shown in Figure 8.3, availability is the most recurrent attribute (S01, S03, S04, S11, S14, and S15), which can be critical to SoS. Security (S01, S03, S04, S11, and S14) and interoperability (S03, S04, S06, S11, and S15) are required as means to ensure the integrity and authenticity in communications between constituents. Modularity (S01, S03, S04, S11, and S16) refers to a clear separation between the data collection module and the data request interfaces, which may be maintained independently for different constituents. Scalability (S01, S03, S11, and S16) and performance (S01 and S16), which also include latency and response time, are also critical and focus on mitigating loss of data.

The other attributes, although important, targeted particular application domains, for instance, the real-time operation is present in crisis contexts, where the SoS must make decisions in critical situations; and reliability is necessary for health domains, where failures could result in fatalities.

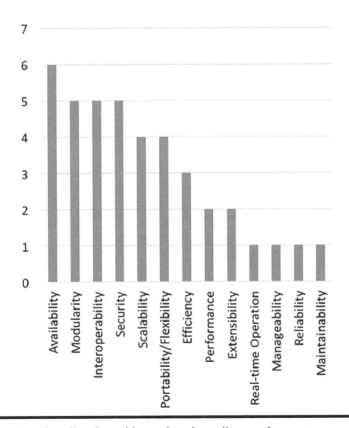

Figure 8.3   Number of studies that addressed each quality requirement.

There are also several architectural patterns being used in the data collection solutions. Among the main patterns, we highlight Service-Oriented Architecture (SOA), orchestration, producer/consumer, shared repository, data as a service, layered, and monitoring (Garcés et al. 2019; Sena et al. 2018; Ingram et al. 2015; Avgeriou and Zdun 2005). The shared repository and data-as-a-service patterns are useful in approaches where data is sent to a central platform and made available to other constituents. Orchestration, producer/consumer, and monitoring are management patterns (used when the central entity must request data from constituents), which control what data needs to be collected and also keep the monitoring of constituents so that whenever a new data is generated, such data is collected and stored. SOA and layered pattern (Richards 2015) allow the modularization and organization of the architecture so that the tasks are modularized to achieve weak coupling. When using SOA, constituents act as services with their independent functionalities, and their communication interface is the unique data input/output port in the SoS.

8.4 Data Integration in Systems of Systems

Data integration is the most challenging task of the entire KD process in SoS due to the dynamism of SoS, i.e., constituents and missions change at runtime, also changing the data that is generated, which may impact on different formats or increase in volume, as also pointed out by the studies addressing this issue (S01, S02, S06, S11, S14, and S15). New constituents emerge, and the new data is often not integrated into the KD process. Since we are dealing with a Big Data context, the volume of data generated directly impacts the variety of data, which requires very complex processes and techniques for the integration to be performed correctly.

In general, there are two main workflows for data integration: continuous flow integration and integration by information queries. In the first case, data is sent to a central platform to be stored in a given format previously defined by operation contracts agreed between the SoS constituents and the central entity. This transformation can occur either in the constituent itself (which is not common because constituents commonly use data in different formats from those of the central entity) or in the communication interface between the constituent and central entity. In fact, the important point of this first workflow is that data is sent continuously and already transformed into the specified format. In the central entity, this data can be stored in several different database architectures (e.g., data lake, relational databases, and nonrelational databases), and storage challenges are minimized because data is already standardized.

In the second workflow, data is stored in its original format/structure in both constituent and shared repository, and the format will only be transformed when an operation requires some specific knowledge. This type of integration increases query processing but prevents unused data from being preprocessed. As an example, study S06 states data should be integrated into an SoS only when necessary, because a previous data integration may require formatting and processing efforts and could not be aligned to accommodate the new data integration; otherwise, performance could be improved when data is already integrated.

In general, in this scenario of data collection and integration, formats must be defined in advance in the operating contracts so that the communication interfaces between the constituents and the central entity know the data format they need to request and receive. Besides, formats can be changed at runtime, but without prior configuration of the collection interface, communication errors will be thrown and the data from that constituent will probably not be collected to support KD.

Among the studies that presented an approach in which data is sent to a central platform, two of them (S2 and S11) proposed the use of a module especially destined to receive data from different constituents and adapt them to be used in the SoS. While S02 proposed this module as a mediator responsible for exchanging formats and keeping the information interoperability among constituents, S11 proposed an adapter service to perform data format transformation between two different formats from the domain connected to the Enterprise Server Business module, a central controller of their specific domain that controls the communication between constituents.

S14 presented a four-tier architecture, in which the second tier is responsible for the communication among constituents, using protocols and communication technologies, such as Wi-Fi and Ethernet. S01 presented an approach composed of two main components: one for collecting data and another for merging the collected data.

Finally, S15 proposed an approach in which the SoS stakeholders establish a shared terminology to keep the knowledge in the same format. In short, this study defines that each constituent must store data in a specific format to be integrated. Therefore, it is important to define an approach to agree on whether the integration will be carried out at the SoS level, establishing a specific format and being controlled by a central entity, or whether the integration will be individually performed by each constituent in a collaborative manner.

There are also patterns being adopted to promote the data integration process in SoS, as summarized in Table 8.2. Regarding the relevant architectural requirements addressed in the data integration process, we found the same ones discussed in Section 8.4; however, addressing different patterns. The patterns and the reason why they were used are summarized in Table 8.2.

Table 8.2 Patterns Used for Data Integration in SoS

Pattern	Reason
Data as a service	In this pattern, all modules need to be constructed as a service to be consumed, including data collection and integration.
Pipe and filters	This pattern creates a flow (pipe) composed of several steps (filters) in which data must pass through, including integration.
Broker	This pattern is used to structure several constituents and guide the flow of data, including data translation.
Orchestration	An orchestration pattern proposes the use of an entity that manages the flow of data, identifying what data should be collected, when to collect such data, and to which constituent it should be sent.
Layered	In a layered architecture, an integration layer between the collection and the knowledge extraction layers is proposed to modularize the implementation according to domain requirements.
Monitoring	This pattern proposes the use of a monitoring entity, which performs data integration whenever it is necessary for the accomplishment of the mission.

8.5 Knowledge Discovery in Systems of Systems

Most studies, except S01 and S06, addressed approaches for KD in SoS and can be classified into two categories according to the objective that guided the knowledge extraction. Eight studies (S02, S05, S07, S08, S09, S11, S12, and S15) focused on extracting knowledge that is useful for a given application domain, for instance: (a) classification of messages from social networks (S11); (b) creation of early warnings for tsunamis (S09); (c) improvement of healthcare data analysis (S12); and (d) forecasting of vacancy risk in neighborhoods and prediction of rent/selling prices (S07). Other studies (S10, S13, S14, S16, and S17) focused on KD for SoS improvements, for instance, S16 turned the systems of the city into smart systems and S14 optimized an energy management system based on a solar power forecast model. In general, the main benefit of knowledge discovery in SoS is to support decision-making. For this reason, some studies that address SoS decision-making based on data and communication between constituents have also been addressed in this topic.

Most studies proposed architectural solutions, except S05 that proposed a logical model, and S08, S10, and S11 that presented systems for specific applications (prediction, regression, classification, and so forth). Regarding the architectural solutions, S03 presented an architectural pattern to extract knowledge from the constituents and composed of three main entities: (a) the services (i.e., the constituents); (b) the messenger and router, responsible for data transmission between services (messenger) and for intercepting and rerouting data; and (c) service/data connectors, which hide the internal structure of the connected services and connect only the ones necessary to provide and expose data. Moreover, S09 reported the development of an architecture for collaborative, complex, and critical decision-making in SoS that enables constituents distributed in heterogeneous environments to communicate through message exchange.

Addressing the layered architectural pattern, S16 presented an architecture containing a specific layer for event/decision management. This architecture provides real-time intelligent decision-making and scalability for the data manipulation. Each technology is used to facilitate processing a huge amount of data and to improve the performance of the application. Another layered architecture was presented in S14, which included a layer with the analytical system responsible for data processing. Moreover, S07 presented a system that can support predictive analytics; for this, there is a generic method for data analysis and knowledge dissemination. S08 proposed an architecture containing two modules: (a) one involving the knowledge acquisition from historical data; and (b) another using the knowledge for automatic risk identification (in this case, of vessels in risk among all in the shipping traffic). S17 introduced an approach for selecting the SoS constituents based on a set of five key attributes (i.e., performance of the prediction, performance of the decision, affordability, scalability, and robustness) to improve intelligent predictions and decisions in a time-series environment.

One of the critical domains in which KD has been explored is healthcare. In S13, the authors proposed a general architecture with not only several services and subsystems, but also technical support units, such as computing facilities for data storage and management, data distribution, networking, processing, and analysis. Besides, S02 presented an architecture with several modules for managing data/information and a module for knowledge extraction. S12 proposed an architecture considering cutting-edge technologies of cloud computing and Big Data. Such architectures are composed of six layers: data resources, file storage, data storage, programming model, data analysis, and platform management. In particular, the data analysis layer is also responsible for data processing, analysis models, business value, and knowledge extraction.

Aiming at supporting the operation and decision-making in SoS, S05 proposed a knowledge-driven logical model composed of eight steps: data ingestion, image archive (for constituents that provide satellite images), browsing engine, image features extraction, inventory, query engine, classification and knowledge acquisition, and interactive learning. Similarly, S04 presented a data-shared architecture with four components: (a) web search, in which users search for and retrieve data; (b) catalog node, which holds the metadata catalog and forwards data requests of users to data repositories or metadata index server; (c) data repository, which provides metadata information to discover, locate, and describe data; and (d) metadata index server, which stores metadata of different domains from other catalog nodes distributed in different geographical areas. The SoS architecture discussed in S11 focuses on the loose coupling of the services in a centralized service management catalog. This architecture proposes: (a) a module for query processing to access the data needed for KD; (b) an enterprise server business module for interaction and communication among services; and (c) an Application Programming Interface (API) management server for external interfaces. Finally, in S10, the authors proposed a system that could be integrated as a constituent in SoS. This system implements Big Data techniques to extract relevant information to derive knowledge and apply such knowledge as a set of requests for constituents.

Regarding the use of knowledge, some initiatives detail how the knowledge could be used to support the SoS operation (S08, S14, S15, and S16). While S08 and S15 proposed an external interface in which SoS stakeholders must evaluate the results before any action, S14 and S16 proposed a layer to receive the knowledge and send it to controller entities (orchestrator and monitor) or SoS stakeholders. Further details of how this knowledge is used could be provided to show how decision-making can be supported by constituent data.

Finally, concerning quality requirements and architectural standards, the same ones found for the data collection and integration have been considered for the discovery of knowledge. In general, no specific attribute falls into this part except for the performance and efficiency required for the execution of the models of KD. Moreover, scalability and availability are still critical in this scenario and must be still investigated to keep the quality of the entire data flow and to adequately fulfill the SoS mission.

8.6 Research Agenda

There are already important advancements in the field of KD in SoS, but there are also several gaps that were identified from the set of existing studies in this field. In addition to the need for robust approaches that support KD in SoS (Aloisio et al. 2005, McDermott et al. 2006; Demchak et al. 2008; and Moßgraber et al. 2013), multiple challenges must be addressed to consolidate such approaches. As perspectives of future lines of research, we highlight the items presented in Table 8.3, divided in the three main research topics: data collection, data integration, and knowledge discovery. In short, we focus on more detailed approaches that address each aspect of knowledge discovery at a more practical level, considering technologies, protocols, and interfaces.

8.7 Final Considerations

The constant evolution of complex systems such as SoS and the growth of the volume of data generated by their constituents, together with the need to extract useful knowledge from these data, have drawn the attention of researchers to the development of approaches that allow KD in SoS.

Table 8.3   Perspectives of Future Works in KD in SoS

Research Topic	Perspective for Future Work
Data collection	Investigate existing approaches in-depth and identify components that can be reused in different types of SoS, e.g., examine how the different protocols of various constituents can be abstracted and the collected data be sent to a repository in which it can be accessed; Identification of recurring problems in SoS architecting and, in turn, architectural patterns that address them, e.g., support the collection of data from different sources, such as sensors, internet, and different systems, while also enabling the adaptation of security settings, query and request forms of each source; and integration of SoS infrastructure and streaming technologies that support real-time data collection while also mitigating potential bottlenecks.
Data integration	Develop approaches that can integrate data efficiently and securely, without losing the context of information and that are adaptable to different types of data; and develop approaches that support the integration of dynamic data types at runtime
Knowledge discovery	Develop systematic methods that enable the extraction of knowledge by detailing the interior of each module, considering the tasks of preprocessing, analysis, and postprocessing; Support the dissemination of knowledge in the SoS as a whole, i.e., to apply the knowledge to fulfill some mission of the whole system (SoS); and develop approaches that support that adaptation of SoS modules to new missions, e.g., to rewire how constituents are connected or the collected data is processed.
Big data	Map different frameworks and technologies that support the management of the V's proposed in the big data scenario (variety, veracity, volume, value, and velocity) to support in the future directions previously described.

Considering the results of our SMS, the number of contributions already made in this field is still low, indicating that there are further gaps to be researched so that the state of the art can move forward. Despite the need for a robust approach that supports KD in SoS (Aloisio et al., 2005; McDermott et al., 2006; Demchak and Krüger, 2008; Moßgraber et al., 2013), many challenges must be still addressed to consolidate such an approach. The existence of these challenges can be justified by the lack of research advances in this field. Besides, all existing approaches consider architectural issues, addressing patterns, quality attributes, and architectures for specific domains. However, these approaches are still immature and have limitations, leaving open several challenges to be addressed.

Acknowledgments

This work was supported in part by FAPESP (Grants 2017/22237-3, 2017/06195-9, and 2019/19730-5), CNPq (Grant 141602/2017-1, 312634/2018-8), and Capes.

References

Agrawal, D., Das, S., & El Abbadi, A. Big data and cloud computing: current state and future opportunities. In *Proceedings of the 14th International Conference on Extending Database Technology*, pp. 530–533. 2011.

Aloisio, G., Cafaro, M., Fiore, S., & Quarta, G. A grid-based architecture for earth observation data access. In *Proceedings of the 2005 ACM Symposium on Applied Computing*, pp. 701–705. 2005.

Appel, S. U., Botti, D., Jamison, J., Plant, L., Shyr, J. Y., & Varshney, L. R. Predictive analytics can facilitate proactive property vacancy policies for cities. *Technological Forecasting and Social Change*, 89, pp. 161–173. 2014.

Avgeriou, P., & Zdun, U. Architectural patterns revisited-a pattern language. 2005.

Batty, M., *"Smart Cities, Big Data."* SAGE Publications, London, England, pp. 191–193. 2012.

Beyer, M. A., & Laney, D. *The Importance of 'Big Data': A Definition.* Gartner, Stamford, CT, 2012.

Cavalcante, E., Cacho, N., Lopes, F., Batista, T., & Oquendo, F. Thinking smart cities as systems-of-systems: A perspective study. In *Proceedings of the 2nd International Workshop on Smart*, p. 1–4. 2016.

Chen, Y., Argentinis, J. E., & Weber, G. IBM Watson: How cognitive computing can be applied to Big Data challenges in life sciences research. *Clinical Therapeutics*, 38(4), pp. 688–701. 2016.

Curry, E. System of systems information interoperability using a linked dataspace. In: *2012 7th International Conference on System of Systems Engineering (SoSE)*, pp. 101–106. 2012.

Curry, D. M., Beaver, W. W., & Dagli, C. H. A system-of-systems approach to improving intelligent predictions and decisions in a time-series environment. In *2018 13th Annual Conference on System of Systems Engineering (SoSE)*, pp. 98–105. 2018.

Demchak, B., & Krüger, I. H. Rich Feeds for RESCUE. In *Proceedings of the 5th International ISCRAM Conference*, v. 5. 2008.

Dersin, P. Systems of systems. IEEE-Reliability Society. Technical Committee on "Systems of Systems". 2014.

Garcés, L., Sena, B., & Nakagawa, E. Y. Towards an architectural patterns language for Systems-of-Systems. In: *26th Conference on Pattern Languages of Programs (PLoP), 2019*, Ottawa, Ontario, Canada, pp. 1–24. 2019.

Goswami, S., Chakraborty, S., Ghosh, S., Chakrabarti, A., & Chakraborty, B. A review on application of data mining techniques to combat natural disasters. *Ain Shams Engineering Journal*, 9(3), pp. 365–378. 2018.

Hassan, M. M., & Huh, E. N. An efficient grid based metadata processing and sharing architecture for GEOSS. In *2008 10th International Conference on Advanced Communication Technology*, v. 3, pp. 2071–2075. 2008.

Hata, Y., Kamozaki, Y., Sawayama, T., Taniguchi, K., & Nakajima, H. A heart pulse monitoring system by air pressure and ultrasonic sensor systems. In *IEEE International Conference on System of Systems Engineering (SoSE'2007)*, p. 1–5. 2007.

Idiri, B., & Napoli, A. The automatic identification system of maritime accident risk using rule-based reasoning. In *2012 7th International Conference on System of Systems Engineering (SoSE)*, pp. 125–130, 2012.

Ingram, C., Payne, R., & Fitzgerald, J. Architectural modelling patterns for systems of systems. *INCOSE International Symposium*, 25(1), pp. 1177–1192. 2015.

Issa, A., Ramadugu, K., Mulay, P., Hamilton, J., Siegel, V., Harrison, C., & Boehmer, T. Deaths related to Hurricane Irma—Florida, Georgia, and North Carolina, September 4–October 10, 2017. *Morbidity and Mortality Weekly Report*, 67(30), 829. 2018.

Jamshidi, M. *System of Systems Engineering: Innovations for the Twenty First Century.* John Wiley & Sons, Hoboken, NJ, 2011.

King, R., Younan, N., Datcu, M., & Nedelcu, I. Innovative data mining techniques in support of GEOSS: A workshop's findings. In *2011 2nd International Conference on Space Technology*, pp. 1–4. 2011.

Lahboube, F., Haidrar, S., Roudiès, O., Souissi, N., & Adil, A. Systems of systems paradigm in a hospital environment: benefits for requirements elicitation process. *International Review on Computers and Software (I. RE. CO. S.)*, 9(10), 1798–1806, 2014.

Luo, N. The impact of natural disasters on global stock market: The case of the Japanese 2011 Earthquake. 2012.

Maier, M. W. Architecting principles for systems-of-systems. *Systems Engineering*, 1, pp. 267–284. 1998.

Majd. S., Marie-Hélène, A., Véronique, M.; Claude, M., & David, V. Integration of brainstorming platform in a system of information systems. In *Proceedings of the 8th International Conference on Management of Digital EcoSystems*, pp. 166–173. 2016.

McDermott, W. J., Robinson, P., & Duncavage, D. P. Knowledge mining application in ISHM testbed. In *2006 IEEE Aerospace Conference*, p. 9. 2006.

Moßgraber, J., Chaves, F., Middleton, S. E., Zlatev, Z., & Tao, R. The seven main challenges of an early warning system architecture. In *ISCRAM*. 2013.

NazariI, S., Sonntag, C., Stojanovski, G., & Engell, S. A modelling, simulation, and validation framework for the distributed management of large-scale processing systems. *Computer Aided Chemical Engineering*, 37, pp. 269–274. 2015.

Ni, J., Chen, Y., Sha, J., & Zhang, M. SoSE architecture of data intensive computing for healthcare information system. In *2015 Eighth International Conference on Internet Computing for Science and Engineering (ICICSE)*, pp. 159–167. 2015a.

Ni, J., Chen, Y., Sha, J., & Zhang, M. Anatomy of functional components of healthcare information system. In *2015 Eighth International Conference on Internet Computing for Science and Engineering (ICICSE)*, pp. 172–180. 2015b.

Nielsen, C. B., Larsen, P. G., Fitzgerald, J., Woodcock, J., & Peleska, J. Systems of systems engineering: Basic concepts, model-based techniques, and research directions. *ACM Computing Surveys (CSUR)*, 48(2), p. 18. 2015.

Paroutis, S., Bennett, M., & Heracleous, L. A strategic view on smart city technology: The case of IBM Smarter Cities during a recession. *Technological Forecasting and Social Change*, 89. pp. 262–272. 2014.

Petersen, K., Vakkalanka, S., & Kuzniarz, K. Guidelines for conducting systematic mapping studies in software engineering: An update. *Information and Software Technology*, 64, pp. 1–18. 2015.

Rathore, M. M., Ahmad, A., Paul, A., & Rho, S. Urban planning and building smart cities based on the internet of things using big data analytics. *Computer Networks*, 101, pp. 63–80. 2016.

Richards, M. (2015). *Software architecture patterns* (Vol. 4). 1005 Gravenstein Highway North, Sebastopol, CA 95472: O'Reilly Media, Incorporated.

Sena, B., Garcés, L., Allian, A., & Nakagawa, E. Investigating the applicability of architectural patterns in big data systems. In *Conference on Pattern Languages of Programs (PLoP 2018)*, Portland. vol. 33, pp. 1–14. 2018.

Silva, B. N., Khan, M., & Han, K. Integration of Big Data analytics embedded smart city architecture with RESTful web of things for efficient service provision and energy management. *Future Generation Computer Systems*, 107, 975–987. 2017.

Spohrer, J., & Maglio, P. P. Service science: Toward a smarter planet. Introduction to service engineering. pp. 3–30. 2010.

Tannahill, B. K., Maute, C. E., Yetis, Y., Ezell, M. N., Jaimes, A., Rosas, R., & Jamshidi, M. Modeling of system of systems via data analytics—Case for "Big Data" in SoS. In *2013 8th International Conference on System of Systems Engineering*, pp. 177–183. 2013.

Tannahill, B. K., & Jamshidi, M. Big data analytic paradigms—From PCA to deep learning. In *2014 AAAI Spring Symposium Series*. 2014.

Wickramasinghe, N., Chalasani, S., Boppana, R. V., & Madni, A. M. Healthcare system of systems. In *2007 IEEE International Conference on System of Systems Engineering*, pp. 1–6. IEEE. 2007.

Wong, R. K., Chi, C. H., Yu, Z., & Zhao, Y. A system of systems service design for social media analytics. In *2014 IEEE International Conference on Services Computing*, pp. 789–796. 2014.

Zheng, Y., Liu, F., & Hsieh, H. P. U-air: When urban air quality inference meets Big Data. In *Proceedings of the 19th ACM SIGKDD International Conference on Knowledge Discovery and Data Mining*, pp. 1436–144. 2013.

CLOUD SERVICES FOR DATA-INTENSIVE SYSTEMS

Chapter 9

The Challenging Landscape of Cloud Monitoring

William Pourmajidi, Lei Zhang, and Andriy Miranskyy
Ryerson University

John Steinbacher and David Godwin
IBM Canada Lab

Tony Erwin
IBM Watson and Cloud Platform

Contents

Cloud Computing, as the most evolved form of deployment platform, is constantly changing the ways that companies deploy their services and products. Advanced features of Cloud Computing (such as elasticity, serverless, and XaaS) make application deployment more time- and cost-effective than before. Cloud users no longer need massive upfront capital and can enjoy the pay-as-you-go billing model of Cloud and use their business revenue to pay for the ongoing cost of Cloud resources.

The low cost of resources on the Cloud has led to the high adoption rate among businesses and organizations. On the Cloud service provider side, such a high rate of adoption translates to an ever-increasing number of required resources. As the number of the deployed resources increases, so does the complexity of underlying architecture. To deal with this complexity, Cloud service providers need to adopt advanced Cloud Management tools to be able to plan, implement, and maintain complex Cloud infrastructures.

Among the most crucial Cloud management tools for maintenance of Cloud resources are monitoring tools that are responsible for offering a holistic view for all kinds of resources on the Cloud, including both the hardware resources (e.g., bare-metal servers, routers, and switches) and the virtual resources (e.g., virtual servers, virtual network devices, and software-defined data centers). The large scale of Cloud deployments translates to hundreds of thousands of components; the generated monitoring data for these components is classified as a Big Data problem due to high volume, velocity, value, and high variety of the generated logs and therefore requires a Big Data solution. Needless to say, monitoring a Cloud infrastructure, with a complex architecture and hundreds of thousands of deployed resources, is not a trivial task and comes with many challenges.

In this chapter, we review the concept of Cloud computing and its key features, its delivery options, and Cloud monitoring challenges in general. Then we focus on Cloud-generated logs, their importance, characteristics, and challenges associated with them. We review a few proposed solutions that other researchers have offered for these challenges.

Finally, we choose two challenges that, to the best of our knowledge, do not have trivial solutions. The *first* one is the preservation of the authenticity, reliability, and usability of Cloud-generated logs. We argue that the critical nature of logs calls for tamper-proof and immutable log-storage and propose a platform on top of existing blockchains to store logs in the immutable blocks of a blockchain.

The *second* one is the creation of the scalable monitoring solutions for large-scale Cloud infrastructure. The monitoring activities of large-scale Cloud platforms are challenging due to the Big Data characteristics of Cloud-generated logs. The entire efforts dedicated to log collection and storage are worthless if logs are not assessed and analyzed promptly. We create a prototype that leverages microservice architecture in conjunction with Publish-Subscribe architectural pattern to create a scalable log collection and analysis funnel. The platform is used to detect anomalies in collected logs and send an alert to the Cloud DevOps team upon detecting an anomaly.

9.1 Introduction

While the term "Cloud" has been used in different contexts such as networking and switching [97], it was Google's CEO Eric Schmidt that used the term in 2006 to refer to a business model that provides various services to consumers over the Internet [87]. With advancements in virtualization and software-defined resources, a few organizations including Amazon and Microsoft became motivated to create massive data centers and use these data centers to convert physical computing resources to virtual resources and then provide them to consumers via Internet. This move fundamentally changed the way that computing resources are constructed and consumed.

The traditional, on-premises paradigm, which required all resources to be physically on-premises, came with many drawbacks. To begin with, the massive upfront cost that is needed to purchase all IT resources and the space that is going to be allocated to host such resources. In addition to IT resources, a company using on-premises infrastructure should implement proper cooling system and equip the server rooms with proper fire prevention systems. Besides, a large in-house IT department is required to look after the deployed resources and ensure the performance, security, and functionality of the entire on-premises platform. Last but not least, the ongoing costs such as enterprise-grade Internet connection and electricity significantly increase the Total Cost of Ownership (TCO) for on-premises model.

In contrast, the off-premises paradigm, known as Cloud computing, offers a unique set of features such as elasticity, just-in-time, and pay-per-use that can be used to offer complex, seamless, and reliable services to consumers. Cloud computing has become an inevitable platform for companies who offer advanced services to their consumers via Internet such as Netflix, Dropbox, and Spotify.

Besides technical advancements, Cloud solutions are known to be far more feasible than traditional infrastructure. This is due to the fact that the main idea of resource pricing on the Cloud is based on renting rather than buying [19]. In other words, Cloud Service Providers (CSPs) need to virtualize all their resources and ensure that their shared pool of virtual resources is highly utilized and is shared among enough tenants. To achieve this high level of utilization, the CSPs rely on state-of-the-art network facilities, advanced hypervisors with complex virtualization features, containerization, software-defined data centers, and advanced Cloud management platforms. To ensure the smooth operation of the Cloud environment, the Cloud-grade management platform should be able to deal with various complications that are common among infrastructures used for large-scale service delivery.

In the following, we review the definition of Cloud computing and identify the key features in its universe of discourse. Additionally, we review the Cloud computing delivery options and their details.

9.1.1 Cloud Computing and Its Key Features

Cloud Computing, as an enabling model, is the most evolved form of deployment infrastructure. The term "Cloud," in its current sense, was first used by the CEO of Google (in 2006), Eric Schmidt. He described Cloud as a business model that allows companies to provide a wide range of services to their clients through the Internet [97]. The National Institute of Standards and Technology (NIST) defines Cloud computing as "cloud computing is a model for enabling ubiquitous, convenient, on-demand network access to a shared pool of configurable computing resources (e.g., networks, servers, storage, applications, and services) that can be rapidly provisioned and released with minimal management effort or service provider interaction" [21].

In the majority of Cloud offerings, two parties are involved. The CSP, who owns a shared pool of configurable computing resources, and the Cloud Service Consumer (CSC), who benefits from the shared computing and storage services and, in exchange, pays a pay-as-you-go service fee.

To be configurable, this physical shared pool of resources should be transformed into virtual resources. CSPs use Hypervisors to achieve this transformation [49]. Hypervisors take control of hardware resources and virtualize them and uniform these virtualized resources in a shared pool of resources, in which resources are shared among CSCs. Advancements in virtualization, as the key technology behind Cloud computing [96], provided a higher utilization ratio for hardware by breaking the physical limitation of allocating a hardware unit to a single user.

In a virtualized environment, the same hardware is shared among multiple users, making it more utilized, resulting in a more appealing financial feasibility. In spite of this high utilization, CSPs afford to offer their resources at a lower price and make it more appealing for CSCs. In addition to lower prices, CSPs offer a pay-as-you-go model to CSCs that makes Cloud computing an unbeatable alternative to on-premises deployments. Here are the key features of a public Cloud offering [75,79].

On-demand self-service: Registration and provisioning of the account as well as administration of Cloud resources happens through an interface (usually a Web-based portal that is known as Cloud Management Dashboard) and is based on the user demand. Additionally, almost all changes are applied either real-time or near-real-time.

Ubiquitous and broad network access: It is possible for CSCs to access Cloud resources via various networks such as VPNs and IPsec tunnels. Additionally, CSCs can use a variety of platforms (Personal Computer, Mobile devices, tablets) to access and control Cloud resources.

Resource pooling: For the CSPs, all virtualized resources, irrespective of their bare-metal origin, become a large pool of virtualized resources, and CSCs can choose their preferred subset of resources from this pool.

Elasticity: Resources on the cloud, based on their virtualized nature, can be configured to support Intelligent Workload Management. That is, resource can expand or shrink based on the resource requirements, hence, the term elasticity.

Just-in-time (JIT): Most operations on the Cloud, except for rare cases such as recovering data from cold backup options, are instantaneous. This feature has significantly contributed to the popularity of Cloud computing platforms among developers and early adopters.

Templating: Following the Object-Oriented (OO) paradigm, many settings on the Cloud can be converted to templates. A template is like an OO Class from which many new objects can be instantiated. An example of use of templating is to create a master server image and instantiate many new virtual servers from that image.

Serverless: As a new execution model, Serverless feature allows the execution of code based on a trigger, where resources are only allocated at the time of execution. In other words, if the application is sitting on a server and is executed only ten times a day, and each time for 100 seconds, all a CSC has to pay is 1,000 seconds of server usage (as opposed to the traditional server-based model that CSP had to pay for the entire time of the server 24×7×365 whether the application was running or not).

Anything-as-a-Service (XaaS): XaaS defines a service offering model in which the CSPs package various platforms and offer it to the CSCs as a service. An example of XaaS is when a CSP decides to host a database on their infrastructure and allocate an instance of that service to a CSP and charge them per hour or per query. The benefit for the CSPs in this case is that they are not responsible for the installation, configuration, or troubleshooting the database instance. In other words, IT support is outsourced to the CSPs.

9.1.2 Cloud Computing Delivery Options

To group the services and create seamless offerings, CSPs categorize their service delivery under three major categories [51] as follows.

1. **Infrastructure-as-a-Service (IaaS):** This is the most advanced level of offering. In this model, the CSP shares all its raw resources to the CSC and the CSC is responsible for deploying Virtual Machine (VM), network and security settings for the created VMs. Obviously, this model requires the CSC to be tech-savvy and aware of all Cloud offerings.
2. **Platform as a Service (PaaS):** In this service model, the CSP provides their customers with a computation platform (usually in the form of a VM) and a set of preinstalled software, application, and development packages. The CSC can choose to develop, test, and deploy any type of application they wish and enjoy Cloud features such as scalability and elasticity.
3. **Software as a Service (SaaS):** In this service model, the entire infrastructure, platform, and running environment are managed by the CSP. In this model, the CSCs are using thin clients (mainly web browsers) to interact with the provided software or application.

It is important to mention that the complexity of service delivery reduces as we move from IaaS to PaaS and to SaaS.

The majority of online distributed systems are deployed on well-known Cloud providers, such as Amazon Web Services (AWS), Microsoft Azure, Google Cloud, and IBM Cloud. These providers use traditional reliability solutions, such as logging and three-way replication [34]. Nevertheless, traditional reliability systems were designed for far less complex information systems and assumed that only a few components require monitoring and only a few components would fail. These assumptions no longer hold, and the scale of the monitoring solutions for Cloud systems has to change [34].

9.1.3 Our Contributions

The work in this chapter capitalizes on our existing work [71–74] in this area and expands it. As our *main contribution*, among the reviewed challenges, we choose two critical challenges that, to the best of our knowledge, do not have trivial solutions. We select these challenges as we believe in a significant impact on the Cloud computing adoption rate.

For decades, information systems have been used to collect and store important client data. The authenticity and provenance of such data are of paramount importance [31,41]. In the past, when the data resided in the private data warehouses, we needed to worry mainly about the integrity of the internal IT personnel. Now, when such data migrate to the Cloud, the number of people and organizations that may access these data increases, which increases the risk of tampering with the data or unauthorized access to the information.

These challenges were combatted by creating logging infrastructure that recorded access to the data events at various levels and locations (e.g., at the operating system or database levels). However, one could tamper with such logs, e.g., by erasing the recorded events. This becomes even more pronounced in the Cloud era, as the CSCs do not know who has access to the systems on which their information is stored. While the CSPs strive to limit access to the client's information, one cannot guarantee that unauthorized access will not happen.

Moreover, the software products these days require continuous access to the data stored in persistent storage on the Cloud, meaning that the Cloud infrastructure should have high availability (HA). CSCs rely on the CSPs to ensure this continuous access and availability. The level of availability is typically governed by the signed Service-Level Agreement (SLA) between CSC and CSP. In the case of an SLA breach, the penalties may be severe. In such a case, CSP personnel may be tempted to tamper with the log records to deflect the blame. Log tampering can happen by adding, removing, or manipulating a part of a log or the entire logs. We argue that while the existing tamper detection solutions can be used to detect any changes in the logs, the critical nature of logs calls for tamperproof and immutable log-storage solutions.

Clients need continuous access to data and services that they store and implement in the Cloud. Thus, the Cloud infrastructure should be highly available, and therefore, the CSPs must continuously monitor their infrastructure to detect problems before a client notices them. Large-scale Cloud platforms can include millions of virtual and physical resources where each resource is continuously generating logs. For all parties involved in a Cloud setting, logs magnify technical issues and, if analyzed carefully and in a timely manner, can be used to detect issues and prevent potential outages and degradation of service. In other words, logs are worthless if they are not assessed and analyzed promptly. Large-scale Cloud infrastructure generates high *volume* and high *velocity* of data. Logs may contain critical information about the operations of each component and therefore have high *value*. Although the majority of logs are textual data, there are many different types of logs. In other words, logs have high variance and *variety*. Evidently, we argue that the scale of Cloud-generated logs falls into the Big Data scale [62,73].

Thus, we have two interrelated challenges: Preserve the authenticity of the logs (either to maintain the audit trail for client data access or to prevent tampering with the logs capturing CSP infrastructure behavior) while being able to cope with the large volume and velocity of these logs, and use these logs to detect issues with the Cloud platform in near-real-time to ensure the HA of the Cloud services for the clients.

To address the first challenge, we propose a platform on top of existing blockchain platforms, to store logs or their signatures in the immutable blocks of a blockchain. Additionally, we propose an alteration for blockchain architecture so that the modified architecture can support a hierarchical structure. This alteration enables us to address the volume and velocity problem. This blockchain of blockchains addresses the scalability issues of the mainstream blockchains, allowing the creation of a tamper-proof log-storage solution for large-scale Cloud platforms.

To tackle the second challenge, we build a prototype of a system, which extracts knowledge from the stream of Cloud logs, and use machine learning to analyze these logs in near-real-time. The proposed prototype leverages microservice architecture in conjunction with the

Publish-Subscribe architectural pattern to create a scalable log collection and analysis funnel. The platform is deployed on the IBM Cloud service infrastructure and is used to detect anomalies in logs emitted by the IBM Cloud services, hence the dogfooding. The prototype efficiency is promising as it takes around 17 seconds or less from the point of receiving a new log record to emitting an alert to the IBM Cloud DevOps team. Based on the DevOps team feedback, this time interval is considered as near-real-time by them.

While the proposed solution is applied to challenges related to Cloud generated logs, we believe that the proposed platform can be applied to scenarios where collected data and its authenticity are of paramount importance. For instance, secure data storage and data retrieval are among key features that are needed for Knowledge Management Systems (KMS) [30].

The rest of the paper is structured as follows. Section 9.2.2 provides details on main challenges of Cloud monitoring and groups these challenges for better comprehension. Section 9.2.1 offers additional details specific to Cloud-generated logs and a few challenges associated with them. Section 9.3 provides a sample of resolved issues followed by technical details about our contribution to the solution domain. Among reviewed challenges, we choose authenticity and reliability of Cloud-generated logs as the first challenge to address and include technical details of our proposed solution in Section 9.3.2. For the second challenge, we choose the monitoring of large-scale Cloud infrastructure and propose a Cloud-based solution that can be used to address large-scale monitoring challenges. We include the technical details of the proposed solution in Section 9.3.3. Section 9.4 concludes the chapter by providing a summary of the proposed solutions.

9.2 Challenges

We have dedicated this section to the details related to the interrelated challenges we have selected to tackle. Section 9.2.1 provides details related to Cloud-generated logs, the importance of log's authenticity, and its role in bringing trust among Cloud participants. Section 9.2.2 describes challenges related to monitoring of large-scale Cloud infrastructure and various factors that make the Cloud monitoring a not-trivial activity.

9.2.1 Cloud-Generated Logs, Their Importance, and Challenges

During the normal operation of a Cloud platform, although many logs are being collected and stored, no one pays attention to collected logs except the technical operation department, which may check these logs periodically. The continuous monitoring of all resources on the Cloud is an effort by the CSP to ensure that the current performance of the Cloud platform and the Quality of Service (QoS) that is provided to CSC match the ones that are promised to them in the signed SLA. When a technical issue arises, or a Cloud service delivery is interrupted, the collected logs become the most important source of the troubleshooting and tracing efforts by the technical operations department.

Depending on the scope of the technical issue, some or many of the departments of the CSP will get involved to analyze the logs and to draw conclusions on important matters such as what has happened, how it has happened, and who is responsible for the incident. Cloud service delivery interruptions or outages can directly impact a CSC; in many cases, the CSC will be one of the parties that become interested in reviewing and assessing the logs. Logs contain very sensitive information and details about offered services. For example, operational logs indicate how and at what capacity a system has been operating, and network logs include all incoming and outgoing packets of a deployed solution on the Cloud platform. These logs hold the truth about the delivered QoS and can be used as legal evidence in the court of law [82]. Logs are generated and collected by various monitoring solutions that a CSP has deployed on the Cloud infrastructure. In fact, full access to all resources (e.g., bare-metal servers, networking components, Cloud management platforms, virtualization tools) is required to deploy holistic monitoring solutions [67], and such access is only available to the CSP.

While the full control over monitoring systems and generated logs allows a CSP to monitor and maintain Cloud services efficiently, it gives them a controversial power over evidential resources that are significantly important to CSCs. That is, logs are generated and stored on a platform that is built, managed, and owned by the CSP. Hence, CSPs have read, write, and modify permissions on all collected logs. The majority of CSPs provide a monitoring dashboard to their CSCs. These dashboards are used by CSCs to view, analyze, and export logs that may seem useful for generating reports or other technical tasks. While using these tools, the CSCs have to trust that the information provided to CSP is genuine and has full integrity, in other words, has not been tampered. Ironically, almost in all cases, the CSCs have no option to test and verify the integrity of the logs that are provided to them. Without an option to verify the integrity of the provided logs, CSCs are in a very weak position at the times of QoS disputes. Such disadvantage causes many trust-related issues. CSPs offer their service to CSCs at a predefined rate and with a predefined set of QoS characteristics. All such characteristics and their acceptable values will be defined in an SLA that legally binds the two parties. Any deviation from the SLA considered a breach of agreement and is subject to a legal action. In addition to QoS characteristics, the responsibility domain of CSPs and CSCs, with respect to any of the three offerings, which were reviewed above, is included in the SLA. Figure 9.1 depicts the CSP and CSC responsibilities related to each service offering. The complex nature of the Cloud landscape calls for exhaustive and comprehensive SLAs [68]. In fact, the continuous monitoring of all resources on the Cloud is an effort by the CSP to ensure that the current performance of the Cloud platform and the QoS that is provided to CSC match the ones that are promised to them in the signed SLA. Here, we list the most important challenges of Cloud monitoring and their details.

9.2.1.1 Ensuring the Authenticity, Reliability, and Usability of Collected Logs

Another major challenge related to Cloud monitoring is that for the collected logs, to be valuable and admissible as digital evidence, their authenticity and reliability have to be guaranteed. Unfortunately, logs and other forms of digital evidence can be easily tampered. To overcome this challenge, many have recommended the use of a Log Management System (LMS) [59,76]. The majority of LMSs promise a set of desirable features, such as tamper resistance, verifiability, confidentiality, and privacy [76]. Interestingly, the authors indicate that while encryption is required to preserve the collected logs, it will cause many search issues. For instance, relying on traditional search techniques would require complete decryption for all the records at the time of the search. Such a requirement by itself creates room for potential unauthorized access. The authors present a design for a log encryption system that allows a designated trusted party, known as audit escrow agent, to construct search capabilities and allow an investigator to decrypt entries matching a keyword. Similarly, Ko and Will [54] acknowledge the complexity and difficulty of preserving data and logs on the Cloud and suggest the use of an internal process to access the data forcing such limitation in all internal system calls. The authors explore additional options, such as the use of signatures, hash creation for records, or hash chaining, but at the end argue that such methods

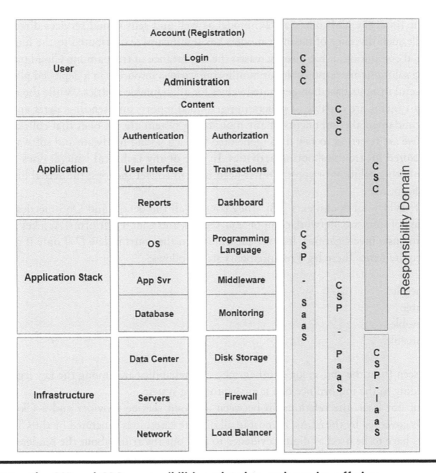

Figure 9.1 **The CSP and CSC responsibilities related to each service offering.**

can cause significant performance issues. In recent years, many verification-as-a-service platforms offer integrity control for the data that are uploaded by the user, but they do need a trusted third party (TTP). For example, arXiv [5] provides a repository for electronic documents and ensures their integrity.

9.2.1.2 Trust Among Cloud Participants

As was indicated at the beginning of this chapter, while building in-house monitoring platforms provides full control over the monitoring systems to the CSPs, it puts them in a very powerful and autocratic position compared to the CSCs. This is because the accuracy of the provided data cannot be assessed by the CSCs as the full control is in the hands of the CSP [84]. The issue becomes more critical when generated metrics and their values are used as the basis for invoice generation. Similarly, if the CSC is complaining about a breach of the SLA, the issue of genuineness of logs becomes a critical matter and can damage the trust between these two parties. In a Cloud computing environment, many different types of suppliers and users exist.

The CSPs (such as Amazon, IBM, Microsoft, and Google) are conglomerates that provide the actual Cloud environment. In the B2B model, the CSCs (such as Netflix [20] and Dropbox [9]) use the services provided by the CSPs to repackage or offer on-demand services to their clients.

At the same time, the CSP offers a B2C model as well and sells Cloud services directly to end users. While such diversity of business models has significantly contributed to the financial success of Cloud computing, it has also increased the importance of trust among Cloud participants. Monitoring solutions are responsible for monitoring various resources in a deployed platform and generate useful insights based on generated values for all definable metrics. While the majority of monitoring systems are capable of generating graphical reports and sending alerts and notifications, the fundamental components of any monitoring system are the ones that collect and store logs. Here we are referring to raw data (generated by each Cloud hardware and software component) and stored for troubleshooting activities. In case of any technical issue, it does not matter which monitoring solution or approach has been used to collect the logs; the actual logs play the most significant role.

Logs are evidential documents [28]. They contain all the details and QoS metrics related to the operation of software, network components, servers, and Cloud platforms. As a key element in computer forensic investigations, logs are presentable in the court of law [77] only if they satisfy the legal requirement. These legal requirements are as follows:

1. Authentic
2. Reliable
3. Believable
4. Admissible

As can be seen from the above, log's authenticity and reliability are among the key legal requirements, yielding to the importance of a tamper-proof log system.

Last but not least, the relationship between a Cloud service provider and a Cloud service consumer is governed by the SLAs. Almost in all dispute cases, logs generated by the Cloud monitoring tools have to be used as digital evidence to find out the truth about the rendered services. Hence, Cloud service providers have additional legal obligations to accurately collect logs and safely store them for both operational and legal use.

9.2.1.3 Log Tampering Prevention/Detection Challenges

Digital forgery and tampering of digital artifacts and files long existed. Many solutions have been proposed to detect or prevent such undesired activities. Since the majority of logs are stored in files, it is vital to explore solutions that are offered for file tamper detection or prevention. Various file verification techniques exist to ensure that the file at hand is not tampered. More than five decades ago, Peterson et al. described the use of cyclic codes to verify that a given array of bits is original or a change has happened [69]. Based on similar principles of cyclic codes, checksum has been widely known and used [38,86]. In particular, checksums are used by many file systems to validate the integrity of files and their related operations, such as copy and move. Checksums are generated by using a checksum function that takes a block of digital data of arbitrary size and in return generates a fixed-size value. The primary issue related to checksumming data is that generating and verifying checksum values will slow down the I/O process [86], a process that is already known to be the slowest among all other processes in a computer [85].

One of the modern favorite hashing techniques is a family of SHA [43], which is used as a means to verify content, authorship, or a property of a digital artifact. As an example, the source code management system git [11] generates a SHA-1 [43] signature for a commit and uses it to trace the commit throughout the entire life cycle of the source code [35]. In this solution, SHA-1 is mainly used for traceability and points out to the person who committed the code and is not used as a means for tamper detection. In recent years, many verification-as-a-service platforms offer integrity control for the data that is uploaded by the user. Verification-or-integrity-as-a-service solutions, such as arXiv [5], provide a repository of electronic documents and ensure their integrity. Similarly, DIaaS uses the service-oriented architecture to release the burdens of data integrity management from users. In the suggested solution, an independent Information Management System (IMS) is in charge of collecting and storing data with a minimal impact on the performance of data storage [66]. As for Cloud solutions, theoretically, many of the mentioned solutions are applicable.

However, the complexity of Cloud environment (in particular, auto-scaling, redundant systems, and load balancers) and the scale of generated logs bring more challenges for the storage, access, and verification of the logs. Sharma [83] points out the complexity of mega-scale Cloud environment and suggests incorporation of various cryptographic algorithms and digital signature to achieve high integrity for storing critical information in the Cloud. Liu et al. [56] focus on the data storage integrity verification for Big Data in the areas of Cloud and IoT, stating that data integrity is critical for any computation-related system. Bharath and Rajashree [33] suggest the use of a mediator that verifies the integrity of the data and sends the integrity report to the users. However, this solution still requires trust in a third party or central authority. The main drawback of these services is that one must trust the central authority that is offering the service. The problem of trusting a third party can be alleviated by a self-contained solution that does not rely on a TTP integrity verification service.

9.2.2 *Cloud Monitoring Challenges*

With many organizations choosing to move from their traditional infrastructure to Cloud, the reliability of services offered by the CSP becomes an important topic. The CSPs need to implement and maintain complex hardware, software, and network infrastructure. The CSPs design and implement this complex platform in several data centers full of homogeneous bare-metal servers equipped with hypervisors that take control of hardware resources, virtualize them, and share them in a configurable pool of resources. These servers and their virtual machines are connected via physical and Software-Defined Networks (SDNs).

To achieve HA, for every critical component, several redundant pairs are considered (e.g., UPSs, routers, switches, firewalls, storage components, and bare-metal servers). Needless to say, the CSPs require advanced monitoring tools that capture several metrics for every deployed component on the Cloud infrastructure. Metrics are collected at predefined intervals and are stored as logs. Logs are among the most important pieces of analytical data in Cloud-based services [59]. Cloud Operational Logs (COLs) are generated during the operation of Cloud platforms and are kept for future analysis. COLs consist of hardware, infrastructure, network, virtualized and application logs. Cloud monitoring tools are responsible to collect and store COLs. Here, we list the most important challenges of Cloud monitoring and their details. Throughout this section, we will be using the term **component** that describes hardware or software component of a Cloud platform, solution, or system. Note that the types of components are numerous and can range from bare-metal computers and network switches, to VMs and containers, to database systems, middleware servers, and front-ends. Moreover, the components may be offered via different service models (e.g., IaaS, PaaS, or SaaS) and vendors (e.g., Amazon, Google, IBM, or Microsoft). While each of these components may have its own unique set of health-related attributes and health states (as well as associated health criteria) [39], the general issues discussed below are applicable to all of them.

9.2.2.1 Monitoring Large-Scale Cloud Infrastructure

It is a common practice for CSPs to design, deploy, and utilize several data centers around the world. These data centers are, intentionally, geographically distributed to be able to serve a wide range of CSCs around the globe. Additionally, the distributed architecture provides the infrastructure needed for HA and efficient content delivery. It is not uncommon for a large data center to have more than 100,000 components, such as servers, network equipment, and storage platforms. And it is not uncommon for each of those components to generate several logs at various time intervals (every second, every minute, etc.). For example, companies such as Netflix deploy large and scalable solutions on the Cloud, and the metrics that need to be monitored can quickly produce more than 10 billion records a day [32], making the data set large enough to be classified as Big Data [62,64].

The high volume of generated logs makes the storage and process of the collected data computationally expensive [62]. The enormous speed at which logs are generated and collected resembles the *Velocity* characteristic of the Big Data. Obviously, the required space to store the collected logs, even in textual format, can quickly evolve to a large space. To put the required volume to store these logs in context, Lemoudden et al. [55] denote that if a service provider has around 5,000 servers, 2,000 routers and switches, 600 security devices (firewalls, VPNs), and around 50,000 desktops, the company generates about 100,000 messages per second. These generated logs translate to 100 GB per hour or about 2.35 TB per day [55]. This volume matches the *Volume* characteristic of the Big Data. The importance of careful collection and storage of logs is due to the fact that they are an effective source of critical information about the operation of each component and the overall quality of the rendered service [98]. The significance of the collected logs matches the *Value* characteristic of the Big Data. Last but not least, although majority of logs are considered as textual data, there are many different types of logs. For example, hardware logs and application logs reflect very different type of logs. The diversity in types of collected logs matches the *Variety* characteristic of the Big Data.

Evidently, we argue that the scale of Cloud-generated logs falls into Big Data scale [62,64]. Hence, monitoring large-scale Cloud infrastructure is one of the major challenges of Cloud monitoring [95].

9.2.2.2 Unique Cloud Characteristics

In addition to the scale of Cloud infrastructure, unique characteristics of Cloud platforms cause various monitoring challenges. The CSPs use Cloud orchestration tools to automate the allocation of resources and their placement, fault management, and storage management [57]. Many monitoring tools need to be aware of the existence of a resource before they can provide a monitoring service for it. Hence, conventional monitoring tools cannot be used in an environment that offers dynamic resource allocation [95] empowered by Cloud orchestration tools.

These challenges are not limited to hardware resources such as CPU and RAM, and the dynamic nature of Cloud networks also causes difficulties for the network monitoring tools [70]. In addition to these challenges, it is important to mention that traditional monitoring tools cannot provide a seamless monitoring solution for the Cloud due to unique Cloud characteristics, such as elasticity, automatic scaling, and dynamic resource management. As a result, CSPs may adopt more than one monitoring system, which by itself brings additional challenges, such as missing on an end-to-end view of operational logs or having to deal with various log formats.

9.2.2.3 Layered Architecture

Cloud platforms consist of several hierarchical layers [90]. The layer at the bottom is the hardware level and consists of data center components. Many software-defined layers are implemented on top of this layer [50]. A common challenge for CSPs is to trace an issue and find out the layer (and a component specific to that layer) that is the root cause of a given problem. Addressing this challenge requires extensive traceability and a holistic view of how layers are interrelated. Interestingly, this layered architecture opens the door for many log tampering opportunities as the logs at each layer are only accessible to the technical team responsible for that layer. The layered architecture adds to the complexity of the Cloud monitoring and makes it more challenging [83].

9.2.2.4 Access Requirement

Another important challenge for Cloud monitoring is that a complete monitoring system requires complete access to the entire Cloud infrastructure and only CSPs have such level of access. As a result, almost all Cloud monitoring solutions are implemented by the CSPs. While this is beneficial to the CSPs, it leaves the CSCs with no options to validate the accuracy of provided monitoring details and logs.

9.2.2.5 Billing and Monitoring Bound

Cloud monitoring tools are mainly implemented by the CSPs, which makes the trustworthiness of the monitoring data questionable [67]. Amazon CloudWatch [1], Google Stackdriver Monitoring [25] are examples of such monitoring systems. The CSPs use Cloud monitoring tools for two important reasons. Firstly, to monitor the status of all deployed components; and secondly, to feed the required details for Cloud charge-back system that converts resource usages into billable items. While the former is often used internally and within the jurisdiction of the Cloud provider, the latter has a significant impact on the customer. Hence, it is critical that the CSCs are aware of the collected metrics, their values, and how they are used to construct their payable invoices.

9.2.2.6 Diverse Service Delivery Options

The existence of various Cloud service deliveries, namely IaaS, PaaS, and SaaS, adds up the complexity of Cloud monitoring requirement. IaaS as the most comprehensive form of delivery requires the most advanced monitoring systems that can cover all the deployed components in an IaaS offering. As for the PaaS, the CSCs have control over one or more VMs and only require access to operating system logs. In contrast, in SaaS, the CSCs only use the software that are provided to them as a service and therefore need very limited monitoring resources. Another challenge for Cloud monitoring tools is to offer different monitoring options to CSCs, based on different delivery types [39].

9.2.2.7 XaaS and Its Complex Monitoring Requirement

To remain competitive, CSPs continuously add new services to their product catalogue. These services are hosted by the CSP and used by the CSCs with minimal IT efforts. In other words, the implementation, monitoring, and the maintenance of these services are managed by CSPs. Needless to say, CSPs need to monitor the state of the offered system continuously to make sure

CSPs' QoS expectations are met. Additionally, as CSPs do not have any type of access to the underlying architecture of the offered service, they need to have a dashboard that allows them to monitor their usage and associated metrics related to their application.

9.2.2.8 Establishing High-Availability Failover Strategies

Defining failover and HA for large distributed systems is a nontrivial task, as the systems generally consist of several clusters, database systems, availability zones, complex networks, and a combination of monolith and microservice architectures. Implementing HA policies and strategies requires extensive monitoring of resources. Monitoring solutions that will be used in HA architecture need to provide a holistic health state of the main site as well as all the backup sites that will be used for failovers. Such a broad coverage tremendously increases the number of elements that a monitoring solution should cover.

While the implemented monitoring solution should handle the collection of such massive number of metrics and elements in real time, it should also remain as responsive as possible, so that the HA components can make decisions based on the latest and the most accurate state of each element. Finding a balance between the minimum number of elements that need to be monitored and the performance of monitoring system requires further research.

Failovers are computationally and commercially expensive and should be only used when necessary. Therefore, deciding whether to failover or keep using the same resources becomes an important topic that requires further exploration. Once it is determined that a failover is required, selecting a failover strategy becomes critical. In the simplest case, we can failover the whole system, say, by redirecting traffic to a different instance of the system residing in a different geographical zone. However, this may dramatically increase load on the instance to which we redirected traffic, causing its performance to degrade (and potentially an outage due to overload).

Probabilistically, rarely all components of a large system will malfunction simultaneously. Thus, potentially one can often failover just a portion of the system rather than the whole system (which may be faster and less expensive than failing over the whole system). Therefore, selecting the portion of the platform that requires failover becomes the most important task. It will be critical to understand what has gone wrong and which components are affected, so a logical failover plan is developed and executed. To the best of our knowledge, no general framework to address this task exists at the time of writing.

When it comes to designing and implementing HA for services (for both monolith and microservice architecture), a major challenge arises if the transactions are distributed among multiple nodes. If one node fails, a usual failover approach may bring back the service, but the state of the transaction may become unknown and/or the data related to that transaction may become inconsistent. A primary goal for failover practices is to retrieve the service as soon as possible, and at times, this may favor service over data consistency. For example, consider a VM that hosts a service that relies on in-memory database. If this service experiences a deadlock situation, restarting the VM would bring back the service at the cost of losing the data and state, which were saved in memory.

The monolith architecture has a somewhat relaxed approach toward the number of business tasks that are handled by each service. It is very common to see a server-side monolithic component that handles all the business tasks and has internal logic to ensure atomicity of processed tasks. In contrast, in the case of microservices, ideally, we would like to keep transaction limited to a particular microservice, which makes failover and transaction rollback straightforward. However, architecturally it is not always possible. In such a case, a potential solution would be to create a monitoring service that satisfies Atomicity, Consistency, Isolation, Durability (ACID) principles and will not allow failovers that would result in data inconsistency. Following a series of predefined rules, in case of a microservice failure, the monitoring system will make a logical decision about failing over one, a group, or all of the microservices based on transactional boundaries.

In addition to the above challenges, each component of the system has a different degree of importance in regard to HA and failover policies. For example, if a VM running a service fails, an acceptable failover policy would be to launch a new VM on another server using the same image. The same logic applies to bare-metal servers. A faulty bare-metal server can be easily replaced by another bare-metal server, or in some cases a VM, in a different server farm. In contrast, when the main load balancer is down, or if the default gateway of a cluster is down, irrespective of the state of each individual component, the failover policy can no longer use the same resources in the cluster as none of them are accessible.

Another potential solution is to use application-specific HA structure. The architects of the application create a tiered structure of components. Then, a set of failover polices will be defined for each tier. At the time of failure, the monitoring application will identify the tier and take necessary actions that are defined within the application-specific HA rules. By adding a context-aware, software-defined monitoring solution, we can define a smart failover plan that:

(a) considers the device and its tier before calling a failover action, (b) can decide whether to failover the entire application or just one microservice, and (c) can prevent data loss in case of failure of a microservice (by applying ACID-like features to the monitoring system, as discussed above).

Finally, changes to the software may cause regression of functionality. Twitter experienced a major outage due to such an event on January 19, 2016 [91]. If the breaking software change has been delivered to both primary and failover systems, then failover will not help and the only remaining course of action is to roll back the change and restart the system. Thus, one should be careful about how the code changes are being rolled out to production systems. Ideally, rollback can be integrated into the HA strategies. However, it is unclear if this can be automated for any type of regression-inducing change. For example, changes to source code of a script can be rolled back automatically with ease. However, changes to a data schema and the data itself may require manual intervention.

9.3 Solutions

In this section, we provide a few examples of solved challenges related to Cloud monitoring and then provide details on two solutions we offer for two major challenges mentioned above.

The importance of authenticity, reliability, and usability of Cloud-generated logs was discussed in Sections 9.2.1.1 and 9.2.1.2. The CSPs and CSCs disputes can be easily addressed by referring to authentic and reliable logs. Given the vital role of logs in Cloud computing, we choose this challenge as the *first* challenge to tackle. We believe this challenge has a significant impact on the growth of Cloud computing, and if resolved, it significantly increases the desirable trust among Cloud participants and reduces the barriers of Cloud adaptability.

Additionally, as reviewed in Section 9.2.2.1, the generated logs using various Cloud monitoring tools in large-scale Cloud deployment (such as public Cloud providers) exhibit Big Data characteristics and should be addressed by Big Data solutions. We argue that the entire process of log collection and storage is wasted if logs are not analyzed in real-time or near-real-time. The operational value of logs declines as the delay in log analysis increases. Therefore, CSPs must analyze collected logs as soon as humanely possible. Our solution to challenge uses Cloud tools and artificial intelligence to review and detect problems and anomalies in near-real-time (around 17 seconds after logs are generated). This solution leverages resources of the Cloud platform that it monitors, hence the *dogfooding*.

9.3.1 Examples of Solved Challenges

Challenges discussed in Section 9.2 have been tackled by researchers. As the Cloud offerings have to scale elastically [95], efforts have been made to build monitoring tools using multitier and peer-to-peer architecture, making the tools more resilient to elasticity than conventional monitoring systems [95].

The massive scale of resources on the Cloud and the number of metrics that needs to be monitored can easily exceed billions of records per day [32]. To preserve space required to store logs, Anwar et al. suggest to avoid storing repetitive values, leading to reduction of the size of stored data by up to 80% [32].

Topology and scale of Cloud networks can change dynamically [70]. Traditional network monitoring tools do not support the dynamic nature of Cloud networks. Pongpaibool et al. [70] built fault-tolerance monitoring system based on clustered architecture, improving performance of monitoring applications for Cloud networks.

Cloud computing is delivered through various enabling services of IaaS, PaaS, and SaaS; each of these delivery methods has a different monitoring requirement. Rodrigues et al. [39] focused on these requirements, acknowledging the need for complex monitoring systems to process complicated monitoring scenarios. They also presented an overview of the Cloud monitoring concepts, structure, and solutions.

Implementation of a complete monitoring system requires full access to the components that will be monitored [67]. Nguyen et al. [67] indicated that only Cloud providers have such level of access to Cloud resources. Therefore, most of the Cloud monitoring solutions are built by Cloud providers. In contrast, Cloud consumers require full details of monitoring data and need a way to verify the monitoring details that are provided by the Cloud provider. To address this issue, Nguyen et al. [67] combined role-based monitoring templates with agent-based monitoring and used event processing engine to refine the collected data and to provide a trustworthy and holistic monitoring solution. Cloud platforms consist of large number of hardware and software components [34,62], generating large volume of logs and metrics data that exceeds the level that a human can interpret [34,63]. To address this challenge,

Bhattacharyya et al. [34] built metrics anomaly detection system (based on recurrent neural networks) successfully detecting up to 98.3% of anomalies.

To summarize, for the first challenge, most existing solutions promote the use of a TTP. Those solutions that suggest the use of blockchain have scalability and performance issues. These solutions suggest partial storage of logs (such as hashes of the logs or the essential log records, e.g., the audit ones). However, given the importance of logs, partial storage of logs may not be good practice for the CSPs. We propose a solution in Section 9.3.2 that focuses on solving blockchain's scalability challenges and allows the full storage of logs in blockchain as an immutable storage option.

Moreover, while the issues related to monitoring large-scale platforms have been tackled, we could not find an end-to-end solution that is both scalable and analyzes the logs in near-real-time. Our proposed solution in Section 9.3.3 is designed and implemented to be scalable (has been able to process up to 120 requests per minute) and analyzes the data in near-real-time (reporting the results of the analysis in ≤ 17 seconds).

9.3.2 Proposed Solution for Authenticity, Reliability, and Usability of Cloud-Generated Logs: LCaaS

As it was indicated in Section 9.2.1.2, the CSPs use continues monitoring to ensure that the current QoS provided to the CSCs matches with the ones in the signed SLA. When a technical issue arises, the CSC will be one of the parties that becomes interested in reviewing and assessing the logs, because logs hold the truth about the delivered QoS and can be used as legal evidence in a court of law [82]. As the Cloud monitoring tools are implemented by the Cloud provider, there are some tamper-motivation scenarios that can be considered.

Here, we define tamper motivation as the desire of one or more of the parties involved in a platform, infrastructure, or Cloud solution to access critical logs and to tamper the logs by adding, removing, or manipulating a part or the entire log. Given the number of logs that are generated by the Cloud monitoring solutions, there are many tampering possibilities. While tamper detection solutions can be used to detect any changes in the logs [80,88], we argue that due to the critical nature of logs, tamper detection is not good enough; one should consider a storage option that offers immutability for all critical logs.

Log tampering may affect CSCs financially and technically. If a CSP tampers the logs related to resource usage and charges the customer with a higher amount or if a CSP hides the breach of one or more criteria of an SLA, the CSC is in immediate need of finding a method or a tool to verify the integrity of provided data by the CSP.

Given the existence of many tamper motivations on the Cloud platforms, the cost of log tampering for the CSCs, and the inadequacy of existing monitoring solutions, we come to the conclusion that an immutable log system that is capable of storing the logs and verifying their integrity can be genuinely beneficial for the CSCs and can be used to establish trust among Cloud participants.

The problem of log tempering can be resolved if a temper-proof storage is employed to store Cloud-generated logs. Given its immutability and distributed nature, **blockchain** offers a solid foundation for log storage. Additionally, a correctly implemented distributed blockchain is an adequate alternative to current practices of using TTPs [58,92,100].

9.3.2.1 Blockchain as a Log Storage Option

Blockchain in the simplest form is a distributed database of records. Records are stored in each copy of the database, known as public ledger, and they are append-only. The most famous application of blockchain is providing the infrastructure to the most controversial currency in the world, i.e., Bitcoin. While Bitcoin is tightly coupled with the blockchain, it is important to mention that Bitcoin is only one of the possible applications of blockchain technologies. In 2008, an individual or a group of the researchers under the alias of Satoshi Nakamoto published a paper titled "Bitcoin: A peer-to-peer electronic cash system" [65]. In this paper, the authors describe a system in which financial transactions can be sent from a sender to a recipient without relying on a trusted financial institute such as a bank. Nakamoto argues that a purely peer-to-peer version of electronic cash transaction eliminates the needs of relying on a financial institution. A Payer needs to digitally sign a transaction to prove the authenticity of the transaction, and the receiver has to verify the transaction to prevent the double-spending problem.

A significant component that allows transactions to be immutable is the use of a timestamp method to mark each transaction with a timestamp. A timestamp server takes a hash of a block of items to be timestamped and widely publishes the hash and its timestamp so that every participant gets to know that the items must have existed at the time of the announcement [65]. A significant component of blockchain that allows transactions to be immutable is the use of the Proof of Work (PoW) verification schema. PoW involves running iterations for finding a particular value that when it is hashed in conjunction with other elements of a block, the calculated hash begins with a certain number of zero bits. The number of zeros is proportional to the time required to complete a PoW. The higher the number of zeros, the longer it will take to complete the PoW. Once the computational effort is dedicated and the hash value is found, all items along with the found value, known as *nonce*, are kept in a block. The content of a block cannot be changed unless the whole PoW process is repeated.

Chaining blocks together using hash binding or hash chaining [44,52,81] significantly increases the amount of computational effort that is needed for changing the content of an earlier block. In a hash binding relationship, the current hash of the previous block is used as the previous hash of the current block. This chain makes any attempt to change the blockchain computationally unfeasible as one needs to reprocess PoW for all the blocks in order to tamper with any of the earlier blocks [60].

Current blockchain implementations of the distributed ledgers already have notary proof-of-existence services [92]. For example, Poex.io [24], launched in 2013, verifies the existence of a computer file at a specific time, by storing a timestamp and the SHA-256 [43] of the respective file in a block that eventually will be added to a blockchain. The service is anonymous as the files are not stored or transferred to the provider's servers. Since the digital signature of the file is permanently stored in a decentralized blockchain, the provider can verify the integrity and existence of such a file (at a point of submission to the blockchain) anytime in the future. Characteristics of cryptographic hash function [78] allow a provider to claim, with high certainty, that if the document had not existed at the time when its hash was added to the blockchain, it would have been very difficult to embed its hash in the blockchain after the fact. Additionally, embedding a particular hash and then adopting a future document to match the embedded hash is also almost impossible [78].

Proof-of-existence solutions cannot be used as scalable LMSs, as they consider files individually, with no search function to locate the appropriate file or block. Moreover, Cloud solutions consist of thousands of components, each of which generates a large volume of logs [73]. The current solutions are not designed to handle the scale that is required to store Cloud-generated logs. Furthermore, the current public blockchains can handle a limited number of concurrent transactions [92].

At its very core, blockchain requires a lot of computational resources to operate. For the creation of every block, on average, many iterations of hash generation are repeated until the desired outcome matches the required difficulty target. This requirement makes blockchain an expensive solution for storage of high volume data such as logs. Hence, using blockchain as an LMS, at least without modifications, is neither financially nor technically feasible.

Although blockchain technology has great potential and can be used in many disciplines, it is dealing with a number of challenges. The scalability remains the most critical challenge [99]. Blockchain heavily relies on consensus algorithms, such as PoW, and such algorithms are computationally expensive. To overcome the scalability issues, a novel cryptocurrency scheme is suggested by [37] where old transactions are removed from the blockchain, and a database holds the values of removed transactions. Although this solution reduces the size of the blockchain, it introduces the same trust issue that traditional databases are suffering from.

PoW requires a great deal of computing resources and higher cost for creating each block. To address the cost associated with PoW, King and Nadal [53] provide an alternative approach to

PoW and name it Proof-of-Stake (PoS). They argue that the security of peer-to-peer cryptocurrency solutions (such as Bitcoin) does not have to depend on cost of energy consumption, and one can mine or validate block transactions according to how many coins he or she holds. Compared to PoW, the proposed alternative works faster and cheaper. Confirming the ownership of a coin (or any digital asset) is fast, easy, and secure. Given the higher efficiency of PoS, some public Blockchain platforms such as Ethereum have decided to migrate from PoW to PoS.

In spite of PoW computational requirement, and given the scalability limitations of blockchains, we suggest a minor architectural change to significantly increase blockchain capacity and make it big-data-ready. The goal of this solution is to create a prototype of an immutable log system (called Logchain) using blockchain technology as a means to store and verify the collected Cloud-generated logs. Our prototype constructs a Logchain-as-a-service (LCaaS) that receives logs or their hashes and stores them in an immutable hierarchical ledger; clients can use its API to interact with the solution and send, verify, and retrieve data from this immutable storage. The details of LCaaS are as follows.

9.3.2.2 LCaaS Technical Details

LCaaS is a hierarchical blockchain framework, graphically shown in Figure 9.2. The figure depicts a two-level hierarchy, but the number of levels can be increased if a use case requires it. Current blockchain consensus protocols require every node of the network to process every block of the blockchain, hence a major scalability limitation. We overcome this limitation by segmenting a

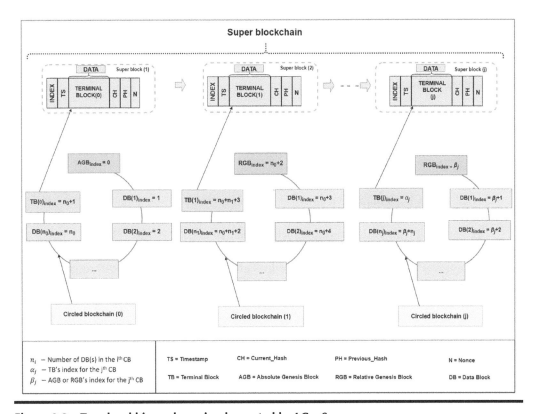

Figure 9.2 Two-level hierarchy as implemented by LCaaS.

portion of a blockchain and locking it down in a block of a higher-level blockchain, i.e., we create a two-level hierarchy of blockchains. Validating the integrity of a high-level block confirms the integrity of all the blocks of the lower-level blockchain and leads to reduction of the number of operations needed to validate the chain.

We have built a prototype application that sits on top of a basic blockchain and converts it to a hierarchical ledger. Our primary goal is to bring scalability to blockchain for the situations in which the number of data items that need to be stored in a blockchain is large (e.g., operational logs of a Cloud platform). At its current state, the prototype supports API-based interactions and log file or their hashes can convert to one or several blocks. Then the prototype will mine the blocks and puts them in a blockchain. Finally, the prototype has the ability to convert the blockchain to circled blockchains and forms a hierarchical ledger.

As mentioned in the legend of Figure 9.2, n_i refers to the number of data blocks in the i-th circled blockchain and α_j is the index of the terminal block of the j-th circled blockchain. β_j is the index for the absolute or relative genesis block of the j-th circled blockchain. The value of α_j will be calculated by

$$\alpha_j \begin{cases} n_0 + 1, & \text{if } j = 0 \\ n_0 + 1 + \sum_{i=1}^{j} (n_i + 2) = n_0 + 1 + 2j + \sum_{i=1}^{j} n_i, & \text{if } j \geq 1 \end{cases} \tag{9.1}$$

and the value of β_j will be calculated by

$$\beta_j = \begin{cases} 0, & \text{if } j = 0 \\ \alpha_{j-1} + 1, & \text{if } j \geq 1 \end{cases} \tag{9.2}$$

Here are the key elements of the LCaaS:

- **Blocks**: are atomic units of storage. Our implementation of blocks is similar to the existing blockchain solutions. A block contains the following variables: nonce, index, timestamp, data, previous _ hash, and current _ hash. nonce is an arbitrary random number that is used to generate[1] a specific current _ hash. index is a unique sequential ID for each block. timestamp indicates the time when the block is created. data is a composite data type and contains information about logs. current _ hash is generated by concatenating all of the above-indicated variables and adding the current _ hash of the previous block, referred to as previous _ hash.

  In other words, the current _ hash of the i-th block becomes the previous _ hash of block $i+1$. One has to iterate through several values of nonce, to generate the current _ hash for a given block that matches the defined difficulty _ target. The target can be set during the initialization of the LCaaS and may be adjusted later, if needed. The difficulty _ target is often defined as the number of zeros that must appear at the beginning of the desired current _ hash; the larger the number of zeros—the longer it will take (on average) to produce current _ hash satisfying the

---

[1] One may use different hashing functions. Currently, the most popular hash function in the blockchain community is SHA-256.

difficulty _ target requirement. Blocks are linked together based on a hash-binding relation. Formally, we show the creation of the current _ hash in Algorithm 1.

- **Blockchains**: blocks that are linked together will result in a blockchain. An i-th block in a blockchain relies on current _ hash of block $i-1$; if data in an earlier block, say, block m is tampered, the link among all the subsequent blocks, $m+1$ to i will be broken and one will have to recompute current _ hash (updating nonce values) of each block from m to i. Mining, as a computationally expensive task, consists of taking the data in the lock, along with its timestamp and previous _ hash and find a nonce that —

Algorithm 1: Generation of Hash and Nonce for a Block. Our Implementation Instantiates Hasher Using SHA-256

Input: block _ index, timestamp, data, previous _ hash
Output: current _ hash, nonce
content = concatenate(index, timestamp, data, previous _ hash);
content = Hasher(content);   // to speedup computing nonce = 0;
repeat
nonce = nonce + 1;
current _ hash = Hasher(concatenate(nonce, content));
until *prefix of current_hash = difficulty_target*;
return current _ hash, nonce;

when put together and hashed—results in a hash that matches the desired difficulty target of a blockchain. The difficulty target is often proposed as the number of required 0s at the beginning of the desired hash. Our implementation of blockchains and mining operations have the same characteristics of any other blockchain.

- **Circled Blockchain (CB)**: is a closed-loop blockchain that has a genesis and a terminal block. The terminal block is the tail of a blockchain and indicates that the blockchain cannot accept any more blocks. The terminal block converts a blockchain to the CB and makes it ready to be submitted to a new Superblock (defined below).

    One needs to specify in advance the maximum number of blocks that can be appended to the CB or the maximum amount of time that CB stays "open" until the terminal block is added to it, whichever comes first. These values would depend on the use case. The goal is to create a CB with a reasonable number of blocks in it (denoted by n_i for the i-th CB). If the frequency of log submission is high—a short window of time is preferred, otherwise, a larger window of time may be beneficial. The maximum amount of time should be fairly short to minimize the risk of tampering the whole CB: say, 24 hours or less.
- **Genesis Blocks (GB)**: is the first block of any blockchain. This block has predefined characteristics. Its previous _ hash and current _ hash are set to zero (as there are no prior blocks), and it has a null data element. Its primary purpose is to indicate the start of a new blockchain. We extended the genesis block definition, creating two different types of genesis blocks.
- **Absolute Genesis Block (AGB)**: is placed as the first block of the first blockchain. An AGB has the same characteristics as GB, with previous _ hash and current _ hash set to zero and data element set to null.

Relative Genesis Block (RGB) is placed at the beginning of every subsequent CB after the first CB. RGB `current _ hash` and `previous _ hash` are set to the `current _ hash` of the terminal block of the previous Superblock.

■ **Terminal Block (TB)**: is similar to a genesis block, but it is added at the end of a blockchain to "close" it and produce a CB. The TB's data element has details about the CB that it has terminated. The elements are as follows. The `aggr _ hash` is created by generating a hash (e.g., using SHA-256) of concatenated `current _ hash` values of all blocks in that CB (AGB or RGB to the block prior to the terminal block). The data element may also store four optional values, namely `timestamp _ from`, `timestamp _ to`, `block _ index _ from`, and `block _ index _ to`. These optional values can be used by the search API to locate the required CB that contains the block or blocks that a user is looking for. Then, as with any other block, we produce a `current _ hash` of the terminal block as per Algorithm 1.

■ **Superblock**: exhibits the features of a regular data block and has `nonce, index, timestamp, data, previous _ hash`, and `current _ hash`. The only differentiator is that its data element stores all of the field of a TB of a CB (`index, data`, etc.).

■ **Superblockchain**: is a blockchain consisting of Superblocks. The blocks are "chained": `current _ hash` of a previous Superblock becomes `previous _ hash` of the next one.

■ **API**: The API, enabling users to interact with LCaaS, is as follows. There are two data submission functions: `submit _ raw` and `submit _ digest`. The former allows the client to submit the actual log file, the latter—just the file's digest (e.g., SHA-based digest computed using OpenSSL `dgst` [22]), thus, preserving the privacy of the log and reducing the amount of transmitted data. Both functions return, on success, timestamp and block_index of the transaction and, on failure, details of the error.

In addition to the file, the user may provide optional parameters that will be preserved in the blockchain, such as log file name, and starting and ending time stamps in this log file. These optional parameters may help to speed up the search for existing record in the blockchain, as discussed below. For verification of an actual log file, one should use function `verify _ raw`, for verification of the digest-based representation of the file—`verify _ digest`. The functions would return the status of submission and number of blocks that matches the submitted data, if no block is found, the API will return zero. In case of an error, the API will return the failed status along with the error's description.

9.3.2.3 LCaaS Summary

In this section, we describe Cloud-based immutable log storage solution, LCaaS, based on the blockchain technology. This solution prevents log tampering, ensuring transparent logging process and establishing trust between all Cloud participants (providers and users). Thus, the solution is of interest to practitioners. LCaaS exhibits the following characteristics.

Distributed Ledger is shared between Cloud users and Cloud providers.

Each participant has read-only and manageable access to some or all of the items in the ledger.

Immutability: hash of each block is created as per pseudo code shown in

Algorithm 1. It incorporates the hash of a previous block; thus, any changes to the previous blocks would "break" the blockchain guarantying immutability.

Cryptographically sealed: nonces are used as a PoW method to ensure that generated hashes meet the configured difficulty target. The hashes include all the elements in a block, including its timestamp, and nonce.

This hierarchical structure and its embedded recursive approach enhance the scalability, accessibility, and privacy of the hierarchical ledger compared to traditional blockchain platforms.

Scalability Improvement: relying on Superblocks, many Superblocks can be generated at the same time and then added to a Superblockchain at the same time. This will bring parallel processing feature for situations where multiple sources of data are generating data that needs to be put in the blockchain. For example, a platform may consist of 20 servers and each server can be associated with one Superblockchain.

Accessibility Improvement: API-based verification is added to the hierarchical ledger so users can submit raw data or digest values to check the consistency of their data.

Privacy Improvement: to improve privacy, an entire Superblockchain is reserved for a client to ensure that blockchains from different clients are not mingled. Furthermore, a user will only need to send the TB to the LCaaS to verify the integrity of the entire CB. Additionally, the option to store the hash value of data as opposed to real data would bring additional confidentially to the clients.

If LCaaS is implemented on a public blockchain, all transaction records are publicly available. This becomes a major privacy concern if the users of LCaaS decide to push their raw logs into the blockchain. Privacy can be improved if the users of LCaaS send the digest of their logs. If higher level of privacy is needed, one can implement LCaaS on a private blockchain.

The proposed LCaaS acts as a hierarchical ledger and repository for all logs generated by the Cloud providers and can be accessed by all the Cloud participants to establish trust among them. Using the provided API, a client can verify the logs provided by the Cloud provider against the records in the LCaaS and find out if the logs were tampered with or remained intact.

9.3.3 Proposed Solution for Monitoring Large-Scale Cloud Infrastructure: Dogfooding

The stability and performance of Cloud platforms are essential as they directly impact customers' satisfaction. Cloud service providers use Cloud monitoring tools to ensure that rendered services match the quality of service requirements indicated in established contracts such as SLAs.

Given the enormous number of resources that need to be monitored, highly scalable and capable monitoring tools are designed and implemented by Cloud service providers such as Amazon, Google, IBM, and Microsoft. Cloud monitoring tools monitor millions of virtual and physical resources and continuously generate logs for each one of them. Considering that logs magnify any technical issue, they can be used for disaster detection, prevention, and recovery. However, logs are useless if they are not assessed and analyzed promptly. Thus, we argue that the scale of Cloud-generated logs makes it impossible for DevOps teams to analyze them effectively. This implies that one needs to automate the process of monitoring and analysis (e.g., using machine learning and artificial intelligence). If the automation will witness an anomaly in the logs—it will alert DevOps staff.

The automatic anomaly detectors require a reliable and scalable platform for gathering, filtering, and transforming the logs, executing the detector models, and sending out the alerts to the DevOps staff. In this work, we report on implementing a prototype of such a platform based on the seven-layered architecture pattern, which leverages microservice principles to distribute tasks among highly scalable, resources-efficient modules. The modules interact with each other via an instance of the Publish-Subscribe architectural pattern. The platform is deployed on the IBM Cloud service infrastructure and is used to detect anomalies in logs emitted by the IBM Cloud services, hence the dogfooding. In particular, we leverage IBM Cloud Functions to deploy the computing modules, IBM Event Streams to establish communication among the modules, and IBM Cloud Object Storage and IBM Cloudant for persistent storage.

The prototype efficiency is promising: it takes the platform 17 seconds or less from the point of receiving a new log record to emitting an alert to the IBM Cloud DevOps team.

9.3.3.1 Challenges of Storing and Analyzing Cloud-Generated Logs

The storage requirement for Cloud-generated logs (discussed above) calls for innovative expansion of Cloud storage features. Vernik et al. [93] suggest the use of federated storage to increase the capacity and performance of Cloud storage to accommodate demanding storage tasks (such as log storage). By nature, logs are redundant, and systems continuously generate and write logs even if the values for monitored metrics do not change. Hence, to preserve space required to store logs, Anwar et al. suggest to avoid storing repetitive values, leading to reduction of the size of stored data by up to 80% [32].

The high volume and velocity of generated monitoring data pose various challenges for monitoring systems. Not only the storage of such data is a challenge, but also the data processing portion is computationally expensive [62,95] and sometimes infeasible [34,63]. Hence, storage and processing the data generated by Cloud monitoring platforms is one of the key challenges of Cloud monitoring [95].

Using the same example provided in Section 9.2.2.1, consider a Cloud log storage platform that stores about 2.35 TB data per day. Simply querying the data (that is, reading it and loading it to any application) by itself is a major challenge. Some researchers have proposed solutions [61,94] based on the combination of Big Data storage and processing tools, such as HDFS [12] and Spark [4], with Cloud monitoring solutions. The data can then be passed to anomaly detecting techniques, such as [29,34,40,45]. Additionally, some researchers have decided to use data science algorithms to analyze Cloud-generated logs to find anomalies [34,48].

As discussed above, Cloud computing issues, especially infrastructure issues, should be detected and fixed as fast as possible. However, this means that issues should be detected in near-real-time so that the IBM DevOps team can be informed about the issue and start their troubleshooting. As a manual observation of logs, at least at the scale of Cloud logs is impossible, our **primary objective** is to design, and implement a platform that can be used for collecting, storing, and analyzing Cloud-generated logs. The platform should have nonfunctional features, such as scalability, reliability, and redundancy.

9.3.3.2 Dogfooding Technical Details

In this section, we provide technical details related to the proposed solution. We indicate the modules that are used, their order, the data flow, and we conclude this section by reviewing the architecture of the proposed solution. The proposed solution has the capability of listening or retrieving data from various Cloud components and offers scalable storage and monitoring infrastructure for log analysis. By using the proposed solution, a massive amount of logs can be collected, transformed to the desired format, and stored in Cloud data storage platforms so they can be fed to analytical tool for further data analysis. Before we dive into details of our proposed solution, let us elaborate on the desired characteristics of a Cloud monitoring platform based on the content provided in Sections 9.2.2 and 9.2.1. The desirable key characteristics of a Cloud-scale monitoring system are as follows.

Scalability: A platform that can monitor several metrics for each of the components in a Cloud platform distributed among several data centers needs to be scalable. The number of resources that needs to be monitored constantly increases, and therefore, only a scalable monitoring platform can be used in Cloud environments.

Elasticity: A platform that should automatically scale up or down with the intensity of the incoming log records.

Reliability and stability: A monitoring platform is mainly implemented to ensure that all other components of a Cloud platform are operating normally.

As collection of data and monitoring of Cloud platform are continuous activities and require 24×7 operation, Cloud platforms should be reliable and resilient to component failure.

Capacity: The scale of generated logs requires a monitoring system with elastic capacity. That is, the size of the collected logs continues to grow and so does the required space to store them.

Support of various log formats: Cloud platforms consist of several different types of components. The logs generated by various components (e.g., servers, routers, and software platforms) are of different types and a Cloud monitoring platform should be able to collect and process various types of logs.

Interconnection feasibility: As Cloud providers continue to add new services, it is very important that the existing monitoring platform can keep up with new demands.

We are basing this solution on the seven-layered architecture for processing online and offline data described in detail in [46,47]. This architecture allows us to use microservices and publish-subscribe software architecture and offers a good balance between scalability and maintainability due to high cohesion and low coupling of the solution. Furthermore, asynchronous communication between the layers makes the seven-layered architecture a building block for a general architecture for processing streaming data.

The detailed description of the seven-layered architecture is given in [46,47]. Below we provide a summary of this architecture, depicted graphically in Figure 9.3. Microservices in odd layers communicate with each other via topics of a publish-subscribe infrastructure in even layers. A microservice in Layer 1 ingests data (e.g., log records and metrics' observations) from external sources and converts them to a unified format that is recognized by the subsequent layers of the architecture; it then publishes the converted data in a message to a topic in Layer 2. A microservice in Layer 3, subscribed to a topic in Layer 2, receives a converted message from the Layer 1 and

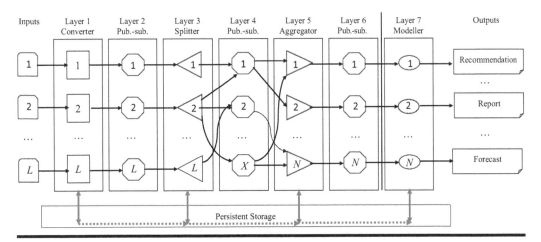

Figure 9.3 A diagram of the seven-layered architecture with *L* input sources, *N* models, and *X* topics of interest. Dashed lines represent publish-subscribe layers. Vertical dash-dotted line separates data preparation layers from the analytics layer. Arrows denote flow of data. Blue arrows between Layers 1, 3, 5, 7 and persistent storage reflect potential communication between microservices (in a given layer) and persistent storage. (Adapted from [47].)

decides what to do with it: either publish a message to topics of interest in Layer 4 or discard the message (if it is not of interest to any model). A microservice in Layer 5, subscribed to topics in Layer 4, aggregates received messages, enriches them with historical data (received from the persistent storage), and transforms the resulting data in the form required by the models in Layer 7. The resulting transformed and enriched data are passed, via topics in Layer 6, to models residing in microservices of Layer 7. The output of the models (e.g., a label deeming given observation anomalous or not) is passed to external services (e.g., a system, such as PagerDuty [23] or Slack [26], notifying Operations team about anomalies).

The microservices interact with the persistent storage for storing and accessing historical data and trained models. Moreover, it is often used for caching batches of data, as the size of a message passed via publish-subscribe software is limited [47]. For example, at the time of writing, Amazon Kinesis and IBM Event Stream maximum message size is 1 MB [17,18]. In practice, batched input data, historical data sets prepared in Layer 5 for retraining models, and the trained models (created and reused in Layer 7) often exceed this limit. One can split the large data into chunks and pass these chunks in separate messages via publish-subscribe. However, given that messages are passed asynchronously, aggregating them on the receiving end becomes problematic. Instead, seven-layered architecture recommends to persist the data (e.g., to object store or database) and pass a message with a pointer to the stored data via publish-subscribe [47].

A scalable and useful Cloud monitoring tool needs to have both "pushing" and "pulling" capabilities so that other components, namely the components that either generate logs or hold logs, can easily interact with the proposed tool.

Layer 1 of the seven-layered architecture is exposed to the outside world for data collection. A RESTful API [42] is designed and implemented, and logs can be pushed to this API. In our prototype of the monitoring system, we leveraged public IBM Cloud services to implement the seven-layered architecture. The relations between the services are represented graphically in Figure 9.4, details are given below.

We chose public multitenant offering of IBM Cloud Event Streams [10] (based on the Apache Kafka [2] software, which implements publish-subscribe pattern). The offering if fully managed, highly available, and is charged by the number of topics and the amount of data passing through them.

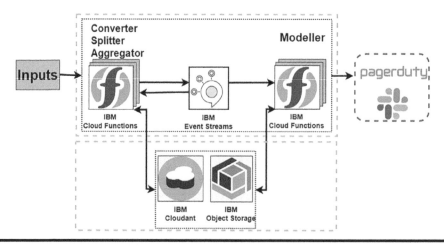

Figure 9.4 Architecture of the proposed solution.

We could have implemented and managed microservices using managed container offering (namely, IBM Cloud Kubernetes Service [15]). However, we decided to leverage fully managed function-as-a-service (FaaS) offering of IBM Cloud Functions [6] (which is implemented based on Apache OpenWhisk [3]). Given that the seven-layered architecture is aimed at the Data Science pipeline, which is typically stateless, this was a natural decision. Solutions on FaaS scale up and down trivially, as the FaaS platform "fires up" individual instances of a Function to process incoming messages: the more messages are in the pipeline, the more messages will be running concurrently. It was also attractive economically: FaaS is billed based on the amount of time a Function is running (proportional to the number of CPUs and memory requested to each Function); thus, we do not have to pay for idle resources.

We implement the Functions (from here on we will use the term "Function" and "microservice in the 7-layered architecture" interchangeably) in Java or Python. Given that the microservices are communicating with each other asynchronously via topics in the IBM Cloud Event Streams, the usage of multiple languages was not an issue.

IBM Cloud Functions have multiple types of triggers to start a Function. Our prototype receives incoming data via RESTful API [13]. IBM Cloud has readily available service to deploy the API and authorize access to it [14]. Triggers are set up to call a corresponding Function in Layer 1 for every POST request coming through the API.

IBM Cloud Functions has a specific type of triggers for the Event Streams. Such trigger listens to an Even Streams' topics and starts an instance of a Function when a message (or a group of messages) is published to this topic. The trigger then passes these messages to the started Function. This is how we activate the Functions in Layers 3, 5, and 7.

Some of the models are retrained periodically[2] rather than online; for those models, we set up timer-based triggers that retrain the models (by firing specialized Functions in Layer 5 periodically).

For persistent storage, we use two services. The first one is fully managed JSON document store IBM Cloudant [16], which elastically scales throughput as well as storage. However, a single document, stored in Cloudant, cannot be larger than 1 MB [8], which implies that we cannot store large transformed data frames (produced in Layer 5) and trained models (used in Layer 7). For these items, we leverage IBM Cloud Object Storage [7], another fully managed and scalable service.

The prototype of our solution was running for a month, analyzing alerts from the 2,000 deployments discussed above. We computed the duration of the time from a message arriving into our system to the message leaving the system (depending on the type of content in the message, we either produce a report in Layer 7 or save it to persistent storage in Layer 3). The statistics of the timing data are shown in Table 9.1 and Figure 9.5.

Table 9.1 Summary Statistics of the Timing Data

Type	Min.	1st Qu.	Median	Mean	3rd Qu.	Max.
Reported	4.1	5.3	7.5	7.7	9.2	17.0
Saved	1.5	1.7	1.9	2.5	2.7	44.5

---

[2] The reason for retraining is the arrival of new features or new values for existing nominal features (e.g., the names of the new customer systems that were deployed, since the previous retraining). In this case, we retrain a Random-Forest-based model [36,89] every 12 hours.

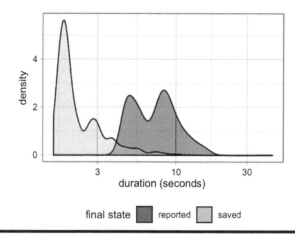

Figure 9.5   Duration of time from a message entering the prototype to the message leaving the prototype.

As we can see, on average it takes 8 seconds for the whole life cycle (from receiving the message to emitting the report); at worst, it takes 17 seconds. Notice that the right tail of the distribution is heavy: in fact, 75% of the reports (3rd Quartile) complete in 9 seconds or less.

Figure 9.5 illustrates the distributions of the duration of time from a message entering the prototype to the message leaving the prototype. If a message left the system in Layer 3 (by being saved to persistent storage), it is deemed "saved." If a message left the system in Layer 7 (via a produced report), it is deemed "reported."

As for historical data (saved in Layer 3), it takes on average 3 seconds (and, at worst, 45 seconds) to reach the persistent storage. The maximum value of 45 seconds is an outlier: 99.87% of messages were saved in 15 seconds or less. Given that most Cloud providers operate on four 9s availability (99.99%, which translates to 52.56 minutes of potential downtime per year) or five 9s availability (99.999%, which translates to 5.26 minutes of potential downtime per year), the process time of 15 seconds or less seems promising and acceptable.

9.3.3.3 Dogfooding Summary

In this section, we reported our experience of creating a prototype of the scalable and resilient platform (based on the seven-layered architecture), for monitoring and analysis of logs emitted by components of IBM Cloud services. To implement the prototype, we leveraged public IBM Cloud services, hence the dogfooding. While the proposed platform uses IBM Cloud services, it is possible and reasonably straightforward for one to implement the same monitoring system using services provided by other Cloud providers, such as Amazon, Microsoft, or Google.

The prototype was tested on the production data. It showed good scalability (has been able to process up to 120 requests per minute) and responsiveness (reporting the results of the analysis in ≤ 17 seconds).

9.4 Conclusions

In the past, application providers had to design and deploy their products on a costly hardware platform. The situation has changed with introduction of Cloud services that led to reduction of upfront costs, improved elasticity, etc. These benefits led to a dramatic increase of popularity in

Cloud services. With a five-year compound annual growth rate (CAGR) of 22.3%, public cloud spending will grow from 229 billion dollars in 2019 to nearly 500 billion dollars in 2023 [27]. To guarantee reliable operation of the Cloud offerings, one must monitor their health.

In this chapter, we highlight some of the challenges posed by the task of monitoring Cloud solutions, platforms, and systems. While some challenges have already been solved, we proposed two solutions for two significant Cloud monitoring challenges that are still open, namely authentication of collected logs and the near-real-time log analysis.

For the former, we propose blockchain-based immutable log storage, which can "notarize" logs in a matter of seconds. In the future, we are planning to test LCaaS with existing blockchain solutions to find integration points that can be used to implement LCaaS on top of such solutions. We plan to integrate this log storage into the IBM platform.

For the latter, we create a scalable microservice-based solution that autoscales with log volume and provides results of the analysis in less than a minute. In the future, we are planning to widen the usage of our platform, by monitoring additional IBM Cloud services and by integrating the monitoring features with our immutable log storage.

Cloud monitoring is a fertile area for novel research and practice. Solving the above challenges will simplify integration of Cloud monitoring into the maintenance and operations phases of the software development life cycle, while reducing the risk of outages, lessening maintenance cost, and decreasing the load on human and computer resources. While we discussed solutions to some of the problems, others are remaining. Thus, we encourage researchers and practitioners to explore this field.

References

1. Amazon cloudwatch - application and infrastructure monitoring. https: //aws.amazon.com/cloud-watch/. (Accessed on 03/10/2020).
2. Apache kafka. https://kafka.apache.org/. (Accessed on 06/25/2019).
3. Apache openwhisk is a serverless, open source cloud platform. https: //openwhisk.apache.org/. (Accessed on 06/25/2019).
4. Apache spark™ - unified analytics engine for big data. https://spark. apache.org/. (Accessed on 06/25/2019).
5. arxiv.org e-print archive. https://arxiv.org/. (Accessed on 07/14/2019).
6. Cloud functions - overview | IBM. https://www.ibm.com/cloud/functions. (Accessed on 06/25/2019).
7. Cloud object storage - pricing | IBM. https://www.ibm.com/cloud/object-storage/pricing/. (Accessed on 10/21/2019).
8. Cloudant: Documents. https://cloud.ibm.com/docs/services/ Cloudant?topic=cloudant-documents. (Accessed on 07/04/2019).
9. Dropbox. https://www.dropbox.com/. (Accessed on 07/18/2019).
10. Event streams - IBM event streams - overview | ibm. https://www.ibm.com/cloud/event-streams. (Accessed on 06/25/2019).
11. Git - distributed version control system. https://git-scm.com/. (Accessed on 07/14/2019).
12. Hdfs architecture guide. https://hadoop.apache.org/docs/r1.2.1/hdfs_design.html. (Accessed on 06/25/2019).
13. IBM api explorer: Cloud functions. https://developer.ibm.com/api/view/cloudfunctions-prod:cloud-functions:title-Cloud_Functions. (Accessed on 07/04/2019).
14. IBM api explorer catalog. https://developer.ibm.com/api/list. (Accessed on 07/04/2019).
15. IBM cloud. https://cloud.ibm.com/kubernetes/overview. (Accessed on 07/04/2019).
16. IBM cloudant - overview - Canada. https://www.ibm.com/ca-en/marketplace/database-management. (Accessed on 06/25/2019).

17. IBM event streams faqs. https://cloud.ibm.com/docs/services/EventStreams?topic=eventstreams-faqs\#max_message_size. (Accessed on 07/04/2019).

18. Kinesis data streams limits - amazon kinesis data streams. https://docs.aws.amazon.com/streams/latest/dev/service-sizes-and-limits.html. (Accessed on 07/05/2019).

19. Mathematical proof of the inevitability of cloud computing. http://www.joeweinman.com/resources/joe_weinman_inevitability_of_cloud.pdf. (Accessed on 02/04/2020).

20. Netflix Canada - watch TV shows online, watch movies online. https://www.netflix.com/ca/. (Accessed on 07/18/2019).

21. Nist sp 800-145, the NIST definition of cloud computing. https://nvlpubs.nist.gov/nistpubs/Legacy/SP/nistspecialpublication800-145.pdf. (Accessed on 07/19/2019).

22. Openssl dgst. https://www.openssl.org/docs/manmaster/man1/dgst.html. (Accessed on 07/14/2019).

23. Pagerduty: Centralize your monitoring data. https://www. pagerduty.com/. (Accessed on 07/04/2019).

24. Poex.io - the original blockchain notary service. https://poex.io/. (Accessed on 07/14/2019).

25. Stackdriver Monitoring - Hybrid Cloud Monitoring.

26. Where work happens | slack. https://slack.com/intl/en-ca/. (Accessed on 07/04/2019).

27. Worldwide public cloud services spending will more than double by 2023, according to IDC. https://www.idc.com/getdoc.jsp?containerId= prUS45340719. (Accessed on 04/04/2020).

28. Rafael Accorsi. Log data as digital evidence: What secure logging protocols have to offer? In *33rd Annual IEEE Int. Computer Software and Applications Conference, COMPSAC'09*, volume 2, pages 398–403. IEEE, Seattle, Washington, DC, 2009.

29. Subutai Ahmad, Alexander Lavin, Scott Purdy, and Zuha Agha. Unsupervised real-time anomaly detection for streaming data. *Neurocomputing*, 262:134–147, 2017.

30. Omar S Al-Kadi. Knowledge management systems requirements specifications. *arXiv preprint arXiv:2004.08961*, 2020.

31. Maryam Alavi and Dorothy Leidner. Knowledge management systems: Issues, challenges, and benefits. *Communications of the Association for Information Systems*, 1(1):7, 1999.

32. Ali Anwar, Anca Sailer, Andrzej Kochut, and Ali R. Butt. Anatomy of cloud monitoring and metering: A case study and open problems. In *Proceedings of the 6th Asia-Pacific Workshop on Systems*, APSys '15, pages 6:1–6:7, New York, NY, USA, 2015. ACM.

33. P. Bharathi and S. Rajashree. Secure file access solution for public cloud storage. In 2014 *International Conference on Information Communication and Embedded Systems (ICI- CES)*, pages 1–5. IEEE, Chennai, India, 2014.

34. Arnamoy Bhattacharyya, Seyed Ali Jokar Jandaghi, Stelios Sotiriadis, and Cristiana Amza. Semantic aware online detection of resource anomalies on the cloud. In *2016 IEEE International Conference on Cloud Computing Technology and Science (CloudCom)*, pages 134–143. IEEE, Luxembourg, 2016.

35. Christian Bird, Peter C Rigby, Earl T Barr, David J Hamilton, Daniel M German, and Prem Devanbu. The promises and perils of mining git. In *6th International Working Conference on Mining Software Repositories, MSR'09*, pages 1–10. IEEE, Vancouver, BC, 2009.

36. Leo Breiman. Random forests. *Machine Learning*, 45(1):5–32, Oct 2001.

37. J.D. Bruce. The mini-blockchain scheme, 2014. *URL:* http://cryptonite.info.

38. Fred Cohen. A cryptographic checksum for integrity protection. *Computers & Security*, 6(6):505–510, 1987.

39. Guilherme Da Cunha Rodrigues, Rodrigo N Calheiros, Vinicius Tavares Guimaraes, Glederson Lessa dos Santos, Marcio Barbosa De Carvalho, Lisandro Zambenedetti Granville, Liane Margarida Rockenbach Tarouco, and Rajkumar Buyya. Monitoring of cloud computing environments: Concepts, solutions, trends, and future directions. In *Proceedings of the 31st Annual ACM Symposium on Applied Computing*, pages 378–383. ACM, Pisa, Italy, 2016.

40. Min Du, Feifei Li, Guineng Zheng, and Vivek Srikumar. Deeplog: Anomaly detection and diagnosis from system logs through deep learning. In *Proceedings of the 2017 ACM SIGSAC Conference on Computer and Communications Security*, pages 1285–1298. ACM, Dallas, TX, 2017.

41. Michael Factor, Ealan Henis, Dalit Naor, Simona Rabinovici-Cohen, Petra Reshef, Shahar Ronen, Giovanni Michetti, and Maria Guercio. Authenticity and provenance in long term digital preservation: Modeling and implementation in preservation aware storage. In *Workshop on the Theory and Practice of Provenance*, San Francisco, CA, 2009.

42. Roy T Fielding and Richard N Taylor. *Architectural styles and the design of network-based software architectures*. University of California, Irvine Doctoral dissertation, 2000.

43. Patrick Gallagher. Secure hash standard (shs). *FIPS PUB*, pages 1–27, 2008.

44. Stuart Haber and W Scott Stornetta. How to time-stamp a digital document. In *Conference on the Theory and Application of Cryptography*, pages 437–455. Springer, Santa Barbara, CA, 1990.

45. Shilin He, Jieming Zhu, Pinjia He, and Michael R Lyu. Experience report: System log analysis for anomaly detection. In *2016 IEEE 27th International Symposium on Software Reliability Engineering (ISSRE)*, pages 207–218. IEEE, Ottawa, ON, 2016.

46. Sheik Hoque and Andriy Miranskyy. Architecture for analysis of streaming data. In *2018 IEEE International Conference on Cloud Engineering (IC2E)*, pages 263–269. IEEE, Orlando, FL, 2018.

47. Sheik Hoque and Andriy Miranskyy. Online and offline analysis of streaming data. In *2018 IEEE International Conference on Software Architecture Companion (ICSA-C)*, pages 68–71, Seattle, WA, 2018.

48. Mohammad Saiful Islam and Andriy Miranskyy. Anomaly detection in cloud components. In *13th IEEE International Conference on Cloud Computing, CLOUD 2020*. IEEE Computer Society, Virtual Event, 2020. (to appear).

49. Nancy Jain and Sakshi Choudhary. Overview of virtualization in cloud computing. In *2016 Symposium on Colossal Data Analysis and Net- working (CDAN)*, pages 1–4. IEEE, Indore, India, 2016.

50. Hui Kang, Michael Le, and Shu Tao. Container and microservice driven design for cloud infrastructure DevOps. In *2016 IEEE International Conference on Cloud Engineering (IC2E)*, pages 202–211, Berlin, Germany, April 2016.

51. Michael J Kavis. *Architecting the Cloud: Design Decisions for Cloud Computing Service Models (SaaS, PaaS, and IaaS)*. John Wiley & Sons, Hoboken, NJ, 2014.

52. John Kelsey and Bruce Schneier. Minimizing bandwidth for remote access to cryptographically protected audit logs. In *Recent Advances in Intrusion Detection*, page 9, 1999.

53. Sunny King and Scott Nadal. Ppcoin: Peer-to-peer crypto-currency with proof-of-stake. *self-published paper*, August 2012. https://decred. org/research/king2012.pdf.

54. Ryan KL Ko and Mark A Will. Progger: An efficient, tamper-evident kernel-space logger for cloud data provenance tracking. In *2014 IEEE 7th International Conference on Cloud Computing (CLOUD)*, pages 881–889. IEEE, Anchorage, AK, 2014.

55. Mouad Lemoudden and Bouabid El Ouahidi. Managing cloud-generated logs using big data technologies. In *2015 International Conference on Wireless Networks and Mobile Communications (WINCOM)*, pages 1–7. IEEE, Marrakech, Morocco, 2015.

56. Chang Liu, Chi Yang, Xuyun Zhang, and Jinjun Chen. External integrity verification for outsourced big data in cloud and IoT: A big picture. *Future Generation Computer Systems*, 49:58–67, 2015.

57. Changbin Liu, Yun Mao, Jacobus Van der Merwe, and Mary Fernandez. Cloud resource orchestration: A data-centric approach. In *Proceedings of the biennial Conference on Innovative Data Systems Research (CIDR)*, pages 1–8. Citeseer, Asilomar, CA, 2011.

58. Michael Mainelli and Mike Smith. Sharing ledgers for sharing economies: An exploration of mutual distributed ledgers (aka blockchain technology). *Journal of Financial Perspectives*, 3(3):38–58, 2015.

59. Raffael Marty. Cloud application logging for forensics. In *Proceedings of the 2011 ACM Symposium on Applied Computing*, pages 178–184. ACM, TaiChung, Taiwan, 2011.

60. Roman Matzutt, Martin Henze, Jan Henrik Ziegeldorf, Jens Hiller, and Klaus Wehrle. Thwarting unwanted blockchain content insertion. In *2018 IEEE International Conference on Cloud Engineering (IC2E)*, pages 364–370. IEEE, Orlando, FL, 2018.

61. Shicong Meng, Arun K Iyengar, Isabelle M Rouvellou, Ling Liu, Kisung Lee, Balaji Palanisamy, and Yuzhe Tang. Reliable state monitoring in cloud datacenters. In *2012 IEEE Fifth International Conference on Cloud Computing*, pages 951–958. IEEE, Honolulu, HI, 2012.

62. Andriy Miranskyy, Abdelwahab Hamou-Lhadj, Enzo Cialini, and Alf Larsson. Operational-log analysis for big data systems: Challenges and solutions. *IEEE Software*, 33(2):52–59, 2016.

63. Andriy V. Miranskyy, Nazim H. Madhavji, Mechelle S. Gittens, Matthew Davison, Mark Wilding, and David Godwin. An iterative, multi-level, and scalable approach to comparing execution traces. In *Proceedings of the 6th Joint Meeting of the European Software Engineering Conference and the ACM SIGSOFT Symposium on the Foundations of Software Engineering*, ESEC-FSE '07, pages 537–540. ACM, Dubrovnik, Croatia, 2007.

64. Audris Mockus. Engineering big data solutions. In *Proceedings of the on Future of Software Engineering, FOSE 2014*, pages 85–99, New York, NY, USA, 2014. ACM.

65. Satoshi Nakamoto. Bitcoin: A peer-to-peer electronic cash system. 2008. Bitcoin. https://bitcoin.org/bitcoin.pdf.

66. Surya Nepal, Shiping Chen, Jinhui Yao, and Danan Thilakanathan. Diaas: Data integrity as a service in the cloud. In *2011 IEEE International Conference on Cloud Computing (CLOUD)*, pages 308–315. IEEE, Washington, DC, 2011.

67. The An Binh Nguyen, Melanie Siebenhaar, Ronny Hans, and Ralf Steinmetz. Role-based templates for cloud monitoring. In *2014 IEEE/ACM 7th International Conference on Utility and Cloud Computing (UCC)*, pages 242–250, London, UK, 2014.

68. Pankesh Patel, Ajith H Ranabahu, and Amit P Sheth. Service level agreement in cloud computing. 2009.

69. William Wesley Peterson and Daniel T Brown. Cyclic codes for error detection. *Proceedings of the IRE*, 49(1):228–235, 1961.

70. Panita Pongpaibool, Aimaschana Niruntasukrat, Chavee Issariyapat, Koonlachat Meesublak, Chumpol Mokarat, and Premrudee Aiumsupucgul. Netham-nano: A robust and scalable service-oriented platform for distributed monitoring. In *Proceedings of the AINTEC 2014 on Asian Internet Engineering Conference*, AINTEC '14, pages 51:51–51:57, New York, NY, USA, 2014. ACM.

71. William Pourmajidi and Andriy Miranskyy. Logchain: Blockchain assisted log storage. In *Proceedings of IEEE International Conference on Cloud Computing (CLOUD 2018)*, San Francisco, CA, 2018.

72. William Pourmajidi, Andriy Miranskyy, John Steinbacher, Tony Erwin, and David Godwin. Dogfooding: Using IBM cloud services to monitor IBM cloud infrastructure. In *Proceedings of the 29th Annual International Conference on Computer Science and Software Engineering*, pages 344–353, Markham, ON, 2019.

73. William Pourmajidi, John Steinbacher, Tony Erwin, and Andriy Miranskyy. On challenges of cloud monitoring. In *Proceedings of the 27th Annual International Conference on Computer Science and Software Engineering*, pages 259–265. IBM Corp., Markham, ON, 2017.

74. William Pourmajidi, Lei Zhang, John Steinbacher, Tony Erwin, and Andriy V. Miranskyy. Immutable log storage as a service. In *Proceedings of the 41st International Conference on Software Engineering: Companion Proceedings, ICSE 2019*, Montreal, QC, Canada, May 25–31, 2019, pages 280–281, 2019.

75. Deepak Puthal, Bibhudutta PS Sahoo, Sambit Mishra, and Satyabrata Swain. Cloud computing features, issues, and challenges: A big picture. In *2015 International Conference on Computational Intelligence and Networks*, pages 116–123. IEEE, Odisha, India, 2015.

76. Indrajit Ray, Kirill Belyaev, Mikhail Strizhov, Dieudonne Mulamba, and Mariappan Rajaram. Secure logging as a service—delegating log management to the cloud. *IEEE Systems Journal*, 7(2):323–334, 2013.

77. D Reilly, Chris Wren, and Tom Berry. Cloud computing: Forensic challenges for law enforcement. In *International Conference for Internet Technology and Secured Transactions (ICITST)*, pages 1–7. IEEE, London, UK, 2010.

78. Phillip Rogaway and Thomas Shrimpton. Cryptographic hash-function basics: Definitions, implications, and separations for preimage resistance, second-preimage resistance, and collision resistance. In *International Workshop on Fast Software Encryption*, pages 371–388. Springer, Delhi, India, 2004.

79. Abdul Salam, Zafar Gilani, and Salman Ul Haq. *Deploying and Managing a Cloud Infrastructure: Real-World Skills for the CompTIA Cloud+ Certification and Beyond: Exam CV0-001*. John Wiley & Sons, Hoboken, NJ, 2015.

80. Masaya Sato and Toshihiro Yamauchi. Vmm-based log-tampering and loss detection scheme. *Journal of Internet Technology*, 13(4):655–666, 2012.

81. Bruce Schneier and John Kelsey. Cryptographic support for secure logs on untrusted machines. In *USENIX Security Symposium*, volume 98, pages 53–62, San Antonio, TX, 1998.

82. Siti Rahayu Selamat, Robiah Yusof, and Shahrin Sahib. Mapping process of digital forensic investigation framework. *International Journal of Computer Science and Network Security*, 8(10):163–169, 2008.

83. Shweta Sharma. A strongly trusted integrity preservance based security framework for critical information storage over cloud platform. *International Journal of Applied Information Systems*, 11(6):3–7, 2016.

84. Melanie Siebenhaar, Ronny Hans, Ralf Steinmetz, et al. Role-based templates for cloud monitoring. In *Proceedings of the 2014 IEEE/ACM 7th International Conference on Utility and Cloud Computing*, pages 242–250. IEEE Computer Society, London, UK, 2014.

85. Abraham Silberschatz, Peter Baer Galvin, and Greg Gagne. *Operating System Concepts Essentials*. John Wiley & Sons, Inc., Hoboken, NJ, 2014.

86. Gopalan Sivathanu, Charles P Wright, and Erez Zadok. Enhancing file system integrity through checksums. Technical report, Citeseer, 2004.

87. Pelle Snickars. The archival cloud. *The YouTube Reader*, 2009.

88. Richard T Snodgrass, Shilong Stanley Yao, and Christian Collberg. Tamper detection in audit logs. In *Proceedings of the Thirtieth International Conference on Very Large Data Bases-Volume 30*, pages 504–515. VLDB Endowment, Toronto, Canada, 2004.

89. Tin Kam Ho. Random decision forests. In *Proceedings of 3rd International Conference on Document Analysis and Recognition*, volume 1, pages 278–282, Montreal, Canada, Aug 1995.

90. Wei-Tek Tsai, Xin Sun, and Janaka Balasooriya. Service-oriented cloud computing architecture. In *2010 Seventh International Conference on Information Technology: New Generations*, pages 684–689, Las Vegas, Nevada, 2010.

91. Twitter. Twitter service issue, 2016. http://twitterstatus.tumblr.com/post/137610751178/service-issue.

92. Sarah Underwood. Blockchain beyond bitcoin. *Communications of the ACM*, 59(11):15–17, October 2016.

93. Gil Vernik, Alexandra Shulman-Peleg, Sebastian Dippl, Ciro Formisano, Michael C Jaeger, Elliot K Kolodner, and Massimo Villari. Data on-boarding in federated storage clouds. In *2013 IEEE Sixth International Conference on Cloud Computing*, pages 244–251. IEEE, Santa Clara, CA, 2013.

94. Jonathan Stuart Ward and Adam Barker. Varanus: In situ monitoring for large scale cloud systems. In *2013 IEEE 5th International Conference on Cloud Computing Technology and Science*, volume 2, pages 341–344. IEEE, Bristol, UK, 2013.

95. Jonathan Stuart Ward and Adam Barker. Self managing monitoring for highly elastic large scale cloud deployments. In *Proceedings of the 6th International Workshop on Data Intensive Distributed Computing*, DIDC '14, pages 3–10, New York, NY, USA, 2014. ACM.

96. Yuping Xing and Yongzhao Zhan. Virtualization and cloud computing. In Future Wireless Networks and Information Systems, pages 305–312. Springer, 2012. https://link.springer.com/chapter/10.1007/978-3-642-27323-0_39.

97. Qi Zhang, Lu Cheng, and Raouf Boutaba. Cloud computing: State-of- the-art and research challenges. *Journal of Internet Services and Applications*, 1(1):7–18, 2010.

98. Yanping Zhang, Yang Xiao, Min Chen, Jingyuan Zhang, and Hongmei Deng. A survey of security visualization for computer network logs. *Security and Communication Networks*, 5(4):404–421, 2012.

99. Zibin Zheng, Shaoan Xie, and Hong-Ning Dai. Blockchain challenges and opportunities: A survey. 2016.

100. Guy Zyskind, Oz Nathan, and Alex 'Sandy' Pentland. Decentralizing privacy: Using blockchain to protect personal data. In *2015 IEEE Security and Privacy Workshops*, pages 180–184, 2015.

Chapter 10

Machine Learning as a Service for Software Application Categorization

Cagatay Catal
Qatar University

Besme Elnaccar
De Facto

Ozge Colakoglu
DHL Supply Chain

Bedir Tekinerdogan
Wageningen University & Research

Contents

10.1 Introduction

Software repositories such as GitHub [1] and SourceForge [2] host thousands of software projects and provide numerous categories to classify them. These categories are necessary to help users to browse and find the intended project easily. The largest category in SourceForge is now the software development category, which has 207,032 projects for only the Windows operating system [3]. This categorization is mainly based on the functionality provided by the projects and is regularly updated. While SourceForge currently includes 21 top-level categories, it included ten top-level categories 2 years ago [4]. Another benefit of this categorization is that it increases reusability because developers can easily find related source code by inspecting these categories and their subcategories.

Project owners in SourceForge specify several features such as the domain, programming language, operating systems, status, user interface, database environment, audience, and license to help people find their projects. Domain information shows the category of the project, which is hosted in the repository. Sometimes newbie system users might select an incorrect category that can adversely affect the reputation of the relevant repository in the long term. Since more and more applications are added to the repositories in the Big Data era, the manual categorization is not a viable option. To overcome the problems with manual categorization of projects, automated approaches can be applied instead [5]. To this end, several approaches have been proposed in the literature [4,6–10]. A popular approach relies on text classification [6], whereby the source code of the project is considered as a textual document, and different identifiers such as variable name and function name are processed. This approach fails in case the source code is absent. In fact, some repositories let users upload only executable files, such as jar files. As such, researchers processed the API (Application Programming Interface) calls of applications by splitting the name of the corresponding package/class/method into tokens. For example, a Java application can use javax.sound.midi package, and when this package name is split into tokens, it generates sound and midi keywords, which helps the machine learning algorithm to classify this software as a music application.

In our previous study [3], we used an ensemble of classifiers approach to automatically categorize software applications into domain categories in the absence of source code and performed our experiments on the ShareJar repository for 745 projects. In this study, we aim to design and implement a cloud-based end-to-end application categorization system using machine learning algorithms to investigate the applicability of cloud computing technology. We focused on projects that have the source code and hosted on SourceForge. Since Azure Machine Learning Studio was preferred as the machine learning platform, four available multiclass classification algorithms, namely logistic regression, decision forest, decision jungle, and artificial neural network, were investigated during the experiments. There was no more algorithm to analyze in the platform at that time, and as such, our experiments included only these algorithms.

After the best algorithm in terms of accuracy parameter was selected, this classification model was transformed into a web service and deployed on a cloud platform. Subsequently, a web-based client application was developed to call this web service and inform the end user about the categorization of the application under test. The following research questions were defined in this project:

- **RQ1:** Is the cloud computing–based application categorization system using machine learning effective for automatically categorizing applications?
- **RQ2:** Which granularity level (i.e., package/class/method) provides better performance for application categorization?

■ **RQ3:** Does the machine learning–based categorization approach provide acceptable performance, and which machine learning algorithm is better in terms of accuracy parameter?

The end-to-end prediction system that we built in this study is a data-intensive software system because the prediction model was built based on numerous data that were collected from existing SourceForge projects. From the knowledge management perspective, our prediction model and the corresponding prediction web service are considered as the critical knowledge in our data-intensive system.

To simplify the access to this knowledge, we utilized the web service technology, which receives and sends data using REST (Representational State Transfer) APIs [21]. Compared to SOAP-based (Simple Object Access Protocol) web services, RESTful web services are implemented and accessed easier, and also, REST fixes several shortcomings of SOAP. In our data-intensive system, the testing data is sent to the web service by using the HTTP protocol, and the web service responds with the classification label. This shows that we followed the request/response approach for the web service implementation instead of the batch execution approach.

The remaining sections are organized as follows: Section 10.2 provides the background and the related work. Section 10.3 explains the system design and the general approach. Section 10.4 presents the results, and Section 10.5 discusses the threats to validity. Finally, Section 10.6 provides conclusions and future work.

10.2 Background and Related Work

Nowadays, machine learning and deep learning techniques are being applied in many different domains. For instance, deep learning algorithms have been applied for face detection, image classification, and object detection problems, and researchers reported state-of-the-art results for these challenging problems [22]. Due to the increasing growth of cloud computing and web services technologies, machine learning–based prediction models have been integrated with cloud computing platforms. These studies can be considered under *machine learning as a service* category.

Ribeiro et al. [23] proposed a service component architecture to design and provide machine learning as a service (MLaaS). They showed the applicability of the proposed approach for energy demand forecasting problems. Hesamifard et al. [24] developed a framework to apply the deep learning algorithms over encrypted data and demonstrated how to train artificial neural networks with encrypted data and return the predictions in an encrypted format. Their approach follows privacy-preserving training and classification and also presents accurate results. Li et al. [25] developed a scalable MLaaS approach for Uber and discussed several scalability challenges when building MLaaS in a company. Assem et al. [26] proposed a high-level approach called TCDC (train, compare, decide, and change) as an MLaaS and showed that their approach is capable of selecting the best performance model across all models. Tafti et al. [27] determined ten MLaaS environments, namely Amazon Machine Learning, Google Cloud Prediction API, IBM Watson Analytics, Microsoft Azure Machine Learning Studio, BigML, Yottamine Analytics, Algorithmia, Ersatz, FICO Analytic Cloud, and Data Robot, and performed a comparison in medical informatics. They also analyzed BigML and Algorithmia environments with respect to quantitative and qualitative features. Bacciu et al. [28] developed a conceptual architecture for the implementation of a machine learning service for the Internet of Things and presented the relevant key guidelines. Loreti et al. [29] proposed a distributed architecture to parallelize the prediction stage of the machine learning pipeline and demonstrated the applicability of the approach with a text mining service. Prist et al. [30] compared the performance of machine learning algorithms implemented in cloud-based Microsoft Azure Machine Learning Studio and on-premise Matlab algorithms. Yao et al. [31] investigated the effectiveness of six MLaaS systems, namely Amazon Machine Learning, PredictionIO, Microsoft Azure Machine Learning Studio, Automatic Business Modeler (ABM), Google Prediction API, and BigML. As we see in these recent papers, machine learning as a service is a hot topic, and as such, we aimed to develop our software application categorization system based on this approach.

This research area, which categorizes software applications into domain categories, became more and more active. There are several studies that focus on the development of a novel approach that can work when the source code of the project is available. Some recent works aimed to develop tools, methods, and techniques in the absence of source code in software repositories [3,8]. Therefore, we can broadly classify research papers into two categories in this area. The first group is the development of models that are dependent on the source code, and the other group of papers does not rely on the source code. The second group of techniques can just work on the bytecode of the application.

Ugurel [10] reported that the Support Vector Machine (SVM) model is a good approach using the words in comments and README files. Kuhn et al. [11] introduced an approach based on Latent Semantic Indexing clustering and demonstrated that it could group source code having a similar vocabulary. Sandhu et al. [12] showed that Singular Value Decomposition (SVD) with Naive Bayes provides the best performance. Kelly et al. [13] used topic modeling approaches to retrieve topics from the source code. Wang et al. [9] showed that the approach that uses the SVM algorithm and online profiles is effective for categorizing applications. Hindle et al. [14] reported that the IBk algorithm is successful for the classification of commits.

Linares-Vasquez et al. [5] demonstrated that API calls from libraries could be used as features of the projects. They reported that linear SVM on the method level is the best approach for Sharejar projects, which do not contain source code, and the Expected Entropy Loss (EEL) algorithm selects the most relevant attributes. EEL is a statistical measure applied for feature selection and calculated for each feature. This measure ranks the features and removes the noninformative terms. A higher score shows more discriminatory features, and it is always nonnegative. To calculate the EEL measure, the prior entropy of the class distribution, the posterior entropy of the class in the case of existence of the feature, and the posterior entropy of the class in the case of absence of the feature must be computed. More information about the theory is provided in an Information Theory and Coding book [51].

Escobar-Avila et al. [15] proposed and validated a model that uses Dirichlet Process Clustering to group bytecode documents in the absence of source code. Also, their approach does not expect that API calls exist in the application. Vargas-Baldrich et al. [8] developed a software tagging approach called Sally for Maven-based projects and reported that Sally generates expressive tags and does not depend on machine learning algorithms. Recently, Al-Subaihin et al. [16] categorized mobile applications in Blackberry and Google app stores using an agglomerative hierarchical clustering method. They evaluated their approach to 17,877 applications and showed that their approach improves existing categorization quality. There is a recent survey on the analysis of app stores in software engineering [17]. It presents very useful future directions to address the open problems on the app store analysis.

Nguyen and Nguyen [18] applied the Deep Neural Network algorithm for software categorization and showed that this algorithm provides better performance than the other machine learning algorithms. Sharma et al. [19] processed readme files from GitHub, and they were used in the LDA-GA algorithm, which is a topic modeling algorithm to identify the domain categories. Chen et al. [20] categorized 13,000 services into 90 classes by using machine learning algorithms.

10.3 Methodology

Manual categorization of software projects into the corresponding categories by system administrators is time-consuming, expensive, and error-prone. When hundreds of projects are submitted to a repository in a day, the categorization of the application into the correct category correctly is not an easy and feasible task. To this end, we present an automated approach that does not require the use of administrators. Instead, the system automatically categorizes the software project, and later, the administrators can check whether the automated categorizations are correct or not. However, this step is not required but can support the automated approach to achieve high accuracy. In this context, accuracy (a.k.a., classification accuracy) is the metric used to evaluate the classification models and calculated by dividing the number of correct predictions over the total number of predictions. For highly imbalanced data sets, other evaluation parameters such as F-measure, Area Under ROC Curve (AUC), False Positive Rate, and False Negative Rate are also used.

In this section, we explain how the data set is generated, and experiments are performed with the help of classification algorithms. In Figure 10.1, we represent the overview of the experimental design. We use the Microsoft Azure cloud computing platform to respond to the client requests and Azure Machine Learning Studio platform for designing our experiments. In Figure 10.1, the SourceForge repository is depicted at the top, but this repository can be replaced with other repositories if necessary, and the overall approach is flexible enough to be used in other cases as well. Since our experiments are based on the data set that includes data from SourceForge, this figure includes this repository.

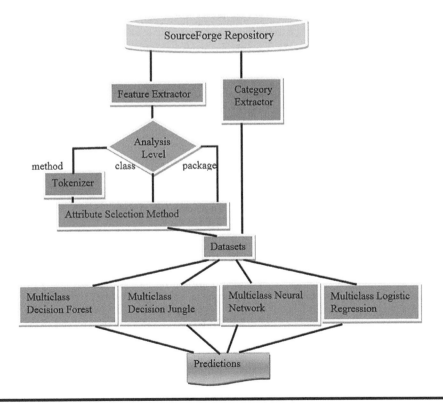

Figure 10.1   An overview of the experimental design.

Before we build and deploy the categorization web service into the Microsoft Azure cloud platform, we first investigated the performance of several multiclass classification algorithms that exist in the Azure Machine Learning Studio platform for this categorization problem. The platform provides four multiclass classification algorithms, namely decision forest, decision jungle, neural network, and logistic regression. From the SourceForge repository, we retrieve the corresponding category data and features regarding the project. Based on the analysis level, the tokenizer tool is executed. This tool is responsible for tokenizing the method names. For instance, the *getMidiMusic* method is divided into get, midi, and music keywords. For class and package levels, the tokenizer tool is not executed. The frequency of each word is considered as a feature in our approach, and as such, we built a dictionary to represent all the words used in the projects. As shown in Figure 10.1, after tokens are generated, an attribute selection method is run, and the most important attributes are selected. The Expected Entropy Loss method was used as the attribute selection approach. By combining features with the category information for all the projects, we generate the data sets on method, class, and package levels.

Our data sets are the same as the data sets used in Linares-Vásquez et al.'s study [5]. However, in Figure 10.1, we showed how a researcher or practitioner could build his/her own data set based on the available projects in a repository or company. This idea can be applied in different contexts with minor modifications. Feature extractor and category extractor tools can be implemented as two different tools, or it can be a single tool that performs these two tasks. This preference is an implementation-level decision and can be adjusted depending on the constraints of the platforms. For the evaluation of the classification algorithms, we performed fivefold cross-validation (CV). In N-fold CV, data is partitioned into N subsets, training is performed on one subset called training set $(N-1)$ and validated on the other subset called testing set (N). This process is repeated N times to reduce variability, and results are averaged to calculate the predictive performance.

We applied to 3,286 Java projects from the SourceForge repository. As the evaluation parameter, we used the accuracy parameter to evaluate the performance of the algorithms. In Table 10.1,

Table 10.1 SourceForge Project Categories

Category	Count	Category	Count
Bioinformatics	323	Education	775
Chat	504	Email	366
Communication	699	Frameworks	1,115
Compilers	309	Front Ends	584
Database	988	Games	607
Graphics	313	Indexing	329
Internet	1,061	Interpreters	303
Mathematics	373	Networking	360
Office	522	Scientific	326
Security	349	Testing	904
Visualization	456	Web	534

domain categories and the number of projects in a category are represented. Since the best performance in terms of accuracy parameter was achieved with the neural network algorithm, the model that is based on this algorithm was transformed into a web service. Subsequently, this web service was deployed into the Azure cloud using the features in the Azure Machine Learning Studio platform. Also, a web-based client application based on ASP.NET technology was implemented to call this categorization web service, inform the end user, and test the system. RESTful web services are preferred while transforming the prediction model into a web service in the machine learning platform that we used. We also selected the request/response approach to implement the web service instead of the batch execution approach. For the classification of a new project, we are able to send this testing data to the prediction web service deployed in the Azure cloud platform and receive the corresponding prediction label from the server. This end-to-end system is easy to maintain and adapt to new conditions because each component in this system is not highly dependent on the other components, and also, with the help of the cloud computing platform, the system is scalable. When the data set should be updated with more projects, the new prediction model should be built and then automatically transformed into a web service and deployed into the cloud platform again.

10.4 Experimental Results

In this section, we present our experimental results. Four multiclass classification algorithms were investigated for the application categorization problem on three granularity levels, namely package level, class level, and method level. Since Java projects can be analyzed based on these three levels, we aimed to see how the classification algorithms perform at these granularity levels. If one of these levels provides superior performance, we can select that level, and as such, we do not need to create data sets based on the other levels. Also, this would shorten the software development process and model building phase. For all the algorithms, we did this type of analysis by considering the granularity levels of projects. In practice, only one of these levels should be sufficient for practitioners.

In Figure 10.2, the experimental results of each algorithm are shown for the package level. It was observed that the Neural Network (NN) algorithm provides the best performance in this case. This NN algorithm is the implementation of the Multi-Layer Perceptron (MLP) topology. Also, the performance of the Decision Forest algorithm is very similar to the performance achieved with NN. The other two algorithms, Logistic Regression and Decision Jungle, did not provide good performance on this granularity level for this problem. Based on these experiments, we can conclude that either NNs or Decision Forest algorithm must be preferred in the case of package granularity level. Decision Jungle and Logistic Regression at this level should not be used due to their very low performance. Although decision jungles are recent extensions to decision forests, it is interesting to observe that the performance of decision jungle is very low compared to the decision forest algorithm. While decision jungles can be considered as an ensemble of decision-directed acyclic graphs, decision forests are an ensemble of decision trees that vote based on the most popular class. Since we have a lot of data for the training stage, the NN algorithm provided very high performance, but if we had less data, probably the performance would not be like this one. NN algorithms are mostly good at modeling complex relationships, and as such, it might have provided the best performance. It is also considered that the implementations of these high-performance algorithms are optimized, and we did not try to add more machine learning components such as parameter tuning to improve the performance.

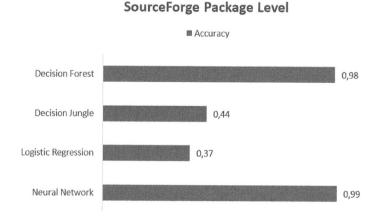

Figure 10.2   Results for the package level.

In Figure 10.3, the experimental results of each algorithm are shown for the class level. In this level, we observed that again NN and Decision Forest algorithms provide good performance compared to the other two algorithms. The best performance was achieved again with the NN algorithm. Compared to the package granularity level, the overall performance is lower in this case. This analysis indicates that researchers and practitioners should prefer the package analysis level instead of class level. The decision jungle algorithm, which is an extension of the decision forest algorithm, provides very low performance compared to the decision forest algorithm. At this analysis level, Decision Forest and NN algorithms can be preferred by the practitioners because of their similar performance. Since we did not optimize the parameters of the algorithms, their performance might be different when the parameters of the models are tuned.

In Figure 10.4, the experimental results of each algorithm are shown for the method level. Like in two other analyses, we observed that the NN algorithm and Decision Forest algorithm provide better performance compared to the other two algorithms. Logistic Regression algorithm again provided the worst performance among four classification algorithms. Based on this analysis, we have similar recommendations like in the previous package and class-level analysis. However,

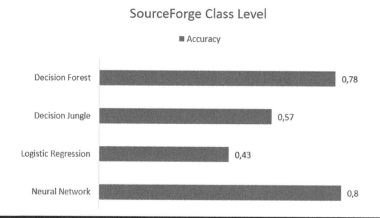

Figure 10.3   Results for the class level.

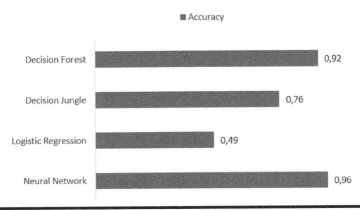

SourceForge Method Level

■ Accuracy

- Decision Forest — 0,92
- Decision Jungle — 0,76
- Logistic Regression — 0,49
- Neural Network — 0,96

Figure 10.4 Results for the method level.

the performance of the Decision Jungle algorithm is better compared to the performance of this algorithm at the other granularity levels.

In Figure 10.5, we show the performance of all the classification algorithms at all levels. The aim of this figure is to consolidate all the observations and present a single picture with all the required information. As we see in this figure, NN and Decision Forest algorithms provide much better performance compared to the other classification algorithms in terms of accuracy parameter. The performance of the method level is better than the class-level performance, and it is similar to the package-level performance. According to our experimental studies based on these three levels, we selected the NN-based categorization model, transformed it into a web service, and published it in the Azure cloud platform.

Responses to the Research Questions are listed as follows:

■ **A-RQ1:** It was shown that the cloud-computing-based categorization system simplifies many tasks with the help of web service capability.

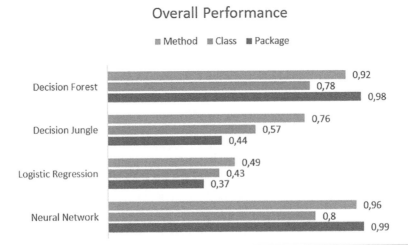

Overall Performance

■ Method ■ Class ■ Package

- Decision Forest — 0,92 / 0,78 / 0,98
- Decision Jungle — 0,76 / 0,57 / 0,44
- Logistic Regression — 0,49 / 0,43 / 0,37
- Neural Network — 0,96 / 0,8 / 0,99

Figure 10.5 An overview of results at three levels.

- **A-RQ2:** We observed that method-level and package-level analyses provide better performance than the class-level analysis for the software application categorization problem.
- **A-RQ3:** The NN-based model provides better performance.

Since the performance of the Decision Forest algorithm is comparable to the performance of the NN algorithm, researchers and practitioners might prefer this algorithm as well. If the implementation simplicity is the main concern of the practitioners, they can build the classification model based on the decision forest algorithm. Another drawback of the NN algorithms is that they work like black-box methods, and it is hard to explain how the model works. However, decision-tree-based algorithms such as decision forest algorithms are based on decision rules, and as such, the explanation of the decision behind these algorithms is relatively manageable. Practitioners should consider this complexity and explainability aspects before starting the implementation of the required prediction system.

10.5 Discussion

This study is an experimental study, and therefore, we should address the threats to validity in this section. As the other experimental software engineering studies, we have certain limitations, and as such, our conclusions are valid under the specified conditions and assumptions. The following issues discuss some of the limitations of our study, and other researchers can focus on some of these limitations to improve the performance of the presented models. Limitations of our study are given as follows:

- Our experiments were performed on a data set, including data from the SourceForge repository. Although this repository contains high-quality open-source projects, different source code repositories, and the other development approaches, such as closed-source development might impact the results of our experiments. Also, our data set contains only Java projects. If it is aimed to work on projects implemented with the other programming languages such as C++ or Python, new software components must be developed to build the data set, and the performance on this new data set may be different than the one reported in this study.
- An accuracy parameter was used to evaluate the performance of algorithms on different levels, such as class level and method level. Since the data set is not unbalanced, the accuracy parameter was suitable in this study. There are many evaluation parameters in the context of machine learning, but the accuracy is the one preferred by the researchers in this problem domain.
- We selected the well-known multiclass classification algorithms, which exist in the Azure Machine Learning Studio, and we applied all the available algorithms in this platform. However, different machine learning frameworks or machine learning as a service platform might contain different multiclass classification algorithms, and researchers might reach better results with different algorithms and settings.
- As the evaluation approaches, we followed the fivefold CV approach. There are other evaluation approaches, such as a hold-out approach (e.g., dividing the data set into training and testing data sets). Also, different K parameters can be preferred for the K-fold CV evaluation approach. The selection of the evaluation approach might have an impact on the performance of the classification algorithms.

■ Classification algorithms have been used with their default parameters. Parameter tuning (a.k.a., parameter optimization) might impact the performance of each classification algorithm, but we aimed to use the algorithms with their default parameters in this study to see the overall performance.

■ As the attribute selection approach, the Expected Entropy Loss method has been applied. However, there are dozens of attribute selection algorithms that can be used. If different attribute selection approaches are applied in our proposed approach, researchers may reach different results.

10.6 Conclusion

Categorizing software applications into domain categories is a challenging research area. In this study, we aimed to develop a cloud-based end-to-end categorization system. We designed several experiments using four classification algorithms, and three granularity levels (i.e., package level, class level, and method level), and the performance of the models was investigated based on the accuracy evaluation parameter.

We used data regarding the projects hosted in the SourceForge repository, which is one of the most popular ones in the software developer community. All the experiments were performed in the Azure Machine Learning Studio platform due to its flexibility, easy-to-use features, and scalability. Since there exist only four multiclass algorithms to apply, we applied all of them during our experiments. We demonstrated that the NN algorithm provides better performance for categorizing applications, and a cloud-based end-to-end categorization system is effective for application categorization problems. In addition to the NN algorithm, we observed that the Decision Forest algorithm also provides comparable performance. Due to the simplicity and explainability of Decision Forest algorithms, practitioners might prefer them instead of NN algorithms. The package granularity level provided the best performance among others, but also the performance of the method level was comparable to the package level.

As part of future work, new experiments can be performed on larger data sets, and deep learning algorithms can be applied. Recently, deep learning algorithms achieved remarkable results on different problems, such as face recognition and object detection. To this end, researchers can analyze the performance of deep learning algorithms such as Convolutional Neural Networks (CNN) [32], Recurrent Neural Networks (RNN) [33] (i.e., Long Short-Term Memory Networks – LSTM [34]), Autoencoders [35], Deep Belief Networks [36], and Boltzmann Machines [37] in addition to other traditional machine learning algorithms.

Other repositories can also be investigated, and new experiments can be performed on new repositories. In this research, we focused on the SourceForge repository, but there are similar repositories that host several open-source projects. Also, companies have many in-house software systems, and therefore, this type of analysis can be performed based on these legacy applications. Researchers and practitioners can prepare new data sets based on these projects, and even they can share them as public data sets with other researchers in some repositories. Since we could only access these public data sets, our experiments were performed on these datasets; however, our analysis can be performed in more data sets later on.

In addition, other ensemble algorithms such as Stacked Generalization (Stacking) [38], Gradient Boosting Machines [39], Gradient Boosted Regression Trees [40], Boosting [41], AdaBoost [42], and Bootstrapped Aggregation (Bagging) [43] can be implemented and investigated on different data sets regarding different repositories. Different feature selection approaches such as filter methods (i.e., Information Gain [44], Chi-square test [45]), wrapper methods (i.e., recursive feature elimination algorithm [46]), and embedded methods (i.e., regularization methods [47]) can be preferred in new research studies [22]. Several parameter optimization techniques such as Grid Search [48], Random Search [49], and Bayesian optimization [50] can also be applied to improve the performance of the prediction models.

The system and experiments can be performed for projects, which do not have the source code. However, in that case, we need to add new components to the system because we should process the bytecode instead of source code. There are several studies that can work on binary data, and as such, those papers must be investigated by the practitioners before the implementation.

References

1. Kalliamvakou, E., Gousios, G., Blincoe, K., Singer, L., German, D. M., & Damian, D. (2014, May). The promises and perils of mining GitHub. In *Proceedings of the 11th Working Conference on Mining Software Repositories* (pp. 92–101).
2. Howison, J., & Crowston, K. (2004, May). The Perils and Pitfalls of Mining SourceForge. In MSR (pp. 7–11). SourceForge. (2020) Sourceforge. [Online]. Available: https://sourceforge.net/directory/os:windows/
3. Catal, C., Tugul, S., & Akpinar, B. (2017). Automatic software categorization using ensemble methods and bytecode analysis. *International Journal of Software Engineering and Knowledge Engineering*, 27(07), 1129–1144.
4. Tian, K., Revelle, M., & Poshyvanyk, D. (2009, May). Using latent dirichlet allocation for automatic categorization of software. In *2009 6th IEEE International Working Conference on Mining Software Repositories* (pp. 163–166). IEEE.
5. Linares-Vásquez, M., McMillan, C., Poshyvanyk, D., & Grechanik, M. (2014). On using machine learning to automatically classify software applications into domain categories. *Empirical Software Engineering*, 19(3), 582–618.
6. Kawaguchi, S., Garg, P. K., Matsushita, M., & Inoue, K. (2006). Mudablue: An automatic categorization system for open source repositories. *Journal of Systems and Software*, 79(7), 939–953.
7. McMillan, C., Linares-Vasquez, M., Poshyvanyk, D., & Grechanik, M. (2011, September). Categorizing software applications for maintenance. In *2011 27th IEEE International Conference on Software Maintenance (ICSM)* (pp. 343–352). IEEE.
8. Vargas-Baldrich, S., Linares-Vásquez, M., & Poshyvanyk, D. (2015, November). Automated tagging of software projects using bytecode and dependencies (N). In *2015 30th IEEE/ACM International Conference on Automated Software Engineering (ASE)* (pp. 289–294). IEEE.
9. Wang, T., Wang, H., Yin, G., Ling, C. X., Li, X., & Zou, P. (2013, September). Mining software profile across multiple repositories for hierarchical categorization. In *2013 IEEE International Conference on Software Maintenance* (pp. 240–249). IEEE.
10. Ugurel, S., Krovetz, R., & Giles, C. L. (2002, July). What's the code? Automatic classification of source code archives. In *Proceedings of the Eighth ACM SIGKDD International Conference on Knowledge Discovery and Data Mining* (pp. 632–638).
11. Kuhn, A., Ducasse, S., & Gírba, T. (2007). Semantic clustering: Identifying topics in source code. *Information and Software Technology*, 49(3), 230–243.
12. Sandhu, P. S., Singh, J., & Singh, H. (2007). Approaches for categorization of reusable software components.
13. Kelly, M. B., Alexander, J. S., Adams, B., & Hassan, A. E. (2011, September). Recovering a balanced overview of topics in a software domain. In *2011 IEEE 11th International Working Conference on Source Code Analysis and Manipulation* (pp. 135–144). IEEE.
14. Hindle, A., German, D. M., Godfrey, M. W., & Holt, R. C. (2009, May). Automatic classication of large changes into maintenance categories. In *2009 IEEE 17th International Conference on Program Comprehension* (pp. 30–39). IEEE.

15. Escobar-Avila, J., Linares-Vásquez, M., & Haiduc, S. (2015, May). Unsupervised software categorization using bytecode. In *2015 IEEE 23rd International Conference on Program Comprehension* (pp. 229–239). IEEE.
16. Al-Subaihin, A. A., Sarro, F., Black, S., Capra, L., Harman, M., Jia, Y., & Zhang, Y. (2016, September). Clustering mobile apps based on mined textual features. In *Proceedings of the 10th ACM/IEEE International Symposium on Empirical Software Engineering and Measurement* (pp. 1–10).
17. Martin, W., Sarro, F., Jia, Y., Zhang, Y., & Harman, M. (2016). A survey of app store analysis for software engineering. *IEEE Transactions on Software Engineering*, 43(9), 817–847.
18. Nguyen, A. T., & Nguyen, T. N. (2017, May). Automatic categorization with deep neural network for open-source Java projects. In *2017 IEEE/ACM 39th International Conference on Software Engineering Companion (ICSE-C)* (pp. 164–166). IEEE.
19. Sharma, A., Thung, F., Kochhar, P. S., Sulistya, A., & Lo, D. (2017, June). Cataloging github repositories. In *Proceedings of the 21st International Conference on Evaluation and Assessment in Software Engineering* (pp. 314–319).
20. Chen, W., Xu, P., Wu, G., Dou, W., Gao, C., & Wei, J. (2017, June). A hierarchical categorization approach for system operation services. In *2017 IEEE International Conference on Web Services (ICWS)* (pp. 700–707). IEEE.
21. Fielding, R. T., & Taylor, R. N. (2000). *Architectural Styles and the Design of Network-Based Software Architectures* (Vol. 7). University of California, Irvine.
22. Brownlee, J. (2019). Deep Learning for Computer Vision: Image Classification, Object Detection, and Face Recognition in Python. Machine Learning Mastery.
23. Ribeiro, M., Grolinger, K., & Capretz, M. A. (2015, December). Mlaas: Machine learning as a service. In *2015 IEEE 14th International Conference on Machine Learning and Applications (ICMLA)* (pp. 896–902). IEEE.
24. Hesamifard, E., Takabi, H., Ghasemi, M., & Wright, R. N. (2018). Privacy-preserving machine learning as a service. *Proceedings on Privacy Enhancing Technologies*, 2018(3), 123–142.
25. Li, L. E., Chen, E., Hermann, J., Zhang, P., & Wang, L. (2017, July). Scaling machine learning as a service. In *International Conference on Predictive Applications and APIs* (pp. 14–29).
26. Assem, H., Xu, L., Buda, T. S., & O'Sullivan, D. (2016). Machine learning as a service for enabling Internet of Things and People. *Personal and Ubiquitous Computing*, 20(6), 899–914.
27. Tafti, A. P., LaRose, E., Badger, J. C., Kleiman, R., & Peissig, P. (2017, July). Machine learning-as-a-service and its application to medical informatics. In *International Conference on Machine Learning and Data Mining in Pattern Recognition* (pp. 206–219). Cham: Springer.
28. Bacciu, D., Chessa, S., Gallicchio, C., & Micheli, A. (2017, October). On the need of machine learning as a service for the internet of things. In *Proceedings of the 1st International Conference on Internet of Things and Machine Learning* (pp. 1–8).
29. Loreti, D., Lippi, M., & Torroni, P. (2020). Parallelizing Machine Learning as a service for the enduser. *Future Generation Computer Systems*, 105, 275–286.
30. Prist, M., Monteriù, A., Freddi, A., Pallotta, E., Ciabattoni, L., Cicconi, P., ... & Longhi, S. (2020, January). Machine learning-as-a-service for consumer electronics fault diagnosis: A comparison between matlab and Azure ML. In *2020 IEEE International Conference on Consumer Electronics (ICCE)* (pp. 1–5). IEEE.
31. Yao, Y., Xiao, Z., Wang, B., Viswanath, B., Zheng, H., & Zhao, B. Y. (2017, November). Complexity vs. performance: Empirical analysis of machine learning as a service. In *Proceedings of the 2017 Internet Measurement Conference* (pp. 384–397).
32. Krizhevsky, A., Sutskever, I., & Hinton, G. E. (2012). Imagenet classification with deep convolutional neural networks. In *Advances in Neural Information Processing Systems* (pp. 1097–1105).
33. Graves, A., Mohamed, A. R., & Hinton, G. (2013, May). Speech recognition with deep recurrent neural networks. In *2013 IEEE International Conference on Acoustics, Speech and Signal Processing* (pp. 6645–6649). IEEE.
34. Malhotra, P., Vig, L., Shroff, G., & Agarwal, P. (2015, April). Long short term memory networks for anomaly detection in time series. In *Proceedings* (Vol. 89). Presses Universitaires de Louvain.

35. Baldi, P. (2012, June). Autoencoders, unsupervised learning, and deep architectures. In *Proceedings of ICML Workshop on Unsupervised and Transfer Learning* (pp. 37–49).
36. Mohamed, A. R., Dahl, G. E., & Hinton, G. (2011). Acoustic modeling using deep belief networks. *IEEE Transactions on Audio, Speech, and Language Processing*, 20(1), 14–22.
37. Hinton, G. E. (2012). A practical guide to training restricted Boltzmann machines. In *Neural networks: Tricks of the trade* (pp. 599–619). Springer, Berlin, Heidelberg.
38. Naimi, A. I., & Balzer, L. B. (2018). Stacked generalization: An introduction to super learning. *European Journal of Epidemiology*, 33(5), 459–464.
39. Natekin, A., & Knoll, A. (2013). Gradient boosting machines, a tutorial. *Frontiers in Neurorobotics*, 7, 21.
40. Persson, C., Bacher, P., Shiga, T., & Madsen, H. (2017). Multi-site solar power forecasting using gradient boosted regression trees. *Solar Energy*, 150, 423–436.
41. Schapire, R. E. (1999, July). A brief introduction to boosting. In *Ijcai* (Vol. 99, pp. 1401–1406).
42. Hastie, T., Rosset, S., Zhu, J., & Zou, H. (2009). Multi-class adaboost. *Statistics and Its Interface*, 2(3), 349–360.
43. Breiman, L. (1996). Bagging predictors. *Machine Learning*, 24(2), 123–140.
44. Lee, C., & Lee, G. G. (2006). Information gain and divergence-based feature selection for machine learning-based text categorization. *Information Processing & Management*, 42(1), 155–165.
45. Jin, X., Xu, A., Bie, R., & Guo, P. (2006, April). Machine learning techniques and chi-square feature selection for cancer classification using SAGE gene expression profiles. In *International Workshop on Data Mining for Biomedical Applications* (pp. 106–115). Springer, Berlin, Heidelberg.
46. Yan, K., & Zhang, D. (2015). Feature selection and analysis on correlated gas sensor data with recursive feature elimination. *Sensors and Actuators B: Chemical*, 212, 353–363.
47. Ng, A. Y. (2004, July). Feature selection, L1 vs. L2 regularization, and rotational invariance. In *Proceedings of the Twenty-First International Conference on Machine Learning* (p. 78).
48. Pontes, F. J., Amorim, G. F., Balestrassi, P. P., Paiva, A. P., & Ferreira, J. R. (2016). Design of experiments and focused grid search for neural network parameter optimization. *Neurocomputing*, 186, 22–34.
49. Bergstra, J., & Bengio, Y. (2012). Random search for hyper-parameter optimization. *Journal of Machine Learning Research*, 13(Feb), 281–305.
50. Snoek, J., Larochelle, H., & Adams, R. P. (2012). Practical bayesian optimization of machine learning algorithms. In *Advances in Neural Information Processing Systems* (pp. 2951–2959).
51. Abramson, N. (1963). *Information Theory and Coding*. MacGraw-Hill, New York.

Chapter 11

Workflow-as-a-Service Cloud Platform and Deployment of Bioinformatics Workflow Applications

Muhammad H. Hilman
Universitas Indonesia

Maria A. Rodriguez and Rajkumar Buyya
University of Melbourne

Contents

11.1 Introduction

Workflow is a computational model that represents the application tasks and its related flow of data in the form of interconnected nodes. The data-intensive applications that utilize the workflow model consist of several complexes, large-scale applications, and involve a vast amount of data. These workflows' characteristics meet the criteria of the Big Data processing, which includes the massive involvement of volume, velocity, and variety of data. Therefore, these workflows are usually deployed in the distributed systems that have massive computational resources such as cluster, grid, and cloud computing environments.

To manage the complexity of executing workflows, its interaction with the users, and its connectivity to the resources in distributed systems, the researchers utilize the toolkit called workflow management system (WMS). The WMS hides the complicated orchestration between those coordinated components. It needs to be noted that the interconnected tasks within a workflow have strict dependencies in which the following tasks can be executed whenever the earlier tasks that become its dependencies have finished their execution. Therefore, the critical responsibility of this WMS includes the management of data movement, the scheduling of tasks and preserving their dependencies, and the provisioning of required computational resources from the external distributed systems.

The latest report by Gartner [1] presented public cloud computing trends in 2020 and its forecast for the next 5 years. It is expected that 60% of organizations all over the world will migrate their computational load to external cloud providers by 2022, and this number is expected to rise as high as 90% by 2025. This means that within 5 years, almost all services will be hosted on clouds. In addition, Gartner estimated that the revenue of cloud providers would grow to US$266.4 billion (A$387.83 billion) in 2020.

Furthermore, the popularity of using workflows to automate and manage complex scientific applications has risen as this increasing trend of migrating computational load from the on-premises data center to the cloud computing environments. This demand drives the market to provide many kinds of computational infrastructure as a service, including but not limited to compute resources, platforms, and the software. Therefore, there is a potential market to provide the execution of workflows as the utility services for the scientific community.

A conventional WMS is designed to manage the execution of a single workflow application. In this case, a WMS is tailored to a particular workflow application to ensure the efficient execution of the workflow. It is not uncommon for a WMS to be built by a group of researchers to deploy a specific application of their research projects. With the advent of the computational infrastructure and the rising trends of workflow model adoption within the scientific community, there is a demand to provide the execution of workflow as a service. Therefore, there is an idea to elevate the functionality of WMS to provide the service for executing workflows in the clouds called the Workflow-as-a-Service (WaaS) cloud platform. To the best of our knowledge, this kind of platform is still in progress, and no working system has provided this particular service to the market yet.

Developing the WaaS cloud platform means scaling up the WMS functionality and minimizing any specific application-tailored in the component of the system. This challenge arises with several issues related to the resource provisioning and scheduling aspect of the WMS. In this work, we focus on designing the resource provisioning and scheduling module within the existing CloudBus WMS [2] for the WaaS cloud platform development. We modify the scheduling modules to fit into the requirements by building on the capability for scheduling multiple workflows.

We evaluate our proposed platform with two bioinformatics workflows. The first workflow is 1,000 Genome workflow to identify overlapping mutations in human genes. It provides a statistical evaluation of potential disease-related mutations. The second workflow is AutoDock Vina – a molecular docking application – to screen a large number of ligand libraries for plausible drug candidates (i.e., virtual screening). These workflows are taken as case study to learn how the platform's prototype manages the execution of multiple workflows.

In summary, the main contributions of this chapter are:

- The development of CloudBus WMS extension for WaaS cloud platform.
- The implementation of EBPSM that can handle multiple workflows scheduling within WaaS cloud platform.
- The performance evaluation of WaaS cloud platform prototype in real cloud computing environments.

The rest of this chapter is organized as follows. Section 11.2 reviews works are related to our discussion. Section 11.3 describes the development of WaaS cloud platform and its requirements. Meanwhile, Section 11.4 explains the case study of execution of multiple workflows in WaaS cloud platform. Finally, the Section 11.5 summarizes the findings and discusses the future directions.

11.2 Related Work

WMS technology has evolved since the era of cluster, grid, and current cloud computing environments. A number of widely used WMSs were initially built by groups of multidisciplinary researchers to deploy the life-science applications of their research projects developed based on the computational workflow model. Each of them has a characteristic tailored to their requirements. However, to the best of our knowledge, the existing WMS systems are not designed for handling multiple workflows execution as it becomes the main requirement for WaaS cloud platform. Therefore, the case study of several prominent WMSs is plentiful and worth to be explored further for the development of such a platform.

ASKALON [3] is a framework for development and runtime environments for scientific workflows built by a group from The University of Innsbruck, Austria. Along with ASKALON, the group released a novel workflow language standard developed based on the XML called Abstract Workflow Description Language (AWDL) [4]. ASKALON has a tailored implementation of wien2k workflow [5], a material science workflow for performing electronic structure calculations using density functional theory based on the full-potential augmented plane wave to be deployed within the Austrian Grid Computing network.

Another project is Galaxy [6], a web-based platform that enables users to share workflow projects and provenance. It connects to myExperiments [7], a social network for sharing the workflow configuration and provenance among the scientific community. It is a prominent WMS and widely used for in silico experiments [8–10].

A lightweight WMS, HyperFlow [11], is a computational model, programming approach, and also a workflow engine for scientific workflows from AGH University of Science and Technology, Poland. It provides a simple declarative description based on JavaScript. HyperFlow supports the workflow deployment in container-based infrastructures such as Docker and Kubernetes clusters. HyperFlow is also able to utilize the serverless architecture for deploying Montage workflow in AWS Lambda and Google Function, as reported by Malawski et al. [12].

Kepler [13] is a WMS developed by a collaboration of universities, including UC Davis, UC Santa Barbara, and UC San Diego, United States. It is a WMS that is built on top of the data-flow-oriented Ptolemy II system [14] from UC Berkeley. Kepler has been adopted in various scientific projects including the fluid dynamics [15] and computational biology [16]. This WMS provides compatibility to run on different platforms, including Windows, OSX, and Unix systems.

Another project is Pegasus [17], one of the prominent WMSs that is widely adopted for projects that make an essential breakthrough to scientific discovery from The University of Southern California, United States. Pegasus runs the workflows on top of HTCondor [18] and supports the deployment across several distributed systems, including grid, cloud, and container-based environments. The Pegasus WMS has a contribution to the LIGO projects involved in the gravitational wave detection [19].

Furthermore, there is also Taverna [20], a workflow management system from The University of Manchester that has been recently accepted under the Apache Incubator project. Taverna is designed to enable various deployment models from the stand-alone, server-based, portal, clusters, grids, to the cloud environments. Taverna has been used in various in silico bioinformatics projects, including several novel Metabolomics research [21,22].

Finally, the CloudBus WMS [2], a cloud-enabled WMS from The University of Melbourne, is the center of discussion in this paper. The CloudBus WMS is comparable to other WMS in terms of its GUI and provenance-supported features. Furthermore, the CloudBus MWS also is equivalent to the majority of MWSs in terms of the support for deployment in grid and cloud computing environments. This detailed comparison can be seen in Table 11.1.

11.3 Prototype of WaaS Cloud Platform

In this section, we discuss a brief development of the CloudBus WMS and the WaaS cloud platform development. The evolving functionality of CloudBus WMS in its first release to handle the deployment in the grid computing environment up to the latest version that provides the cloud-enabled functionality is described to give an overview of how the distributed systems change how the WMS works. Furthermore, we present the extension related to the scheduler component of this existing WMS to support the development of the WaaS cloud platform.

11.3.1 CloudBus Workflow Management System

The earliest version of the WMS from the CLOUDS lab was designed for grid computing environments under the name of GridBus Workflow Enactment Engine in 2008. The core engine in this WMS was called a workflow enactment engine that orchestrated the whole workflow execution. The engine interacts with users through the portal that manages workflow composition and execution planning. This engine also equipped with the ability to interact with grid computing environments through the grid resource discovery to find the possible grid computational infrastructure, the dispatcher that sends the tasks to the grids for the execution, and the data movement to manage data transfer in and out through HTTP and GridFTP protocols. The Gridbus Workflow Enactment Engine was tested and evaluated using a case study of fMRI data analysis in

Table 11.1 Summary of Various WMS Features

Main Features		Askalon	Galaxy	HyperFlow	Kepler	Pegasus	Taverna	CloudBus
Workflow engine	Service-oriented	✓	✓	-	✓	✓	✓	✓
	GUI-supported	✓	✓	-	✓	✓	✓	✓
	Provenance-empowered	✓	✓	✓	✓	✓		✓
Distributed environments	Grid-enabled	✓	✓	✓	✓	✓	✓	✓
	Cloud-enabled	✓	✓	✓	✓	✓	✓	✓
	Container-enabled	-	✓	✓	-	✓	-	-
	Serverless-enabled	-	-	✓	-	-	-	-

the medical area. The architectural reference to this Gridbus Workflow Engine and its case study can be referred to in the paper by Yu and Buyya [23].

The second version of the GridBus Workflow Enactment Engine was released in 2011, built with plugin support for deployment in cloud computing environments. In this version, the engine is equipped with the components that enable it to utilize several types of external computational resources, including grid and cloud environments. Therefore, it was renamed to CloudBus Workflow Engine. In addition to this functionality, the CloudBus Workflow Engine was tested and evaluated for scientific workflow execution on top of the Aneka Cloud Enterprise platform [24] and Amazon Elastic Compute Cloud (EC2) using a case study of evolutionary multiobjective optimization technique based on a genetic algorithm. We suggested that readers refer to the architectural design and case study implementation published by Pandey et al. [25].

The latest release of the CloudBus Workflow Engine in 2016 was the implementation of a comprehensive cloud-enabled functionality that allows the engine to lease the computational resources dynamically from the IaaS cloud providers. This version introduces a Cloud Resource Manager module that enables the platform to manage the resources (i.e., Virtual Machines (VMs)) from several IaaS cloud providers related to its automated provisioning, integrating to the resource pool, and terminating the VMs based on the periodic scanning of the implemented algorithm. Along with the dynamic functionality of cloud resources management, the WMS is also equipped with a dynamic algorithm to schedule workflows, which is able to estimate the tasks' runtime based on the historical data from the previous workflows' execution. This version is known as the CloudBus WMS. The architectural reference and its case study on Astronomical application Montage can be referred to in the paper by Rodriguez and Buyya [2].

11.3.2 WaaS Cloud Platform Development

The CloudBus WMS is continuously adapting to the trends of the distributed systems' infrastructures from cluster, grid, to the cloud environments. With the increasing popularity of the computational workflow model across scientific fields, we extend the CloudBus WMS to serve as a platform that provides the execution of workflow as a service. Therefore, we design the reference to the WaaS cloud platform based on the structure of CloudBus WMS. Five entities compose the WaaS cloud platform, they are portal, engine, monitoring service, historical database, and plugins to connect to distributed computing environments. This structure is similar to the previous CloudBus WMS architecture. The architectural reference for the platform can be seen in Figure 11.1.

Portal: an entity that is responsible for bridging the WaaS cloud platform to the users. The portal serves as the user interface in which users can submit the job, including composing, editing, and defining the workflow QoS requirements. It interacts with the engine to pass on the submitted workflows for scheduling. It also interacts with the monitoring service so that the users can monitor the progress of the workflows' deployment. Finally, the engine sends back the output data after it finished the execution through this entity. The change from the previous CloudBus WMS functionality is the capability of the portal to handle the workload of multiple workflows.

Monitoring Service: an entity that is responsible for monitoring the workflow execution and resources running within the WaaS cloud platform that is provisioned from the clouds. Five components in this entity are the *Workflow Monitor* that tracks the execution of the jobs, the *Resource Monitor*, which tracks the VMs running in the platform, the *Cloud Information Services* that discover the available VM types and images of the IaaS clouds profile, the *Cloud Resource Manager* that manages the provisioning of cloud resources, and the *VM Lifecycle Manager*, which keeps tracking the VMs' status before deciding to terminate them.

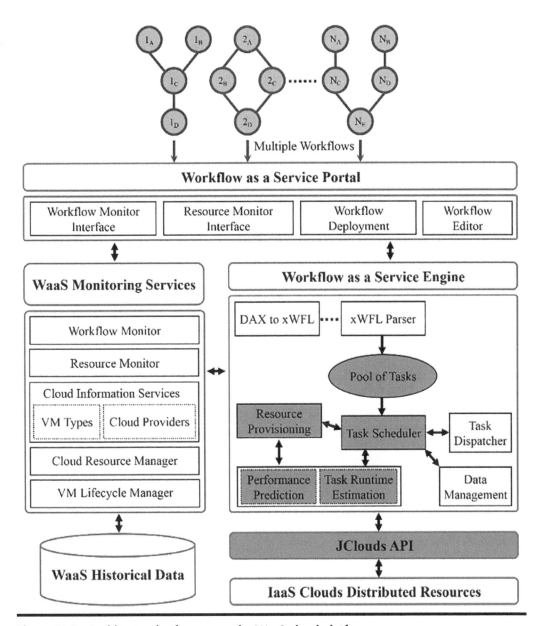

Figure 11.1   Architectural reference on the WaaS cloud platform.

This entity interacts with the portal to provide the monitoring information of workflows' execution. On the other hand, it also interacts with the engine to deliver the status of job execution for scheduling purposes and the state of the computational resource availability. We changed the provisioning algorithm, which is managed by the cloud resource manager and the VM life cycle manager, based on the EBPSM. Both the cloud resource manager and the VM life cycle manager control the VMs provisioning by keeping track of the idle status of each VM. They will be terminated if the idle time exceeded the *threshold*$_{idle}$. This provisioning algorithm is depicted in Algorithm 1. Finally, this entity saves the historical data of tasks' execution into the historical database based on an HSQL database where the information is used to estimate the tasks' runtime.

Algorithm 1: Resource Provisioning

> **procedure** manageResource
> VM_{idle} = all leased VMs that are idle
> $threshold_{idle}$ = idle time threshold
>   **for** each $vm_{idle} \in VM_{idle}$ **do**
> t_{idle} = idle time of vm
>   **if** $t_{idle} \geq threshold_{idle}$ **then**
>   terminate vm_{idle}
>   **end if**
>   **end for**
> **end procedure**

Engine: an entity that is responsible for the orchestration of the whole execution of workflows. This entity interacts with the other objects of the WaaS cloud platform, including the third-party services outside the platform. Moreover, it takes the workflows' job from the portal and manages the execution of tasks. The scheduler that is part of this entity schedules each task from different workflows and allocates them to the available resources maintained by the monitoring service. It also sends the request to the plugins, JClouds API, for provisioning new resources if there is no available idle VMs to reuse.

Task scheduler, the core of the engine, is modified to adapt to the EBPSM that manages the scheduling of multiple workflows. Within the task scheduler, there is a component called the *WorkflowCoordinator* that creates the *Task Manager(s)* responsible for scheduling each task from the pool of tasks. To manage the arriving tasks from the portal, we create a new class *WorkflowPoolManager* responsible for periodically releasing ready tasks for scheduling and keeping track of the ownership of each task.

Prediction component within the task scheduler is responsible for estimating the runtime of the task, which becomes a prerequisite of the scheduling. We modify the *PredictRuntime* component to be capable of building an online incremental learning model. This learning model is a new approach for estimating the runtime for scientific workflows implemented in the WaaS cloud platform. In the previous version, it utilizes statistical analysis to predict the tasks' runtime.

Historical database: an HSQL database used to store the historical data of tasks' execution. The information, then, is used to estimate the tasks' runtime. In this platform, we add the submission time variables to the database, since this information is used to build the prediction model to estimate the runtime.

Plugins: a JClouds API responsible for connecting the WaaS cloud platform to third-party computational resources. Currently, the platform can connect to several cloud providers, including Amazon EC2, Google Cloud Engine, Windows Azure, and OpenStack-based NeCTAR clouds. It sends the request to provision and terminates resources from the cloud providers.

Finally, the modified components within the WaaS cloud platform from the previous version of the CloudBus WMS are marked with the dark-filled diagram in Figure 11.1, and the class diagram reference to the WaaS cloud platform scheduler extension is depicted in Figure 11.2.

11.3.3 Implementation of Multiple Workflows Scheduling Algorithm

EBPSM is a dynamic heuristic algorithm designed for WaaS cloud platform. The algorithm was designed to schedule tasks from multiple workflows driven by the budget to minimize the makespan. EBPSM distributes the budget to each of its tasks in the first step, and then, it manages the

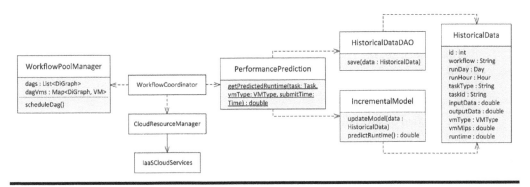

Figure 11.2   Class diagram reference on the scheduler extension of the WaaS cloud platform.

tasks from different workflows to schedule based on its readiness to run (i.e., parents' tasks finished the execution).

Furthermore, the algorithm looks for idle resources that can finish the tasks as fast as possible without violating its assigned budget. This algorithm enforces the reuse of already provisioned resources (i.e., VMs) and sharing them between tasks from different workflows. This policy was endorsed to handle the uncertainties in the clouds, including VM performance variability, VM provisioning, and deprovisioning delays, and the network-related overhead that incurs within the environments. Whenever a task finishes, the algorithm redistributes the budget for the task's children based on the actual cost. In this way, the uncertainties, as mentioned earlier from cloud computing environments, can be further mitigated before creating a snowball effect for the following tasks.

The scheduling phase of the EBPSM was mainly implemented in the task scheduler, a part of the engine. The *WorkflowPoolManager* class receives the workflows' jobs and distributes the budget to the tasks as described in Algorithm 2. It keeps track of the workflows' tasks before placing the ready tasks on the priority queue based on the ascending Earliest Finish Time (EFT). Then, the *WorkflowCoordinator* creates a task manager for each task that is pooled from the queue. In the resource provisioning phase, the task scheduler interacts with the cloud resource manager in the monitoring resource to get the information of the available VMs.

The task scheduler sends the request to provision a new VM if there are no VMs available to reuse. The implementation of this phase involves several modules from different components of the WaaS cloud platform. The details of this scheduling are depicted in Algorithm 3.

The post-scheduling of a task ensures budget preservation by calculating the actual cost and redistributing the workflows' budget. This functionality was implemented in the task scheduler with additional information related to the clouds from the cloud information service, which maintains the cloud profile such as the VM types, and the cost of the billing period. The details of the budget redistribution procedure are described in Algorithm 4.

Algorithm 2: Budget Distribution

    procedure distributeBudget (β, T)
        S = tasks' estimated execution order
        T = set of tasks in the workflow
        l = tasks' level in the workflow
        β = workflow's budget

    for each *task* $t \in T$ **do**
      allocateLevel(t, l)
      initiateBudget(0, t)
    end for
    for each level *l* **do**
      T_l=set of all tasks in level *l*
      sort T_l based on ascending EFT
      put(T_l, S)
    end for
    while $\beta > 0$ **do**
      t=*S.poll*
      C^t_{vmt}=cost of task *t* in *vmt*
      vmt=chosen VM type
      allocateBudget($C^t_{vmt,}$ t)
      $\beta = \beta - C^t_{vmt}$
    end while
    end procedure

Algorithm 3: Scheduling

    procedure scheduledQueuedTasks(*q*)
      sort *q* by ascending EFT
      while *q* is not empty **do**
        t=*q.poll*
        vm=*null*
        if there are idle VMs **then**
          VM_{idle}=set of all idle VMs
          vm=*vm* $\in VM_{idle}$ that can finish *t* within *t.budget* with the fastest execution time
        else
          vmt=fastest VM type within
          t.budget
          vm=*provisionVM(vmt)*
        end if
        scheduleTask(t, vm)
      end while
    end procedure

Algorithm 4: Budget Update

    procedure scheduledQueuedTasks(*q*)
      sort *q* by ascending EFT
      while *q* is not empty **do**
        t=*q.poll*
        vm=*null*
        if there are idle VMs **then**
          VM_{idle}=set of all idle VMs
          vm=*vm* $\in VM_{idle}$ that can finish *t*within *t.budget* with the fastest execution time

      else
          vmt=fastest VM type within*t.budget*
          vm=*provisionVM(vmt)*
      end if
      scheduleTask(t, vm)
    end while
  end procedure

In this work, we implemented a version of the EBPSM without the container. We did not need the container-enabled version as we only used bioinformatics workflow applications that did not have conflicting software dependencies and libraries. The enablement for microservices and serverless-supported WaaS cloud platform is left for further development. For more details on the EBPSM versions and their budget distribution strategies, we suggested the readers to refer to the papers by Hilman et al. [26,27].

11.4 Case Study

In this section, we present the case study of multiple workflows execution within a WaaS cloud platform prototype. We address the workload of bioinformatics workflows and its preparation for the execution. Furthermore, we also describe the technical infrastructure and its experimental design to deploy the platform and present the results from the experiment.

11.4.1 Bioinformatics Applications Workload

Many bioinformatics cases have adopted the workflow model for managing its scientific applications. An example is myExperiments [7] that has a broader scope to connect various bioinformatics workflows' users. This social network for scientists who utilize the workflows for managing their experiments stores almost 4,000 workflows software, configurations, and data sets with more than 10,000 members. We explored two prominent bioinformatics workflows in the area of genomics analysis [28] and drug discovery [29] as a case study for this work.

11.4.1.1 Identifying Mutational Overlapping Genes

The first bioinformatics case was based on the 1000 Genomes Project[1], an international collaboration project to build a human genetic variation catalogue. Specifically, we used an existing 1000 Genome workflow[2] to identify overlapping mutations in humans' genes. The overlapping mutations were statistically calculated in a rigorous way to provide an analysis of possible disease-related mutations across human populations based on their genomics properties. This project has an impact on evolutionary biology. Examples include a project related to the discovery of full genealogical histories of DNA sequences [30].

    The workflow consists of five tasks that have different computational requirements [31]. They are *individuals*, *individuals_merge*, *sifting*, *mutations_overlap*, and *frequency*. *Individuals* performs data fetching and parsing of the 1000 genome project data that listed all Single Nucleotide

---

[1] http://www.internationalgenome.org/about.
[2] https://github.com/pegasus-isi/1000genome-workflow.

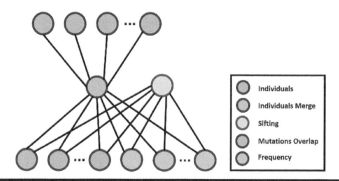

Figure 11.3 1000 Genome workflow.

Polymorphisms (SNPs) variation in the chromosome. This activity involves a lot of I/O reading and writing system call. *Individuals_merge* showed similar properties, as it was a merging of *individuals* outputs that calculate different parts of chromosomes data. Furthermore, *sifting* calculates the SIFT scores of all SNPs variants. This task has a very short runtime. Finally, *mutations_overlap* calculates the overlapping mutations genes between a pair of individuals while *frequency* calculates the total frequency of overlapping mutation genes between several random individuals.

The 1000 Genome workflow takes two inputs, the chromosome data and its haplotype estimation (i.e., phasing) using the shapeit method. The entry tasks were *individuals*, which extract each individual from chromosome data, and *sifting* that calculates the SIFT scores from the phasing data. Furthermore, in the next level, *individuals_merge* merged all output from *individuals*, and then, its output along with the *sifting* output becomes the input for the exit tasks of *mutation_overlap* and *frequency*. For our study, we analyzed the data corresponding to two chromosomes (chr21 and chr22) across five populations: African (AFR), Mixed American (AMR), East Asian (EAS), European (EUR), and South Asian (SAS). Furthermore, the structure of the workflow is shown in Figure 11.3.

11.4.1.2 Virtual Screening for Drug Discovery

The second bioinformatics case used in this study was the virtual screening workflow. Virtual screening is a novel methodology that utilized several computational tools to screen a large number of molecules' libraries for possible drug candidates [32]. In simple terms, this (part of) drug discovery process involves two types of molecules, target receptors, and ligands that would become the candidates of drugs based on its binding affinity to the target receptor. This technique rises in popularity as the in silico infrastructure and information technology are getting better. The virtual screening saves many resources of scientists for in vitro and in vivo that require wet-lab experiments.

There are two main approaches in carrying out the virtual screening: ligand-based and receptor-based virtual screening [33]. The ligand-based virtual screening relies on the similarity matching of ligands' libraries to the already known active ligand(s) properties. This activity is computationally cheaper than the other approach, as it depends only on the computation of the features of the molecules. On the other hand, the receptor-based virtual screening requires the calculation for both of the target receptors and the ligands to evaluate the possible interaction between them in a very intensive simulation and modeling. However, since the error rate of ligand-based virtual

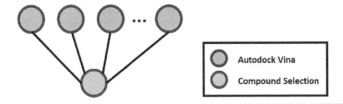

Figure 11.4   AutoDock Vina workflow.

screening is relatively higher than the structure-based, this approach is applied as a filter step when the number of ligands involved in the experiments is quite high.

In this study, we used a virtual screening workflow using AutoDock Vina [34], a molecular docking application for structure-based virtual screening. In particular, we took a virtual screening case of one receptor and ligands with various sizes and search spaces of the docking box taken from the Open Science Grid Project developed by the Pegasus group[3]. The receptor-ligand docking tasks in this workflow can be executed in parallel as in the bag of the tasks application model. Moreover, AutoDock Vina is a CPU-intensive application that can utilize the multi-CPU available in a machine to speed up the molecular docking execution. Therefore, two-level parallelism can be achieved to speed up the workflows, the parallel execution of several receptor-ligand docking tasks on different machines, and the multi-CPU parallel execution of a docking task within a machine. The structure of the virtual screening workflows is depicted in Figure 11.4.

11.4.2 Workload Preparation

The Pegasus group has developed the tools to generate both the 1000 Genome and Virtual Screening workflow based on the XML format. We converted the DAG (Direct Acyclic Graph) generated from the tools into the xWFL, the format used by the WaaS cloud platform. Based on this converted DAG, we prepared two versions of the 1000 Genome workflows, which take two different chromosomes of chr21 and chr22 as input. Furthermore, we created two types of workflows that take as input two different sets of seven ligand molecules for Virtual Screening.

We installed five applications for the 1000 Genome workflow in a custom VM image for the worker nodes. These applications are based on the Mutation_Sets project[4] and are available in the 1000 Genome workflow project[5]. It needs to be noted that the *mutation_overlap* and *frequency* tasks were python-based applications and have a dependency on the *python-numpy* and *python-matplotlib* modules. On the other hand, the only application that needs to be installed for the Virtual Screening workflow was AutoDock Vina[6], which can be installed without any conflicting dependencies with the other workflow applications. Therefore, in this scenario, we did not encounter the conflicting dependencies problem.

We composed a workload that consists of 20 workflows with the types as mentioned earlier of applications that were randomly selected based on a uniform distribution. We also modeled four different arrival rates of those workflows based on a Poisson distribution from 0.5 workflows per

---

[3] https://github.com/pegasus-isi/AutoDock-Vina-Workflow.

[4] https://github.com/rosafilgueira/Mutation_Sets.

[5] https://github.com/pegasus-isi/1000genome-workflow.

[6] http://vina.scripps.edu/.

Table 11.2 Various Budgets Used in Evaluation

Name	β_1	β_2	β_3	β_4
1000 Genome Workflow				
chr21	$0.1	$0.25	$0.45	$0.65
chr22	$0.1	$0.25	$0.45	$0.65
Virtual Screening Workflow				
vina01	$0.05	$0.15	$0.25	$0.35
vina02	$0.01	$0.04	$0.06	$0.08

minute (wf/m), which represents the infrequent requests, up to 12 wf/m that reflects the busiest hours. Each workflow was assigned a sufficient budget based on our initial deployment observation. We defined four different budgets for each workflow from β_1 to β_4, which represent the minimum to the maximum willingness of users to spend for particular workflows' execution. These budgets can be seen in Table 11.2.

11.4.3 Experimental Infrastructure Setup

Three components need to be deployed to ensure the running of the WaaS cloud platform. The first is the master node containing the core of the workflow engine. This master node is the component that manages the life cycle of workflows' execution and responsible for the automated orchestration between every element within the platform. The second component is a storage node that stores all the data involved in the execution of the workflows. This storage manages the intermediate data produced between parents and children tasks' execution and acts as a central repository for the WaaS cloud platform. Finally, the worker node is the front-runner to execute the workflows' tasks submitted into the platform. The worker node(s) provisioning and life spans are controlled based on the scheduling algorithms implemented in the core of the workflow engine.

For this experiment, we arranged these components on VMs with different configurations and setup. The master node was installed on Ubuntu 14.04. 6 LTS VM running in a local HP Laptop with Intel(R) Core(TM) i7-56000 CPU @ 2.60 GHz processor and 16.0 GB RAM. This VM was launched using VMWare Workstation 15 player with 8.0 GB RAM and 60.0 GB hard disk storage. Moreover, we deployed the storage node on a cloud instance provided by The Melbourne Research Cloud[7] located in the *melbourne-qh2-uom* availability zone. This VM was installed on Ubuntu 14.04.6 LTS operating systems based on the *uom. general.1c4g* flavor with 1 vCPU, 4 GB RAM, and an additional 500 GB hard disk storage.

Furthermore, the worker nodes were dynamically provisioned on Amazon EC2 Asia Pacific Sydney region using a custom-prepared VM image equipped with the necessary software, dependencies, and libraries for executing 1000 Genome and Virtual Screening workflows. We used four different types and configurations for the worker nodes based on the family of T2 instances. The T2 instances family equipped with the high-frequency processors and have a balance of compute,

---

[7] https://gateway.research.unimelb.edu.au/resources/platforms-infrastructure-and-equipment/research-computing-services/services/research-cloud.

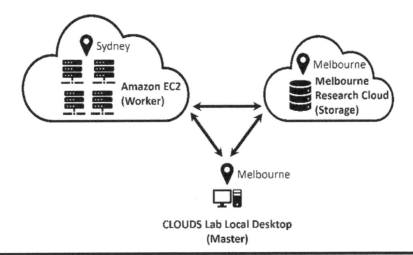

Figure 11.5 Architectural reference on the WaaS cloud platform nodes deployment.

Table 11.3 Configuration of Virtual Machines Used in Evaluation

Name	vCPU	Memory	Price per Second
CLOUDS Lab Local Desktop			
Master Node	4	8,192 MB	N/A
Melbourne Research Cloud			
Storage Node	1	4,096 MB	N/A
Amazon EC2			
Worker Node			
t2.micro	1	1,024 MB	$0.0000041
t2.small	1	2,048 MB	$0.0000082
t2.medium	2	4,096 MB	$0.0000164
t2.large	2	8,192 MB	$0.0000382

memory, and network resources. Finally, the architectural reference for the nodes' deployment and its configuration are depicted in Figure 11.5 and Table 11.3 respectively.

11.4.4 Results and Analysis

In this section, we present the comparison of EBPSM and First Come First Serve (FCFS) algorithm, as the default scheduler, in a single workflow and homogeneous settings to ensure the fair evaluation. Then, it was followed by a thorough analysis of the EBPSM performance on a workload of multiple workflows in a heterogeneous environment represented by different arrival rates of workflows to the WaaS cloud platform.

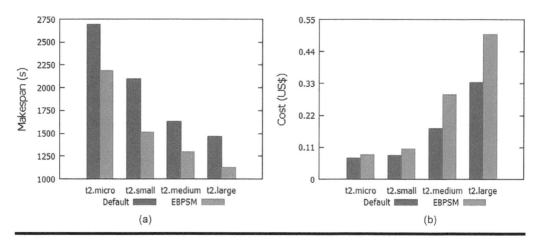

Figure 11.6   Makespan and cost of 1000 Genome (chr22) workflow in homogeneous environment.

11.4.4.1 More Cost to Gain Faster Execution

The purpose of this particular experiment is to evaluate our proposed EBPSM for the WaaS platform compared to the default scheduler of the CloudBus WMS. This default scheduler algorithm did not rely on an estimate of tasks' runtime. It scheduled each task based on the first-come, first-served policy into a dedicated resource (i.e., VM) and terminated the resource when the particular task has finished the execution. Furthermore, this default scheduler was not equipped with the capability to select the resources in heterogeneous environments. Therefore, it only works for homogeneous cluster settings (i.e., clusters of one VM type only). Then, to have a fair comparison to the default scheduler, we modified the EBPSM to work for a single workflow in a homogeneous environment. We removed the module that enables EBPSM to select the fastest resources based on the task's subbudget and let the algorithm provision a new VM if there are no idle VMs available to reuse, which means hiding the budget-driven ability of the algorithm.

In Figure 11.6a, we can see that the homogeneous version of EBPSM was superior to the default scheduler on all scenarios. In this experiment, the default scheduler provisioned 26 VMs for each situation, while EBPSM only leased 14 VMs. In this case, we argue that the delays in initiating the VMs, which include the provisioning delay and delays in configuring the VM into the WaaS platform, have a significant impact on the total makespan. Therefore, the EBPSM can gain an average speed of 1.3× faster compared to the default scheduler. However, this enhancement comes with a consequence of additional monetary cost.

Figure 11.6b shows that there is an increase in monetary cost for executing the workflows. The EBPSM lets the idle VM to be active for a certain period before being terminated, hoping that the next ready tasks would reuse it. This approach produced a higher cost compared to the immediate resource termination of the default scheduler approach. The average increase was 40% higher than the default scheduler. Is it worth to spend 40% more cost to gain 1.3× faster makespan? Further evaluation, such as Pareto analysis, needs to be done. However, more rapid responses to events such as modeling the storm, tsunami, and bush fires in the emergency disaster situation, or predicting the cell location for critical surgery are undoubtedly worth more resources to be spent.

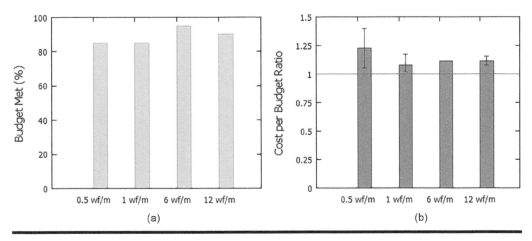

Figure 11.7 Cost and budget analysis on workload with different arrival rate.

11.4.4.2 Budget Met Analysis

To evaluate the budget-constrained multiple workflows deployment, we analyzed the performance of the EBPSM against its primary objective, meeting the budget. Two metrics were used in this analysis: the number of successful cases in meeting the budget and the cost per budget ratio for any failed ones.

In this experiment, we observed the EBPSM performance in various arrival rate scenarios to see if this algorithm can handle the workload in both peak and nonpeak hours. Figure 11.7a shows that in the nonpeak hours, the EBPSM could achieve 85% of the budget met while in the busier environment, this percentage increases up to 95%. In the peak hours, there are more VMs to reuse and less idle time that makes the platform more efficient. However, it needs to be noted that there might exist some variability in the Amazon EC2 performance that might impact the results. Thus, the graphs did not show a linear convergence. Nevertheless, 85% of the budget-met percentage showed satisfactory performance for the algorithm.

The result of failed cases is depicted in Figure 11.7b. From this figure, we can confirm the superiority of EBPSM for the peak-hours scenarios. The violation of the user-defined budget was not more than 15% in the peak hours while the number increases up to 40% can be observed in the nonpeak hours' settings. On average, the budget violation was never higher than 14% for all arrival rate schemes. Still and all, this violation was inevitable due to the performance variation of the Amazon EC2 resources.

11.4.4.3 Makespan Evaluation

It is essential to analyze the impact of scheduling multiple workflows on each of the workflows' makespan. We need to know whether sharing the resources between various users with different workflows is worth it and more efficient compared to a dedicated resource scenario in deploying the workflows. Before we discussed further, let us revisit the Figure 11.6a, which shows the result of a single 1000 Genome (chr22) workflow execution in a homogeneous environment. Then, we compared it to the Figure 11.8b that presents the result for the same 1000 Genome (chr22) workflow in multiple workflows scenario and heterogeneous environment. If we zoomed-in to the two

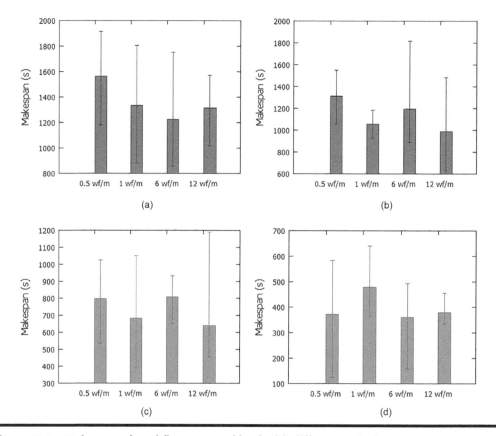

Figure 11.8 Makespan of workflows on workload with different arrival rate.

Table 11.4 Comparison of 1000 Genome (chr22) Workflow in Two Environments

	Makespan (s)		Cost ($)	
Name	*Minimum*	*Maximum*	*Minimum*	*Maximum*
Single – Homogeneous	2,187	1,125	0.084	0.499
Multiple – Heterogeneous	1,819	1,013	0.062	0.471

figures, we could observe that EBPSM can further reduce both the makespan and the cost for the workflow in the latter scenario. We extracted these details of both scenarios into Table 11.4.

Let us continue the discussion for the makespan analysis. Figure 11.8a–d depicts the makespan results for 1000 Genome (chr21, chr22) and Virtual Screening (vina01, vina02) respectively. If we glanced, there was no linear pattern showing the improvement of EBPSM performance over the different arrival rates of workflows. Nevertheless, if we observed further and split the view into two (i.e., peak hours and nonpeak hours), we can see that the EBPSM, in general, produced

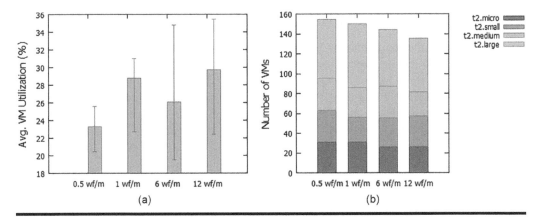

Figure 11.9   Average VM utilization and VM usage on workload with different arrival rate.

better results for the peak-hour scenarios except for some outlier from 1000 Genome (chr22) and Virtual Screening (vina01) workflows. We thought that this might be caused by the number of experiments and the size of the workload. This is an important note to be taken as, due to the limited resources, we could not deploy workload with the scale of hundreds, even thousands, of workflows.

11.4.4.4 VM Utilization Analysis

Finally, the last aspect to be evaluated regarding the EBPSM performance was VM utilization. It was the most important thing to be pointed out when discussing the policy of sharing and reusing computational resources. In Figure 11.9a, we can see the increasing trend in VM utilization percentage along with the arrival rate of workflows on the platform. The average utilization upsurge for each scenario was 4%. The minimum utilization rate was 20% produced by the 0.5 wf/m scenario and the maximum of 36% for the 12 wf/m scenario.

We argue that the VM utilization rate had a connection to the number of VMs used during the execution. Figure 11.9b depicted the number of VMs used in this experiment. We can observe that the overall number of VMs was declining along with the arrival rate of workflows. The average number of decrease was 20% for all VM types. The lowest drop was for the *t2.large* by 15%, and the highest drop was for the *t2.medium* by 25%. Meanwhile, the *t2.small* decreased by 22% and *t2.micro* by 16%, respectively. The EBPSM is always preferred to the fastest VM type, and it recalculates and redistributes the budget after each task finished execution. Hence, in this case, the exit tasks might use more VMs of the cheapest type if the budget has been used up by the earlier tasks. Therefore, *t2.large* as the fastest VM type along with *t2.micro* as the cheapest would always be preferred compared to the other VM type.

From this experiment, we concluded that in the WaaS cloud platform where the number of workflows involved is high, the scheduling algorithm must be able to maintain the low number of VMs being provisioned. Any additional VM leased means the higher possibility of incurring more delays related to the provisioning, initiating, and configuring the VMs before being allocated for executing the abundance of tasks.

11.5 Conclusions and Future Work

It is important to understand that this chapter primarily focused on designing the WaaS scheduler functionality. We found out that the performance of dynamic scheduling algorithms for multitenant users in WaaS cloud platforms is greatly impacted by the stability of the surrounding environments. The developer must consider the performance variability of cloud resources, which are the main computational backbone of the platform, the high possibility of overhead delays in the networks between the nodes involved in the platform, and the number of tenants submitting the jobs into the platform. These three factors are dynamically changing. Therefore, the algorithms must be able to adapt and react accordingly at any given time to the changes.

Further development of the WaaS cloud platform would be focused on developing the WaaS portal. It is the interface that connects the platform with the users. In this case, the users are expected to be able to compose and define their workflow's job, submit the job and the data needed, monitor the execution, and retrieve the output from the workflow's execution. Finalizing the server-based functionality is another to-do list so that the WaaS cloud platform can act as a fully functional service platform in the clouds.

Additional feature to be implemented in the future is to enable the WaaS cloud platform on microservices technology such as container technology, serverless computing, and unikernels system to accommodate the rising demand of the Internet of Things (IoT) workflows. This IoT demand is increasing along with the shifting from centralized infrastructure to distributed cloud computing environments. The shifting is manifested through the rising trends of edge and fog computing environments.

References

1. Gartner, "Gartner Forecasts Worldwide Public Cloud Revenue to Grow 17% in 2020," 2019.
2. M. A. Rodriguez and R. Buyya, "Scientific workflow management system for clouds," In R. Bahsoon, M. Heisel, B. Maxim, N. Ali and I. Mistrik (eds.) *Software Architecture for Big Data and the Cloud*, Morgan Kaufmann, Burlington, MA, 2017, pp. 367–387.
3. T. Fahringer, R. Prodan, R. Duan, J. Hofer, F. Nadeem, F. Nerieri, S. Podlipnig, J. Qin, M. Siddiqui, H.-L. Truong, A. Villazon and M. Wieczorek, "ASKALON: A development and grid computing environment for scientific workflows," In *Workflows for e-Science: Scientific Workflows for Grids*, London, Springer, 2007, pp. 450–471.
4. J. Qin and T. Fahringer, *Scientific Workflows: Programming, Optimization, and Synthesis with ASKALON and AWDL*, Springer, Heidelberg, 2014.
5. P. Blaha, K. Schwarz, G. K. Madsen, D. Kvasnicka and J. Luitz, *WIEN2K, An Augmented Plane Wave+ Local Orbitals Program for Calculating Crystal Properties*, Vienna University of Technology, Vienna, 2001.
6. J. Goecks, A. Nekrutenko and J. Taylor, "Galaxy: A comprehensive approach for supporting accessible, reproducible, and transparent computational research in the life sciences," *Genome Biology*, vol. 11, no. 8, p. R86, 2010.
7. C. A. Goble, J. Bhagat, S. Aleksejevs, D. Cruickshank, D. Michaelides, D. Newman, M. Borkum, S. Bechhofer, M. Roos and P. Li, "myExperiment: A repository and social network for the sharing of bioinformatics workflows," *Nucleic Acids Research*, vol. 38, pp. 677–682, 2010.
8. D. R. Bharti, A. J. Hemrom and A. M. Lynn, "GCAC: Galaxy workflow system for predictive model building for virtual screening," *BMC Bioinformatics*, vol. 19, no. 13, p. 550, 2019.
9. M. W. C. Thang, X. Y. Chua, G. Price, D. Gorse and M. A. Field, "MetaDEGalaxy: Galaxy workflow for differential abundance analysis of 16s metagenomic data," *F1000Research*, vol. 8, p. 726, 2019.

10. D. Eisler, D. Fornika, L. C. Tindale, T. Chan, S. Sabaiduc, R. Hickman, C. Chambers, M. Krajden, D. M. Skowronski, A. Jassem and W. Hsiao, "Influenza classification suite: An automated galaxy workflow for rapid influenza sequence analysis," Influenza and Other Respiratory Viruses, vol. 14, pp. 358–362, 2020.

11. B. Balis, "HyperFlow: A model of computation, programming approach and enactment engine for complex distributed workflows," *Future Generation Computer Systems*, vol. 55, pp. 147–162, 2016.

12. M. Malawski, A. Gajek, A. Zima, B. Balis and K. Figiela, "Serverless Execution of Scientific Workflows: Experiments with HyperFlow, AWS Lambda and Google Cloud Functions," *Future Generation Computer Systems*, vol. 110, pp. 502–514, 2017.

13. I. Altintas, C. Berkley, E. Jaeger, M. Jones, B. Ludascher and S. Mock, "Kepler: An extensible system for design and execution of scientific workflows," In *Proceedings of the 16th International Conference on Scientific and Statistical Database Management*, 2004.

14. J. Davis, M. Goel, C. Hylands, B. Kienhuis, E. A. Lee, J. Liu, X. Liu, L. Muliadi, S. Neuendorffer and J. Reekie, "Overview of the Ptolemy Project," 1999.

15. P. Korambath, J. Wang, A. Kumar, J. Davis, R. Graybill, B. Schott and M. Baldea, "A smart manufacturing use case: Furnace temperature balancing in steam methane reforming process via kepler workflows," *Procedia of Computer Science*, vol. 80, pp. 680–689, 2016.

16. P. C. Yang, S. Purawat, P. U. Ieong, M. T. Jeng, K. R. DeMarco, I. Vorobyov, A. D. McCulloch, I. Altintas, R. E. Amaro and C. E. Clancy, "A demonstration of modularity, reuse, reproducibility, portability and scalability for modeling and simulation of cardiac electrophysiology using kepler workflows," *PLOS Computational Biology*, vol. 15, no. 3, pp. 1–19, 2019.

17. E. Deelman, K. Vahi, M. Rynge, R. Mayani, R. daSilva, G. Papadimitriou and M. Livny, "The evolution of the pegasus workflow management software," *Computing in Science Engineering*, vol. 21, no. 4, pp. 22–36, 2019.

18. D. Thain, T. Tannenbaum and M. Livny, "Distributed computing in practice: The condor experience," *Concurrency - Practice and Experience*, vol. 17, no. 2–4, pp. 323–356, 2005.

19. E. Deelman, C. Kesselman, G. Mehta, L. Meshkat, L. Pearlman, K. Blackburn, P. Ehrens, A. Lazzarini, R. Williams and S. Koranda, "GriPhyN and LIGO, building a virtual data grid for gravitational wave scientists," In *High Performance Distributed Computing*, 2002.

20. K. Wolstencroft, R. Haines, D. Fellows, A. Williams, D. Withers, S. Owen, S. Soiland-Reyes, I. Dunlop, A. Nenadic, P. Fisher, J. Bhagat, K. Belhajjame and F. Bacall, "The taverna workflow suite: Designing and executing workflows of web services on the desktop, web or in the cloud," *Nucleic Acids Research*, vol. 41, no. 1, pp. 557–561, 2013.

21. B. B. Misra, "Open-source software tools, databases, and resources for single-cell and single-cell-type metabolomics," In *Single Cell Metabolism: Methods and Protocols*, New York, Springer, 2020, pp. 191–217.

22. R. Tsonaka, M. Signorelli, E. Sabir, A. Seyer, K. Hettne, A. Aartsma-Rus and P. Spitali, "Longitudinal metabolomic analysis of plasma enables modeling disease progression in duchenne muscular dystrophy mouse models," *Human Molecular Genetics*, vol. 29, pp. 1–11, 2020.

23. J. Yu and R. Buyya, "Gridbus workflow enactment engine," In J. Chen, L. Wang, and W. Jie (eds.) *Grid Computing: Infrastructure, Service, and Applications*, CRC Press, Boca Raton, FL, 2018.

24. C. Vecchiola, X. Chu and R. Buyya, "Aneka: A software platform for.NET-based cloud computing," In W. Gentzsch, and L. Grandinetti (eds.) *High Speed and Large Scale Scientific Computing*, IOS Press, Amsterdam, 2009, pp. 267–295.

25. S. Pandey, D. Karunamoorthy and R. Buyya, "Workflow engine for clouds," In R. Buyya, J. Broberg, and A. Goscinski (eds.) *Cloud Computing*, John Wiley & Sons, Ltd, Hoboken, NJ, 2011, pp. 321–344.

26. M. H. Hilman, M. A. Rodriguez and R. Buyya, "Task-based budget distribution strategies for scientific workflows with coarse-grained billing periods in IaaS clouds," In *Proceedings of the 13th IEEE International Conference on e-Science*, Auckland, 2019.

27. M. H. Hilman, M. A. Rodriguez and R. Buyya, "Resource-sharing Policy in Multi-tenant Scientific Workflow as a Service Platform," arXiv, 2019.

28. M. P. Mackley, B. Fletcher, M. Parker, H. Watkins and E. Ormondroyd, "Stakeholder views on secondary findings in whole-genome and whole-exome sequencing: A systematic review of quantitative and qualitative studies," *Genetics in Medicine*, vol. 19, no. 3, pp. 283–293, 2017.

29. D. Dong, Z. Xu, W. Zhong and S. Peng, "Parallelization of molecular docking: A review," *Current Topics in Medicinal Chemistry*, vol. 18, no. 12, pp. 1015–1028, 2018.

30. J. Kelleher, Y. Wong, A. W. Wohns, C. Fadil, P. K. Albers and G. McVean, "Inferring whole-genome histories in large population datasets," *Nature Genetics*, vol. 51, no. 9, pp. 1330–1338, 2019.

31. M. H. Hilman, M. A. Rodriguez and R. Buyya, "Task runtime prediction in scientific workflows using an online incremental learning approach," In *Proceedings of the 11th IEEE/ACM International Conference on Utility and Cloud Computing*, Zurich, 2018.

32. A. Gimeno, M. J. Ojeda-Montes, S. Tomás-Hernández, A. Cereto-Massagué, R. Beltrán-Debón, M. Mulero, G. Pujadas and S. Garcia-Vallvé, "The light and dark sides of virtual screening: What is there to know?," *International Journal of Molecular Sciences*, vol. 20, no. 6, p. 135, 2019.

33. C. Grebner, E. Malmerberg, A. Shewmaker, J. Batista, A. Nicholls and J. Sadowski, "Virtual screening in the cloud: How big is big enough?," Journal of Chemical Information and Modeling, vol. 60, no. 9, pp. 4274–4282, 2019.

34. O. Trott and A. J. Olson, "AutoDock vina: Improving the speed and accuracy of docking with a new scoring function, efficient optimization, and multithreading," *Journal of Computational Chemistry*, vol. 31, no. 2, pp. 455–461, 2010.

CASE STUDIES

Chapter 12

Application-Centric Real-Time Decisions in Practice: Preliminary Findings

Patrick Tendick
Ingredion Inc.

Audris Mockus
University of Tennessee Knoxville

Wen-Hua Ju
Avaya Inc.

Contents

12.1 Introduction

Arguably, the two biggest drivers of technology in the 21st century are machine learning (ML) and interactive software applications or apps. The former has led to an explosion in the use of artificial intelligence (AI), with myriad applications in areas as diverse as natural language understanding and medical diagnosis. The latter include websites, mobile apps, voice assistants, chat bots, interactive voice response (IVR or voice menu) applications, streaming services, online gaming, and automotive infotainment systems.

Increasingly, businesses and other organizations interact with customers and employees through applications. Indeed, many companies are synonymous with their apps. It seems obvious that organizations would seek to use ML and predictive analytics to guide interactions with customers and other users of software apps. The goal would be to use the increasing volume of available data to learn how to alter the behavior of an app in real time. For example, an e-commerce site might want to decide whether to offer a customer free shipping on an item. Such a decision might consider things such as how many times the customer has viewed that product in the current session and other products the customer has viewed. While traditional data analysis and ML are inherently offline processes, making decisions in real time is fundamentally different and may involve the evaluation of a previously fitted model or the application of some other kind of business logic [11]. Enabling this have been *decisioning engines* (rules engines that evaluate business rules) [6] and *scoring engines* (servers that evaluate statistical models), which have emerged over the past 20 years, providing the ability to apply a ruleset or previously fitted model to new data, often in milliseconds [2,5]. More recently, many commonly used ML platforms provide the ability to evaluate trained ML models (perform *inference*) as a service, and many MLaaS (ML as a Service) solutions are available.

Despite these advances, there are many challenges that hinder the use of ML to change the real-time behavior of apps. Interactive applications are almost always event-driven, which means that the modules and routines of the app execute at unpredictable times and in an unpredictable order according to the whims of the user. Still, data scientists generally take a *model-centric* approach, in which a specific type of model is considered outside of the context of the application. Under this approach, the data scientist typically trains a model that somehow produces a prediction or score, and the application developer must adapt this output to the app using an interface specified by the data scientist. However, a model-centric approach is hard to implement on the application side and tends not to address the range of decisions made by the application nor leverage the data that is available to the app in real time. Of course, large companies in the tech sector have found and will continue to find ways around these challenges by nature of their ample technical teams, but most businesses will have trouble integrating real-time inference into their applications.

In [10], we described a possible framework for incorporating data-driven decision-making into software applications. This chapter describes our experiences implementing such a framework as a research prototype and validating the approach by applying the framework to a simple e-commerce system. In doing so, it partially addresses the future work described in [10]. The framework consists of a client library to be used by an application, a decision broker that receives and processes requests from the application, a data store that stores the potentially massive amounts of client requests and responses, and an administrative user interface (UI) that can be used to manage the way that the framework handles application requests. We have found that this implementation works surprisingly well, albeit for an artificially simple example. Furthermore, the framework facilitates the process of incorporating real-time decisions into an application and highlights some of the inherent difficulties in doing so.

To illustrate and evaluate the proposed framework, we conduct an exploratory case study implementing a simple application using this framework. Section 12.2 provides motivation for this work, Section 12.3 provides a detailed description of the approach, Section 12.4 describes the case study approach used, Section 12.5 details the implementation, Section 12.6 discusses knowledge management (KM) considerations, and Section 12.7 summarizes our findings.

12.2 Opportunities and Challenges

Commercial enterprises have always sought to increase business performance and improve user experience (UX). However, for applications targeted toward consumers, the need to provide a compelling UX is much greater. Unlike traditional transaction processing systems for which the user base consists of business employees, consumers may simply opt to not use a website or mobile app if it does not provide a satisfactory experience. The principle of evidence-based design says that we should use empirical observations to guide software implementation [7]. A common, concrete example of this is the practice of performing content experiments or A/B testing to choose between two or more interface design elements based on the random assignment of candidate designs to users, with the resulting data being used to select the design that results in the best expected outcome, e.g., click through rates or conversions [8]. Techniques such as A/B testing enable applications to adapt to user preferences.

Whereas the result of evidence-based design and A/B testing is typically a static change in the software application logic or content, we may instead use data to guide dynamically how a system reacts or makes decisions in real time. For example, next best action is the principle of using predictive models, ML, or some other mechanism to select the best action to take at the current instant, given all the information currently available. Next best offer is a special case of next best action that seeks the best product or service to offer a customer, based on all the information known at the moment. For example, a customer booking an airline flight on a travel site might be offered travel insurance or a first-class upgrade, depending on things the site knew about the customer previously and also depending on inputs the customer has made while selecting the flight. Next best action and next best offer provide opportunities to use predictive analytics or ML to find the best decision in a given situation.

Scoring engines are server applications that evaluate predictive models or ML algorithms on new observations. Most scoring engines now have the capability to return results for a single new observation in real time, typically with latency measuring in milliseconds. Scoring engines are available that work directly with analytical languages or frameworks and also based on the predictive model markup language (PMML) standard for describing predictive models [2]. Decisioning engines, in contrast, are specifically intended to render business decisions, typically through the execution of business rules. For example, the decision to offer a home loan often involves the application of business rules that describe lending policies. Decisioning engines may also evaluate statistical models or execute other algorithms in the process of providing a decision. Decisioning engines have become commonly available through Decisions as a Service (DaaS) as part of an Enterprise Decision Management (EDM) approach [9], in which a central service provides decisions for a variety of applications across the enterprise. Still, the approaches used with decisioning engines generally are not data-driven in that they do not leverage the data available in the application to build data sets and train models. In contrast, over the last few years, the proliferation of ML models and applications has led to an explosion of ML tools and services, particularly cloud services. These MLaaS services typically also enable trained models to be evaluated on new data in real time.

All of the aforementioned types of services are typically available through a web services interface, and henceforth, we will use the term *scoring service* generically to refer to them. Since a scoring service typically relies on some tools or framework to train the models or build the decision rules, we will use the term *analytical framework* generically to refer to a scoring service and other tools or frameworks used in conjunction with it.

The use of data-driven methods (statistical models or ML) to improve application performance in real time typically requires the involvement of two disparate roles: the data scientist and the application developer. The data scientist collects data, analyzes it, and fits models, or performs other types of learning. Typically, the data scientist seeks to make predictions based on predictors, which are known attributes of the user or interaction that can be shown to predict future outcomes. The application developer, in contrast, is responsible for delivering and maintaining a working operational system. There may be additional or different roles involved in the process, such as systems engineer, knowledge engineer, or business analyst. These two roles (data scientist and application developer) have very different skill sets, tools, philosophies, and worldviews and follow very different processes that use very different terminology.

In the authors' own experiences, one consequence of this disconnect is that analytical algorithms built into applications often are not modified after the initial release, can be poorly documented, and are prone to staff turnover. Furthermore, code written by data scientists often does not meet the application development organization's requirements, including

- Languages
- Platforms, e.g., standalone programs vs. services and containers
- Programming models
- Coding style
- Testing and analysis tools
- Code metrics

So, as a result, the code written by analysts is often refactored. But the development organization really doesn't understand what the algorithm code does, and the data scientist no longer understands the code either, because it has been rewritten! The result is software that is very difficult to maintain.

We would argue that successful integration of analytical decision-making into applications requires *separation of concerns*, that is, a division of work and software between the diverse roles involved. Evidence of the importance of separation of concerns may be found in the success of analytical frameworks [5]. The solution presented here provides separation of concerns and makes it much easier to incorporate data-driven decision-making into apps by hiding the processes and mechanisms for analyzing data, training, and decision-making from the application. In turn, it also hides the internals of the app from the analysis and decision-making processes. The solution does this by providing a universal API for apps that works across analytical tools and languages, along with a central gateway that collects data that can be used for training and that also invokes analytical tools.

12.3 Application-Centric Decision Enablement

The approach typically used with analytical frameworks is model centric, that is, a data scientist or analyst uses these frameworks with a specific prediction problem or decision in mind. Applications must then conform to the interface for the appropriate scoring service and decide how to incorporate the output of that service into their processing. In contrast, we have proposed an *application-centric* approach, in which an application identifies the decisions it must make and then queries a simple API or service to provide those decisions. The use of the API and the provided decisions provide *instrumentation* (capture of data) and *control* (the ability to affect the behavior of the application), an approach used in *instrumentation and control engineering* (ICE), which is applied to a wide variety of systems [1,3]. The ability to collect data from and control the application enables us to use a *stimulus-response* approach to understand how the application reacts to the control. Figure 12.1 provides a visual comparison of the model-centric and application-centric approaches.

We call this approach *application-centric decision enablement*, which is provided through a *decision framework*. Figure 12.2 shows the architecture of the decision framework. The goal of application-centric decision enablement is to enable an application to request decisions that make sense in terms of its internal logic, based on the information it has at the time. The decisions could be of any data type, including Boolean, numeric or string-valued, or URL or object-valued. The values returned could represent yes/no decisions, the index of a choice from a list, a list of options to offer the end user, or HTML links or content to display.

Henceforth, we will refer to a system on which an application runs as an *application system*. Importantly, application systems are session-aware, that is, they somehow track user sessions and maintain some memory about what the user has done previously in a session. An example of such a system is a web application framework. We will use the term application system interchangeably

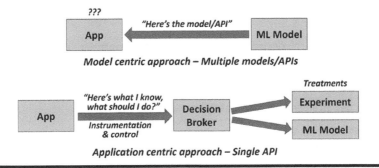

Figure 12.1 Comparison of model-centric and application-centric approaches.

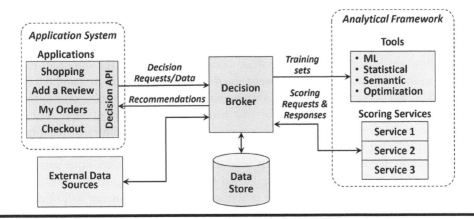

Figure 12.2 Architecture of the decision framework. © 2020 Avaya Inc. All Rights Reserved.

to mean either a computing system on which applications run or the combination of software, device, user, and user's environment. Figure 12.2 shows an application system running several applications (Shopping, Add a Review, My Orders, and Checkout). An application uses a *decision API* to send *decision requests* to a central *decision broker*. The decision API provides a single library and interface that is independent of any ML models used. An app requests a decision from the broker and specifies the decision requested and provides the data currently known to the app. The decision broker:

■ Uses information in the decision request to capture information about the application system, application, decision being requested, and data known to the application at that point in time.
■ Stores the data provided in the request in a *data store*.
■ Routes the request to a *treatment*, which is a prespecified way of handling the request.
■ May incorporate data from *external data sources* such as a data lake.
■ May generate *training sets* to be used by analytical frameworks to do things such as train ML models.

The treatments to which a request is routed may:

■ Simply return a *default response* if no model has been trained to handle the request.
■ Return a random response as part of an *experimental design* such as those used in A/B testing.
■ Convert the request into a *scoring request* to evaluate a previously trained model to obtain a decision and then return the resulting inference back to the app.

An important function of the decision API is the automatic capture of data. Typically, interactive applications such as web apps use platforms or frameworks specifically designed to run those apps. Examples of such platforms or frameworks include:

■ Web platforms and frameworks
■ IVR systems
■ Automated text chat and voice assistant platforms

Many mobile apps and other applications use web platforms or frameworks on the back end, accessing them using web services. Something all these platforms and frameworks have in common is the ability to maintain *session variables* or *session attributes* during a user session. Session variables enable the app to remember data between calls to back-end code. This is because the frameworks are event-driven and the application code itself has no ability to remember anything between calls to the back end. This is important because, for example, the app needs to remember what is in the user's shopping cart between the time they add an item to it and the time they go to checkout. Knowledge of these mechanisms enables us to develop framework-specific APIs (as opposed to just language-specific APIs) that make instrumentation of applications quite a bit easier. For the frameworks above, which are very widely used, we can easily capture the session variables, reducing the burden on the app to know what data to provide. In the case of the sample application, servlet code stores data it needs later in the form of key/value pairs in session attributes. The API used for the sample application is specifically designed to capture data from servlet sessions. It can be argued that most of the important data in an app will be captured in session attributes, since data that is important probably needs to be recalled in future calls to the back-end code.

We will test the proposed approach by applying it to a fictitious web e-commerce site called BuyStuff, which is operated by a fictitious company, Acme Commerce. The BuyStuff system consists of a home page that presents a list of products. The user can select a product to view that product's page, where the user can specify the quantity to buy and choose whether to make a purchase. The user can add or remove items from their cart and view different items. From the page for a product, the user can either make a purchase or log out without buying anything. Choosing either of these options ends the session, which started when the user first accessed the home page. The site may choose to offer free shipping on an item to incent the user to buy. While the site still makes money with free shipping, it reduces the profit margin on the item substantially.

The application system consists of a servlet running in a servlet container, along with several static HTML pages. When a user navigates to the page for a product, the page places a request to the servlet to retrieve information about that product, including the product name, product code, price, and shipping cost. When the servlet provides the product information, it can optionally decide to offer free shipping. Once free shipping has been offered on a product, it must be offered on every subsequent page view for that product. The point in the servlet code where the application system decides whether to offer free shipping is called a decision point. This system has only one decision point, but there are other points in the code at which data may be collected without necessarily making a decision, for example, when the user makes a purchase or logs out. These latter code locations are called *capture points*. Every decision point is a capture point, but the converse is not true.

The decision broker is implemented in the Java® (*Oracle and Java are registered trademarks of Oracle and/or its affiliates. Other names may be trademarks of their respective owners.*) language and exposed as a web service using a servlet. The broker accepts various types of requests from applications and does so in the context of sessions in the application system. More specifically, the broker receives requests that do one or more of the following:

- Authenticate the client (the BuyStuff site) and establish the start of the session on the application system.
- Establish that the application system is executing in a particular application such as shopping.
- Request a decision.
- Provide data without requesting a decision.
- Notify the broker that the application system session is ending.

If the broker receives a decision request, it can respond either by returning a default response or by providing one of several possible treatments that an analyst has specified for that decision point. These treatments could invoke an external system to obtain a decision, or they could return a random answer if the goal is to experiment. Experimentation is a critical step in the collection of the data required to develop decision rules that reflect the behavior of the system and its users.

The decision framework provides an API specifically built for servlets. The app calls the API at the decision points to provide decisions. The API performs several functions:

- It authenticates the client (the BuyStuff site) and establishes the start of the session on the client system.
- It enables an app to request a decision or capture data.
- It captures basic information about the decision point or capture point, specifically, the name of the application, the system on which it is running, the name or identifier of the decision point or capture point, and a description of the desired decision for a decision point.
- At capture points, it automatically captures servlet session attributes.

◼ It enables the client to signal the end of the user session.

The decision framework includes a UI that enables a data scientist or other user to do the following:

◼ Manage accounts used by application systems, including authentication and privileges.
◼ Identify and manage application systems.
◼ Identify and manage decision points, including the management of treatments applied to those decision points.
◼ Manage the variables to be used for training and in obtaining decisions from external scoring services.
◼ Generate data sets for training.

Interactive applications such as web apps, online games, mobile apps, IVR apps, and chat bots typically do not simply engage in isolated interactions with a user. Instead, each interaction (which would typically correspond to a single invocation of an event handler) is part of a larger session that may encompass multiple applications. Business enterprises are often concerned with providing a unified customer experience, one that takes into account everything that has happened to the user recently. For this reason, the decision API and decision broker also keep track of entire user sessions and not just individual decision requests. This includes tracking the beginning and end of the session and keeping track of the application from which each decision request is made. The broker also tries to keep track of the time a user spends in a particular application, something we will call an application session. One session may be broken into many application sessions, each associated with an application, and a given application may be associated with multiple application sessions in a given session. In this context, the notion of an application is somewhat vague and arbitrary, since the entire site could be viewed either as one application or as a collection of apps. In contrast, the notion of a session is usually pretty precise, since sessions must be managed precisely by the environment in which the apps run.

The data store stores *activities*, which are complex objects that typically represent client sessions or time spent in applications within a session. The activities that make up the basic building blocks of the broker's data are designed to be nested. So the activity that represents a session can contain other activities and can also be part of a larger activity that represents, e.g., an extended customer journey. The data store is implemented in a document-oriented NoSQL database. The broker stores and manipulates the data using a document object model (DOM) based on JSON. The JSON DOM approach is suitable because of its inherent tree structure and because application data is provided in JSON format. A tree structure is required because of the nested nature of client sessions: Sessions contain application sessions (contiguous periods spent in a single application), which in turn contain client requests, which in turn contain application data.

Modern interactive applications operate at web scale, and business decisions need to be made in real time, so the decision broker needs to be lightweight, horizontally scalable, and have high availability and low latency. The broker service, being implemented as a web service, can be deployed horizontally and load balanced across many nodes to provide scalability and high availability. The NoSQL database used for the data store can be sharded and distributed across many nodes to provide high availability and scalability. And the time required to process a request, ignoring network latency and the time required to access an external scoring service, is typically just a few milliseconds.

The application-centric approach has several advantages. It enables applications to focus on incorporating decisions into their logic, without worrying about how those decisions are made.

It focuses the data scientist or analyst on making decisions that are relevant to the application and are based on data that is available at the time the decision is made. By moving decisions out of application logic, application systems become more agile and robust. For example, a decision about whether to grant a loan that is to be consumed by an online loan application can be easily modified to account for new models or data or include additional business rules without changing the loan app itself.

12.4 Method

To evaluate the feasibility of our approach, we conducted an exploratory case study. The exploratory case study [7,12] investigates distinct phenomena characterized by a lack of detailed preliminary research, especially formulated hypotheses that can be tested, or by a specific research environment that limits the choice of methodology. Since there have been few, if any, prior studies of creating frameworks to separate concerns of developers and data scientists, it was premature to conduct the investigation of effectiveness of the approach. We started from the very basic approach of trying to implement a simple application using our framework. The primary results of the case study involve detailed description of various design decisions we had to take and challenges that we faced. More specifically, the primary research question we tried to answer was whether the framework provided a feasible approach to implementing data-driven decision-making in contemporary applications through the analysis of user behavior. The secondary research questions are:

- What are unforeseen issues involved when using the proposed framework?
- Does the approach deliver meaningful separation of concerns and potential for improved maintainability?

Below we describe the implementation of the application that can serve both as an elaboration of the framework and as a way to illustrate the issues and advantages it may provide in practice.

12.5 Initial Experiences

12.5.1 Accounts

How can we ensure security and control access in an environment in which many different application systems and applications may be using the broker? The first step involved in integrating an application system with the framework is to create an account that the system can use to invoke the broker service. Account creation is a straightforward process like that of many other systems. An account can be used to invoke the broker from an application or to access the UI. It would seem that one account per application system is appropriate, where an application system is defined to be an entity that encompasses user sessions. An example of such a system is a web application framework. Figure 12.3 shows a screen shot of the Accounts list. In the figure, there are two accounts: one for administering the decision broker (admin), which was used to access the UI and create the second account (acme), which is to be used by the BuyStuff application system.

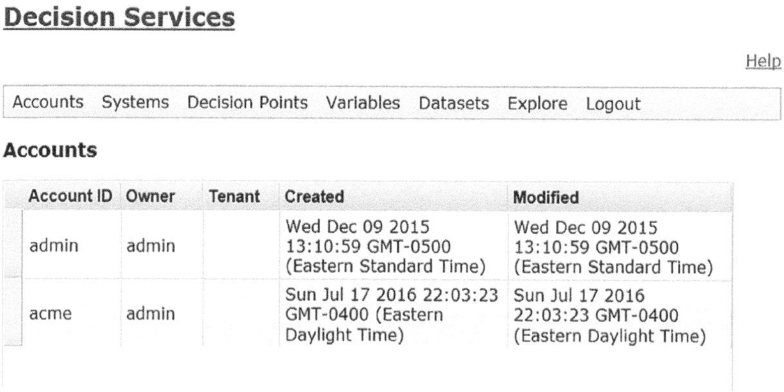

Decision Services

Help

| Accounts | Systems | Decision Points | Variables | Datasets | Explore | Logout |

Accounts

Account ID	Owner	Tenant	Created	Modified
admin	admin		Wed Dec 09 2015 13:10:59 GMT-0500 (Eastern Standard Time)	Wed Dec 09 2015 13:10:59 GMT-0500 (Eastern Standard Time)
acme	admin		Sun Jul 17 2016 22:03:23 GMT-0400 (Eastern Daylight Time)	Sun Jul 17 2016 22:03:23 GMT-0400 (Eastern Daylight Time)

Figure 12.3   Accounts. © 2016 Avaya Inc. All Rights Reserved.

12.5.2 Instrumentation and Control

The BuyStuff app is implemented as a single servlet class. This class implements the following standard servlet methods:

- **init**: Initializes the servlet. This is where we set parameters used to access the service. Figure 12.4 shows a code snippet from this method.
- **doGet**: Handles GET requests. This method serves up the static web pages. Figures 12.5 and 12.6 show code snippets from this method.
- **doPost**: Handles POST requests. This method handles other requests, including requests for product information. Figure 12.7 shows a code snippet from this method.

The API provides its capabilities through a class called ServletRecommender, which implements the Recommender interface. The Recommender interface describes the methods that enable an application to make requests to the broker. The line of interest in Figure 12.4 simply calls a static method to set parameters that will be needed by individual sessions when connecting to the service.

```
// **** DaaS CALLS ****
ServletRecommender.setAttributes(this, "http://localhost:8080/Service/server",
    "Acme Commerce", 1000000,           ,           );
// **** END DaaS CALLS ****
```

Figure 12.4   Initialization of the API. © 2016 Avaya Inc. All Rights Reserved.

```
// Get the session and set the content type.
HttpSession session = request.getSession();
response.setContentType("text/html");

// Get the cart.
Cart cart = getCart(session);

// **** DaaS CALLS ****
Recommender recommender = ServletRecommender.getRecommender(session, "Shopping", "1.0", "doGetStart");
// **** END DaaS CALLS ****
```

Figure 12.5   Instrumentation of doGet. © 2016 Avaya Inc. All Rights Reserved.

```
CartItem cartitem = cart.get(product);
if (cartitem==null)
    cartitem = cart.add(product, quantity, false);
else
    cartitem.setQuantity(quantity);

cartitem.setBuy(true);
session.setAttribute("cartitem", cartitem);
session.setAttribute("buy", true);

// **** DaaS CALLS ****
recommender.close("BuyClose");
// **** END DaaS CALLS ****
```

Figure 12.6   Instrumentation of doGet. © 2016 Avaya Inc. All Rights Reserved.

```
// **** DaaS CALLS ****
if (!cartitem.getFreeShipping())
    // If not offering free shipping, get recommendation.
    cartitem.setFreeShipping(recommender.offerRecBoolean(
        false, "Shopping", "1.0", "FreeShipping 1", "Should we offer free shipping?"));
else
    // Otherwise, continue w/free shipping and just capture data.
    recommender.capture("FreeShipping 2");
// **** END DaaS CALLS ****
```

Figure 12.7   Instrumentation of doPost. © 2016 Avaya Inc. All Rights Reserved.

More specifically, the setAttributes method takes the URL of the broker service, the name of the system, the session timeout in milliseconds, and the login credentials for the acme broker account and stores them in servlet attributes (not to be confused with session attributes). The code in Figure 12.5 is called at the beginning of the doGet method, and the line of interest (labeled "DaaS Calls") calls the getRecommender static method to obtain a Recommender object, establishing a connecting with the broker if necessary. getRecommender also tells the broker that the application system is in version 1.0 of the Shopping application, at the location with label doGetStart. The code in Figure 12.6 is called later in the doGet method and is in a block of code that handles the event that the user decides to buy a product. The line of interest uses the recommender object to call the close method, which tells the broker that the user's session is ending. The close method includes a label, in this case "BuyClose," which identifies the place in the program at which the session was ended. Another call to the close method, not shown, handles the case in which the user logs out without making a purchase. The lines of interest in Figure 12.7 are in a block of code that handles a request for product information and deals with the question of whether to offer free shipping. This is managed with a call to the method offerRecBoolean, which asks for a Boolean decision as to whether to offer free shipping. offerRecBoolean is only called if the user has not previously been offered free shipping and takes the following arguments:

- **defaultvalue**: The default value to be returned if the broker does not know how to handle this request, in this case false (don't offer free shipping).
- **appname**: The name of the current application, in this case Shopping.
- **version**: The version of the application.
- **requestlabel**: A label that identifies the location in the program (decision point).
- **description**: A short description of the request.

offerRecBoolean also records and sends session variables to the broker automatically. Other variables can be recorded as well, as long as they are registered with the recommender using other methods not discussed here. If the user has previously been offered free shipping on the item, then there is no decision to make, and the application simply calls the capture method, which records that a particular point in the program was reached, and also records and sends variables.

An important part of application-centric decision enablement is the collection of data. If the goal is next best action or next best offer, then the decision framework needs to collect predictor variables that potentially predict the outcome of the interaction. In addition, if the goal is to make a decision that leads to the best outcome, then the decision framework also needs to collect variables that represent the outcome of the interaction. The decision framework also needs to collect variables representing the recommendations made. The application might not actually use the recommendation provided, however. In this case, the decision framework would need to collect the action actually taken by the application. If a decision rule is to be based on an ML model, then the decision framework needs to collect observations that can then be used to construct training sets and also must provide the relevant predictor variables in real time to provide a decision.

Application data is serialized into JSON format before being sent to the broker, using commonly available methods for serializing objects. Typically, basic types such as strings and integers are converted into their JSON equivalent types, while complex objects are converted to documents whose elements are the objects' serialized properties. Arrays are converted to JSON arrays, with the elements serialized appropriately. Because we are serializing into JSON, the broker deals in JSON data types, which are platform-independent.

When an application requests a decision, it may ask for a response of a variety of types, including Boolean, string, integer, number, url, and object. Except for url, these are all JSON types. The url type is simply a string that is understood to represent a URL. The application could also request more than one value. For example, the application could request a recommendation consisting of an array of links to present to the user. When the broker makes a recommendation, it stores that recommendation along with the request. If the application chooses to report the action it takes back to the broker, then the broker stores that information also. For example, the app could request an array of five items to present to the user and then inform the broker about the item actually selected. The selection reported back to the broker could be the array index of the items selected, or it could be the actual value used. For example, if a customer service web chat application requests a recommended response to a customer's message, an agent could use the recommendation as is or modify it in some way.

12.5.3 Discovery

Having created an account and modified the application, we can now run the BuyStuff application system. The home menu appears as in Figure 12.8, and the page for the product Acme TV Box appears as in Figure 12.9. The decision broker only knows about applications, application systems, and decision points through the requests it receives from the application. One of the functions of the decision broker is to discover the application systems, applications, and decision points associated with these requests and store the resulting metadata or *schema*. This schema may then be used to configure the broker to respond in different ways to handle different decisions on behalf of applications. There is no indication of free shipping in Figure 12.9 because initially the broker has not been configured to handle the decision point in the app and therefore returns the default value of **false**. In addition, the broker needs to discover the variables that are being provided by the applications and through data integration.

Welcome to BuyStuff!

Products:

Acme TV Box

Figure 12.8   The BuyStuff home page. © 2016 Avaya Inc. All Rights Reserved.

Product	Acme TV Box
Product Code	acmetvbox
Price	99
Shipping	10
Quantity	1
Total Cost	109

Add to Cart   Remove from Cart

Change quantity + -

Buy it!

Log Out

Figure 12.9   The Acme TV Box product page. © 2016 Avaya Inc. All Rights Reserved.

Decision Services

Help

Accounts   Systems   Decision Points   Variables   Datasets   Explore   Logout

Systems

System Name	Owner	Channel	Tenant	Created	Modified
Acme Commerce	acme	...	...	Mon Jul 18 2016 07:58:56 GMT-0400 (Eastern Daylight Time)	Mon Jul 18 2016 07:58:56 GMT-0400 (Eastern Daylight Time)

Figure 12.10   Systems. © 2016 Avaya Inc. All Rights Reserved.

After we have exercised the application, we can use the UI to manage the application systems and decision points. If we select the Systems item on the main menu, we now see the application system Acme Commerce, which is owned by the account acme (Figure 12.10). If we then select the Decision Points item on the main menu, we can see the newly discovered decision point Free Shipping 1 in the Shopping application in the Acme Commerce application system (Figure 12.11). There could be many decision points, applications, etc. At this point, the broker knows about the decision point but does not know how to handle it.

12.5.4 Experimentation

To obtain useful predictions, it is not enough simply to collect a large amount of data. In the shipping cost example, we would not be able to learn from the data to whom and when to offer free shipping if the site never offered free shipping or if it were only offered to members of a loyalty program. An

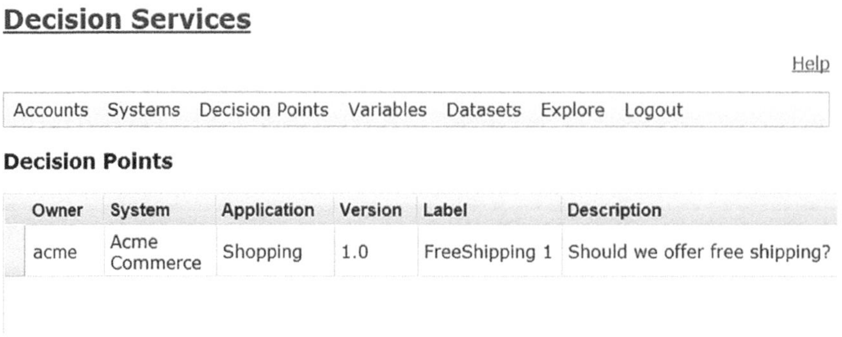

Decision Services

Help

| Accounts | Systems | Decision Points | Variables | Datasets | Explore | Logout |

Decision Points

Owner	System	Application	Version	Label	Description
acme	Acme Commerce	Shopping	1.0	FreeShipping 1	Should we offer free shipping?

Figure 12.11   Decision points. © 2016 Avaya Inc. All Rights Reserved.

often-overlooked component of statistical reasoning is experimentation. The broker implements experiments by randomly assigning treatments to decision requests. A treatment is just a particular way of handling a decision request from an application. A treatment could always return the same recommendation, or it could return a randomized recommendation. Or, it could invoke a scoring service to evaluate a trained model or render a decision in some other way. To manage the handling of the decision point, we need to configure treatments for it. If there are multiple treatments for a decision point, the broker will select one at random using weights that we provide. For example, we could specify one treatment that uses the default value and another that makes a recommendation based on a predictive model and specify that the predictive model should only be used 10% of the time until it has been deemed successful. The decision to include the ability to choose the treatment for a decision request at random was based on the need to perform ongoing experimentation after a model has been developed and deployed and is consistent with standard MLOps (the practice of managing ML deployments in production). The treatments for a decision point are stored in the schema for the application system.

If we choose to create a new treatment, we get a screen like that shown in Figure 12.12. We can enter a name, version, description, and handler. The handler is an extension that actually handles the treatment. Handlers are configured via an XML file and loaded at run time. There could be different handlers that interface with different scoring services or other tools. An important design decision was to make the implementation, configuration parameters, and configuration UI highly extensible. The handler we have chosen is called NoReplacementHandler, and it makes a recommendation selected randomly from

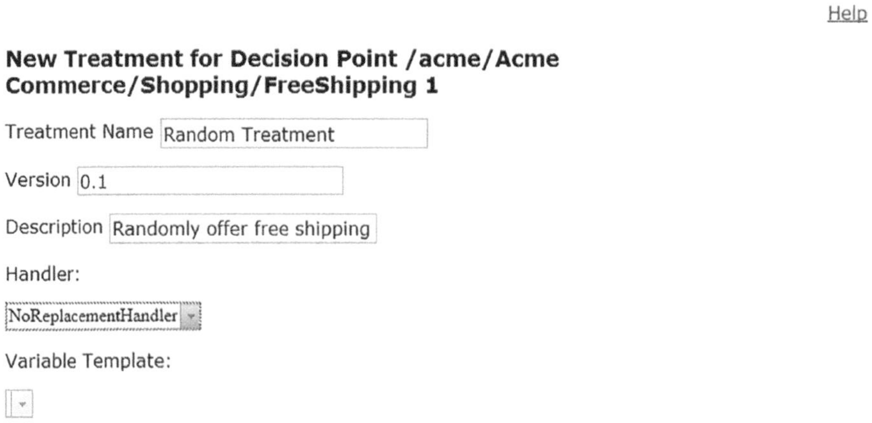

Help

New Treatment for Decision Point /acme/Acme Commerce/Shopping/FreeShipping 1

Treatment Name Random Treatment

Version 0.1

Description Randomly offer free shipping

Handler:

NoReplacementHandler ▾

Variable Template:

▾

Figure 12.12   A random treatment for a decision point. © 2016 Avaya Inc. All Rights Reserved.

the choices given by the application, in this case **true** and **false**. In other words, it randomly decides whether to offer free shipping. The decision to include a handler that randomly selects from a list of possible choices is essential to support experimentation. In this screen there is also an item called Variable Template. *Variable templates* will be described in more detail in the next section, but they specify the data to be passed to the handler by the broker. In this case, the handler makes its decision completely at random and does not need any input data. If we click OK in this screen, we get another page for configuring the handler. Since handlers are extensions that could be written by third parties, each has its own configuration parameters, and each can have its own web page for configuration. The configuration page for NoReplacementHandler (Figure 12.13) enables us to enter the probabilities for the possible choices. In the Boolean case, this reduces to specifying the probability of choosing **true** as the response. We will enter 0.3 so that the treatment recommends free shipping 30% of the time. If we now return to the BuyStuff application system (after restarting the BuyStuff and broker services) and access the Acme TV Box page several times, we eventually see the screen in Figure 12.14, which includes the text "You qualify for free shipping on this item!!!" and shows a shipping cost of zero.

12.5.5 Analysis and Training

In addition to discovering application systems and decision points, the broker also discovers the variables provided by the apps in decision requests. For example, a decision request might include variables called **productcode, cost, price, productname**, and **shippingcost**.

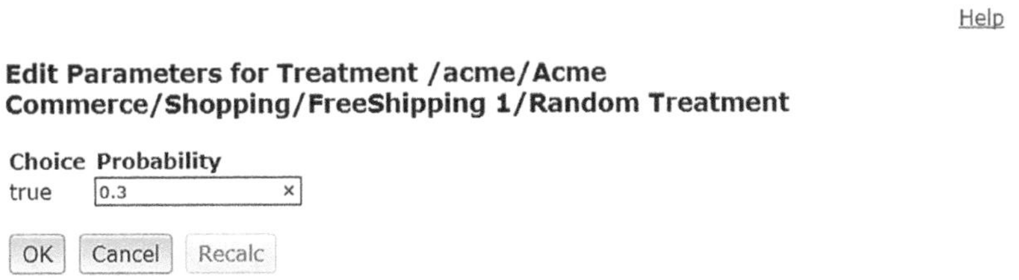

Figure 12.13   Parameters of the random treatment. © 2016 Avaya Inc. All Rights Reserved.

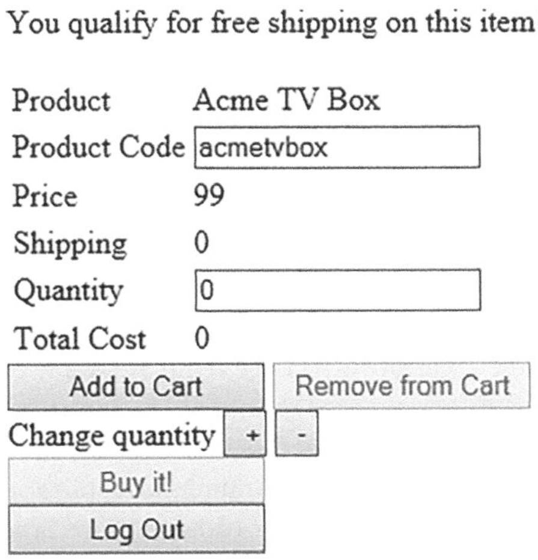

Figure 12.14   The Acme TV Box product page with free shipping offer. © 2016 Avaya Inc. All Rights Reserved.

The broker records information about these variables (metadata), including the variable name and data type, in the schema for the application system. Of course, the broker does not know what these variables actually represent. Variables are identified according to the application system, decision point or capture point, and their position in the DOM tree of the JSON document provided with a request. This metadata may then be used to specify the data to be included in a training set or scoring request. The decision to represent captured variables this way was driven by the need to capture the context of the variable and to differentiate between different variables with the same name in different parts of the system.

Once we have performed an experiment to collect data on how users respond to different inputs, we can analyze the data and train models. The broker has already identified the decision points and variables. Once the data is available, the broker can help a data scientist to extract data sets for analysis and training. The broker will probably collect more variables than the data scientist needs, so the data scientist must select the variables of interest. Also, the data collected by the broker tends to be semistructured and follows a document tree structure (sessions contain application sessions, which contain decision requests, which contain complex application objects, etc.), so the data needs to be *flattened*, that is, converted into a flat record format for consumption by analytical tools.

As mentioned in the previous section, data to be passed to a treatment handler must be specified in a variable template. A variable template describes how to flatten the data and can also be used to describe the rows of a data set to be generated by the broker. A variable template defines the variables (outputs) to be provided and the parts (inputs) to be used to calculate them.

The most complex functions of the broker relate to the discovery, specification, and processing of variables. Data that the analyst might view as one variable could be represented as different variables in the application depending on where the data was captured. For example, a product code could be identified variously as "productcode," "sku," or "upc" in different applications or even in different parts of the same app. Also, note that although a variable template may be applied at a specific point in the application, the data used to calculate the variables may have been observed in the past, present, or future with respect to that point. For example, in deciding whether to offer free shipping, a decision algorithm may want to know both the current product being viewed by the user (present) and previous products viewed in the same session (past). Also, when developing and training an algorithm for the free shipping example, the analyst would want to have a data set that includes the outcome of the user's session, that is, whether they bought the product or not (future). Because the data used to calculate a variable could have been collected at multiple points in time, the variable template can include a window (which time points to include relative to the current time point) and an aggregation method such as sum, average, min, or max (how to combine possibly multiple data points).

The Variables item on the main menu is a pull-down menu containing several items. By selecting the item Discover Variables, we cause the broker to identify variables in the data that has been captured. Once this has been done, the variables in the captured data will be available to include in variable templates. To create a variable template, we use the screen in Figure 12.15 to specify a name, version, and description for the variable template. To add a variable, we use a screen containing a tree that depicts the variables that have been discovered by the broker (Figure 12.16). By expanding the tree, we can drill down through the application system owner (account), application system, application, decision point or capture point, and then down through the hierarchy of objects until we reach the **productname** property of the product property of the **currentitem** session variable. We'll select the **productname** property as a source for a new variable called **productname**.

Help

New Variable Template

Template Name Shipping Cost 1

Version 1.0

Description Variables for analyzing shi ×

Figure 12.15 Variable template. © 2016 Avaya Inc. All Rights Reserved.

Help

Select a Variable Part

- acme (Owner)
  - Acme Commerce (System)
    - (Application)
    - Shopping (Application)
      - 1.0 (Version)
        - FreeShipping 1 (Decision)
          - Data
            - session_attribs (Object)
              - productcode (String)
              - currentitem (Object)
                - product (Object)
                  - productcode (String)
                  - cost (Integer)
                  - price (Integer)
                  - productname (String)
                  - shippingcost (Integer)
                - quantity (Integer)
                - buy (Boolean)
                - freeshipping (Boolean)
              - action (String)
              - cart (Object)
            - Request Variables
          - doGetStart (Data Capture)

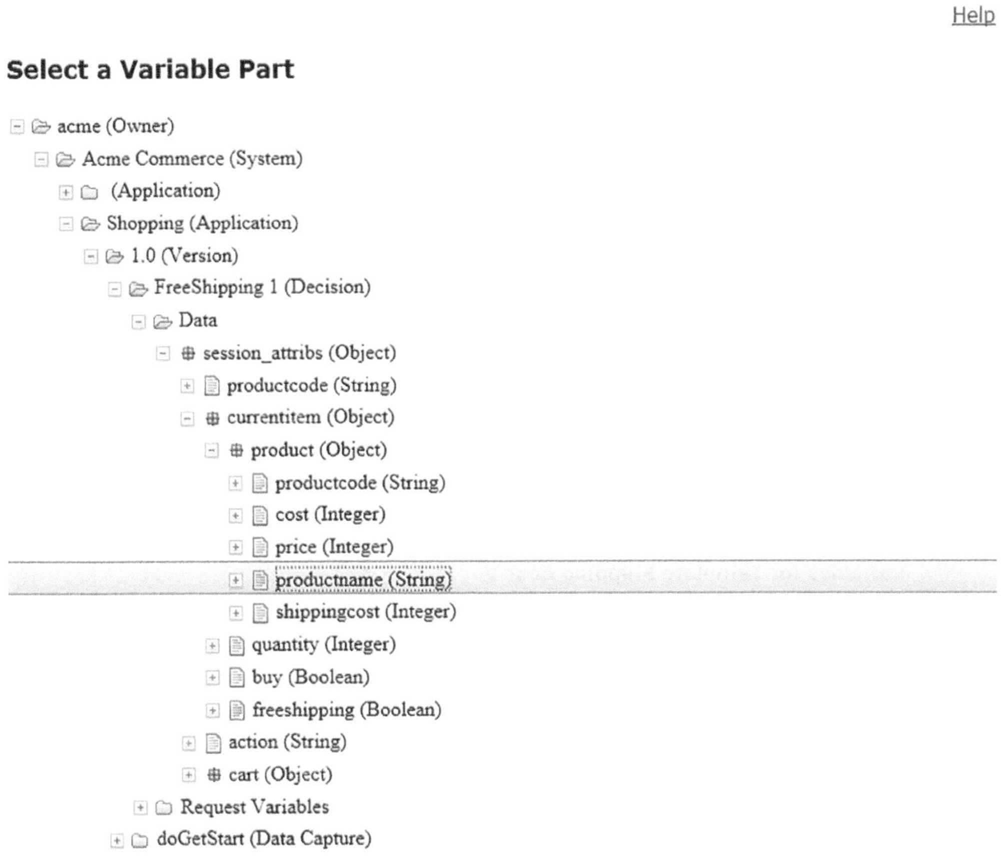

Figure 12.16 Discovered variable parts. © 2016 Avaya Inc. All Rights Reserved.

Once we have selected the source of the new variable, we can specify the properties of that variable (Figure 12.17). It is here that we can give the variable a name that will be used when it is marshalled in a call to a treatment handler or output in a data set. We can also specify a data type, aggregate, window type (current item, first, last, previous, or next), and window size. The data type can be any of the JSON data types (Boolean, integer, number, string, object, or array). As an example, if the aggregate is sum, the window type is first, and the window size is 2, then the variable will be calculated by summing the first two values observed in the session. Additional information can be entered to specify how to handle arrays, such as the data type of the elements, and how to aggregate the elements of an array. We will set the data type to string, the aggregate to

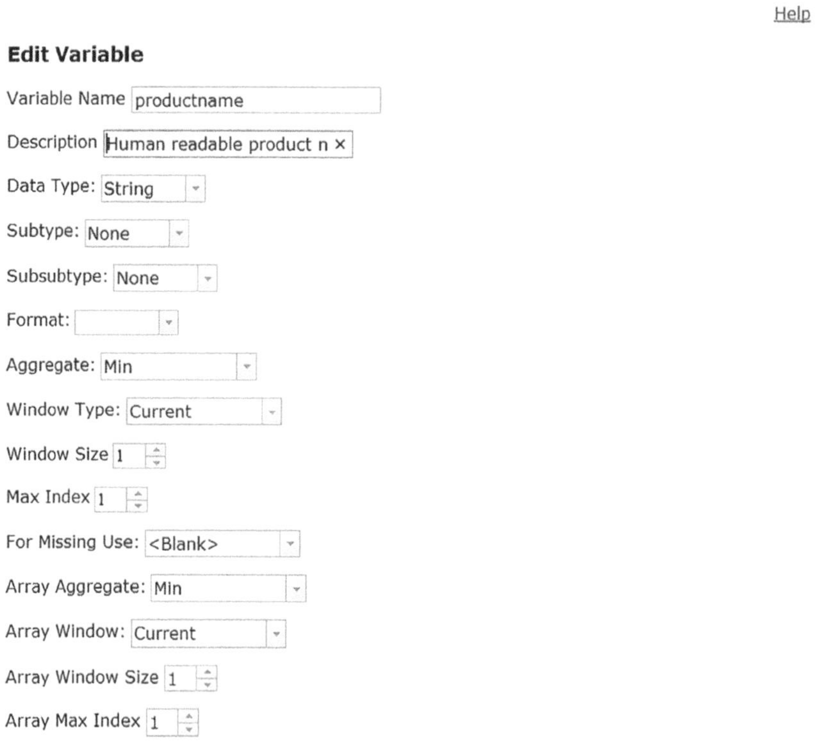

Edit Variable

Variable Name productname

Description Human readable product n ×

Data Type: String

Subtype: None

Subsubtype: None

Format:

Aggregate: Min

Window Type: Current

Window Size 1

Max Index 1

For Missing Use: <Blank>

Array Aggregate: Min

Array Window: Current

Array Window Size 1

Array Max Index 1

Figure 12.17 Properties of variable productname. © 2016 Avaya Inc. All Rights Reserved.

Variables for Template Shipping Cost 1

Variable Name	Data Type	Subtype	Description	Aggregate	Window
productname	string	none	Human readable product name	min	current
cost	number	none	Wholesale cost of the item	min	current
price	number	none	The price charged for the item	min	current
shippingcost	number	none	The shipping cost of the item	min	current
quantity	number	none	The quantity currently selected	min	current

Figure 12.18 Shipping cost variables. © 2016 Avaya Inc. All Rights Reserved.

min, and the window type as current (the current item only). Once we have set the properties of the new variable, we could specify more program variables from which **productname** could be calculated, but instead we will add more variables to the template (Figure 12.18).

After experimentation, the next step is training. For this step, we need a data set, which we can construct using the variable template we just created. Before we can generate a data set, we need to describe its contents and how it will be generated. We will first create a new *data set spec*, a specification of the data and format to be used for the data set, using the screen in Figure 12.19.

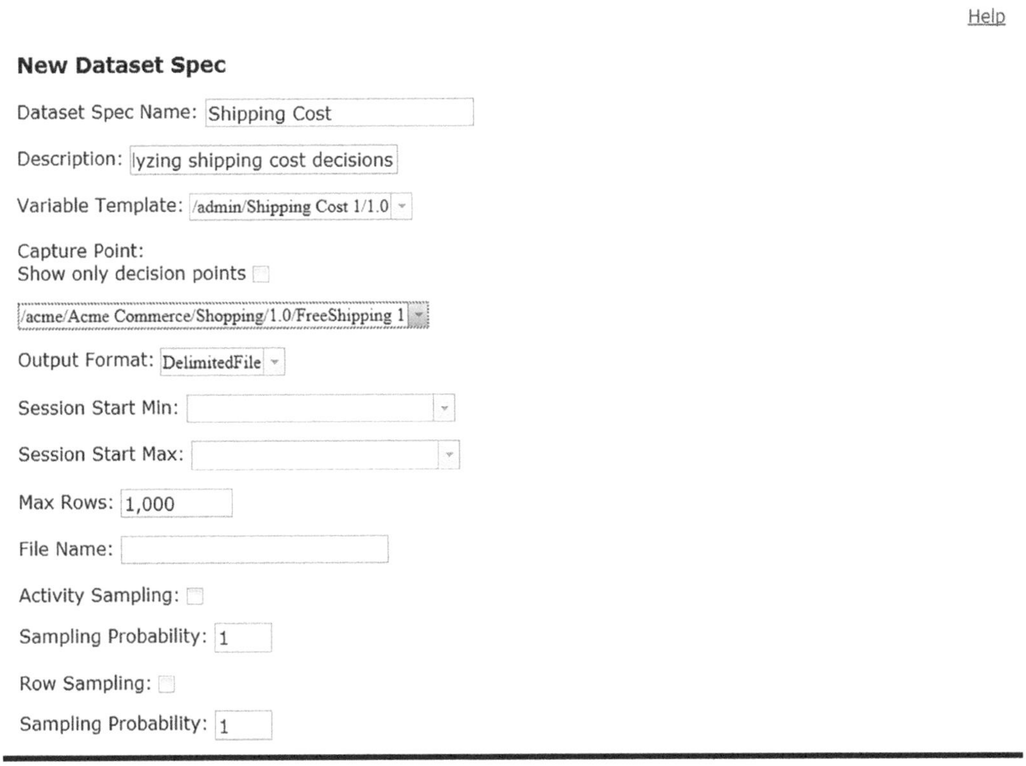

New Dataset Spec

Dataset Spec Name: Shipping Cost

Description: lyzing shipping cost decisions

Variable Template: /admin/Shipping Cost 1/1.0 ▼

Capture Point:
Show only decision points ☐

/acme/Acme Commerce/Shopping/1.0/FreeShipping 1 ▼

Output Format: DelimitedFile ▼

Session Start Min: ▼

Session Start Max: ▼

Max Rows: 1,000

File Name:

Activity Sampling: ☐

Sampling Probability: 1

Row Sampling: ☐

Sampling Probability: 1

Figure 12.19 Shipping cost data set spec. © 2016 Avaya Inc. All Rights Reserved.

In this screen, we can specify a name for the data set spec, a description, a variable template, an output format, an output file name, and a variety of other parameters that determine how the data set is generated:

■ A range of date/time values for the session start.
■ The maximum number of records to extract.
■ Whether to sample activities (sessions). If this box is checked, the user can specify a sampling probability. If there is a very large amount of data, we may only want to sample, say, 1% of the sessions.
■ Whether to sample rows (capture points). If this box is checked, the user can specify a sampling probability. If there are a lot of decision points in a session, say in a gaming or video streaming app, then we may only want to sample only 10% of the decision points.

These options are useful for narrowing down the records to use in the analysis, for example, to reflect only those to which a certain experiment applies and also to reduce the sheer number of records in the case in which the volume of data is too large to allow for analyzing all of it. There are many other ways the data could be filtered. For example, we could just sample from the decision points at which the user first viewed a product. Note that when the broker extracts data for a decision point (row), it looks at the entire session in which that decision point occurred. The output file parameter is really the name of a program extension that is loaded at runtime. The extension processes each row to produce the right format, output, or action. The decision to have the file or

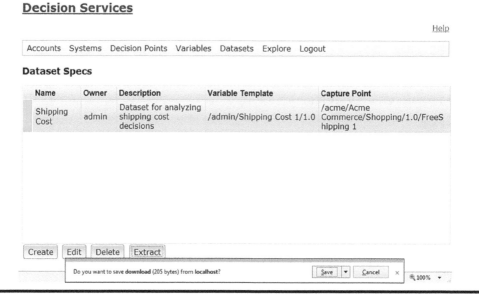

Figure 12.20 Extracting a data set. © 2016 Avaya Inc. All Rights Reserved.

other output created by an extension was based on the need to allow for a wide variety of output formats. To generate a data set, we simply click the Extract button on the Dataset Specs screen (Figure 12.20). The resulting data set can be opened in Microsoft Excel, for example. The data set generated can now be imported into an analysis program for analysis and training. In the example above, the file format was CSV, but an appropriate extension could produce a different format instead. The result of the analysis and training process is a scoring service.

After analysis and training have been performed to obtain a scoring service, the broker must be configured to invoke the service as part of a treatment that it applies in response to a decision request. To invoke a scoring service, the broker must marshal the variables required by that service, which entails a similar flattening process to that used when extracting data sets. Once a scoring service has been developed from the data, the same variable template can be used to specify the data used by the treatment. ML frameworks often have two distinct capabilities: The ability to fit a model or train a classifier based on a data set and the ability to apply that model or classifier to a smaller data set (perhaps containing only one observation) with the same structure as the original data set. This means that a model obtained using an exported data set can be applied to a new data set with the same structure created by the treatment handler. In this way, the data scientist can be freed from worrying about the format or structure of the data provided to a scoring service by a treatment handler if the variable template specified for the treatment is the same as that used in the data set spec used to create the data set. Indeed, the data scientist need not even be aware of the broker and still be able to develop a scoring service that will work.

12.6 Knowledge Management

The field of KM had grown out of the struggles of large organizations in preserving, sharing, and propagating knowledge and ideas. There are many definitions of KM [4], reflecting the 30-plus-year evolution of the field. Earlier definitions focused on the recording and sharing of knowledge (information management), whereas more recent work has focused on the generation of knowledge based on the thesis that knowledge is something that exists only in people's minds. Current KM efforts center on the notion of conversational leadership, which is based on the observation that people acquire knowledge and develop new ideas particularly well in conversational settings.

Despite the increased importance of apps to businesses, businesspeople (people whose primary responsibility is the running of the business rather than those of more technical roles such as application developer and data scientist) have little visibility into the workings of applications or the data science that could be used to guide those applications. In addition, the role of UX designer has grown rapidly in recent years. The input of businesspeople and UX designers is critical for bridging the gap between ML models and the business and UX decisions required by applications. The proposed decision framework provides a twofold solution to this problem:

- It records the kinds of decisions made by the app and the information known to the app and the business in real time.
- It provides a mechanism for adding new decision logic to apps based on business needs.

By making explicit the decisions made and the information on which they are based, the framework enables stakeholders (app developers, data scientists, businesspeople, and UX designers) to understand how well an app is helping to meet business goals. Even more importantly, the decision framework gives stakeholders a structure for conversations about what the app *should* do to achieve better business outcomes and user experiences and how best to go about doing it. In this way, the framework supports both ends of the KM spectrum: information management and conversational leadership. In short, the decision framework provides a mechanism by which businesspeople and UX designers can achieve greater visibility into and control over the apps upon which the business depends.

12.7 Conclusions

We have shown that the approach proposed in [10] can be applied to a simple e-commerce web application, and the example application is of the exact type envisioned in that paper. The process of instrumenting the application was straightforward with the servlet-specific API, and session variables were captured successfully. The broker successfully discovered the decision points and capture points of the application, and the web UI made it easy to configure a simple randomized treatment for the decision point. Furthermore, the broker was able to successfully discover the variables captured, and the UI made it possible to define how those variables could be flattened into meaningful data that could be used for analysis and decision-making. Finally, we were able to extract a small data set based on actual application data and the variable template created in the UI.

The prototype system provided a good separation of concerns between the application developer and the data scientist, since the data scientist needed little or no understanding of the internals of the app to collect data or develop models. However, the roles of application developer and data scientist alone are probably not sufficient to provide for better decisions, since many of those decisions would be motivated by businesspeople or UX designers. And despite the separation of concerns, collaboration between the different roles is essential. The following are some other observations and learnings.

The outputs of ML or statistical models are often too low level to provide actionable decisions. For example, a predictive model might provide a probability that the customer will not renew their contract. While useful information, this number in itself does not provide an action to be taken.

Instead, the app needs to know, e.g., whether to offer a discount or to start a chat session with a retention specialist. Obtaining an actionable decision may require not just evaluating the model, but also calling business rules and performing other calculations.

One unforeseen issue centered on the identification of capture points (including decision points) and, by extension, identification of the variables associated with them. Originally, capture points were identified by their owner, the application system, application, application version, module (e.g., package), submodule (e.g., class), routine (e.g., method), and line number. Although the module, submodule, routine, and line number could be captured automatically by the API in the Java case, the approach proved to be too fragile, since any change to the code that caused the line number, method, class, etc., of the capture point to change would result in a new capture point. To remedy this, we switched to identifying decision points and capture points by the owner, application system, application, application version, and label, where the label was explicitly specified by the app developer.

Another unforeseen issue was the sheer complexity of the data captured, due to the hierarchical nature of sessions, capture points, and the data in the app. For example, the captured data could include a shopping cart, which is a Map object, within which there are items (objects) containing the product code, quantity, price, and shipping cost. In the authors' experience, real systems contain even more complex data. A related unforeseen issue was the complexity of specification of variables to be used in analysis and decision-making and the complexity of the extraction of the data. This was by far the most complex part of the process and would appear to be not so much a result of the broker and UI design as it is due to the inherent complexity in identifying the correct variables for predicting future outcomes.

Since captured variables are serialized into JSON, and since that JSON is used to discover the variable metadata, it is impossible to tell whether a given item is a variable or an object instance. For example, we might see items in a JSON object with keys "red," "green," and "blue". We have no way of knowing just from this information whether red, green, and blue represent three different variables or three instances of a single variable called color. The reason for this is that the properties of a Java object will be serialized into items within the corresponding object, as would the key/value pairs of the entries in a map containing instances of objects keyed by color. Also, session variables might very well be stored in a map for convenience. For this reason, it may be necessary to provide a capability in the UI to specify whether something is a variable or an instance of a different variable.

Since the decision broker captures variables from different capture points, apps, and application systems, a given piece of information could be named differently in different application systems or apps. For this reason, and because of the need to capture information about the meaning of the data captured, a domain model of the captured data would be extremely helpful. For example, one application system may have a variable called **mobile** that represents the customer's mobile number, while another application system might store the mobile number in a variable called **phonenum**. A domain model might have a variable called **mobileNumber** that would be defined to be the customer's mobile number. The discovered variable **phoneNum** could then be mapped to the domain model item **mobileNumber**. Rather than building a data set from a list of discovered variables, a data scientist could instead select the corresponding domain model variables.

The automatic data capture mechanism employed (capturing session attributes and possibly other session context) works extremely well, but one downside of this is that the mechanism could easily capture more information than desired. For example, the data capture mechanism could capture highly confidential information such as social security numbers, authentication credentials, mobile numbers, etc. Or, the mechanism might capture a large amount of information that has no prediction value. For this reason, there is a need to be able to limit the data captured by the API. For example, a data scientist or app developer might specify a list of variables that may be captured or a list of variables that cannot be captured. These lists could refer to the specific variables captured at a capture point, or they could refer to the corresponding items in a domain model. They could also protect the broker from being overloaded by incoming data by limiting data capture to a well-defined set of variables. This could happen if the amount of data known to the application system grew unexpectedly.

Although a customer's mobile number might be considered too sensitive to capture as is, it may still be very useful for linking data from different sessions for the same customer. A solution to this problem would be to record an encrypted version of the mobile number, using a known cryptographic hash scheme. The encrypted mobile number would still be useable for linking sessions, since it would always encrypt to the same value, but it would be virtually impossible for someone to extract the true mobile number from the encrypted value.

In the simplified example presented, discovery, experimentation, and data capture all take place on the same application system environment. In practice, this would most probably not be the case. Instead, discovery would be done with a development or test environment, and experimentation and data capture would be done on a production system. Because of this, a practical version of the decision broker would need the capability to take the schema discovered in a development or test environment and use it for a production system and to disable discovery in the production system. That way, the data scientist would be working with a fixed, locked-down view of the decision points and variables.

The decision broker service is stateful, in the sense that it keeps track of information about a user session on the application system between requests. This becomes an issue when the broker is scaled horizontally by adding more broker instances, since each instance must maintain or access the data captured in previously calls to the broker in a user session. The prototype decision framework used servlet session cookies to identify sessions in calls to the broker. With multiple sessions behind a load balancer, sticky sessions could be used to ensure that the calls to the broker would always be routed to the same broker instance within a session.

In practice, 21st century big data analytics is built around automated and reproducible data pipelines. These pipelines extract data from source systems, transform it somehow, and then deliver it to various repositories. An automated data pipeline and the systems that manage it would require some sort of machine interface to the decision broker, such as a REST interface or a command line interface (CLI). Such interfaces could easily be built into the decision broker to enable the extraction of training data sets or the querying of the schema for a system.

In the example, random sampling for experimentation is done by making a random choice between **true** and **false** when deciding whether to offer free shipping. This is equivalent to randomly selecting the decision points for which free shipping will be offered. In other words, the *sampling units* (the items sampled at random to construct a sample) for experimentation were decision points. One obvious drawback of this sampling scheme is that the customer could simply keep viewing the page for an item until they were offered free shipping, as we did. There are several alternative sampling schemes, which include sampling sessions or customers. Here are some possible choices for sampling units:

1. **Decision points**, in which the random choice of whether to offer free shipping is made for each decision point (given that the customer has not previously been offered free shipping).
2. **Application sessions**, in which a random choice about whether to offer free shipping is made every time the customer enters the shopping app.

3. **Application system sessions**, in which the customer would always be offered free shipping in a sampled application system session (visit to the BuyStuff site).
4. **Customers**, in which a sampled customer would always be offered free shipping.

References

1. William Bolton. *Instrumentation and Control Systems*, Second Edition. Elsevier, Oxford, 2015.
2. John Chaves, Chris Curry, Robert L Grossman, David Locke, and Steve Vejcik. Augustus: The design and architecture of a PMML-based scoring engine. In *Proceedings of the 4th International Workshop on Data Mining Standards, Services and Platforms*, pages 38–46. ACM, 2006.
3. G P Frost, T J Gordon, M N Howell, Q H Wu. Moderated reinforcement learning of active and semi-active vehicle suspension control laws. *Proceedings of the Institution of Mechanical Engineers, Part I: Journal of Systems and Control Engineering*, 210(4): 249–257, 1996.
4. John Girard, and JoAnn Girard. Defining knowledge management: Toward an applied compendium. *Online Journal of Applied Knowledge Management*, 3(1): 1–20, 2015.
5. Alex Guazzelli, Kostantinos Stathatos, and Michael Zeller. Efficient deployment of predictive analytics through open standards and cloud computing. *ACM SIGKDD Explorations Newsletter*, 11(1):32–38, 2009.
6. Sue Hildreth. Rounding up business rules. *Computerworld*, 39(21):24–26, 2005.
7. Barbara A Kitchenham, Tore Dyba, and Magne Jorgensen. Evidence-based software engineering. In *Proceedings of the 26th International Conference on Software Engineering*, pages 273–281. IEEE Computer Society, 2004.
8. Ron Kohavi, Randal M Henne, and Dan Sommerfeld. Practical guide to controlled experiments on the Web: listen to your customers not to the HIPPO. In *Proceedings of the 13th ACM SIGKDD International Conference on Knowledge Discovery and Data Mining*, pages 959–967. ACM, 2007.
9. James Taylor and Neil Raden. *Smart Enough Systems: How to Deliver Competitive Advantage by Automating Hidden Decisions*. Prentice Hall, Upper Saddle River, NJ, 2007.
10. Patrick Tendick and Audris Mockus. Decisions as a service for application centric real time analytics. In *Proceedings of the 2nd International Workshop on BIG Data Software Engineering*, pages 1–7. ACM, 2016.
11. Patrick H Tendick, Lorraine Denby, and Wen-Hua Ju. Statistical methods for complex event processing and real time decision making. *Wiley Interdisciplinary Reviews: Computational Statistics*, 8(1):5–26, 2016.
12. Robert K Yin. *Case Study Research Design and Methods*, Third edition. Sage Publications, Thousand Oaks, CA, 2003.

Chapter 13

Industrial Evaluation of an Architectural Assumption Documentation Tool: A Case Study

Chen Yang
Wuhan University
University of Groningen
IBO Technology (Shenzhen) Co., Ltd

Peng Liang
Wuhan University

Paris Avgeriou
University of Groningen

Tianqing Liu and Zhuang Xiong
Wuhan University

Contents

13.1 Introduction

According to Kruchten et al. [1], the concept of architectural knowledge *consists of architecture design as well as the design decisions, assumptions, context, and other factors that together determine why a particular solution is the way it is.* In this work we adopt the definition of architectural assumption (AA) from our previous work: AAs are architectural knowledge taken for granted or accepted as true without evidence [2]. This definition of AA emphasizes the characteristic of uncertainty in architectural knowledge: stakeholders believe but cannot prove, for instance, the importance, impact, or correctness of specific architectural knowledge. In addition to being a type of architectural knowledge, assumptions are also a type of artifact. As defined by Kroll and Kruchten [3]: *An artifact is a piece of information that is produced, modified, or used by a process.* Since AAs are produced (i.e., made), modified, and used during software development, we advocate treating AAs as a type of software artifacts, similarly to requirements, design decisions, etc.

AAs are important in both software architecting and software development in general [4,5]. However, AAs are usually not well managed and remain implicit or become invalid,[1] leading to a multitude of issues (e.g., architectural mismatch, architectural misunderstandings, and

---

[1] An AA is invalid if its properties are incorrect or imprecise, or it is not an AA any longer.

system failures) [6–8]. In our recent systematic mapping study (SMS) on assumptions and their management [9], we identified 12 assumption management activities (e.g., Assumption Making, Documentation, Evaluation, and Maintenance), in which Assumption Documentation was the second most frequently discussed activity (89 out of 134 studies, 66.4%). As also evidenced in our industrial survey (with 112 practitioners) and two industrial case studies (with 12 architects and 24 architects respectively), performing AA Documentation effectively and systematically is of paramount importance in software development [4,2,10]. The importance of AA Documentation is also supported by other studies. As an example, Landuyt and Joosen [7] mentioned that currently early AAs (i.e., AAs made in requirements engineering) are usually undocumented. Therefore, it is difficult to distinguish AAs from requirements, as well as analyze relationships between AAs and requirements. Later it would hinder the transition from requirements engineering to architecting (e.g., connecting AAs and design decisions).

Within all the challenges in AA Documentation, the lack of dedicated tool support is one of the most important concerns raised by practitioners. For example, in our earlier work [2], we proposed an approach: Architectural Assumption Documentation Framework (AADF) for documenting AAs in software development and evaluated its effectiveness through a case study with a number of architects from different industries and domains. In that case study, we took the first step in providing tool support: an MS Excel template that implements AADF. The results of the case study show that although architects considered AADF as beneficial for AA Documentation as well as software development, the lack of a specialized tool is a major obstacle when using the approach.

In this chapter, we present such a specialized tool in order to promote the practice of AA Documentation in industry: Architectural Assumptions Manager (ArAM). ArAM was developed as a plugin of Enterprise Architect,[2] which is a Unified Modeling Language (UML) modeling tool widely used in software development, and implemented AADF (the reason of choosing AADF as the basis of ArAM is provided in Section 3.1). To validate the usefulness and ease of use of ArAM, we conducted an industrial case study in Beijing and Shenzhen, China, with 16 software architects from ten companies. The results of the case study show that ArAM is generally useful and easy to use in AA Documentation as well as in software development, though there are several issues to be addressed; as an example, the tool should support automatic analysis (e.g., finding missing relationships between AAs) and verification (e.g., verifying the correctness of existing assumptions) in software development.

13.1.1 Relation to Our Previous Work on Architectural Assumption and Their Management

This chapter is part of a number of works we did on AAs and AA management. Table 13.1 lists all our related publications and provides details for each regarding its contribution, contribution type, publication year, and its relation to our previous work. The contribution of this chapter is the implementation of the ArAM tool and its empirical validation in industry. Related to our previous work, ArAM is the tool support for AADF, which in turn extended the simplified conceptual model [11]. This work is also partially based on the state of research (see [9]) and state of practice (see [4] and [10]), using as input from both industrial needs and research problems/concerns in order to derive requirements for the ArAM tool. This tool can be used to support the AA management process [12].

---

[2] http://www.sparxsystems.com.au/products/ea/.

Table 13.1   Relationship between this Work and Our Previous Work on AAs and Their Management

Previous Work	Contribution	Contribution Type	Publication Year	Relation to Previous Work
[11]	A simplified conceptual model with a lightweight approach for AA Documentation in agile development, and preliminary evaluation of the approach.	Conceptual model and its empirical validation	2014	First work with an initial idea of documenting AAs
[9]	State of the research regarding assumptions and their management in software development from literature.	State of research	2018	Literature review focusing on general assumption management
[10]	State of the practice regarding AAs and their management from architects' perception.	State of practice	2017	Building on [9], but narrowing the scope from assumption management to AA management
[12]	An AA management process and evaluation of the process.	Management process and its empirical validation	2018	A general AA management process that encompasses the activities identified in [9] and [10], as such an approach was lacking.
[4]	State of the practice regarding AA Identification and Documentation from practitioners' perception.	State of practice	2016	[12] showed the need to provide dedicated approaches for individual activities of the process, especially for AA Documentation. Before being able to propose a solution for AA Documentation, a specific analysis was required of how this activity is performed in practice.

(Continued)

Table 13.1 (*Continued*) Relationship between this Work and Our Previous Work on AAs and Their Management

Previous Work	Contribution	Contribution Type	Publication Year	Relation to Previous Work
[2]	An approach: Architectural Assumption Documentation Framework (i.e., AADF), an MS Excel template, and industrial evaluation of the approach.	Documentation framework and its empirical validation	2017	[4] confirmed that AA Documentation (or lack thereof) is a real problem in industry, and the existing approaches are not able to satisfy certain stakeholders concerns in describing AAs in development. This also confirmed the earlier results obtained from [9] and [10]. Therefore, we proposed a systematic method for AA Documentation.
This work	ArAM (a tool based on Enterprise Architect that implements AADF) and industrial evaluation of the tool.	Tool support and its empirical validation	N/A	The evaluation of AADF in [2] showed that it could benefit AA Documentation, but the lack of tool support was a critical problem to adopt AADF and AA Documentation in practice. Thus, this study offers tool support for AADF.

The rest of the chapter is organized as follows: Section 13.2 describes the assumption concept in detail. Section 13.3 provides related work on AA Documentation. Section 13.4 introduces ArAM. Section 13.5 details the design of the case study. The results of the case study are presented in Section 13.6 and discussed in Section 13.7. Section 13.8 assesses the threats to the validity of the study, and conclusions with future directions are provided in Section 13.9.

13.2 Assumptions in Software Development

This section briefly introduces assumptions in software development. In addition to the uncertain nature of assumptions (as mentioned in the Introduction section), we summarize the other four main characteristics of assumptions (including AAs) in software development:

1. **Subjective:** Many researchers and practitioners pointed out that whether a piece of information is an assumption or not is rather subjective (e.g., [2,9,13,14]). This is the major reason that stakeholders may have a different understanding of the assumption concept. Many studies also mention that it is difficult to draw a line between assumptions and other types of software artifacts. As an example, Roeller et al. [13] mentioned: *From one perspective or stakeholder, we may denote something as an assumption, while that same thing may be seen as a design decision from another perspective.*

2. **Intertwined with certain types of artifacts:** Assumptions are not independent in software development, but intertwined with many other types of software artifacts. For example, when managing assumptions in software design (e.g., [7,15–17]), assumptions are commonly related to requirements, design decisions, components, etc.

3. **Dynamic:** Assumptions have a dynamic nature, i.e., they can evolve over time [2,18,8]. For example, during software development, a valid assumption can turn out to be invalid or vice versa, or an assumption can transform to another type of software artifact or vice versa.

4. **Context-dependent:** Assumptions are context-dependent [2,10]. For example, the same assumption could be valid in one project and invalid in another project because the context changes; or an assumption in one project is not an assumption in another project. Unless the information is expressed in an explicit way (e.g., using phrases such as *it is assumed that*), it is difficult to judge whether the information is an assumption or not, without considering its context [2].

In this work, we advocate the necessity and importance on denoting assumptions explicitly as such, during software development. However, this often does not happen in practice, and stakeholders need to judge whether a piece of information is an assumption or another type of artifact. To assist making this distinction, we further provide **six lessons learned** based on our previous work on assumptions and their management from an industrial survey [4], case studies [2,10], and an SMS [9]. These may increase the possibility of classifying something correctly as an assumption, but there are no definitive rules for doing so. The six lessons learned also act as a theoretical background for assumption management that can help in understanding better the framework (AADF) and its supporting tool (ArAM) presented in Section 13.4.

1. Although other types of artifacts may also include uncertainty, uncertainty is not the core (or emphasis) of such artifacts. For example, when talking about a design decision, stakeholders usually do not debate whether it is uncertain, but focus on addressing the related problems. In contrast, assumptions are usually made in order to deal with uncertainties.

2. The content of an assumption and other types of artifacts is different. For example, the content of a decision is usually about employing a solution to a problem, while the content of an assumption is more about something that is true, correct, important, suitable, etc.

3. Look at the context and not just the content. In our recent SMS [9], we identified many examples of assumptions claimed by the authors of the studies (e.g., *The system will be available during normal working hours* [19]; *There is a subsystem that is responsible for receiving emergency calls and forwarding them to an available Coordinator* [15]; *If thread i holds the lock in read mode, then x cannot be changed by another thread* [20]). We argue that it is difficult to treat such examples as assumptions by only reading these statements. However, if we dig deeper in the studies, paying attention to the context of those examples, it becomes clear why the authors of those studies considered the examples as assumptions, instead of other types of artifacts, such as requirements.

4. Every assumption should be characterized by uncertainty; if something is certain or has strong evidence supporting its validity, it is not an assumption. Despite this inherent uncertainty, an assumption is still taken for granted or accepted as true. Therefore, if such characteristic can be found in a piece of information, it increases the possibility that the information is an assumption. For example, in the early phases of software development, an architect had to make decisions regarding the architecture of a system. However, in that project, even for customers, some information was uncertain in such early phases, and the project team could not wait for eliminating all the uncertainties. In order to meet the schedule and deadlines of the project, the architect came up with several AAs (e.g., *The number of concurrent users of the system will exceed 1 million*) and made architectural design decisions based on those AAs. Considering the example of concurrent users, the architect was not sure about its correctness, but took it for granted during system design. This AA would exist until its uncertainty was eliminated (e.g., the number of concurrent users indeed exceeds 1 million). Assumptions are not equal to uncertainties in software development: instead uncertainties can lead to assumptions, i.e., one way to deal with uncertainties is to make implicit or explicit assumptions [21]. Other ways could also be employed, depending on the project context, such as actively looking for evidence (e.g., diving into documents, conducting surveys, and communicating with related stakeholders) or alternatives in order to address uncertainties.

5. Stakeholders should reach a consistent understanding on what is an assumption in their projects. Only paying attention to the properties of an assumption (e.g., validity and rationale) is not enough. Stakeholders need to further consider or explain to the crowd why such a statement is an assumption, instead of another type of artifact.

6. Sometimes the line between an assumption and another type of artifact is vague. Instead of struggling with the "correct" answer of a statement (whether the statement is an assumption), stakeholders should focus on reaching an agreement on the statement within the team. This means that if stakeholders agree that a statement is an assumption, it can be managed as an assumption in the project. Later if the stakeholders find more evidence, they can make adjustments accordingly (e.g., transforming the assumption to another type of artifact).

13.3 Related Work on AA Documentation

This section first presents related work regarding approaches and tools used for AA Documentation, followed by a comparison between AA management and management of other types of artifacts. Finally, to make the contribution of this work explicit, we compared this work with our previous work on AAs and their management.

13.3.1 Approaches used for AA Documentation

Besides AADF (the framework that ArAM is based on), Table 13.2 lists a number of other approaches used for AA Documentation. Note that the column "Details" refers to whether the study provides details on the approach proposed or just merely mentions that an approach could be used to document AAs; "First class" refers to whether the approach treats AAs as first-class entities or only as a type of by-product. We see the following limitations of those approaches: (a) Different stakeholders have various AA concerns (e.g., *Which AAs have been made?* and *What risks are caused*

Table 13.2 Approaches Used for AA Documentation

Authors	Approaches	Details	First class	Reference
Garlan et al.	Architecture views, description languages, etc., for AA Documentation	No	Yes	[6]
Van Landuyt and Joosen	A metamodel and an instantiation strategy based on quality attribute scenarios and use cases to document AAs	Yes	Yes	[7]
Ordibehesht	An approach based on an architectural analysis and description language to document AAs	Yes	Yes	[23]
Mamun et al.	Alloy language for AA Documentation	Yes	Yes	[24]
Tang et al.	A rationale-based architecture model (documenting AAs as a type of architectural rationale)	Yes	No	[25]
Welsh et al.	REAssuRE (documenting assumptions made at design time)	Yes	Yes	[26]
Faily and Fléchais	Assumption personas (a description of the behavior of a typical user with assumptions)	Yes	Yes	[27]
Habli and Kelly	Architecture design replay through derivational analogy (documenting AAs as a type of design knowledge)	Yes	No	[28]
Hesse and Paech	A decision documentation model (including AA Documentation)	Yes	No	[29]
Heyman et al.	A formal architectural modeling and analysis method (including AA Documentation)	Yes	Yes	[30]
Lago and van Vliet	A metamodel for AA Documentation	Yes	Yes	[31]
Yang and Liang	A simplified conceptual model for AAs with a lightweight approach for AA Documentation	Yes	Yes	[11]

(Continued)

Table 13.2 (*Continued*)   Approaches Used for AA Documentation

Authors	Approaches	Details	First class	Reference
Yang et al.	An AA management process that includes AA Documentation as an AA management activity	Yes	Yes	[12]
Rizkiyanto	A software architecture design reasoning model that uses a template to document AAs	Yes	No	[32]
Rahimi et al.	An approach: Assumption Diagnostics and Rationale Process (ADRP) model for safety-critical assumption management (including documentation)	Yes	Yes	[33]
Tang et al.	A software architecture design reasoning model that uses cards to document AAs	Yes	No	[16]
EL Fassi et al.	An assumption network-based approach used to allocate and manage design margins (including an object-oriented approach for AA Documentation)	Yes	Yes	[17]
Yang et al.	An adapted AA management process (based on [12]) using agile practices that includes AA Documentation as an AA management activity	Yes	Yes	[34]

by assumption A?), but the existing approaches, techniques, and tools only address few of them, and the connections between AA concerns and stakeholders are not clear; and (b) it is unclear which AA concerns are addressed by the proposed approaches, techniques, and tools, and how they address those concerns. Compared with the existing approaches used for AA Documentation, (a) AADF is the first approach that proposes a systematic framework based on ISO/IEC/IEEE Std 42010-2011 [22]; (b) AADF addresses 23 AA concerns of stakeholders; and (c) AADF draws a clear connection between the 23 AA concerns and 8 types of stakeholders (e.g., project manager and architect). Therefore, we chose AADF as the basis of ArAM.

13.3.2 Tools used for AA Documentation

General tools such as MS Word[3] and MS Excel[4] are commonly used in software development for various purposes and can also be used to document AAs. For example, in our previous work [2], we implemented AADF through an MS Excel template and used this template in an industrial case study. There are tools that aim at managing other types of software artifacts, such as design decisions, but include AA Documentation. For example, Manteuffel et al. [35] developed a tool for documenting design decisions, with which AAs can be documented as forces of decisions in that tool. A force is any aspect that affects architects when they make decisions [36]. Finally, there are

---

[3] https://products.office.com/en-us/excel.
[4] https://products.office.com/en-us/word.

several tools that focus on other AA management activities (e.g., AA Evaluation), but can be used for AA Documentation. We provide three examples as follows. Heyman et al. [30] used Alloy (a modeling language) to describe AAs and a tool (Alloy Analyzer[5]) that implements Alloy for AA Evaluation. Rahimi et al. [33] used an Assumption Diagnostics and Rationale Process (ADRP) tool to analyze whether safety-critical assumptions are omitted or invalid in new products, which includes documentation of the assumptions. Fu et al. [37] used a tool called Unspecified Assumption Carrier Finder (UACFinder) to automatically identify undocumented assumptions in system design models through potential syntactic carriers (e.g., constant variables, frequently read or updated variables, and frequently executed action sequences).

The aforementioned tools are either generic or developed for different purposes; thus they may not be suitable or effective for documenting AAs. Moreover, Landuyt and Joosen [7] developed a prototype tool that implements AspectU+ for managing early AAs. Early AAs are a subset of AAs, and the tool is bound to, for example, use cases, which is particularly suitable for managing AAs in requirements engineering. However, the tool may not work for all types of AAs (e.g., AAs made in later phases such as architecting). To the best of our knowledge and based on our recent SMS [9], ArAM is the first tool that advocates treating AAs as first-class entities and is specifically developed for AA Documentation by implementing AADF.

13.3.3 Relation to Requirements and Architecture

AAs are related to different types of artifacts, including requirements and architectural design decisions. However, AAs require their own management approaches and tools for the following reasons.

1. As discussed in Section 13.2, AAs, requirements, architectural design decisions, etc., are different artifacts with different characteristics, properties, etc. As an example, the essence of an assumption is uncertainty, which is not the emphasis in a requirement or a decision.
2. The focus (or concerns) of managing different types of artifacts is diverse, leading to different approaches and tools. These differences include both the tasks that compose the approach or tool and what artifacts are created and consumed and what stakeholders do in a specific task. As an example, Evaluation in requirements engineering, architecting, and AA management has completely different meanings. In requirements engineering, Evaluation means *to go back to the system stakeholders and check if the requirements are what they really need.* [38] In architecting, Evaluation refers to *ensuring that the architectural design decisions made are the right ones, and the candidate architectural solutions proposed in Architectural Synthesis are measured against the architecturally significant requirements collected in Architectural Analysis.* [39] However, in AA management, Evaluation *ensures that the description and analysis of AAs are correct and accurate.* [9] It is possible to integrate AA management into, for example, architecting, but AAs will always require their own management approaches and tools.

As a specific example, AADF can be compared to other Architecture Frameworks, such as the Architecture Decision Documentation Framework proposed by van Heesch et al. [40]. The only common element between these two frameworks is that both of them follow the same standard – ISO/IEC/IEEE Std 42010-2011 [22]; all the other parts of the design of the two frameworks are different. First, the two frameworks were developed based on different motivations. The

---

[5] http://alloy.mit.edu/alloy/.

motivation of AADF is based on our industrial survey on AAs [4] and an SMS on assumptions and their management in software development [9]. Furthermore, the two frameworks used different processes for identifying and selecting concerns. We collected 78 concerns on assumptions from the existing literature. Twenty-three AA concerns were finally selected, and four categories of the concerns (i.e., addressed by the four AADF viewpoints) were classified by using Constant Comparison [41]. Finally, the metamodels in the two frameworks are completely different.

In summary, we argue that though there are existing approaches and tools for managing certain types of software artifacts (e.g., in requirements engineering and architecting), there is still a need to design specific processes, approaches, and tools for managing AAs in software development.

13.4 Architectural Assumptions Manager – ArAM

This section first introduces the necessary background of ArAM (including AADF) and subsequently introduces ArAM in detail, especially regarding the implementation of the AADF and the corresponding viewpoints. For more details on AADF, we refer interested readers to our previous work ([2] and [42]).

13.4.1 Background

AADF follows the guidelines for architecture frameworks proposed in ISO/IEC/IEEE Std 42010:2011 [22]. It comprises four viewpoints: the AA Detail viewpoint, the AA Relationship viewpoint, the AA Tracing viewpoint, and the AA Evolution viewpoint, as shown in Figure 13.1. Each viewpoint frames a set of AA concerns of stakeholders: the Detail viewpoint documents the characteristics (e.g., pros and cons) of each AA; the Relationship viewpoint provides an overview of relationships between AAs; the Tracing viewpoint also shows relations but between AAs and other types of software artifacts (e.g., requirements and architectural design decisions); finally, the Evolution viewpoint tracks the evolution of AAs along software development. The metamodels of the viewpoints are provided in the next subsection alongside the description of the tool.

ArAM was developed as a plugin of Enterprise Architect, which is a UML-based platform for designing and developing software systems. Enterprise Architect supports various modeling objectives and covers the whole software development life cycle. It also supports traces through software development models, for example, from the design phase to the testing or maintenance phase. ArAM is completely flexible and customizable: users of ArAM do not need to use all the viewpoints and elements in ArAM. Instead they can choose specific elements in certain viewpoints to be documented. For instance, they can document only key information according to their project

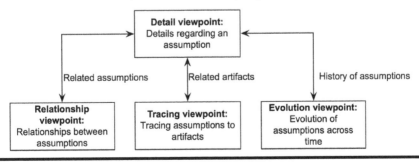

Figure 13.1 Viewpoints of Architectural Assumption Documentation Framework.

context in order to save time and effort. The user guide of ArAM can be found in a short online video,[6] while more information (i.e., user guide, developer guide, and installation information) about ArAM and Enterprise Architect can be found in [42].

13.4.2 ArAM in Detail

AA management should be teamwork: although architects and designers have the major responsibility of managing AAs, other types of stakeholders (e.g., project managers) in development should also be involved [2,9]. Therefore, users of ArAM are mainly architects and designers, but also other types of stakeholders that are actively involved in AA management.

We will walk through the different viewpoints in ArAM using a simple but real industrial example, from the domain of Internet of Things at IBO Technology, which is the employer of the first author. IBO Technology is a Chinese company headquartered in Shenzhen, China, and focuses on IT services (e.g., system integration services) and Internet of Things. The example is from a project that aims to develop a gas cylinders management system. Consider a system that manages a number of gas cylinders and trucks used to carry the gas cylinders. Functions of the system include identifying gas cylinders and tracking the expiry date, validity, etc., of each gas cylinder. There is a Gas Cylinders Identification component in the system, which is used to identify gas cylinders (see Figure 13.2). Initially, the architects *assumed* that gas cylinders can be identified through three different ways (Step 2): active tags, passive tags, and barcodes. This is an architecturally significant issue, as the identification method cannot easily be changed later. This

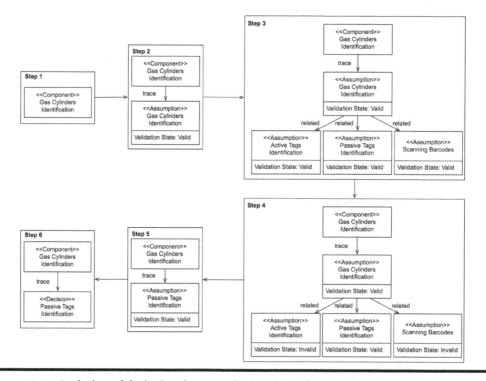

Figure 13.2 Evolution of designing the gas cylinders identification function with AAs.

---

[6] https://youtu.be/LOCTfRbNUyA.

AA can be further decomposed into three AAs (Step 3): "Active Tags Identification," "Passive Tags Identification," and "Scanning Barcodes." During evaluation of the AAs, "Scanning Barcodes" and "Active Tags Identification" were identified as invalid (Step 4), i.e., they were not accepted as true as the identification of gas cylinders with barcodes and active tags proved unsuitable. On the contrary, "Passive Tags Identification" was evaluated as valid. Later, "Scanning Barcodes" and "Active Tags Identification" were removed; the uncertainty of "Passive Tags Identification" was eliminated (Step 5), and this AA transformed into a design decision (Step 6).

13.4.2.1 AA Detail Viewpoint

The AA Detail viewpoint provides an overview of each AA, including all the information about the specific AA that is found in other viewpoints (i.e. the information of this viewpoint is a superset). In AADF, the metamodel of the AA Detail viewpoint is shown in Figure 13.3 and the elements of the AA Detail viewpoint are shown in Table 13.3. As aforementioned, ArAM

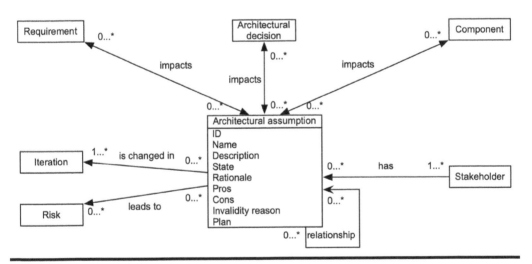

Figure 13.3   Metamodel of the AA Detail viewpoint.

Table 13.3   Elements of the AA Detail Viewpoint

Element	Description
ID	The identification of an AA. It is implicit to users.
Name	The name of the AA.
State	There are two types of State, i.e., Validation State and Action State. Validation State includes three subtypes as "Valid," "Invalid," "Unknown"; Action State includes four subtypes as "Added," "Modified," "Transformed," "Removed".
Version	The version of the AA. It can be adapted to, for example, version of product.

(Continued)

Table 13.3 (*Continued*)   Elements of the AA Detail Viewpoint

Element	Description
Modified on	The date of the AA being modified last time.
Invalidity reason	The reason about why the AA is invalid.
Description	The description of the AA.
Rationale	The reasons for making the AA.
Pros	How the AA positively impacts the system, development, or project.
Cons	How the AA negatively impacts the system, development, or project.
Stakeholders	The stakeholders who are involved in the AA.
Plan	The plan for the AA, for example, "to be removed."
Related assumptions	The relationships between the AA and other assumptions.
Traces	The relationships between the AA and other types of software artifacts.
Evolution	The evolution of the AA.

does not mandate filling in all the details for an assumption; instead the users can choose which details they want to document. This is in line with related work on architectural knowledge management tools, where the input of information can be minimal to accommodate for lean/agile approaches [43].

The aforementioned redundancy in the AA Detail viewpoint serves the purpose of aggregating all information from all viewpoints in one place, without requiring users to input information twice: for example, when updating the AA Relationship and Tracing viewpoint, the AA Detail viewpoint is automatically updated accordingly. An example of a Detail view for the AA "Scanning Barcodes" mentioned in Section 13.4.2 is illustrated in Figure 13.4.

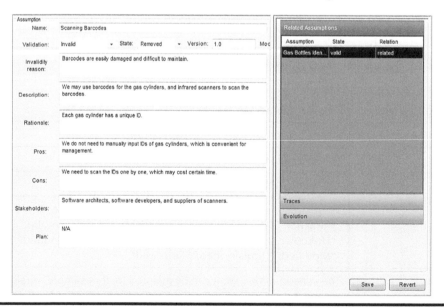

Figure 13.4   An AA Detail view in ArAM.

13.4.2.2 AA Relationship and Tracing Viewpoint

In AADF, the metamodels of the AA Relationship viewpoint and the AA Tracing viewpoint are shown in Figures 13.5 and 13.6, respectively.

We combined the AA Relationship viewpoint and the AA Tracing viewpoint of AADF into a single viewpoint in ArAM: the AA Relationship and Tracing viewpoint. By doing this, the combined viewpoint can show not only the relationships between AAs or AAs and other types of software artifacts independently, but also a combination of the two. A valid (invalid) AA is represented by a rounded green (red) rectangle with the name of the AA as a label. Figure 13.7 illustrates the Gas Cylinders Identification component tracing to the corresponding AA, but also the relation between the latter and the three AAs corresponding to identification through active tags, passive tags, and barcodes.

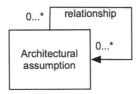

Figure 13.5   Metamodel of the AA Relationship viewpoint.

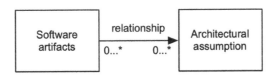

Figure 13.6   Metamodel of the AA Tracing viewpoint.

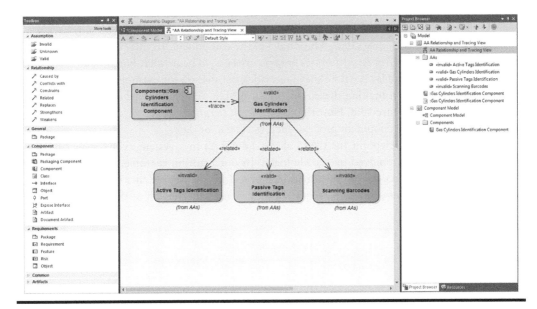

Figure 13.7   An AA Relationship and Tracing view in ArAM.

Table 13.4   Relationship Types of the AA Relationship and Tracing Viewpoint

Relationship	Description
Caused by	Assumption B causes the making of Assumption A.
Conflicts with	A symmetrical relationship that indicates that two assumptions A and B are mutually exclusive.
Constrains	Assumption B is tied to Assumption A. If Assumption A is changed, then Assumption B should be revisited.
Replaces	Assumption A and B can be a substitute of each other.
Strengthens	Assumption A increases the possibility of Assumption B being valid.
Weakens	Assumption A decreases the possibility of Assumption B being valid.
Related	There is a relation between two assumptions, and the type of this relationship is not covered by the types listed above.

As shown in Table 13.4, ArAM provides seven specific types of relationships based on AADF (e.g., "caused by" and "conflicts with"). Double clicking on an AA in an AA Relationship and Tracing view can show the Detail view of the AA. Through using the AA Relationship and Tracing views of ArAM, stakeholders can have a fair understanding of the relationships between AAs and trace AAs to other types of software artifacts in a system, which can further facilitate understanding of the system (e.g., its architecture).

13.4.2.3 AA Evolution Viewpoint

AAs have a dynamic nature: the context of a project (e.g., business environment), as well as the software system itself, is changing over time, making formerly valid AAs invalid, which results in a number of issues in system development [9]. For example, consider a stakeholder assuming that a third-party component can be used in her/his project. However, during development, the stakeholder discovers that some problems caused by the component cannot be addressed, because of the lack of key information (e.g., design rationale) of the component. In this case, the original AA: *the third-party component can be used in this project* turns out to be invalid. Furthermore, AAs may be invalid in the first place (at the time they are made), because of, for example, the lack of knowledge or information when making these AAs [9]. In AADF, the metamodel of the AA Evolution viewpoint is shown in Figure 13.8. Note that the concept *iteration* can represent a number of other variables in a software development process, such as version or date.

The AA Evolution viewpoint in ArAM shows how AAs in a system evolve over time (e.g., from valid to invalid or removed by stakeholders). In our running example, the Evolution view of the AA "Scanning Barcodes" is illustrated in Figure 13.9. By double clicking on an AA in the AA Evolution view, a user can see the specific iteration, e.g., the version of the AA as well as the

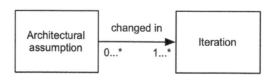

Figure 13.8   Metamodel of the AA Evolution viewpoint.

Figure 13.9   An AA Evolution view in ArAM.

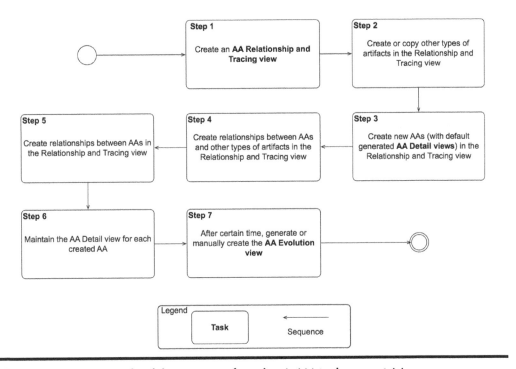

Figure 13.10   An example of the sequence for using ArAM to document AAs.

modified time of the AA. An AA evolution view could be either manually created or automatically generated from the modification history of the AAs.

13.4.2.4 *Putting It All Together*

To illustrate how a stakeholder (e.g., an architect) might use ArAM, Figure 13.10 depicts a number of steps that could be followed. To make these steps more concrete, we use once more the running example of identifying gas cylinders:

1. We create a new AA Relationship and Tracing view within the project pertaining to the cylinders management system.
2. Assuming that components of the system have already been documented in other views, we drag the existing Gas Cylinders Identification component into the AA Relationship and Tracing view.

3. We create four valid AAs to the AA Relationship and Tracing view and name them as "Gas Cylinders Identification," "Active Tags Identification," "Passive Tags Identification," and "Scanning Barcodes," respectively.
4. We create a "trace" relationship between the Gas Cylinders Identification component and the Gas Cylinders Identification assumption.
5. We create three "related" relationships between the Gas Cylinders Identification assumption and the other three AAs.
6. We fill in the AA Detail view of the four AAs with their specific information.
7. During the course of time, we generate or manually create the AA Evolution view for each AA.

The aforementioned process is flexible and customizable. For example, stakeholders can also create AAs and their relationships before they create other types of artifacts (e.g., requirements, design decisions, and components).

13.5 Case Study

This section presents the design of the case study, which followed the guidelines proposed by Runeson and Höst [44].

13.5.1 Goal and Research Questions

ArAM is a tool for AA Documentation aiming at covering the needs of practicing architects. In this study, the goal is to gauge the likelihood that the tool will be adopted in an industrial setting. Davis [45] suggested that "Perceived usefulness" (i.e., *the degree to which a person believes that using a particular system would enhance his or her job performance*) and "Perceived ease of use" (i.e., *the degree to which a person believes that using a particular system would be free of effort*) are two determinants that impact how stakeholders accept or reject information technologies; these two factors constitute the Technology Acceptance Model (TAM). Venkatesh and Davis [46] extended TAM and proposed TAM2, which decomposes "Perceived usefulness" into three social factors, four cognitive instrumental factors, and "Experience." Venkatesh and Bala [47] further extended TAM2 to TAM3, which decomposes "Perceived ease of use" into four anchor factors and two adjustment factors. Table 13.5 lists the factors used in TAM3.

Table 13.5 Factors used in TAM3

Factors (Usefulness)	Factors (Ease of Use)
Subjective norm	Computer self-efficacy
Voluntariness	Perceptions of external control
Image	Computer anxiety
Job relevance	Computer playfulness
Output quality	Perceived enjoyment
Result demonstrability	Objective usability
Experience	Experience

We adopted the factors (explained in the following paragraphs) of TAM3 and used the Goal-Question-Metric approach [48] to formulate the objective of this work: to **analyze** ArAM **for the purpose of** evaluation **with respect to** the perceived usefulness and ease of use **from the point of view of** software architects **in the context of** industrial software development in China. The research questions (RQs) of this study are presented below.

RQ1: How useful is it to use ArAM in software development?

From all the factors of "Perceived usefulness" proposed in TAM3, we studied "Job relevance" (i.e., to what extent ArAM is relevant to the subjects' work), "Output quality" (i.e., to what extent the outputs of ArAM can benefit the subjects' work), "Result demonstrability" (i.e., to what extent the results of using ArAM are communicable), and "Experience" (i.e., to what extent the experience, for example, architecting experience, can impact the perceived usefulness of ArAM).

The following factors were excluded: "Subjective norm" (i.e., to what extent people important to the subjects would suggest that they should (not) use ArAM), "Voluntariness" (i.e., to what extent using ArAM is voluntary or not), and "Image" (i.e., to what extent using ArAM can improve, for example, social status and prestige of the subjects in their companies). We did not apply the factors "Subjective norm" and "Voluntariness" because architecture and design tools were optional for the subjects in their companies, i.e., the subjects were not required to use a specific tool to design software; also, no one would suggest the subjects (not) to use a tool such as ArAM in their companies. Furthermore, since all the subjects were software engineers (architects) in their companies, we argue that using tools, such as ArAM, could not improve social status and prestige (i.e., "Image") of the subjects. Finally, since TAM3 is a general model for technology acceptance, we added a new aspect "Others" in RQ1 to aggregate the factors specifically related to ArAM.

RQ2: How easy is it to use ArAM for AA Documentation?

From all the factors of "Perceived ease of use" proposed in TAM3, we studied "Computer self-efficacy" (i.e., to what extent the subjects can use ArAM without any help), "Perceptions of external control" (i.e., to what extent the existing project resources, for example, requirements documents, can facilitate the use of ArAM), "Perceived enjoyment" (i.e., to what extent using ArAM is pleasant and enjoyable), and "Experience," (i.e., to what extent the experience, for example, architecting experience, can impact the perceived ease of use of ArAM).

The following factors were excluded: "Objective usability" (i.e., the comparison of effort between novices and experts when using ArAM), "Computer anxiety" (i.e., to what extent the subjects are afraid to use computers), and "Computer playfulness" (i.e., to what extent the subjects can interact with computers). The reasons for excluding these factors were: (a) this case study is not a comparative study; (b) the subjects had no fear of using computers and their degree of computer playfulness was high because they were professional software engineers and by definition worked with computers. Furthermore, since TAM3 is a general model for technology acceptance, we added a new aspect "Others" to aggregate the factors specifically related to ArAM.

13.5.2 Case and Subject Selection

This case study is explanatory [44] because it aims at evaluating the usefulness and ease of use of ArAM in software development.

13.5.2.1 Case Description and Units of Analysis

A case is a contemporary phenomenon in its real-life context [44,49], such as a project, a group of stakeholders, or a technology. The distinction between these types of cases is not always clear [50]. In this work, we did not conduct the case study within the software development life cycle.

Instead we asked each subject (i.e., architect) to select one real and nontrivial project related to software-intensive systems from their previous work and used ArAM in the context of the selected projects through workshops. Thus, all the AAs documented by the subjects through ArAM were from real-life projects. We considered this study as a preliminary evaluation of the usefulness and ease of use of ArAM in an industrial setting.

Furthermore, the case study was conducted with 16 architects. Instead of studying the AAs documented by the subjects, we focused on their opinions on the usefulness and ease of use of ArAM. Therefore, both the cases and the units of analysis are the architects, i.e., one unit of analysis for each case and 16 cases in total. Therefore, the case study is multiple and holistic [44].

13.5.2.2 Case Study Procedure

The procedure of the case study is presented as the following.
  Before the workshop

> **T1 Preparation of the case study:** The researchers prepared the documents of the tutorial, questionnaire, interview, the needed devices (e.g., laptops with ArAM installed, recording devices, and a projector), etc.
> **T2 Projects selection:** To create a real context of the case study, we asked each subject to choose a real and nontrivial project related to software-intensive systems from their previous work, which would be used in the workshop.
> **T3 Questionnaire:** The researchers used a questionnaire (see Section 13.5.3) to collect background information of the subjects as well as details of the selected projects.
> **T4 Projects review:** The researchers reviewed the selected projects to ensure that they are nontrivial and related to software-intensive systems.
> **T5 User guide:** The researchers provided both a printed and an MS Word user guide (in Chinese) of ArAM for each subject.

Workshop (4 hours)

> **T6 Tutorial (30 minutes):** The researchers provided the subjects with a tutorial (in Chinese) regarding an introduction to ArAM, including the AA concept and AADF.
> **T7 Discussion (20 minutes):** The researchers discussed with the subjects to ensure that they had a fair understanding of ArAM.
> **T8** Break (10 minutes).
> **T9 Using ArAM (90 minutes):** The subjects used ArAM to document AAs (including related artifacts, such as requirements, design decisions, components, and risks) based on their selected projects. The researchers provided each subject with a laptop in which ArAM was installed.
> **T10 Interview (30 minutes per subject; 60 minutes in total):** Three researchers interviewed (one-to-one and semistructured) the subjects in parallel according to the RQs (see Section 13.5.3).
> **T11 Focus group (30 minutes):** The researchers organized a focus group to further discuss ArAM based on the RQs (see Section 13.5.3).

Figure 13.11 shows the overview of the case study, concerning the process with the tasks and the inputs and outputs of each task.

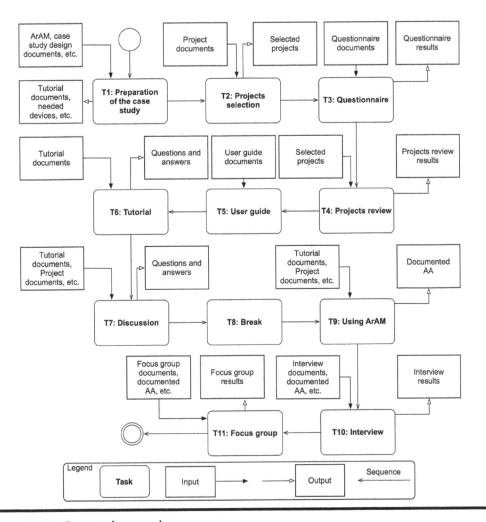

Figure 13.11 **Case study procedure.**

We organized three workshops (4 hours per workshop) in Beijing and Shenzhen with 16 subjects in total. The time of each workshop was strictly limited (see tasks T6–T11 above). For example, the time for interviews (one-to-one) was 1 hour per workshop. The three workshops followed exactly the same procedure (i.e., the 11 tasks mentioned above). The discussions, interviews, and focus groups in the workshops were recorded through recording devices.

13.5.3 Data Collection and Analysis

We used a questionnaire to collect background information of each subject as well as details of each selected project as shown in Tables 13.9 and 13.11 of the Appendix. The subjects were interviewed one by one (semistructured, see the predefined questions as shown in Table 13.10 of the Appendix). Furthermore, we conducted a focus group in each workshop with the subjects to discuss ArAM in depth according to the RQs. The first author acted as the moderator in these focus groups. Because of the limited time of the workshops, as well as the nature of interviews and focus groups, we focused on collecting qualitative instead of quantitative data for the RQs.

Table 13.6 Relationships Among the Data Collection Methods, Data Analysis Methods, and RQs

Data Collection Method	Data Analysis Method	RQs
Questionnaire	Descriptive statistics	Background information
Interview	Constant Comparison	RQ1, RQ2
Focus group	Constant Comparison	RQ1, RQ2

We employed descriptive statistics (e.g., the details of the selected projects) and Constant Comparison [41] (e.g., coding and classifying the data to answer the RQs) to analyze quantitative and qualitative data, respectively. The first, fourth, and fifth authors performed Constant Comparison in parallel through an iterative process. The second author acted as a reviewer to verify the results of Constant Comparison in each iteration. Problems were discussed and addressed among all the authors. Furthermore, MAXQDA[7] was used for the analysis of the qualitative data. The mapping between the data collection methods, data analysis methods, and RQs is shown in Table 13.6.

13.5.4 Pilot Study

We conducted a pilot study with one architect (not any of the authors) in Wuhan, China. The subject had no experience of ArAM before the pilot study. We used the same case study procedure in the pilot study except for the focus group because we could not conduct a focus group with only one subject. The aim of the pilot study was to improve the design of the case study. The pilot study resulted in the following improvements:

1. We refined the tutorial of ArAM. For instance, we used ArAM to create an example of AA documentation based on a real project from industry and presented the example in the tutorial.
2. We included one more assistant for the workshops, i.e., one moderator and two assistants in total.
3. We prepared contingency plans for various situations during the workshops, e.g., we made plans in case a subject could not come or would be late.

13.6 Results

This section provides an overview of the case study as well as results of the RQs.

13.6.1 Overview of the Case Study

The experience of the subjects in software-intensive systems and architecting (or design) is generally classified into three levels as shown in Figure 13.12. Most of the subjects (14 out of 16, 87.5%) have at least 5 years of experience in software-intensive systems, while half of them (8 out

---

[7] http://www.maxqda.com/.

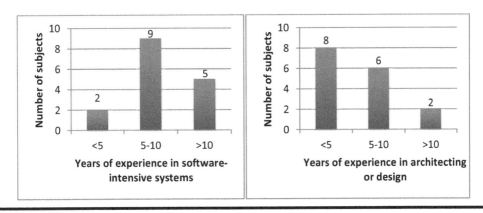

Figure 13.12 Years of experience of the subjects in software-intensive systems and architecting or design.

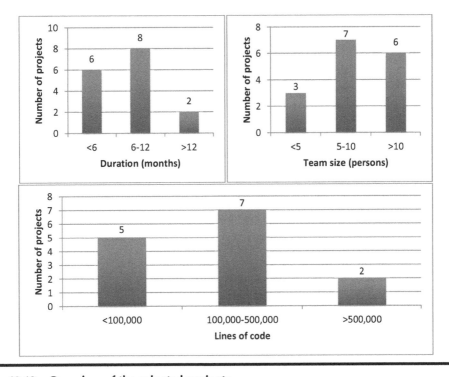

Figure 13.13 Overview of the selected projects.

of 16, 50.0%) have at least 5 years of experience in architecting (or design). Furthermore, few subjects (3 out of 16, 18.8%) stated that they had architecture training.

Figure 13.13 shows duration, team size, and lines of code of the selected projects. Note that two projects were in progress when we conducted the workshops, and therefore, lines of code of these two projects were not counted. More details can be found in Table 13.12 of the Appendix.

The projects are from different domains: Printing, Telecommunications, Security, E-commerce, Management Information Systems, Finance, Petrochemical Industry, Office Automation, and

Geographic Information Systems. In addition to the example detailed in Section 13.4.2 (which was extracted from the case study data), we provide another five examples from the case study data as follows:

1. Development of an intrusion prevention system (IPS). An IPS monitors the network, detects possible malicious incidents, and prevents the identified threats.
2. Development of a ticketing system. This system is used by touristic spots, travel agents, related suppliers, etc.
3. Development of an order management system for network construction, operation, and maintenance (including both broadband and mobile network).
4. Development of an embedded system for printing. The system was used to control the print-head in a printer.
5. Development of a prisoner management system, which uses Radio Frequency Identification Device (RFID) and computer vision techniques to track each prisoner in a prison (e.g., location and health conditions).

The AAs documented by the subjects in their projects are various, and we provide five examples as follows:

1. Assuming that junior engineers were not familiar with the Intel Data Plane Development Kit (DPDK), and introducing DPDK in the development might decrease the performance of the system as well as delay the project.
2. Assuming that there is a need to easily update the system interfaces (i.e., good scalability).
3. Assuming that making all the ordering processes (e.g., generating, arranging, and executing orders) in the order management system execute in 1 s would be suitable according to the project context.
4. Assuming that the printing speed of the printhead should be at least 1.2 m/s.
5. Assuming that it is able to use a 125 KHz module to wake up the system (from the low-power mode) in the embedded device at any time if needed.

Considering the development processes employed in the selected projects, Waterfall Model (including traditional Waterfall Model and adapted Waterfall Model, 8 out of 16, 50.0%) is far ahead of the others (e.g., Hybrid Method, Agile Development, and Iterative Development).

Note that due to privacy concerns by the subjects, we did not collect any further information about their companies.

13.6.2 Results of RQ1

The subjects considered that overall ArAM was useful, though there are several points for improvement. Note that the data related to the RQs was collected through interviews and focus groups, and therefore, for some points, a subject might not mention them at all. As an example, there were eight (out of 16, 50.0%) subjects who thought that the outputs of ArAM would be easy to be understood by another stakeholder, while another five (out of 16, 31.3%) subjects did not mention anything regarding that. We summarized all the "Not mentioned" situation in Section 13.6.4. We further detail the results in five aspects adopted from TAM3:

1. Job relevance

"Job relevance" means to what extent ArAM is relevant to the subjects' work. Fourteen subjects (out of 16, 87.5%) agreed that ArAM is useful for AA Documentation and mentioned several elements in ArAM that are important for documenting AAs, such as the relationship types provided in the tool. As one subject stated: *After making some AAs, these AAs could be connected with relationships (e.g., caused by). In this case, especially when the AAs conflict with or constrain each other, I might need to make certain trade-offs based on the AAs. By doing this, I could intuitively and quickly make more reasonable design decisions.* On the other hand, five subjects (out of 16, 31.3%) thought that some elements in ArAM do not contribute to AA Documentation, which should be simplified or removed. As one subject put it: *I think there is an overlap between rationale, pros, and cons of an AA. Sometimes I just copied and pasted the content from one to another.*

Eleven subjects (out of 16, 68.8%) mentioned that ArAM could contribute to software design and architecting. As one subject put it: *I could have a fair understanding of the AAs made as well as the architecture in a project through those diagrams, instead of spending much time on reading documents.* As another subject stated: *Your tool can help me to identify and evaluate AAs as well as related risks, step by step, just like doing a jigsaw puzzle or brainstorm, which is useful for software design.*

Eleven subjects (out of 16, 68.8%) further mentioned the usefulness of ArAM in other activities of software development, including requirements engineering, testing, risk management, and general project management. As one subject explained: *In the early phases of software development, I would have a lot of AAs, and with the progress of the project, many AAs turn to be invalid. I can document all the information of those AAs through using ArAM, which is useful for system operation and maintenance.* As another subject mentioned: *I think the tool can facilitate requirements engineering and testing: if I want to implement requirements, I have to make AAs; after documenting AAs through the tool, I can give them to testers and ask them to test these AAs.*

Finally, seven subjects (out of 16, 43.8%) mentioned that the usefulness of ArAM would be diverse for different types of stakeholders. As one subject explained: *I do not think the tool is useful for programmers, since programmers do not need to consider AAs, but requirements engineers, architects, designers, and testers can benefit from using the tool.*

2. Output quality

"Output quality" means to what extent the outputs of ArAM can benefit the subjects' work. Fourteen subjects (out of 16, 87.5%) mentioned that the overall quality of ArAM outputs was good. As one subject put it: *Considering AA Documentation, I think the outputs include all the information I need.* On the other hand, four subjects (out of 16, 25.0%) mentioned that the outputs regarding documentation of AA history (e.g., in the AA Detail viewpoint) were not satisfying: *I need to see all the information regarding the evolution of AAs in the AA Detail view, for example, what exactly the previous versions of an AA are, instead of only showing me the state and modified date.* Moreover, two subjects (out of 16, 12.5%) stated that they need information concerning importance and criticality of AAs.

Furthermore, we also asked the subjects when providing the AAs documented through ArAM by them to another stakeholder, whether the stakeholder can understand the documented AAs or not. Eight subjects (out of 16, 50.0%) gave a positive answer: *If AAs are documented like this, I think other people can absolutely understand them.* On the other hand, three subjects (out of 16, 18.8%) stated that it is difficult to say whether other stakeholders can understand the documented AAs through only reading the ArAM outputs. The reason is that stakeholders may have different understandings on those outputs.

Finally, four subjects (out of 16, 25.0%) mentioned that the output quality of ArAM depends on the users, i.e., if the users document AAs without paying attention to the details of AAs, the output quality may be decreased: *For example, if the person only says something like 'based on experience' without elaborating the underlying rationale, this does not help to understand the documented AAs.*

3. Result demonstrability

"Result demonstrability" means to what extent the results of using ArAM are communicable. Eleven subjects (out of 16, 68.8%) mentioned that they were able to present the results of using ArAM to their colleagues: *I only need half an hour to tell my colleagues about the results of using the tool*; only one subject (out of 16, 6.3%) stated that he could not explain the results of the tool clear to other stakeholders: *I still have some uncertain aspects about the tool.*

One subject (out of 16, 6.3%) further considered that different strategies should be used to describe the results of using ArAM for different types of stakeholders: *When you talk to an architect, it could be easy, because architects should have knowledge regarding AAs, and you can just explain the results of using ArAM to the architect. On the other hand, when you talk to a tester, then you should explain the results from the perspective of testing.*

4. Experience

"Experience" means to what extent the experience, for example, architecting experience, can impact the perceived usefulness of ArAM. Thirteen subjects (out of 16, 81.3%) stated that experience of architecting (or design) should be of paramount importance for the perceived usefulness of ArAM. As one subject put it: *If I do not have much experience of architecting, I cannot think, for example, what AAs I have in a project. If you ask me to use ArAM, to some extent, I would not know what to create.*

5. Others

Ten subjects (out of 16, 62.5%) emphasized that clearly presenting the motivation, objectives, and benefits of using ArAM as well as how to use ArAM is of significant importance for the perceived usefulness of the tool. As one subject mentioned: *Considering relationships between AAs, for example, 'conflict', should I identify conflicts when making AAs, or after making AAs?*

Moreover, five subjects (out of 16, 31.3%) connected project context with the usefulness of using ArAM. They pointed out that the tool was context-dependent and may not work well in certain contexts. As one subject mentioned: *AAs are related to many other types of artifacts. If such artifacts are not available in a project, then this tool may not be useful in that case.* Five subjects (out of 16, 31.3%) further mentioned personal preference would be a factor for the usefulness of using ArAM (e.g., one subject preferred to see more quantitative data regarding AAs).

Finally, 13 subjects (out of 16, 81.3%) suggested several aspects to improve the usefulness of ArAM, including quantitative management of AAs (e.g., presenting statistic data regarding AAs), automatic analysis (e.g., finding omitted relationships between AAs based on the existing data), automatic verification (e.g., verifying the correctness of existing AAs), integration with other tools (e.g., being compatible with tools used by stakeholders). As one subject put it: *If the tool can automatically verify AAs, for example, checking if there are conflicting AAs in a diagram, that would be very helpful.* As another subject stated: *It is important to integrate ArAM to the existing tools we are using.*

13.6.3 Results of RQ2

The subjects considered that overall ArAM was easy to use, though there are several issues to consider. We further elaborate on the results in five aspects adopted from TAM3:

1. Computer self-efficacy

"Computer self-efficacy" means to what extent the subjects can use ArAM without any help. Fourteen subjects (out of 16, 87.5%) considered that they could use ArAM independently in their work, while two subjects (out of 16, 12.5%) thought that they needed further training on the tool. The subjects mentioned two factors that influence this aspect. First, the time of the workshop was limited. Though the subjects could use ArAM independently, they were not familiar with it, and therefore, more practice of the tool was needed. Second, ArAM was developed as a plugin of Enterprise Architect. During the workshop, we only focused on the usage of ArAM. Therefore, the unfamiliarity of Enterprise Architect may impede the usage of ArAM in projects. As one subject explained: *This is the first time I use ArAM. Through the tutorial, I had a fair understanding of the tool, and I could use it by myself. However, for some details of the tool or the functions that you did not introduce today, I would still have problems.*

Eight subjects (out of 16, 50.0%) mentioned that the usage of ArAM was clear to them, including its objective, rationale, concepts, and functions, as one subject stated: *Basically, I can understand the tool as well as how to use it. The clarity of the tool is fine for me.* Furthermore, six subjects (out of 16, 37.5%) considered that the layout of ArAM was complicated. As one subject put it: *There are so many items in the tool, which increases the difficulty of using it.* On the other hand, two subjects (out of 16, 12.5%) disagreed: *The tool is not complicated. Basically, you just need to draw some simple boxes with several lines.* Table 13.7 shows the easy and difficult parts of using ArAM pointed out by the subjects.

Table 13.7 Easy and Difficult Parts of Using ArAM

Difficult Part	No. of Subjects (%)	Easy Part	No. of Subjects (%)
Managing relationships between AAs or AAs and other types of software artifacts	9 (56.3%)	Making AAs	5 (31.3%)
Describing AAs	3 (18.8%)	Managing relationships between AAs or AAs and other types of software artifacts	4 (25.0%)
Being aware of the AAs made and their relationships	3 (18.8%)	Basic functions of Enterprise Architect (e.g., double clicking)	3 (18.8%)
Basic functions of Enterprise Architect (e.g., double clicking)	2 (12.5%)	Maintaining AAs	1 (6.3%)
Making AAs	1 (6.3%)	Describing AAs	1 (6.3%)

One subject (out of 16, 6.3%) emphasized that in real life, ArAM should be used from the early phases of software development: *I think the tool is easy to use, if it is used from the early phases of software development. Otherwise, it would be more complicated, because it is rather difficult to recover and document all the AAs made earlier in the project.*

2. Perceptions of external control

"Perceptions of external control" means to what extent the existing project resources, for example, requirements documents, can help the subjects to use ArAM. As we found through the case study, project materials (including requirements, design, and general project documents) were considered helpful for the application of ArAM. As one subject stated: *If I am not familiar with a project, then design documents, including flow charts and description of relationships between the project and other projects, would help me to use the tool.*

3. Perceived enjoyment

"Perceived enjoyment" means to what extent using ArAM is pleasant and enjoyable. Eleven subjects (out of 16, 68.8%) agreed that ArAM was pleasant and enjoyable to use; they could easily understand the usage of ArAM. As one subject put it: *I think the tool was pleasant to use; everything was easy to understand.*

4. Experience

"Experience" means to what extent the experience, for example, architecting experience, can influence the perceived ease of use of ArAM. Thirteen subjects (out of 16, 81.3%) considered that it is easier to use ArAM with certain experience on Enterprise Architect or similar tools (e.g., MS Visio[8]). For example, as one subject stated: *It would be more acceptable and easy for me to use a tool, if I am familiar with the layout. In this case, the layout of your tool looks like MS Visio, which is good for me.*

Eight subjects (out of 16, 50.0%) considered that project experience would help to increase the ease of using ArAM. For example, as one subject put it: *Since I am familiar with the selected project, using ArAM in the project was easy.* Furthermore, one subject (out of 16, 6.3%) mentioned that 1 or 2 years of project experience is enough for using ArAM.

Moreover, eight subjects (out of 16, 50%) thought that experience of design or architecting is not important for increasing the ease of using ArAM, as one subject stated: *If you have certain architecting experience, it's enough. I have only two years of architecting experience, while I think it's easy for me to use the tool.*

5. Others

Fourteen subjects (out of 16, 87.5%) mentioned five aspects regarding learning ArAM, which can influence the ease of using the tool: (a) The tutorial of ArAM was important. As the subjects suggested, a tutorial through a workshop, a well-designed and documented user guide, and Q&A regarding ArAM should be included. (b) Several subjects considered that the examples of AA and the use of ArAM were not very clear and rather complicated: *We need something simple from the beginning, and then you can show me the real example of the usage of ArAM afterwards. As people learn the C language, they always start with Hello World.* (c) All the elements of ArAM were in English, which impeded several subjects from learning and using the tool: *My English is not good, so I prefer a tool in Chinese. Especially considering the terms used in ArAM, it was not easy to understand them in English.* (d) More practice and time of ArAM were needed to make the tool easier to use.

---

[8] https://products.office.com/en-us/visio.

Furthermore, 15 subjects (out of 16, 93.8%) expected that ArAM can be improved in the following aspects, i.e., layout, instructions inside the tool, and shortcut keys. As one subject stated: *The tool includes so many widgets. Sometimes it was difficult to find specific widgets in the tool.*

13.6.4 Summary of Results of RQs

ArAM is generally useful and easy to use in AA Documentation as well as in software development, though there are several issues to be addressed. We summarize the aforementioned results of the RQs as shown in Table 13.8.

13.7 Discussion

This section presents the interpretation of the results of the RQs, as well as the implications for researchers and practitioners.

13.7.1 Interpretation of the Results

Usefulness: Fourteen subjects (out of 16, 87.5%) agreed that ArAM is useful for AA Documentation. The reason is that one major benefit of using ArAM is to make AAs explicit in a systematic way. How to express an AA is a critical problem especially in industry. Without using ArAM (e.g., using MS Word instead), it is possible that the same AA is expressed in different ways by various stakeholders during development, leading to inconsistencies in projects.

The results show that ArAM not only has a high relevance regarding architecting and design, but also can benefit other software development activities, such as requirements engineering. One reason is that AAs are intertwined with various types of software artifacts (e.g., requirements and design decisions), and their life cycle spans the entire software development [4,2,9]. Moreover, since all the subjects were architects, though they were involved in both architecting and other software development activities, the usefulness of ArAM in the whole software development life cycle needs more evidence.

Although most of the subjects considered that the output quality of ArAM was good, they pointed out several aspects for improvements of the tool. One potential reason is that stakeholders may have different preferences and interests when using the tool. Another reason is that the output quality is not only related to the tool itself, but also affected by the users. For example, if a user documents an AA through ArAM without paying enough attention to the details of the AA, the output quality of ArAM would be low.

Furthermore, though architecting (or design) experience was considered not important for the ease of use of ArAM, it has a paramount influence on the usefulness of the tool. One reason could be that there is a significant difference between junior and experienced architects, as junior architects may not even be aware of the AAs made in their projects [2].

Finally, there may be large variations regarding the usefulness of ArAM in various project contexts or between different types of stakeholders. For example, for specific types of projects, such as small projects, documenting AAs may not be necessary, and therefore, ArAM would not be useful in such situation.

Table 13.8 Summary of Results of the RQs

RQ	Aspect	Subaspect	Results
RQ1: Usefulness	Job relevance	AA Documentation	Useful (14 out of 16, 87.5%); Not mentioned (2 out of 16, 12.5%)
		Software design and architecting	Useful (11 out of 16, 68.8%); Not mentioned (5 out of 16, 31.3%)
		Other activities in software development	Useful (11 out of 16, 68.8%); Not mentioned (5 out of 16, 31.3%)
		Types of stakeholders	The perceived usefulness of ArAM would be diverse for different types of stakeholders (7 out of 16, 43.8%)
	Output quality	Quality (overall)	Good quality (14 out of 16, 87.5%); Not mentioned (2 out of 16, 12.5%)
		Expected improvements	Improving the outputs of AA Detail viewpoint (4 out of 16, 25.0%); Improving the quality of the diagrams created in ArAM (2 out of 16, 12.5%); Missed information in ArAM: Importance and criticality of AAs (2 out of 16, 12.5%)
		Understanding outputs by other stakeholders	Easy (8 out of 16, 50.0%); Difficult (3 out of 16, 18.8%); Not mentioned (5 out of 16, 31.3%)
		Other	The output quality of ArAM depends on the users (4 out of 16, 25.0%)
	Result demonstrability		Communicable (11 out of 16, 68.8%); Not communicable (1 out of 16, 6.3%); Not mentioned (4 out of 16, 25.0%)
	Experience	Experience of design or architecting	Important (13 out of 16, 81.3%); Not mentioned (3 out of 16, 18.8%)

(Continued)

Table 13.8 (Continued) Summary of Results of the RQs

RQ	Aspect	Subaspect	Results
	Others	Tutorial	A well-designed tutorial helps better understanding the usefulness of ArAM (10 out of 16, 62.5%)
		Project context	The usefulness of ArAM is different in different project context (5 out of 16, 31.3%)
		Personal preference	The perceived usefulness of ArAM depends on personal preference (5 out of 16, 31.3%)
		Expected improvements regarding functions	Quantitatively management of AAs (1 out of 16, 6.3%); Automatic analysis (e.g., finding omitted relationships between AAs based on the existing data) (1 out of 16, 6.3%); Automatic verification (e.g., verifying the correctness of existing AAs) (4 out of 16, 25.0%); Integration with existing tools (9 out of 16, 56.3%)
RQ2: Ease of use`	Computer self-efficacy	Usage	Without help (14 out of 16, 87.5%); Need help (2, out of 16, 12.5%)
		Clarity	Clear (8 out of 16, 50.0%); Not mentioned (8 out of 16, 50.0%)
		Complexity of layout	Complicated (6 out of 16, 37.5%); Not complicated (2 out of 16, 12.5%); Not mentioned (8 out of 16, 50.0%)
		Easy parts	Making AAs (5 out of 16, 31.3%); Managing relationships between AAs or AAs and other software artifacts (4 out of 16, 25.0%); Basic functions of Enterprise Architect (e.g., double clicking) (3 out of 16, 18.8%); Maintaining AAs (1 out of 16, 6.3%); Describing AAs (1 out of 16, 6.3%)

(Continued)

Table 13.8 (Continued)   Summary of Results of the RQs

RQ	Aspect	Subaspect	Results
		Difficult parts	Managing relationships between AAs or AAs and other software artifacts (9 out of 16, 56.3%); Describing AAs (3 out of 16, 18.8%); Being aware of the AAs and their relationships (3 out of 16, 18.8%); Basic functions of Enterprise Architect (e.g., double clicking) (2 out of 16, 12.5%); Making AAs (1 out of 16, 6.3%)
	Perceptions of external control	When to use	ArAM would be easy to use, if it is used from the early phases of software development (1 out of 16, 6.3%)
			Requirements documents (4 out of 16, 25.0%), design documents (4 out of 16, 25.0%), and general project documents (8 out of 16, 0.0%) are useful for AA Documentation using ArAM
	Perceived enjoyment		Pleasant and enjoyable (11 out of 16, 68.8%); Not mentioned (5 out of 16, 31.3%)
	Experience	Experience on Enterprise Architect or similar tools	Important (13 out of 16, 81.3%); Not mentioned (3 out of 16, 18.8%)
		Project experience	Important (8 out of 16, 50.0%); Not mentioned (8 out of 16, 50.0%)
		Experience of design or architecting	Not important (8 out of 16, 50.0%); Not mentioned (8 out of 16, 50.0%)
	Others	Learning	Impeding ArAM learning: A not well-organized tutorial (7 out of 16, 43.8%); Inappropriate examples of AA and ArAM (6 out of 16, 37.5%); Poor English of users (3 out of 16, 18.8%); Lack of practice (4 out of 16, 25.0%); Lack of time (3 out of 16, 18.8%)
		Expected improvements	Layout (10 out of 16, 62.5%); Instructions inside the tool (6 out of 16, 37.5%); Shortcut keys (7 out of 16, 43.8%);

Ease of use: ArAM is in general easy to use. This is partly due to the reason that ArAM is a plugin of Enterprise Architect (a UML-based platform for designing and developing software systems), which is a mature and popular tool used in industry. Moreover, UML is a common modeling language used in software development. In the case study, architecting (or design) experience was considered insignificant for the ease of use of ArAM by the subjects. This further implies that different types of stakeholders (e.g., requirements engineers and project managers) can easily use ArAM in their work.

The subjects (15 out of 16, 93.8%) have discussed issues regarding basic functions of ArAM. The major reason is that stakeholders may have different preferences and interests when using a tool. For example, in our study, some subjects criticized the layout of ArAM, while others did not see any issues with the layout. Moreover, another reason is that ArAM is only a plugin of Enterprise Architect, and some functions are not adaptable but limited by Enterprise Architect. However, we have compiled a list of feature requests based on the received feedback, and these are gradually being implemented in the next versions of ArAM.

13.7.2 Implications for Researchers

Experience plays a significant role regarding the usefulness of ArAM. There is often a significant difference between junior and senior engineers in AA Documentation; for example, junior engineers may not even be aware of the AAs made in projects or understand their significance. This could mean that dedicated tools such as ArAM benefit senior engineers more than junior engineers. How experience impacts using tools in AA Documentation is an interesting research direction. We advise researchers to adapt their tools for users with different level of experience in order to maximize the benefits for each level.

Concerns of AA management: Though ArAM provides support for AA management, in the case study, we identified three additional concerns of AA management from the subjects: quantitative AA management, automatic analysis and verification, and integration into existing tools.

1. Quantitative AA management

    This includes two aspects. One aspect is using tools to provide quantitative data when managing AAs, including how many AAs have been made and how many AAs are invalid in projects. Another aspect is to make tools "smart": Researchers could (a) collect related data of AAs from a number of projects, (b) analyze the data quantitatively to come up with AA models and patterns, and (c) offer tools that support these models and patterns, in order to improve the effectiveness of AA management with knowledge and experience. However, the significant problem here is that (a) AAs are subjective in nature, and (b) many AAs are implicit and undocumented in existing projects. For example, we looked into open-source communities such as GitHub,[9] where we found that unless the owner of a piece of information explicitly mentions that the information is or includes an AA, it is difficult for us to determine that. Even if a piece of information is explicitly mentioned as an AA, it is usually laconic, i.e., lacking enough context information for further analysis. One possible solution is to create a knowledge base of AAs through (a) mining AA-related data from open-source communities and (b) encouraging both researchers and practitioners to share their AA-related data publically or within an organization.

---

[9] http://github.com/.

2. Automatic analysis and verification

The documented AAs need to be further analyzed and verified automatically by tools, including identifying missing relationships between AAs or AAs and other types of artifacts, and verifying whether a statement of an AA is correct or precise. This is a way to reduce manual effort and improve the return on investment of AA management. However, the important issue here is that currently AAs and their management are not well integrated in software development. Though many researchers advocate connecting AAs with other types of software artifacts (independently whether AAs are considered as first-class entities or not), we argue that it is not the practice in most projects. Therefore, how to perform automatic analysis and verification of AAs still needs further investigation.

3. Integration into existing tools

On the one hand, stakeholders need a dedicated tool to manage AAs in projects, while on the other hand, they do not need a "new" tool, since they are familiar and comfortable with the tools they already use. One solution for this problem is integrating AA management into existing tools (e.g., in this work, we developed ArAM as a plugin of Enterprise Architect). However, stakeholders may use other tools such as Microsoft Visual Studio[10] in their projects. Due to the cost, it is almost impossible to develop plugins for every broadly used tool in software development. How to maximize the return on investment of developing a plugin for an existing tool or toolchain requires further investigation.

Stakeholders in AA management: In the case study, we found that ArAM can benefit not only architecting (or design), but also other development activities. However, we have no evidence on the actual usefulness of ArAM for other types of stakeholders (e.g., requirements engineers and project managers), since all the subjects in this case study were architects. Therefore, how different types of stakeholders can be involved in AA management is another interesting topic for further research.

13.7.3 Implications for Practitioners

Understanding of the AA concept: The AA concept is subjective, which could be a problem in managing AAs. We suggest that practitioners within the same project or an organization reach a consensus on the understanding of the AA concept.

AA management: Not every AA is worth managing (e.g., by ArAM). Stakeholders need to first identify the AAs they perceive important in projects. Moreover, when managing AAs using tools, stakeholders may have different concerns. ArAM is not "perfect" but adaptable. Stakeholder can further maintain ArAM to meet their specific concerns. Finally, as identified in the case study, we suggest stakeholders using requirements documents, design documents, and general project documents to manage AAs if applicable. Additionally, according to the results of the case study, we identified three factors that have an impact on managing AAs when using ArAM.

1. Tutorial

Tutorial is the first and important step of using ArAM to manage AAs. This is not only regarding the quality of tutorial materials or tutorial methods used, but more importantly, stakeholders should pay enough attention to understand the AA concept as well as the motivation of managing AAs.

---

[10] https://www.visualstudio.com/.

2. Project context

AA management is influenced by project context. For example, it may not be worth to spend effort on managing AAs in small or "stable" projects (e.g., a project that is similar to a finished project), since there could be only a few AAs in such types of projects. Therefore, we suggest that practitioners should first evaluate the need and value of managing AAs before using tools (e.g., ArAM).

3. When to manage AAs

Though this factor was only mentioned by one subject, we believe that it should be considered in projects. According to the results of the case study, as well as related literature (e.g., [15]), we suggest that stakeholders manage AAs (e.g., using ArAM) from early phases of software development.

Users of ArAM: AA management is teamwork. Though architects are responsible for managing AAs, other types of stakeholders should be involved (e.g., in AA Evaluation). In the case study, we found that architecting experience would not play an important role regarding the ease of use of ArAM. Therefore, ArAM can be used by different types of stakeholders (e.g., in AA Evaluation). Moreover, as mentioned in Section 13.7.2, there are variations between, for example, junior and experienced architects regarding AA management (e.g., the usefulness of ArAM). Practitioners need to be aware of such variations, which may cause problems (e.g., low quality of documented AAs) in projects.

13.8 Threats to Validity

We followed the guidelines proposed by Runeson and Höst [44] to discuss the threats to the validity of the case study. We excluded internal validity because we did not study causality.

Construct validity reflects to what extent the research questions and the studied operational measures are consistent [44]. We listed related threats as follows.

1. A threat is that the subjects tried to use ArAM without a fair understanding of the AA concept and AADF. To reduce this threat, during the workshops, the subjects were encouraged to raise questions about ArAM; the first, fourth, and fifth authors answered all these questions from the subjects. Moreover, we organized a short discussion about ArAM with the subjects to ensure their appropriate understanding of the tool.
2. A threat is that whether the RQs can be properly answered by the collected data. To mitigate this threat, we used both interview and focus group in this study, iteratively developed the protocol of the case study, and discussed the protocol in a meeting with seven external researchers on software engineering. We also conducted a pilot study to improve the design of the case study.
3. Since all the subjects in the case study are Chinese, there is a threat that the translation from English to Chinese of the related documents (e.g., the questionnaire) and from Chinese to English of the collected data from questionnaires, interviews, and focus groups could have resulted in information vaporization and erosion. To mitigate this threat, the first, second, fourth, and fifth authors (native Chinese speakers) were responsible for the translation. This translation was conducted iteratively.
4. The workshop context of the case study introduced several threats. First, AA management is a continuous activity in software development, and the subjects might act differently

in a workshop compared to their real work. An example is that the subjects did not talk much regarding the AA Evolution viewpoint. We considered this study as a preliminary evaluation of ArAM in an industrial setting. Conducting a longitudinal and comparative study is a solution to address such threat. Furthermore, to avoid bias from the user guide and tutorial step, we carefully designed the related materials. We also asked each subject to select one real and nontrivial project related to software-intensive systems from their previous work and used ArAM in the context of the selected projects through the workshops.

5. A threat is that the collected data from a subject who used ArAM incorrectly would add much less value. To reduce the threat, besides ensuring that each subject had a fair understanding of the AA concept and AADF, we also carefully reviewed all the data from questionnaires, interviews, focus groups, and documentation. As an example, we reviewed the models created by the subjects after the workshops. If a model created by one subject does not make any sense to the authors, we removed all the data from the subject in the case study. Such review ensured that the subjects used ArAM correctly.

External validity concerns the generalization of the findings [44]. This case study was conducted with 16 architects from ten companies in Beijing and Shenzhen, China; we argue that the results are applicable in projects with same or similar context (e.g., domain). However, considering the generalization of the findings to other context, replication of the case study is a solution to address this issue. To improve the external validity, we made the materials of this work online (note that part of the materials are in Chinese) [42].

Reliability focuses on whether the study would yield the same results when other researchers replicate it [44]. To reduce the threat to reliability, we recorded the entire workshops through audio-recording devices to avoid information vaporization and erosion. The first, fourth, and fifth authors performed Constant Comparison for qualitative data analysis in parallel through an iterative process. The second author acted as a reviewer to verify the results of Constant Comparison in each iteration. Moreover, we also conducted a pilot study to refine the case study design and to mitigate the ambiguities and misunderstandings in the execution of the case study. The case study protocol was reviewed by the authors iteratively and also by an external reviewer to reduce bias in the case study design.

13.9 Conclusions and Future Work

The importance of knowledge management in software development has been emphasized by both researchers and practitioners over the past years. As an important type of architectural knowledge, AAs need to be well managed in projects. In this chapter, we present a specialized tool for AA Documentation named ArAM, which was developed based on the AADF method and as a plugin of Enterprise Architect to support practicing architects and designers. Using the ArAM tool can improve knowledge management related to AAs in software development through various aspects, e.g., knowledge identification, documentation, sharing, and reuse. Specifically, the ArAM tool can help stakeholders to: (a) become aware of the AAs made in projects as well as avoid potential problems (e.g., risks) caused by implicit and invalid AAs; (b) trace AAs to other types of artifacts, which can also help system analysis (e.g., impact analysis of design decisions); (c) prevent knowledge vaporization in software development through making AAs explicit and well-documented, which can further facilitate maintenance and handover within projects; and (d) mitigate misunderstandings and ineffective communications between stakeholders, in order to facilitate a better understanding of both the architecture and system within a project team.

There are however several points for improving ArAM, including support for automatic analysis (e.g., finding missing relationships between assumptions) and verification (e.g., verifying the correctness of existing assumptions). Future work includes adapting and refining ArAM according to the issues identified in the case study as well as the suggestions by the subjects. Furthermore, since this study is a preliminary evaluation of ArAM, we also consider a longitudinal and comparative study as future work. Finally, we plan to employ ArAM and evaluate its use in supporting the AA management process in software development (see [12]).

Acknowledgments

This work is partially sponsored by the National Key R&D Program of China with Grant No. 2018YFB1402800 and the Ubbo Emmius scholarship program by the University of Groningen. The authors wish to thank Daan van Driel and Jeroen Brandsma for their participation in the development of ArAM, Wei Ding for his participation in the pilot study, Fangchao Tian for his participation in the workshop of Beijing, and Zengyang Li for reviewing an earlier version of this chapter.

Appendix

See Tables 13.9–13.12.

Table 13.9 Questions used for Collecting Background Information of the Subjects

Question
Your Name?
What is your experience (in years) working in software-intensive systems?
What is your experience (in years) in software architecting?
Have you ever received any professional training (i.e., excluding higher education) related to software architecture or software design?
Can you describe the selected project?
What is the duration of the selected project?
What is the team size of the selected project?
What is the size of the selected project?
What is the code size of the selected project (KLOC)?
What is the development process employed in the selected project?

Table 13.10 Questions used in Interviews and Their Data Items

Question	Data Item
RQ1: How useful is it to use ArAM in AA Documentation?	
Perceived Usefulness	
To what extent ArAM can help you to document AAs?	Helpful / Moderate / Not helpful
What are the reasons?	Text
Does ArAM cover all the aspects of AA Documentation?	Yes / No
If no, which aspects are missed?	Text
Which parts of ArAM are the most related to AA Documentation?	Text
Why these parts of ArAM are the most related to AA Documentation?	Text
Which parts of ArAM are the least related to AA Documentation?	Text
Why these parts of ArAM are the least related to AA Documentation?	Text
Job Relevance	
Which parts of ArAM are the most related to your work?	Text
Why these parts of ArAM are the most related to your work?	Text
Which parts of ArAM are the least related to your work?	Text
Why these parts of ArAM are the least related to your work?	Text
Output Quality	
Can you understand the output of ArAM?	Yes / No
If no, which parts of the output are you unsure of?	Text
How would you rate the quality of the output?	Good / Moderate / Bad
What are the reasons?	Text
Result Demonstrability	
To what extent can you communicate the results of using ArAM to other stakeholders in your company?	I can / To some extent / I cannot

(Continued)

Table 13.10 (*Continued*)   Questions used in Interviews and Their Data Items

Question	Data Item
What are the reasons?	Text
Experience	
How important is architecting experience for the usefulness of ArAM?	Important / Moderate / Not important
How does the experience impact the usefulness of ArAM?	Text
Other Factors	
Are there any other factors that can impact the usefulness of ArAM?	Text
RQ2: How easy is it to use ArAM in AA Documentation?	
Perceived Ease of Use	
How would you rate the clarity of the interactions with ArAM?	Clear / Moderate / Not clear
Which parts of ArAM are you unsure of?	Text
Which parts would you require further training?	Text
When using ArAM to document AAs, was the effort acceptable for you?	Yes / No
Which parts of ArAM were difficult to use?	Text
Why were these parts difficult to use?	Text
Which parts of ArAM were easy to use?	Text
Why were these parts easy to use?	Text
Computer Self-efficacy	
To what extent are you able to use ArAM in your projects without any help?	I can / To some extent / I cannot
What are the reasons?	Text
Perceptions of External Control	
Did you use any other resource from your project (e.g., organizational and technical resources)?	Yes / No
Which resources would be helpful for using ArAM?	Text
Is ArAM compatible with the tools you used?	Yes / No

(Continued)

Table 13.10 (*Continued*)   Questions used in Interviews and Their Data Items

Question	Data Item
Perceived Enjoyment	
To what extent do you think ArAM is pleasant and enjoyable?	Pleasant and enjoyable / Moderate / Not pleasant and enjoyable
What are the reasons?	Text
Experience	
How important is architecting experience for the ease of use of ArAM?	Important / Moderate / Not important
How does the experience impact the ease of use of ArAM?	Text
Other Factors	
Are there any other factors that can impact the ease of use of ArAM?	Text

Table 13.11   Data Items of Background Information

Data Item	Scale Type	Unit	Range
Name	N/A	N/A	Text
Experience working in software-intensive systems	Ratio	Years	>= 0
Experience in software architecting	Ratio	Years	>= 0
Professional training of architecture or design	Nominal	N/A	Yes / No
Project description	N/A	N/A	Text
Project duration	Ratio	Months	>= 0
Team size	Ratio	Persons	>= 0
Project size	Ratio	Person-months	>= 0
Code size	Ratio	Lines	>= 0
Development process	N/A	N/A	Text

Table 13.12   Duration, Team Size, and Lines of Code of the Selected Projects

ID	Duration (Month)	Team Size (Person)	Lines of Code (Thousand)
Project 1	3	10	20
Project 2	4	10	> 500
Project 3	3	8	22
Project 4	10	30	200
Project 5	4	8	400–500
Project 6	48	12	N/A
Project 7	20	7	100
Project 8	11	19	100
Project 9	12	50	10
Project 10	6	4	100
Project 11	6	9	40
Project 12	11	8	100
Project 13	2	4	10
Project 14	12	13	> 500
Project 15	12	15	100
Project 16	4	4	N/A

References

1. P. Kruchten, P. Lago, and H. van Vliet. Building up and reasoning about architectural knowledge. In: *Proceedings of the 2nd International Conference on Quality of Software Architectures (QoSA)*, Västerås, Sweden, pp. 43–58, 2006.
2. C. Yang, P. Liang, P. Avgeriou, U. Eliasson, R. Heldal, P. Pelliccione, and T. Bi, An industrial case study on an Architectural Assumption Documentation Framework. *Journal of Systems and Software*, 134(12): 190–210, 2017.
3. P. Kroll and P. Kruchten. *The Rational Unified Process Made Easy: A Practitioner's Guide to the RUP*. Boston, MA: Addison-Wesley Professional, 2003.
4. C. Yang, P. Liang, and P. Avgeriou. A survey on software architectural assumptions. *Journal of Systems and Software*, 113(3): 362–380, 2016.
5. D.V. Landuyt and W. Joosen. A descriptive study of assumptions made in LINDDUN privacy threat elicitation. In: *Proceedings of the 35th Annual ACM Symposium on Applied Computing (SAC)*, Brno, Czech Republic, pp. 1280–1287, 2020.
6. D. Garlan, R. Allen, and J. Ockerbloom. Architectural mismatch: Why reuse is still so hard. *IEEE Software*, 26(4): 66–69, 2009.
7. D. Van Landuyt and W. Joosen. Modularizing early architectural assumptions in scenario-based requirements. In: *Proceedings of the 17th International Conference on Fundamental Approaches to Software Engineering (FASE)*, Grenoble, France, pp. 170–184, 2014.
8. G. Zhang. Product Manager View on Practical Assumption Management Lifecycle about System Use. Faculty of Computing, Blekinge Institute of Technology, 2017.

9. C. Yang, P. Liang, and P. Avgeriou. Assumptions and their management in software development: A systematic mapping study. *Information and Software Technology*, 94(2): 82–110, 2018.

10. C. Yang, P. Liang, P. Avgeriou, U. Eliasson, R. Heldal, and P. Pelliccione. Architectural assumptions and their management in industry – An exploratory study. In: *Proceedings of the 11th European Conference on Software Architecture (ECSA)*, Canterbury, UK, 2017, pp. 191–207, 2017.

11. C. Yang and P. Liang. Identifying and recording software architectural assumptions in agile development. In: *Proceedings of the 26th International Conference on Software Engineering and Knowledge Engineering (SEKE)*, Vancouver, Canada, pp. 308–313, 2014.

12. C. Yang, P. Liang, and P. Avgeriou. Evaluation of a process for architectural assumption management in software development. *Science of Computer Programming*, 168(12): 38–70, 2018.

13. R. Roeller, P. Lago, and H. van Vliet. Recovering architectural assumptions. *Journal of Systems and Software*, 79(4): 552–573, 2006.

14. X. Wang, J. Mylopoulos, G. Guizzardi, and N. Guarino. How software changes the world: The role of assumptions. In: *Proceedings of the 10th IEEE International Conference on Research Challenges in Information Science (RCIS)*, Grenoble, France, pp. 1–12, 2016.

15. D.V. Landuyt, E. Truyen, and W. Joosen. Documenting early architectural assumptions in scenario-based requirements. In: *Proceedings of the Joint Working IEEE/IFIP Conference on Software Architecture (WICSA) and European Conference on Software Architecture (ECSA)*, Helsinki, Finland, pp. 329–333, 2012.

16. A. Tang, F. Bex, C. Schriek, and J.M.E.M. van der Werf. Improving software design reasoning–A reminder card approach. *Journal of Systems and Software*, 144: 22–40, 2018.

17. S. El Fassi, M.D. Guenov, and A. Riaz. An assumption network-based approach to support margin allocation and management. In: *Proceedings of the Design Society Conference (DESIGN)*, Zagreb, Croatia, pp. 2275–2284, 2020.

18. G.A. Lewis, T. Mahatham, and L. Wrage. Assumptions Management in Software Development. Technical Report, Carnegie Mellon University, 2004.

19. V. Page, M. Dixon, and I. Choudhury. Security risk mitigation for information systems. *BT Technology Journal*, 25(1): 118–127, 2007.

20. C. Flanagan, S.N. Freund, and S. Qadeer. Thread-modular verification for shared-memory programs. In: *Proceedings of the 11th European Symposium on Programming (ESOP)*, Grenoble, France, pp. 262–277, 2002.

21. H. Ziv, D. Richardson, and R. Klösch. The Uncertainty Principle in Software Engineering. Technical Report, 1997.

22. ISO. ISO/IEC/IEEE Std 42010-2011, Systems and Software Engineering - Architecture Description, 2011.

23. H. Ordibehesht. Explicating critical assumptions in software architectures using AADL. Master Thesis, University of Gothenburg, 2010.

24. M.A.A. Mamun, M. Tichy, and J. Hansson. Towards Formalizing Assumptions on Architectural Level: A Proof-of-Concept. Research Report, University of Gothenburg, 2012.

25. A. Tang, Y. Jin, and J. Han. A rationale-based architecture model for design traceability and reasoning. *Journal of Systems and Software*, 80(6): 918–934, 2007.

26. K. Welsh, P. Sawyer, and N. Bencomo. Towards requirements aware systems: Run-time resolution of design-time assumptions. In: *Proceedings of the 26th IEEE/ACM International Conference on Automated Software Engineering (ASE)*. Lawrence, KS, USA, pp. 560–563, 2011.

27. S. Faily and I. Fléchais. The secret lives of assumptions: Developing and refining assumption personas for secure system design. In: *Proceedings of the 3rd International Conference on Human-Centred Software Engineering (HCSE)*, Reykjavik, Iceland, pp. 111–118, 2010.

28. I. Habli and T. Kelly. Capturing and replaying architectural knowledge through derivational analogy. In: *Proceedings of the 2nd Workshop on Sharing and Reusing Architectural Knowledge Architecture, Rationale, and Design Intent (SHARK-ADI)*. Minneapolis, MN, USA: Article No. 4, 2007.

29. T.M. Hesse and B. Paech. Supporting the collaborative development of requirements and architecture documentation. In: *Proceedings of the 3rd International Workshop on the Twin Peaks of Requirements and Architecture (TwinPeaks)*, Rio de Janeiro, Brazil: pp. 22–26, 2013.

30. T. Heyman, R. Scandariato, and W. Joosen. Security in context: Analysis and refinement of software architectures. In: *Proceedings of the 34th Annual IEEE Computer Software and Applications Conference (COMPSAC)*. Seoul, South Korea, pp. 161–170, 2010.

31. P. Lago and H. van Vliet. Explicit assumptions enrich architectural models. In: *Proceedings of the 27th International Conference on Software Engineering (ICSE)*, St. Louis, Missouri, USA, pp. 206–214, 2005.

32. Rizkiyanto. Better Design Rationale to Improve Software Design Quality. Information and Computer Science, Utrecht University, 2016.

33. M. Rahimi, W. Xiong, J. Cleland-Huang, and R. Lutz. Diagnosing assumption problems in safety-critical products. In: *Proceedings of the 32nd IEEE/ACM International Conference on Automated Software Engineering (ASE)*, Urbana-Champaign, IL, USA, pp. 473–484, 2017.

34. C. Yang, P. Liang, and P. Avgeriou. Integrating agile practices into architectural assumption management: An industrial survey. In: *Proceedings of the International Conference on Evaluation and Assessment in Software Engineering (EASE)*, Copenhagen, Denmark, pp. 156–165, 2019.

35. C. Manteuffel, D. Tofan, P. Avgeriou, H. Koziolek, and T. Goldschmidt. Decision architect - A decision documentation tool for industry. *Journal of Systems and Software*, 112(2): 181–198, 2016.

36. U. van Heesch, P. Avgeriou, and R. Hilliard. Forces on architecture decisions-a viewpoint. In: *Proceedings of the Joint Working IEEE/IFIP Conference on Software Architecture (WICSA) and European Conference on Software Architecture (ECSA)*, Helsinki, Finland, pp. 101–110, 2012.

37. Z. Fu, C. Guo, Z. Zhang, S. Ren, and L. Sha. UACFinder: Mining syntactic carriers of unspecified assumptions in medical cyber-physical system design models. *ACM Transactions on Cyber-Physical Systems*, 4(3): 1–25, 2020.

38. I. Sommerville. Integrated requirements engineering: A tutorial. *IEEE Software*, 22(1): 16–23, 2005.

39. C. Hofmeister, P. Kruchten, R.L. Nord, H. Obbink, A. Ran, and P. America. A general model of software architecture design derived from five industrial approaches. *Journal of Systems and Software*, 80(1): 106–126, 2007.

40. U. van Heesch, P. Avgeriou, and R. Hilliard. A documentation framework for architecture decisions. *Journal of Systems and Software*, 85(4): 795–820, 2012.

41. B.G. Glaser and A.L. Strauss. *The Discovery of Grounded Theory: Strategies for Qualitative Research*. New York: Aldine Publishing, 1967.

42. Description of ArAM and Replication Package for the Case Study. https://www.dropbox.com/sh/rtxadvun24f44ke/AABkY4x1lBeqHefmdqrAM-zTa?dl=0.

43. R. Capilla, A. Jansen, A. Tang, P. Avgeriou, and M. Ali Babar. 10 years of software architecture knowledge management: Practice and future. *Journal of Systems and Software*, 116: 191–205, 2016.

44. P. Runeson and M. Höst. Guidelines for conducting and reporting case study research in software engineering. *Empirical Software Engineering*, 14(2): 131–164, 2009.

45. F.D. Davis. Perceived usefulness, perceived ease of use, and user acceptance of information technology. *MIS Quarterly*, 13(3): 319–340, 1989.

46. V. Venkatesh and F.D. Davis. A theoretical extension of the technology acceptance model: Four longitudinal field studies. *Management Science*, 46(2): 186–204, 2000.

47. V. Venkatesh and H. Bala. Technology acceptance model 3 and a research agenda on interventions. *Decision Sciences*, 39(2): 273–315, 2008.

48. V. Basili, G. Caldiera, and D. Rombach. The goal question metric approach, in *Encyclopedia of Software Engineering*, J.J. Marciniak, Editor, New York: John Wiley & Sons, 1994.

49. R.K. Yin. *Case Study Research: Design and Methods*, 3rd Edition. London: Sage, 2003.

50. P. Runeson, M. Host, A. Rainer, and B. Regnell. *Case Study Research in Software Engineering: Guidelines and Examples*. Hoboken, NJ: John Wiley & Sons, 2012.

Glossary

Matthias Galster
University of Canterbury

Bruce R. Maxim
University of Michigan

Ivan Mistrik
Independent Researcher

Bedir Tekinerdogan
Wageningen University

Abstraction: establishing a level of simplicity that hides all but the relevant information in order to reduce complexity and increase efficiency.

Accessibility: information a person or an organization has a right or a privilege to obtain, under what conditions and with what safeguards.

Accuracy: description of the difference between a result or observed data and a true value.

Agile Software Development: software creation that relies on iterative processes that are highly responsive to requirement changes through the collaborative effort of self-organizing cross-functional teams.

Architectural Assumption: architectural knowledge taken for granted or accepted as true without evidence.

Architectural Decision: describes a concrete, architecturally significant design issue for which several potential alternative solutions exist.

Architectural Knowledge: captures architecture design as well as the design decisions, assumptions, context, and other factors that together determine why a particular software solution is the way it is.

Artificial Intelligence: intelligence demonstrated by machines, in contrast to the natural intelligence displayed by humans and animals.

Augmented Analytics: use of machine learning and natural language processing to enhance data analytics, data sharing, and business intelligence.

Big Data: field that treats ways to capture, curate, manage, analyze, systematically extract information from, or otherwise deal with data sets that are too large or complex to be dealt with by traditional data-processing application software within a tolerable elapsed time; data characterized by volume, variety, variability, velocity, and veracity.

Big Data System: software system that handles Big Data.

Business Intelligence: strategies and technologies used by enterprises for the data analysis of business information; provides historical, current, and predictive views of business operations.

Cloud Computing: on-demand availability of computer system resources, especially data storage and computing power, without direct active management by the user.

Cloud Service: any service made available to users on demand via the Internet from a cloud computing provider's servers as opposed to being provided from a company's own on-premises servers.

Cloud Service Consumer: consumer of a cloud service.

Cloud Service Provider: service provider that offers customers storage or software services available via a private or public network; usually, the storage and software are available for access via the Internet.

Communication: creation of shared understanding through interaction among people, computing devices, or computer programs.

Component: in software engineering, refers to a self-contained piece of code that addresses or provides a focused amount of functionality.

Continuous Integration: software development practice where developers integrate code into a shared repository frequently, preferably several times a day; each integration can be verified by an automated build and automated tests.

Cybersecurity: protection of computer systems and networks from the theft of or damage to their hardware, software, or electronic data, as well as from the disruption or misdirection of the services they provide.

Data Fusion: process of integrating multiple data sources to produce more consistent, accurate, and useful information than that provided by any individual data source.

Data-intensive System: software system that needs to handle large amounts of often diverse data.

Data Mining: practice of examining large pre-existing databases or data sets in order to generate new information and insights, typically using automated tools and involving methods at the intersection of machine learning, statistics, and computer science.

Data Science: interdisciplinary field that uses scientific methods, processes, algorithms, and systems to extract knowledge and insights from many structural and unstructured data, often involving Big Data.

Data Scientist: someone who knows how to extract meaning from and interpret data, which requires both tools and methods from statistics and machine learning, as well as being human; spends a lot of time in the process of collecting, cleaning, and munging data, because data is never clean.

Data Warehouse: system for data analysis and reporting; core part of business intelligence.

Decision Making: action or process of making important decisions, typically involving decision alternatives and trade-offs; steps include identifying a decision, gathering relevant information, identifying alternatives, weighting the evidence, choosing among alternatives, taking action, and reviewing decision.

Decision Point: point in space and/or time when a person anticipates making a key decision concerning a specific course of action.

Deployment: all activities that make a software system available for use; typically involves several interrelated activities (at the producer side and/or the consumer side) with possible transitions between them.

Design: process by which a software developer creates a specification of a software artifact, intended to accomplish goals, using a set of primitive components and subject to constraints.

Documentation: written text or illustration that accompanies computer software or is embedded in the source code; documentation explains how the software operates or how to use it and may mean different things to people in different roles.

Ecosystem: interaction of a set of actors on top of a common technological platform that results in a number of software solutions or services.

Elasticity: measurement of the proportional change of a variable in response to a change in another; ability to change and adapt; adaptability.

Ethics: branch of philosophy that concerns matters of value and involves systematizing, defending, and recommending concepts of right and wrong conduct; moral principles that govern a person's behavior or the conducting of an activity.

Failure: inability of a software system to perform its required functions within specified performance requirements.

GIS: geographic information system; framework for gathering, managing, and analyzing geographic data.

Instrumentation: collective term for measuring instruments that are used for indicating, measuring, and recording quantities in software systems; may involve measure of a product's performance, to diagnose errors, and to write trace information; typically implemented in the form of code that monitors specific components in a system.

Internet of Things (IoT): interconnection via the Internet of computing devices embedded in everyday objects, enabling them to send and receive data.

Interoperability: characteristic of a software system or software, whose interfaces are completely understood, to work (exchange and make use of information) with other products or systems or components, at present or in the future, in either implementation or access, without any restrictions.

Knowledge Application: use correct information and knowledge to complete a task or make a decision.

Knowledge Adaption: updating evolving knowledge to remain current or forgetting knowledge when it becomes obsolete or proven incorrect.

Knowledge Acquisition: capture knowledge in explicit forms (e.g., in manuals, client directories, competitor intelligence, patents, licenses, and project artifacts).

Knowledge-based System: computer program that contains large amounts of knowledge, rules, and reasoning mechanisms to provide solutions to real-world problems.

Knowledge Creation: continuous combination, transfer, and conversion of different kinds of knowledge; software development organizations create knowledge through learning, problem-solving, innovation, and importing it from outside sources.

Knowledge Discovery: process of extracting useful knowledge from data.

Knowledge Distribution: distributes or transfers knowledge to others through training programs, automated knowledge repositories, or social networks of experts; transforms an individual's knowledge into knowledge that can be used by others.

Knowledge Engineering: field within artificial intelligence that develops knowledge-based systems; process of eliciting an expert's knowledge, in order to construct a knowledge-based system or an organizational memory.

Knowledge Identification: process of proactively identifying internal organization knowledge needed for the task at hand. Once relevant knowledge has been identified, knowledge can be acquired, created, and shared.

Knowledge Management: enables the knowledge sharing between people, where one person translates their knowledge to another one; in software engineering, knowledge management embraces all aspects of software construction and typically involves knowledge identification, knowledge creation, knowledge acquisition, knowledge organization, knowledge distribution, knowledge application, and knowledge adaption.

Knowledge Organization: organize and transform knowledge in both written form and digital knowledge repositories so that it can be located, searched, and shared with third parties without the involvement of the original knowledge creator.

Logging: process of continuously recording and keeping a record of all data input, processes, data output, and final results in a program.

Machine Learning: study of computer algorithms that improve automatically through experience; seen as a subset of artificial intelligence.

Maintainability: ease with which a computer program can be maintained in order to correct defects or their cause, repair or replace faulty components, prevent unexpected working conditions, maximize a computer program's useful life, maximize efficiency, reliability, and safety, meet new requirements, make future maintenance easier, or cope with a changed environment.

Monitoring: regular observation and recording of activities taking place in a software project or computer program.

Monolithic System: software system in which functionally distinguishable aspects (for example, data input and output, data processing, error handling, and the user interface) are all interwoven, rather than containing architecturally separate components.

Motivation: experience of desire or aversion; as such, motivation has both an objective aspect and an internal or subjective aspect.

Natural Language Processing: subfield of linguistics, computer science, information engineering, and artificial intelligence concerned with the interactions between computers and human languages, in particular how to program computers to process and analyze large amounts of natural language data.

Neural Networks: set of computing systems and algorithms, modeled loosely after the human brain, that are designed to learn to perform tasks and recognize patterns by considering examples (and generally without being programmed with task-specific rules); algorithms interpret sensory data through a kind of machine perception, labeling or clustering raw input.

NoSQL: mechanism for storage and retrieval of data that is modeled in means other than the tabular relations used in relational databases.

Platform: environment in which a piece of software is executed; may be the hardware or the operating system, even a web browser and associated application programming interfaces, or other underlying software, as long as the program code is executed with it.

Privacy: degree of information about one's self or one's associations a person must reveal to others, under what conditions and with what safeguards.

Property: description of who owns information and what just and fair prices for its exchange are.

Real-time: characteristic of computer programs which require receiving data, processing them, and returning the results sufficiently quickly to affect the environment at that time.

Refactoring: process of restructuring existing computer code, changing the factoring, without changing its external behavior; intended to improve the design, structure, and/or implementation of the software, while preserving the functionality of the software.

Server: a computer or computer program that manages access to a centralized resource or service in a network.

Serverless Architecture: software design pattern where applications are hosted by a third-party service, eliminating the need for server software and hardware management by the developer; utilizes cloud computing execution model in which the cloud provider runs the server, and dynamically manages the allocation of machine resources.

Service-oriented Architecture (SOA): style of software design where services are provided to the other components by application components, through a communication protocol over a network.

Software Artifact/Artifact: one of many kinds of tangible by-products produced during the development of software; some artifacts help describe the function, architecture, and design of software, other artifacts are concerned with the process of development itself (such as project plans, business cases, and risk assessments).

Software Engineering: the application of a systematic, disciplined, adaptable, quantifiable approach to the development, operation, and maintenance of software.

Software-intensive System: any system where software influences to a large extend the design, construction, deployment, and evolution of the system as a whole.

Software Quality: functional quality reflects how well a computer program complies with or conforms to a given design, based on functional requirements or specifications (degree to which the correct software was produced); structural quality refers to how a computer program meets nonfunctional requirements that support the delivery of the functional requirements, such as robustness or maintainability (degree to which the software works as needed).

Software Repository: storage location where you can store software packages and related metadata; software packages can be accessed and installed, when required, on computers in the network; repositories facilitate easy storage, maintenance, and backup of software packages.

Software Requirements: description of features, functionalities, and the quality of the target system; convey expectations of users from the software product; requirements can be obvious or hidden, known or unknown, expected or unexpected from client's point of view.

Systems of Systems: collection of task-oriented or dedicated systems that pool their resources and capabilities together to create a new, more complex system, which offers more functionality and performance than simply the sum of the constituent systems.

Technical Debt: concept in software development that reflects the implied cost of additional rework caused by choosing an easy (limited) solution now instead of using a better approach that would take longer.

Telemetry: collection of measurements or other data at remote or inaccessible points (e.g., in the cloud) and their automatic transmission to receiving equipment or software for monitoring and analysis.

Traceability: ability to trace work items such as requirements, design, and code across the development and life cycle of a computer program.

Training Data: in machine learning, training data is an initial set of data used to help a program understand how to apply technologies such as neural networks to learn and make data-driven predictions or decisions on data (typically through building a mathematical model from input data); may be complemented by subsequent sets of data called validation and testing sets.

Value: characteristic of Big Data, which refers to the utility that can be extracted from the data.

Variability: characteristic of Big Data, which refers to data whose value or other characteristics are shifting in relation to the context they are being generated.

Variety: type and nature of data; helps people who analyze data to effectively use resulting insights; Big Data draws from text, images, audio, video, and completes missing pieces through data fusion.

Velocity: speed at which data is generated and processed to meet the demands and challenges that lie in the path of growth and development; Big data is often available in real time and produced continually; two kinds of velocity in Big Data: the frequency of generation and the frequency of handling, recording, and publishing data.

Veracity: characteristic of Big Data, which refers to the data quality and the data value.

Volume: quantity of generated and stored data; size of the data determines the value and potential insight, and whether it can be considered Big Data or not.

Web Service: either a service offered by an electronic device to another electronic device, communicating with each other via the World Wide Web, or a server running on a computer device, listening for requests at a particular port over a network, serving web documents (HTML, JSON, XML, images) and web applications services, which solve specific domain problems over the Web (WWW, Internet, HTTP).

Index

Note: **Bold** page numbers refer to tables and *Italic* page numbers refer to figures.